THE *United States* AND International Law

MAX HILAIRE, PH.D.
Professor & Chair, Department of Political Science & International Studies
Morgan State University

KENDALL/HUNT PUBLISHING COMPANY
4050 Westmark Drive Dubuque, Iowa 52002

Cover and title page images:
Eagle: Image © Robin Phinizy, 2009. Used under license from Shutterstock, Inc.
U.S. Capitol: Image © JupiterImages, Corporation.
United Nations building: Image © SVLumagraphica, 2009. Used under license from Shutterstock, Inc.
United Nations building 2: Image © Newphotoservice, 2009. Used under license from Shutterstock, Inc.
White House: Image © Albert de Bruijn, 2009. Used under license from Shutterstock, Inc.
Flag: Image © Brandon Jennings, 2009. Used under license from Shutterstock, Inc.

ISBN: 978-0-7575-6069-9

Printed in the United States of America
10 9 8 7 6 5 4 3 2 1

CONTENTS

PREFACE

This project began in the wake of the September 11 terrorist attacks on the United States and the response of the Bush administration. The idea for such an exercise started after a series of lectures in Luanda, Angola, as part of a speaking engagement I did for the Public Affairs division of the United States Embassy in Angola. The issue of the legality of the war in Afghanistan and the pending invasion of Iraq drew a great deal of interest and controversy. The audiences were in disagreement about the legality of a United States invasion of Iraq and the war on terror in general. The topic attracted particular attention because at the time Angola was one of the countries on the Security Council that was undecided about the legality of a U.S. invasion of Iraq.

In response to the terrorist attacks the President invoked his executive authority to grant himself expansive power to execute his war on terror. Congress also gave the President authorization to use force to apprehend those responsible for the terrorist attacks. President Bush used his Constitutional authority coupled with authorization from Congress to assume extraordinary powers in framing his response to terrorism, raising questions about his Constitutional responsibility and his international and legal obligations. The President asserted unchecked powers for himself and claimed that there should be no Congressional oversight or judicial review of his actions. The President assumed broad powers to detain indefinitely foreign nationals and American citizens captured on the "battlefield" as enemy combatants and to deny them the right of *habeas corpus*. The President also acted like he was above the law and that all decisions regarding treatment of detainees, interrogation methods and pursuing the war on terror were not subject to Congressional oversight, judicial review or international scrutiny. It is unprecedented for an American President to assume such broad powers in a system carefully designed to prevent any one branch of the government from asserting unchecked powers. Mr. Bush finds himself isolated on a number of international legal issues due to his blatant disregard of international law and his narrow view of the world and the role of multilateral institutions in global diplomacy. Mr. Bush's action has severely damaged the reputation of the United States. This book is an attempt to shed light on the current state of international law in American foreign policy, with emphasis on the Bush administration and its disdain for international law.

I want to express my sincere gratitude to the faculty and staff at the Augustino Neto University Faculty of Law and the Catholic University in Angola who inspired me to write this book, as well as to my students in the Czech Republic who were always so attentive to my views on the subject. Finally, I am grateful to Ambassador Pamela Bridgewater, United States Ambassador to Ghana, on whose invitation to lecture in Ghana in 2006, I was able to finalize my thoughts on the subject.

I Dedicate this Book in Memory of
Dr. Frank Przetacznik;
My Mentor, Professor & Friend

INTRODUCTION

The foreign policy of the current Bush administration has raised serious concerns about the United States' commitment to the rule of law in international affairs and to American global leadership in international institutions. Indeed, the disdain the current Bush administration is showing toward international law and international institutions is not a new phenomenon in United States foreign policy. Recent Presidents, including Reagan, the first Bush and Clinton, have all harbored suspicion or similar hostility toward international law and institutions. President Bush is basically continuing a longstanding tradition in American foreign policy, which calls for the United States to disregard international law when it constrains U.S. behavior or conflicts with U.S. national interest. The history of American foreign policy is replete with examples of such conduct, which in some ways contradicts what the U.S. stands for and the image it projects as a champion of the rule of law in international affairs.

The United States has simultaneously promoted and undermined the rule of law in international affairs while at the same time calling on other states to comply with international law. When the United States was still a weak nation in the eighteenth century, it played a leadership role in the development of international law. The U.S. was a strong supporter of the two Hague Conventions of 1899 and 1907, a chief architect of the League of Nations and the co-sponsor of Paris Pact of 1928. The United States also helped defend against European intervention in Latin America, and it mediated debt and territorial disputes between Latin American nations and Europeans. During the American Civil War the United States developed the Lieber Code, which sought to regulate the conduct of soldiers and to protect the civilian population during the war. The Lieber Code became one of the key components of the Geneva Conventions of 1949. The Jay Treaties with Britain after the Civil War helped institutionalize binding arbitration as a peaceful mechanism for settling interstate disputes.

Following its victory over Spain in the Spanish-American War, the United States invaded a number of countries in the Western Hemisphere, which it initially defined as its sphere of influence. The United States invaded Mexico in 1912 and occupied Mexico City for several years. The United States illegally invaded and occupied Haiti and the Dominican Republic in the 1930s. The United States conspired to overthrow President Abenz of Guatemala in 1954 and the regime of Fidel Castro of Cuba in 1961. The United States invaded the Dominican Republic in 1965 initially to rescue American citizens, but the real reason for the invasion was to prevent a pro-Communist regime from coming to power.

Chapter one explores the recent histories of presidential conduct in foreign affairs to show how Presidents Reagan, Bush and Clinton flouted international law and international institutions to advance their foreign policy goals and objectives. Chapter two examines the status of international law in the United States and how the United States as a young nation embraced international law. It also looks at the contribution of the United States Supreme Court in the development of international law as law in the United States. Chapter three provides an assessment of President Bush's record on international law to date and makes a comparison between President Bush's record and those of his three recent predecessors. Chapters four to nine are case studies that detail President Bush's position on economic and trade issues, on the war on terror, on human rights, the promotion of democracy and the rule of law, relations with the United Nations, global public health policy and the global environment. The analysis will show that President Bush has not deviated very much from the policies of his predecessors and that the difference is in style, not substance. The exercise concludes by showing how the 9/11 terrorist attacks drastically transformed the foreign policy perspective of the U.S. and how it places the United States on a collision course with its traditional allies and the rest of the world. The administration's so-called "war on terror" has caused considerable damage to U.S. standing in the world and created a climate of lawlessness and instability in the international system unforeseen since the Reagan presidency.

chapter 1

THE HISTORICAL RECORD OF PAST PRESIDENTS

Under President Reagan the United States pursued a unilateralist foreign policy that considered international law and institutions hostile to American interest. Reagan took several actions that were blatant violations of international law: He invaded Grenada, following a bloody coup that led to the death of the Prime Minister and several members of his cabinet;[1] he bombed Libya in response to a terrorist attack on a Berlin discotheque that wounded several American servicemen; and he commandeered an Egyptian airliner and forced it to land in Italy in order to arrest the suspected terrorists who had previously hijacked an Italian cruise liner, the Achille Lauro and dumped an American citizen overboard.[2] President Reagan was also responsible for the downing of Iran Air Flight 655 over the Persian Gulf during the Iran-Iraq war in the 1980s, which killed all 290 passengers and crew on the flight.[3] Prior to that incident Reagan reflagged Kuwaiti oil tankers to provoke an attack from Iran, which in turn gave the United States a legitimate justification to retaliate against Iran for attacking American vessels.

President Reagan withdrew the United States from UNESCO in response to attempts by Third World countries to get the agency to adopt a "New World Information Order" that the administration contended would restrict press freedom around the world.[4] President Reagan also withheld portions of United States annual dues and peacekeeping funding to the United Nations in response to the anti-American and Israeli sentiments of the organization.[5] Reagan pressed for structural reform of the United Nations and refused to pay U.S. dues until these reform measures became implemented. The President's action violated U.S. international legal obligations and forced the United Nations to scale back on some of its overseas operations.

Reagan refused to submit the United Nations Convention on the Law of the Sea (UNCLOS III) to the Senate for ratification in opposition to Part XI of the convention, which dealt with exploration and mining of the deep seabed, as he felt it was contrary to free market principles. Part XI of UNCLOS requires mining companies, including American companies, to provide mining technology to the International Seabed Authority (ISA), which it could then transfer to developing countries.[6] In spite of his opposition to UNCLOS, Reagan issued a proclamation in 1989 to extend the jurisdiction of U.S. territorial sea from three to twelve miles in accordance with the convention.[7]

Reagan also stirred controversy when he openly supported and funded anti-communist insurgencies in Nicaragua, El Salvador, Angola and Afghanistan in an attempt to overthrow regimes he considered communist and hostile to the United States' national interest. After Nicaragua filed suit in the International Court of Justice (ICJ) against the United States for funding and arming the Nicaraguan *Contras* and for mining its harbors, the United States withdrew from the Compulsory Jurisdiction Clause (Art. 36 (2)) of the Statute of the court and subsequently withdrew from the entire process.[8] Despite U.S. non-appearance and opposition to the court's decision to pursue Nicaragua's claim, the ICJ concluded that the Reagan administration had indeed violated international law by aiding and directing the Contra war in Nicaragua. The ICJ attributed the activities of the Contras to the United States and said that without U.S. support the Contras could not have carried out such extensive military operations on their own. Despite Nicaragua's efforts before the ICJ, Reagan continued to provide financial, military and logistical support to the Contras. Reagan also intensified his hostilities toward the Soviet Union and Cuba, and he supported Congressional effort to tighten the economic embargo against the Castro regime. Reagan embarked on the development of a space-based missile defense initiative (Star Wars) program, which contradicted the spirit of the Anti-Ballistic Missile Treaty (ABM Treaty), the core of the US/USSR arms control treaties during the Cold War era.

When President George H. W. Bush took office in January 1989, he continued Reagan's foreign policy agenda but made some minor modifications. However, given the unexpected turn of events in the world following the end of the Cold War and the collapse of the Soviet empire, Bush Sr. adjusted American foreign policy consistent with the changing international environment. With Soviet President Gorbachev more willing to cooperate with the United States and the United Nations on resolving international crises, the Bush Sr. administration became persuaded to work with him and the international community to manage regional conflicts. President Bush agreed to give the United Nations a greater role in resolving the conflicts in Afghanistan, Angola, Cambodia, Mozambique and Namibia. The United States also allowed the United Nations to broker a comprehensive peace agreement with the warring factions in Nicaragua, Guatemala and El Salvador.

Former President Bush used the United Nations multilateral framework to counter Iraq's invasion and occupation of Kuwait and to impose comprehensive economic sanctions and harsh ceasefire conditions on Iraq. These measures in essence stripped Iraq of its full sovereignty by placing it under the tutelage of the United Nations.[9] In the immediate aftermath of the Gulf War, Kurds and Shiites led spontaneous rebellions against Hussein's rule. Iraq's military crushed the rebellions, killing many Kurds and Shiites. The military campaign led to a mass exodus of Kurdish refugees across Iraq's northern border and into Turkey. In response to this humanitarian crisis the United States, Britain and France co-sponsored a resolution in the Security Council to condemn Hussein's military operation. At the behest of the United States, the Security Council adopted resolution 688 (1991) which said it was "gravely concerned by the repression of the Iraqi civilian population in many parts of Iraq, including most recently in Kurdish-populated areas, which led to a massive flow of refugees towards and across international frontiers and to cross-border incursions which threaten international peace and security in the region."[10] Although the resolution invoked Chapter VII language, the Security Council did not adopt the resolution under Chapter VII. However, that did not prevent former President Bush from invoking Resolution 688 (1991) to launch military strikes against Iraqi forces in the north of the country and to establish "safe havens" for Kurdish refugees who were fleeing into neighboring Turkey. President Bush also invoked the resolution to justify the establishment of no-fly zones over northern and southern Iraq. This was a clear violation of Resolution 688 (1991), which did not authorize such measures.[11]

In 1992, former President Bush spearheaded a United Nations humanitarian intervention in Somalia to create a safe environment for the distribution of food and emergency relief to the civilian population.[12] Bush acted after the United Nations Operation in Somalia (UNOSOM) was unable to implement its mandate because the warring factions refused to comply with a United Nations-imposed ceasefire agreement. As an alternative to UNOSOM, the United States agreed to lead an International Task Force (ITF) under a Chapter VII mandate with the authority to use all necessary means to secure a safe environment for the distribution of humanitarian assistance to the civilian population.

Under former President Bush the United States was actively involved in a number of multilateral negotiations on critical global issues. In 1988, the Bush administration participated in the United Nations conference to combat the spread of illicit drugs. The administration later signed the UN Convention against Illicit Traffic in Narcotic Drugs and Psychotropic Substances as a vital component of its war on drugs.[13] The United States also played an active role in the United Nations Conference on Environment and Development held in Rio in 1992. Later that year former President Bush transmitted to the Senate for ratification the United Nations Framework Convention on Climate Change, which the United States signed at the Rio Summit.[14] President Bush objected to other provisions of Agenda 21 and did not sign the conventions on deforestation, desertification and biodiversity.[15]

In spite of his commitment to multilateralism, former President Bush did not always comply with international law, especially when it was not in the U.S.'s national interest to do so. Bush continued Reagan's policy of withholding funds for the United Nations regular and peacekeeping budgets; he did not take the United States back into UNESCO; and he refused to recognize the judgment of the International Court of Justice against the United States in the *Nicaragua Case*. However, Bush negotiated an agreement with the newly elected president of Nicaragua, Violeta Chamorro, to vacate the ICJ judgment in exchange for a $250 million aid package.

Former President Bush did not submit important human rights treaties to the Senate for ratification, such as the Convention on the Rights of the Child (CROC), the International Covenant on Civil and Political Rights (ICCPR) and the Convention on the Elimination of All Forms of Discrimination Against Women (CEDAW). President Bush also breached international law when he invaded Panama and captured General Manuel Noriega, the country's legitimate leader at the time who was extradited to the United States by authorities in the Dominican Republic. Since Panama's constitution forbids the extradition of its nationals, officials had to transport Noriega to the Dominican Republican where they could officially extradite him to the United States to face drug trafficking charges. Noriega, who retained his prisoner of war status, later went to trial where he received conviction for drug trafficking charges in United States Federal Court in Miami and a sentence of twenty-five years in prison.[16] The General Assembly swiftly condemned the U.S. invasion as a flagrant violation of international law.[17] Britain, France and the United States vetoed a similar resolution in the Security Council to condemn the invasion.[18]

Noriega completed his sentence in September 2007, and the U.S. ordered him extradited to France to face trial on money laundering charges. Noriega had petitioned the court for a writ of habeas corpus to challenge the U.S. decision to extradite him to France on the grounds that it would violate the Geneva Convention, which requires that the detaining country send a prisoner of war back to his home country at the end of the conflict and upon completion of his sentence. However, the judge in the case ruled that Article 12 of the Geneva Convention allows one party to extradite a prisoner to a third country if it receives assurances that the country will respect the prisoner's Geneva Convention rights.

People expected President Clinton, who succeeded Bush as the first Democratic president in twenty years, to reverse some of the Republican hostility toward international law and institutions. Indeed, Clinton's presidency ushered in a new era in American foreign policy and raised expectations of greater multilateral cooperation by the United States. Clinton successfully completed negotiations with Mexico for its entry into the North American Free Trade Agreement (NAFTA), and he secured passage of the Uruguay Round to establish the World Trade Organization Agreement (WTO). Clinton endorsed the U.S.-led United Nations humanitarian operation in Somalia, and he later supported efforts in the Security Council to deepen the involvement of the international community in Somalia's civil war.

By the time Clinton took office in January 1993, the Cold War had ended and Russia was no longer a threat to the United States and its allies, Clinton continued the policy of his predecessor to integrate Russia into the international community. When Clinton assumed the presidency the world was in the midst of a democratic renaissance and a peace dividend. The United States and Russia were cooperating on resolving a number of outstanding international issues. Both Clinton and President Yeltsin of Russia agreed to continue to support the United Nations in its effort to resolve longstanding regional conflicts that the US/USSR Cold War rivalry had fueled for many years. The United Nations had somewhat settled the civil wars in Afghanistan, Angola, Cambodia, Mozambique, Nicaragua and El Salvador, and the bush war in Namibia. However, the standoff with Iraq over its disarmament program, the ethnic conflicts in Bosnia and Rwanda, the crisis in Haiti over the removal of the democratically elected government of Jean Bernard Aristide, and wars in Liberia and Sierra Leone all posed serious challenges to the United Nations and threatened to derail the gains made resolving other conflicts. These post-Cold War conflicts would have enormous implications for American foreign policy and the U.S. attitude toward international law and institutions.

Within months of taking office President Clinton ran into difficulty with Congressional Republicans following a deadly ambush on American forces participating in the United Nations mission in Somalia. The ambushers killed or injured several American soldiers and dragged the bodies of some of the dead through the streets of Mogadishu. Public humiliation of the incident, which CNN broadcast live, and pressure from Congress, forced Clinton to call for the premature withdrawal of U.S. and U.N. troops from Somalia. The incident would significantly change Clinton's attitude toward United Nations peacekeeping.

In the wake of the Somalia fiasco, President Clinton issued Presidential Decision Directive 25 (PDD 25) to impose strict constraints on future U.S. participation in United Nations peacekeeping.[19] The United States subsequently sponsored a resolution in the Security Council to terminate the United Nations Operation in Somalia (UNOSOM) ahead of schedule.[20] The United States also opposed efforts in the Security Council to deploy new peacekeeping missions in regional conflicts. This shift in American policy had disastrous consequences for the people of Bosnia and Rwanda.

By the time Clinton took office the conflict in the former country of Yugoslavia had significantly escalated. During the campaign Clinton criticized his opponent for not doing more to end the conflict and vowed to use military force to end the violence. However, once elected, Clinton was perplexed by the conflict and basically continued the policy of his predecessor. Clinton did not endorse the Vance-Owen Peace Plan, and he submitted no new peace plan of his own. As the fighting in Bosnia escalated, killing or displacing more civilians, Clinton supported United Nations peace initiatives and the work of the United Nations Protection Force (UNPROFOR) to protect civilians and to enforce the ceasefire and the arms embargo. However, he refused to send U.S. troops to Bosnia.[21]

Without U.S. support UNPROFOR was not adequately equipped to do battle with well-armed Serb paramilitaries, and it could not protect Bosnian civilians against Serbian attacks. The arms embargo made it extremely difficult for the Bosnian Muslims to defend themselves against a superior Serbian army backed by the Yugoslav Army (JNA). Serb forces subsequently overran the civilian safe havens established by the United Nations, took the Dutch contingent of UNPROFOR hostage, and later massacred thousands of Bosnian Muslim civilians in one of Europe's worse atrocities since World War II.[22] In spite of these horrors Clinton refused to send U.S. troops to Bosnia. Britain and France opposed the use of NATO air strikes for fear that Serbian paramilitary forces would retaliate against their peacekeepers. The Clinton administration also opposed giving UNPROFOR the additional military support it needed to implement its mandate. A subsequent Serbian attack on the central market in Sarajevo would lead to a turning point in the war.

Soon after the market attack, Clinton authorized air strikes against Serbian military targets, which forced the Serbs to surrender and to accept a new United States-brokered ceasefire agreement. Clinton's Special Envoy, Richard Holbrooke, soon thereafter convened an all-party conference in Dayton, Ohio, to negotiate a permanent ceasefire and a comprehensive peace accord between the various warring factions. After several weeks of difficult negotiations, they signed the Dayton Accords. The accords basically legitimized the existing de facto ethnic divide of Bosnia. In addition, the accords called for a permanent ceasefire and the deployment of a NATO force to implement them, as well as for the appointment of a High Representative to oversee implementation of the agreement, with the authority to veto laws and to fire politicians.[23] On December 15, 1995, the Security Council adopted resolution 1031 (1995) to endorse the accords and to authorize the deployment of a NATO-led multinational implementation force (IFOR) to assist in implementing the territorial and security provisions of the Peace Agreement.[24] The Security Council also created the International Police Task Force (IPTF) to carry out civilian police duties in Bosnia.[25] The failure of the United States to intervene in Bosnia earlier may have contributed to the ethnic cleansing and killing of thousands of civilians carried out with impunity by Serbs.

Following the death of the Presidents of Burundi and Rwanda in April 1993, Hutu extremists went on a rampage and within a hundred days killed over half a million civilians in Rwanda, the majority of them Tutsis. The United States vehemently opposed efforts in the Security Council to augment the mandate of the existing United Nations Assistant Mission for Rwanda (UNAMIR) to increase the troop level or to authorize the deployment of a new force under a Chapter VII mandate in order to stop the violence.[26] The Clinton administration lobbied other Security Council members to prevent the United Nations from calling the violence in Rwanda genocide, and it instructed all U.S. diplomatic missions to refrain from doing so.[27] The United States maintained this position in light of the overwhelming evidence made public by human rights organizations and the United Nations Secretary General that the atrocities committed in Rwanda were indeed acts of genocide.[28]

Clinton did not push for Senate ratification of pending human rights treaties, including the Convention on the Elimination of Discrimination Against Women (CEDAW), the Protocol to the International Covenant on Civil and Political Rights (ICCPR) and the Convention on the Rights of the Child (CRC). President Clinton did not return the United States to UNESCO or the ICJ Compulsory Jurisdiction Clause. Clinton opposed signing the United Nations Anti-Personnel Mine Convention (Ottawa Landmine Convention), and he did not lobby the United States Senate vigorously to secure ratification of the 1996 Comprehensive Test Ban Treaty (CTBT) and the Biological and Chemical Weapons Conventions. Clinton sought to renegotiate Part XI of the United Nations Convention on the Law of the Sea, which his predecessors had opposed. The 1994 Agreement on the Implementation of Part XI of the United Nations Convention on the Law of the Sea altered the institutional structure of the International Seabed Authority (ISA), dismantled the production ceilings and limitation originally accepted and did away with the transfer of technology to the "Enterprise" and to developing countries.[29] President Clinton subsequently submitted the revised Law of the Sea Treaty to the Senate Foreign Relations Committee (SFRC) for advice and consent, but the committee did not schedule hearings until October 2003.[30] In 2004, the committee forwarded the treaty to the full Senate for approval, but the Senate took no action. Finally, Clinton reluctantly signed the Rome Statute for the International Criminal Court weeks before he left office. Clinton was aware of the opposition to the treaty by Senators on both sides of the aisle; however, he signed the treaty knowing full well that its chance of ratification by the Senate was slim.

During the Presidency of Bill Clinton, Congress passed a number of measures that raised questions about the extraterritorial application of United States law and the possible violation of international law. In 1996, Clinton signed into law the D'Amato Act to impose sanctions and to restrict foreign investment in Iran and Libya (Iran and Libya Sanctions Act of 1996),[31] and the Helms-Burton Act (the Cuban Liberty and Democratic Solidarity or Libertad Act) to prevent third-country companies from investing in nationalized property in Cuba.[32] The Helms-Burton Act also threatened court action against foreign corporations, and it denied entry into the United States of officers of such foreign corporations. A controversial provision of the Act called for prosecuting in U.S. courts foreign nationals who "traffic in" property confiscated from American citizens.[33] After strong protest from Canada, Mexico and the European Union (EU), and a threat of taking the United States to NATFA and the WTO, Clinton reached a compromised agreement with

Congress that allowed him to suspend Titles III and IV of the Act against Canada, Mexico and the EU.[34] Finally, Clinton signed into law the Inter-American Convention for the Protection and Conservation of Sea Turtles. But the WTO ruled the measure was in violation of GATT Article XX of 1994.[35] It is against this background that one can assess the attitude of President George W. Bush toward international law and institutions to determine whether his policy is a new phenomenon or simply a continuation of an old practice in American diplomatic tradition.

This project assesses the importance of international law in U.S. foreign relations and the attitude of the current Bush administration toward international law and institutions. Recent controversies surrounding prisoner abuse in Afghanistan, Guantánamo Bay, Cuba and Iraq, the Bush administration's conduct of its so-called "war on terror" and President Bush's decision to invade Iraq without Security Council authorization have led observers to believe that the United States is no longer committed to a rule-based international order. More importantly, the refusal of the Bush administration to sign the Kyoto Protocol, the Rome Statute of the International Criminal Court (ICC), the Landmine Treaty and a number of human rights conventions conveys an image of the administration that is not consistent with U.S. global commitments and with America's longstanding diplomatic tradition. Finally, the Bush administration's decision to withdraw from the Anti-Ballistic Missile Treaty (ABM Treaty) with Russia has fueled speculation around the world that President Bush is pursuing a policy of legal exceptionalism. This means that the United States expects other countries to play by the rules but believes it should be exempted when international rules constrain U.S. behavior.[36] The first part of this exercise looks at international law in U.S. foreign relations from the birth of the republic. It underscores the emphasis the Founding Fathers placed on law in general, and upon international law in particular, in framing the Constitution of the United States. The Framers of the U.S. Constitution conceived international law, or the law of nations as they called it then, as the "law of the land," and they gave it the same status as domestic law. In some instances they even elevated international law to a higher standard than domestic law. The Framers were of the view that the sovereignty of the United States was embedded in international law; hence international law took precedent over domestic law and Congressional statutes. Part One further shows how international law was invoked to protect the new nation of the United States from European powers and to defend U.S. interests around the world.

Endnotes

1. Gilmore, William C. 1984. *The Grenada intervention,* 32.
2. For a chronology of this event, see Cassese, Antonio. 1989. *Terrorism, politics, and law: The Achille Lauro affair.*
3. See Agora. 1989. The downing of Iran Air Flight 655, *AJIL* 88:318.
4. Hoffer, Peri A. 1986. Upheaval in the UN system: The United States' withdrawal from UNESCO, 12 Brook. *J. Int'l. L.,* 161; Dobbs, Michael, et al. 1985. U.S. quits UNESCO; Move seen as blow to controversial agency. *Washington Post,* Jan. 1.
5. Murphy, John F. 2004. *The United States and the rule of law in international affairs,* 124.
6. Klein, Pierre. 2003. The Effects of U.S. predominance on the elaboration of treaty regimes and on the evolution on the law of treaties. In *United States hegemony and the foundations of international law,* ed. Michael Byers and Georg Nolte, 363, 366.
7. Proclamation No. 5928, 54 Fed. Reg. 777 (Dec. 27, 1989), 3 C.R.F. 547 (1989), reprinted in 43 U.S.C. #1331 note (1994).
8. Murphy, *supra* note 5, 257.
9. Senate Res. 687. 1991.
10. Senate Res. 688. 1991, para. 3.
11. Senate Res. 688. 1991. This resolution was not adopted under Chapter VII; hence it was not legally binding.
12. Senate Res. 794. 1992.
13. UN Doc. E/CONF.82/15. 1988. Reprinted 1989 in *ILM* 28:493.
14. Nash, Marian (Leich). 1993. Contemporary practice of the United States relating to international law. *AJIL* 87:103.
15. See Phillipe Sands. 2003. *Principles of international environmental law,* 55–56.
16. *United States v. Noriega,* 808 F. Supp. 791, 795 (S.D. Fla. 1992).
17. A/Res. 44/240, December 29, 1989.
18. *Yearbook of the United Nations.* 1989. 43:175.
19. Sewall, Sarah B. 2002. Multilateral Peace Operations. In *Multilateralism and U.S. foreign policy,* ed. Stewart Patrick and Shepard Forman, 191, 196.
20. Senate Res. 954. 1994.
21. Senate Res. 713. 1991.
22. Damrosch, Lori et al. 2001. *International law,* 4th ed., 1040.
23. See General Framework Agreement for Peace in Bosnia and Herzegovina, signed on Dec. 14, 1995, U.N. Doc. (S/1995/999, annex).
24. Senate Res. 1031. 1995.
25. See Senate Res. 1035. 1995.
26. Neuffer, Elizabeth. 2002. *The key to my neighbor's house,* 123.
27. Ibid, 124.

28. See Report of Independent Inquiry into the Actions of the United Nations during the 1994 Genocide in Rwanda (Dec. 15, 1999).
29. Pierre Klein, *supra* note 6.
30. See Accession to the 1982 Law of the Sea Convention and Ratification of the 1994 Agreement Amending Part XI of the Law of the Sea Convention and Ratification of the 1994 Agreement Amending Part XI of the Law of the Sea Convention: Hearing Before the Senate Committee on Foreign Relations, 108 Cong. (Oct. 21, 2003). http://foreign.senate.gov/hearings/2003/hrg031021a.html.
31. *ILM.* 1996, 35:1273.
32. *ILM.* 1996, 35:357.
33. See Agora. 1996. The Cuban Liberty and Democratic Solidarity (Libertad) Act. *AJIL* 90: 419.
34. Scott, Shirley V. *The impact of international law on U.S. noncompliance, supra* note 6, 430–431.
35. United States-import prohibition of certain shrimp and shrimp products AB 1998-4. Report of the Appellate Body WT/DS58/AB/R, Oct. 12, 1998. Reprinted 1999 in *ILM* 38:121.
36. See Alvarez, Jose E. Legal unilateralism. In *Wars on terrorism and Iraq,* ed. Thomas G. Weiss, Margaret E. Crahan and John Goering, 188.

chapter II

THE STATUS OF INTERNATIONAL LAW IN THE UNITED STATES

From its birth as a nation the United States has been a strong advocate of international law and a rule-based international legal order that would have as its core respect for the principles of international law. The framers of the U.S. Constitution recognized the importance of international law in the domestic affairs of the United States. They got their inspiration from other nations and were conscious of very universal principles, such as "due process," "equal protection," and the prohibition against "cruel and unusual punishment," which they incorporated into the Constitution. They also borrowed from the law of nations the authority to declare war, to negotiate treaties, to raise an army and navy, and to send and receive ambassadors. It is quite obvious that the Framers did not draft the Constitution in a vacuum; they took international law into consideration in formulating the various provisions of the Constitution.[1] Nor did they totally ignore the practices of other nations that came into existence before the United States. The framers recognized the value of international law and its higher authority. Hence, they elevated international law to the same status as domestic law and Congressional Statutes.[2]

Under Article I of the Constitution the framers grant Congress the power "[t]o define and punish Piracies and Felonies committed on the high Seas, and Offenses against the Law of Nations." Under Article II they granted the President "Executive Authority," the authority to negotiate treaties, the power of Commander-in-Chief, and the power to send and receive ambassadors. In Article III of the Constitution the framers grant the Supreme Court power to adjudicate all cases related to treaties made between the United States and other states, to cases related to other public Ministers and Consuls, and to cases of admiralty and maritime jurisdiction. Article VI recognizes treaties under the authority of the United States as the supreme law of the land. This is significant, as there are few other national constitutions where international law is held in such high esteem. These references are a clear indication that the framers took international law into consideration in framing the Constitution of the United States.

In the early years of the republic, the United States sponsored or supported a number of international agreements in all spheres of international law. The United States Supreme Court also adjudicated a number of legal disputes in which it affirmed the status of international law in the United States. In a famous decision in the *Paquete Habana* case the Supreme Court ruled against the United States for violating the "law of nations" when the U.S. Coast Guard seized two Cuban fishing vessels (*Paquete Habana* and *Lola*) on the high seas as war prizes and ordered them sold by the U.S. federal court as prize vessels. In a suit by the original owners before the Supreme Court, the court held that the seizure of the vessels violated customary international law, which protects fishing vessels at sea in times of war.[3] The Court opined that:

> International law is part of our law, and must be ascertained and administered by the courts of justice of appropriate jurisdiction, as often as questions of right depending upon it are duly represented for their determination. For this purpose, where there is no treaty, and no controlling executive or legislative act or judicial decision, resort must be had to the customs and usages of civilized nations. . . .[4]

The Supreme Court subsequently reaffirmed the core principle in the *Paquete Habana* case by reversing a lower court ruling in the *Banco Nacional de Cuba v. Sabbatino* case. The lower court initially ruled that Cuba's expropriation decree violated international law. The Supreme Court invoked the "Act of State Doctrine," which prohibits the courts of one state from ruling on the legality of legislations passed by the national government of another state.[5]

More recently the federal courts have been less willing to intervene in international law disputes involving the executive branch. When international law conflicts with the Constitution or with Congressional statutes, federal courts will generally give priority to domestic law instead of relying on the "last in time" rule. Additionally, federal courts will either defer to the executive branch or go along with the political interpretation of international law adopted by the President. The Supreme Court has seldom challenged the executive branch on its interpretation of

U.S. treaty obligations or on customary international law.[6] The Supreme Court has also rendered decisions in which it narrowly interpreted international law, hence leaving the executive branch free to violate customary international law or U.S. international treaty obligations.[7] The courts have skillfully avoided ruling on executive branch violations of international law by declaring the issue a "political question."[8] Federal courts have also invoked the doctrine of "Standing" to deny those who file suits against the government. More recently the federal courts have refused to give effect to decisions of the International Court of Justice, which faulted the United States for violating the Vienna Convention on Consular Relations.[9]

Federal courts, however, have ruled on some controversial legal issues in disputes between the United States and foreign governments and between American citizens and foreign governments. In a groundbreaking decision that had tremendous implications for governmental accountability for human rights violations, a federal court in New York decided in 1980 in *Filartiga v. Pena Irala* that Pena Irala of Paraguay was liable for atrocities committed against families of Filartiga while serving in the Paraguayan military. Justice Kaufman upheld the validity of the Alien Tort Statute of 1789 (ATS), which allows foreign nationals to bring civil suits in U.S. courts against foreign government officials for a tort committed in violation of the law of nations.[10] Following that landmark decision the Act has been invoked against a number of foreign government officials, U.S. corporations and non-state foreign entities.[11] Judgments by the courts in these cases have encouraged victims of torture and gross violations of human rights to press their claims in U.S. courts. However, in a major decision in *Sosa v. Alvarez Machain*, and *United States v. Alvarez Machain*, the Supreme Court reversed the decision of the 9th Circuit Court of Appeal, which initially ruled in Machain's favor on the grounds that Jose Francisco Sosa and other Drug Enforcement Administration (DEA) agents had violated the ATCA and the Federal Tort Claims Act (FTCA) by illegally abducting Machain in Mexico and transporting him to the U.S. to face trial for his involvement in the torture and death of a DEA agent.[12] The Supreme Court limited the scope under which individuals can file human rights law suits under ATS by excluding Alvarez Machain's claim of arbitrary arrest and detention as not falling within the standards established by the ATS.[13]

This was the second case involving Alvarez Machain to come before the Supreme Court. Machain, who alleged he was abducted, drugged and unlawfully transported to the United States to face trial for his involvement in the torture and death of a U.S. DEA agent, initially challenged the jurisdiction of the District Court in California to try him in light of his abduction and arbitrary detention. The

District Court affirmed its jurisdiction in the case, but on appeal the 9th Circuit Court of Appeal reversed that ruling on the basis that Machain's abduction violated customary international law and the United States-Mexico Extradition Treaty.[14] The U.S. Government appealed that decision to the Supreme Court. In a surprise ruling the Supreme Court affirmed a long established practice in the U.S. court that the manner of apprehending a defendant is not relevant for establishing criminal jurisdiction. Hence the Supreme Court ruled that Machain's abduction did not violate the U.S.-Mexican Extradition Treaty, as the treaty did not explicitly prohibit the practice.[15] However, the District Court later acquitted Machain on the basis that the evidence against him was insufficient to secure a guilty plea. Machain was then deported to Mexico where he subsequently filed his civil suit against the U.S. Government.

In 1996 Congress passed the Antiterrorism and Effective Death Penalty Act (AEDPA) of 1996 by which it amended the Foreign Sovereign Immunities Act (FSIA) to restrict the scope of sovereign immunities for foreign states that engage in acts that result in the wrongful death or injury of American citizens by means of torture, extra-judicial killing, aircraft sabotage, hostage taking or giving material support or resources to groups to carry out these acts.[16] Following passage of the AEDPA a number of human rights lawsuits have been filed in federal district courts against foreign states and entities for their involvement in or support for such acts.[17] Iran was a party in most of the cases, but it invoked its sovereign immunity and did not appear before the court. The judges in these cases entered default judgments against the defendant state. Although the plaintiffs won judgments against Iran in a majority of these cases they were unable to enjoin Iranian assets in the United States. The U.S. Government sought to prevent plaintiffs from collecting monetary damages in a number of these lawsuits on the grounds that it violated the Algiers Accords, which settled the hostage crisis between Iran and the United States.[18] In other cases the United States argued that seizure of Iranian assets in U.S. possession would violate the Vienna Convention on Diplomatic Relations.

The federal court in New York was also forced to step into a dispute between the Reagan administration and the PLO over the closing of the PLO Mission to the United Nations in New York. The Antiterrorism Act in 1986 called on the President to close the PLO office in Washington and its mission to the United Nations in New York. Passage of the Act conflicted with a U.S. treaty obligation, the 1946 Headquarters Agreement between the U.S. and the United Nations. According to U.S. law the last rule to take effect overrules the existing law. This means the Congressional Statute would take precedent over the 1946 Headquarters

Agreement. However, Judge Palmieri of the federal district court in New York avoided the issue. Instead, he ruled that it was not the intent of Congress to violate the Headquarters Agreement.[19]

As a young nation the United States invoked international law to protect itself from more powerful European nations who had refused to recognize it. For the next century the United States continued to be a strong advocate for international law. The founders of the United States had a keen interest in international law, and they made frequent reference to international law to justify their revolution against British colonialism in order to subsequently win the support and recognition of other nations. One can find numerous references to international law in the writings of the leaders of the American Revolution.[20] The Founders of the United States saw international law as both a protector of their new nation and a restraint against future British aggression. They invoked international law in the Declaration of Independence and incorporated that body of law into the laws of the United States.[21] For the Founding Fathers international law was synonymous with the sovereignty of the new nation.[22] In the early years of the Republic the promotion of and respect for international law became a key pillar of American foreign policy.

The United States was the leading sponsor of the postwar orders established after World Wars I and II. President Wilson's Fourteen Points provided the framework for the creation of the League of Nations and gave birth to several new nations in Central and Eastern Europe.[23] Principles such as the Fourteen Points ultimately became principles of customary international law. The Atlantic Charter signed between President Franklin D. Roosevelt and Prime Minister Churchill of the United Kingdom, and later the Dumbarton Oaks proposal, became the blueprint for the Charter of the United Nations. The United States made sure that international law formed the basis upon which the predication of these post-war orders would take place.[24] Although the United States did not join the League of Nations, it became a member of organizations affiliated with the League, such as the International Labor Organization (ILO) and the World Health Organization (WHO). The United States was a strong proponent of the right of self-determination for the peoples under imperial rule in Eastern and Central Europe and for the dismantling of European colonial empires. During the interwar period the United States and France concluded the Kellog-Briand Pact, which banned war as an instrument of national policy. Although they never ratified the Pact, it has since become part of customary international law. The United States also championed the concept of open diplomacy and the peaceful settlement of disputes. Both the

League Covenant and the Charter of the United Nations incorporated the U.S. vision of a just world order.

After the Second World War the United States provided the leadership that led to the creation of the United Nations and its network of specialized agencies. The United States also provided the financial support to help these organizations get started and to thrive. The United States remains the biggest contributor to the activities of the United Nations and its specialized agencies. The United States called for the dismantling of colonial empires and for the granting of independence to colonial peoples in Africa and Asia. The United States was the chief advocate for prosecuting war criminals from Germany and Japan and was behind the creation of the Nuremberg and Tokyo Tribunals. The United States was also a key architect of the body of international humanitarian law known as the Geneva Conventions. The post-World War II order has the imprimatur of the United States all over it, and it remains very much an American invention.

Although the United States Constitution recognizes international law as the "supreme law of the land" and places it on a par with domestic law and Congressional Statutes, the Founding Fathers remained ambivalent about U.S. involvement in international affairs. The framers of the Constitution established a system of checks and balances between the executive branch and Congress over the conduct of the nation's foreign affairs. In some areas, such as treaty making, war and the appointment of diplomats, they divided the authority between the two political branches.[25] They gave Congress exclusive authority to regulate commerce between the U.S. and other nations and to punish violations of the law of nations.[26] They defined the President's authority in foreign affairs more ambiguously. The Constitution grants the President authority as Commander-in-Chief, but it gives Congress the power to declare war. The President has the authority to negotiate treaties, but treaties can only become law with the support of two-thirds of the Senators present and voting. However, the President's powers in foreign affairs have evolved as a result of Supreme Court decisions affirming the President's authority as the "sole organ" in foreign affairs and granting sovereign authority to the President. One can find additional powers in the President's "Executive Power," in his authority to appoint and receive Ambassadors and negotiate international agreements, and in his oath of office, which calls on him to "take care that the laws are faithfully executed." The President also has inherent powers implied in the Declaration of Independence of the United States as a sovereign nation.[27]

The ascendancy of the United States as a super power after World War II brought with it a shift in the focus of international relations away from Europe to

North America, the Soviet Union, Asia and Africa. As a result of the Cold War the U.S. maintained a strong military presence in Europe. However, a number of new issues, such as decolonization, Soviet expansionism and regional conflicts, would dominate the global agenda. Simultaneously, the authority of the U.S. President in foreign affairs increased, and he became a more dominant figure in the conduct of American foreign policy. The United States abandoned its isolationist policy to become more involved in the creation of a post-war order. United States global reach and the spread of American corporations abroad created a need for greater U.S. involvement in the promulgation of new rules to protect American citizens and business interest overseas. The United States also needed to ensure protection of its network of military bases and military personnel overseas.

With United States interest now spread across the globe, it was important for the United States to promote international law as a means for maintaining a stable international environment and to protect its interest abroad. However, it soon became obvious that the United States was not willing to completely abandon its unilateralist policy, and the post-war planning and the role the U.S. crafted out for itself reflected that attitude. The United States granted itself and the four other permanent members of the Security Council a veto that prevents the United Nations from taking action against a permanent member.[28] The United States initiated a system of weighted voting in the Bretton Woods system that awarded a vote to each member equal to the percentage of its shares in the World Bank and the International Monetary Fund. This voting formula gives the United States 25 percent of the total votes and a virtual veto over decisions of both the Bank and the Fund.[29]

Endnotes

1. Neuman, Gerald. 2004. The uses of international law in constitutional interpretation, *AJIL* 98:82–83.
2. See in general Koh, Harold Kongju. 2004. International law as part of our law, *AJIL* 98:43.
3. Murphy, John F. 2004. *The United States and the rule of law in international affairs*, 98.
4. 175 U.S. 677 (1900) at 700.
5. 376 U.S. 398, 423 (1964); See Curtis Bradley and Jack Goldsmith. 2006. *Foreign relations law*, 91–92.
6. See *Sumitomo Shoji America, Inc. v. Avagliano*, 457 U.S. 176 (1982) at 184–85.
7. See *Sale v. Haitian Centers, Inc.*, 113 S.Ct. 2549 (1993).
8. For an understanding of the Political Question Doctrine, see, *Baker v. Carr*, 369 U.S. 186 (1962); *Goldwater v. Carter*, 444 U.S. 996 (1979).

9. See *Breard v. Greene,* 523 U.S. 371 (1998).
10. *Filartiga v. Pena Irala,* 630 F. 2nd 876 (2d Cir., 1980).
11. See *Wiwa v. Royal Dutch Petroleum Co.,* 226 F. 3d 88 (2d Cir., 2000), *Kadic v. Karadzic,* 70 F. 3d 232 (2nd Cir., 1995), *Lafontant v. Aristide,* 844 F. Supp. 128 (E.D.N.Y., 1994), *Tel-Oren v. Libya Arab Republic,* 726 F. 2d 774 (D.C. Cir., 1984).
12. *Alvarez Machain v. U.S.,* 331 F. 3d 604 (9th Cir., 2003).
13. *Sosa v. Alvarez Machain; United States v. Alvarez Machain,* 124 S.Ct. 2739 (June 29, 2004).
14. *Alvarez Machain v. United States,* 331 F. 3d 604, 610 (9th Cir., 2003) (*en banc*).
15. *United States v. Alvarez Machain,* 504 U.S. 655 (1992).
16. Pub. L. No. 104-132, §221, 110 Stat. 1214, 1241 (1996).
17. *Campuzano v. Iran,* 281 F. Supp. 2d 258 (D.D.C., 2003); *Regier v. Iran,* 281 F. Supp. 2d 87 (D.D.C. 2003); *Dammarell v. Iran,* 281 F. Supp. 2d 105 (D.D.C., 2003); *Cronin v. Iran,* 238 F. Supp. 2d 222 (D.D.C., 2002).
18. Declaration of the Democratic and Popular Republic of Algeria Concerning the Settlement of Claims by the Government of the United States and the Government of the Islamic Republic of Iran, Jan. 19, 1981.
19. *United States v. Palestinian Liberation Organization,* 695 F. Supp. 1456 (S.D.N.Y., 1988).
20. See Pacificus [Hamilton]-Helvidius [Madison] debates on the nature of the foreign Relations power 1793; Reprinted in Jean Smith, *The Constitution and foreign policy* (1989), 48.
21. See Article VI of the Constitution of the United States.
22. Syrett, Harold C., ed. 1961. *The papers of Alexander Hamilton,* 550.
23. Wood, Robert S. 1971. The League of Nations in retrospect: The legal doctrines and political conceptions. In *The process of international organization,* ed. Robert S. Wood, 61.
24. Ibid, 71.
25. See the U.S. Constitution, Article 2, Section 2.
26. Ibid, Article 1, Section 8.
27. *United States v. Curtiss-Wright Export Corporation,* 299 U.S. 304 (1936).
28. Bailey, Sydney D. 1971. Veto in the Security Council. In *The process of international organization,* ed. Robert S. Wood, 224.
29. Spero, Joan Edelman. 1977. *The politics of international economic relations,* 33.

chapter III

THE UNITED STATES AS LAW ENFORCER AND/OR LAW BREAKER

Despite its strong advocacy of the rule of law in international relations, the United States was also a major violator of international law. The United States attacked Libya to stop the practice of Barbary pirates seizing U.S. vessels and holding the crew for ransom. In 1823, the United States issued the pronouncement of the Monroe Doctrine in response to European intervention in the Western Hemisphere. The Doctrine gave the United States an absolute right to intervene in any Latin American states to counter the re-imposition of European colonial rule. In 1812 and 1848 the United States went to war with Mexico, occupied Mexico City and gained control of the southwest territories. In 1898 the United States went to war with Spain over Spanish rule in Cuba. Following its victory in the Spanish-American War, Spain ceded the Philippines and Puerto Rico to the United States. The United States also received an indefinite lease over Guantánamo Bay, Cuba. The war established the dominance of the United States in the western hemisphere, commencing the rise of the United States as a world power.[1]

Other U.S. foreign adventures included support for the rebellion against Colombia that led to the secession of Panama from Colombia. In return the United States received an indefinite lease over the Panama Canal Zone. The United States invaded and occupied Haiti from 1915 to 1939; it overthrew the democratically elected government of Guatemala in 1954; and it orchestrated and funded the Bay of Pigs invasion of Cuba in 1961 in an attempt to overthrown the Castro regime. The United States also attempted to assassinate Fidel Castro numerous times. The

United States invaded the Dominican Republic in 1965, and in 1973 it conspired with the Chilean military to overthrow the elected government of Salvador Allende. The United States intervened in Vietnam and fought a decade-long conflict in Indo-China against Communist insurgents. The United States subsequently bombed Cambodia and Laos and used chemical agents against the civilian population in breach of international humanitarian law.

Between 1980 and 1990 the United States carried out a number of illegal covert military operations in Latin America, Africa and Afghanistan in violation of international law. In 1983, the United States invaded Grenada after the brutal murder of Prime Minister Maurice Bishop and several members of his cabinet following a military coup. President Reagan's initial justification was the protection of American students on the island. But the real motive for the invasion of Grenada was the removal of the radical New Jewel Movement from power because of its close alliance with Cuba and to stop construction of a new airport that Grenada said it needed to boost its tourist industry but which Reagan claimed was a Cuban military base. President Reagan also said that the U.S. had authorization to invade Grenada on the invitation of the Governor General and the collective defense treaty of the Organization of East Caribbean States (OECS). In spite of these claims the United Nations General Assembly overwhelmingly condemned the U.S. invasion as a flagrant violation of international law.[2]

President Reagan was also responsible for mining Nicaragua's harbor and funding and supporting the Nicaraguan *Contras* in their war against the Sandinista government of Daniel Ortega. In 1984, Nicaragua sued the United States before the International Court of Justice (ICJ). In response Reagan withdrew from the court's Compulsory Jurisdiction Clause, which gives state parties the right to file suit against another state without informing the defending state in advance.[3] The United States participated in the first phase of the proceedings but later boycotted the court after the court determined that it had jurisdiction to continue the case against the United States. In 1986, the ICJ ruled against the United States. The ICJ agreed with Nicaragua that the United States had violated international law in mining Nicaragua's harbor and funding the *Contras*.[4]

In 1989, President Bush invaded Panama after General Manuel Noriega annulled the results of a democratic election and defied him. Tension between the United States and Panama further deteriorated after Noriega accused the U.S. of declaring war on Panama and after the beating of an American soldier and his family in the Canal Zone. A United States court in Florida had also indicted General Noriega on drug charges and issued a warrant for his arrest. United States forces overwhelmed Panama's military and captured the capital. A new government was quickly installed, which issued an invitation for U.S. forces to remain in Panama. Bush later justified the invasion of Panama on the basis of (i) the invitation of the government of Panama; (ii) U.S. obligation under the Panama Canal Treaty to defend the canal from external threats; (iii) the need to protect American citizens whose lives were threatened by General Noriega's regime; and (iv) the necessity of bringing General Noriega to justice in the United States.[5] Britain, France and the United States vetoed a resolution in the Security Council condemning the U.S. invasion of Panama. However, a similar resolution in the United Nations General Assembly condemned the U.S. invasion as a flagrant violation of international law.[6]

The United States was also involved in a number of other incidents in violation of international law. In 1982, President Reagan bombed Libya in response to a terrorist attack on a Berlin discotheque that injured several American servicemen. In 1983, Reagan ordered U.S. warplanes to commandeer an Egyptian airline and force it to return to Italy so Italian authorities could arrest and charge the hijackers of an Italian cruise liner who were responsible for killing an American on board the vessel. Between 1981 and 1988 Reagan supported the UNITA rebels of Angola in their civil war against the Cuban-backed Angolan government. Reagan not only supported the apartheid regime of South Africa but blocked efforts in the Security Council to impose economic sanctions against the white minority regime. The United States repeatedly violated the 1977 arms embargo the Security Council imposed on South Africa. The United States overlooked and in some cases contributed to severe human rights violations and atrocities committed by its anti-communist allies in the Third World. In some instances the United States contributed to these abuses by allowing the use of American weapons to clamp down on dissent. In spite of the evidence of U.S. violations of international law, the United States defended its actions as permissible under the United Nations Charter and customary international law. The United States blocked efforts by the United Nations to investigate these atrocities or to condemn them. The United States never admitted to violating international law, and even in cases where the violations were blatant the United States continued to maintain that it acted legally.

Since taking office President Bush has adopted a very hostile attitude toward international law and institutions. Bush has shown tremendous disdain for international law and institutions and has only complied with international law when it advances a very narrowly defined, short-term interest of the United States as articulated by a small group of ideologues in the administration. Many in President Bush's administration argue that the President can disregard international law if he is fulfilling his statutory obligation under the Constitution.[7] Bush and his supporters believe international law constrains the ability of the United States to conduct foreign affairs. The administration also sees the United States as the sole global power and believes it should have the freedom to operate in the global arena without the restrictions imposed on states by international law and institutions. The Bush administration has made it clear that it can violate international law when it is in the U.S. national interest to do so. The September 11 terrorist attacks on the United States gave the Bush administration an excuse to disregard international law in pursuit of its war on terror and to operate in the global arena with impunity.

Indeed, the current attitude of the United States toward international law preceded President Bush. The support of the United States for international law and international institutions and its compliance with its international legal obligations was on the decline long before President Bush took office. President Clinton was responsible for unprovoked military attacks on Sudan and Iraq.[8] He called for a premature withdrawal of U.S. and U.N. forces from Somalia and opposed a direct military intervention in Bosnia to stop the atrocities against Bosnian Muslims and in Rwanda to stop the genocide against Tutsis. Clinton also imposed strict conditions on the United Nations' ability to deploy forces in conflict zones. President Clinton signed but did not submit to the Senate the Kyoto Protocol to the United Nations Framework Convention on Climate Change (UNFCCC) due to opposition from the Chairman of the Senate Foreign Relations Committee, Jesse Helms, who threatened to derail the treaty.[9] He reluctantly signed the Rome Statute for the International Criminal Court (ICC) in his final days in office without submitting it to the Senate for approval.[10]

President Clinton did not lobby hard enough for passage of the Comprehensive Test Ban Treaty (CTBT), which the Senate rejected. He did not submit to the Senate for ratification a number of human rights treaties the United States had previously signed but had not ratified. President Clinton did not sign the Convention on the Prohibition of the Use, Stockpiling, Production and Transfer of Anti-personnel Mines and Their Destruction (the Landmines Convention) after the rejection of a U.S. request for an exemption to certain provisions of the treaty.[11] Clinton signed the Convention on Biodiversity and the amended Convention on the Law of the Sea, but the Senate ratified neither.[12]

When President Bush took office the United States' record on international law and its commitment to multilateralism was already on the decline. President Bush's attitude toward international law and international institutions is ideologically driven and far exceeds the arrogance displayed by his predecessors. Although

Bush tends to be more vocal in his opposition to international law, he has basically continued the practice of American exceptionalism begun in the early 1800s with the pronouncement of the Monroe Doctrine, which became more popular after the Second World War with the growth of American military and economic power.[13] The Bush administration's treatment of detainees at Guantánamo Bay, Bagram and Abu Graib, its invasion of Iraq without United Nations authorization and its rejection of the Rome Statute for the ICC and the Kyoto Protocol have exposed the administration to public criticism from traditional allies and foes alike as being hostile to international law and institutions.[14] Although President Bush's record indicates a President who is acting consistent with traditional U.S. foreign policy and diplomatic relations, his decision to invade Iraq without authorization from the United Nations Security Council and the difficulty managing the postwar situation in Iraq further eroded the image of the U.S. as a major contributor to international legal development and an enforcer of international law. In invading Iraq the Bush administration claimed it was enforcing Security Council resolutions. However, nothing in Security Council resolution 1441 (2003) authorized the United States to act unilaterally on behalf of the United Nations. The legal justifications provided by the Bush administration for the invasion of Iraq were inconsistent with international law and the United Nations Charter. The United States therefore was a lawbreaker, not an enforcer of international law.

Endnotes

1. Schlesinger, Arthur M. 1973. *The imperial presidency,* 82.
2. A/Res/38/7, of Nov. 2, 1983; the vote was 108 to 9, with 27 abstentions, 1983 UNYB, at 214.
3. Article 36 (2) of the Statute of the International Court of Justice.
4. Military and Paramilitary Activities in and Against Nicaragua (*Nicaragua v. United States of America*), Judgment (1986), at *http://icj-cij.org.*
5. Chesterman, Simon. 1989. Rethinking Panama: International law and the U.S. invasion of Panama. In *The reality of international law,* ed. Guy S. Goodwin-Gill and Stefan Talmon (eds.), 60.
6. A/Res/44/240, of December 29,1989, by a vote of 75 to 20, with 64 abstentions. 1989 UNYB, 175.
7. Bolton, John. 2002. Is There Really 'Law' in International Affairs? *Transnat'l L. & Contemp. Probs.,* 10:1.
8. Kohen, Marcelo G. *The use of force by the United States after the end of the cold war, and its impact on international law, supra* note 6 at 197, 203.

9. Deller, Nicole, Arjun Makhijani and John Burroughs, ed. 2003. *Rule of power or rule of law?* 105.
10. Krisch, Nico. *More equal than the rest? Hierarchy, equality and the U.S. predominance in international law, supra* note 6 at 135, 169.
11. The United States had sought an exemption in order to maintain landmines in the Demilitarized Zone on the Korean Peninsula to defend against a possible attack from North Korea.
12. See in general Nico Krisch. 2002. Weak as a constraint, strong as a tool: The place of law in U.S. foreign policy." In *Unilateralism & U.S. Foreign Policy,* ed. David Malone and Yuen Foong Khong.
13. For a critique of U.S. exceptionalism, see in general Peter Malanczuk. 2001. The International Criminal Court and Landmines: What are the Consequences of Leaving the U.S. Behind? *European Journal of International Law,* 11:77.
14. The United States has become increasingly isolated from its traditional allies, including the UK, as the only industrialized country not to sign major multilateral treaties.

chapter IV

INTERNATIONAL LAW AND THE CURRENT BUSH ADMINISTRATION

During the 2000 presidential campaign, candidate Bush displayed little understanding of international law and institutions. He vowed to reverse some of President Clinton's achievements in foreign affairs, particularly U.S. involvement in United Nations peacekeeping activities, humanitarian missions and nations-building initiatives.[1] Bush opposed ratification of the Rome Statute for the International Criminal Court and vowed to withdraw the U.S. signature from the treaty, if elected. He also voiced skepticism about the Kyoto Protocol and said the United States would not ratify it. Bush, like many of his Republican backers, objected to signing multilateral treaties that they felt would constrain the United States' ability to project its power in a unipolar world. Bush favored a selected brand of multilateralism that would allow him to pick and choose which treaties best served the national interest of the United States and therefore were worthy of backing.[2] Bush said he would withdraw from the Anti-Ballistic Missile Treaty (ABM) and review U.S. participation in all United Nations peacekeeping missions. For Bush, the United States should dictate the rules of international conduct but be exempted from following them.

Following his inauguration after the controversial 2000 election, President Bush's first act was to immediately cancel support for the United Nations Fund for Population Activities (UNFPA).[3] The measure was a clear violation of an important U.S. treaty obligation. The President sided with the more conservative wing of the Republican Party that opposed abortion and believed UNFPA encourages abortion as a family planning measure. President Bush refused to submit to the Senate for ratification the Kyoto Protocol for reducing greenhouse gases. Bush disputes the scientific evidence that human activity is in part responsible for the greenhouse gases that contribute to the depletion of the ozone layer and drastic climate change.[4] Although U.S. negotiators considered the treaty flawed, and many Senators had voiced opposition to it, Bush, like Clinton, made no effort to have the treaty renegotiated to make it acceptable to the United States Senate. President Bush believes that the Kyoto Protocol would adversely affect U.S. economic competitiveness and deems it unacceptable to the United States in its present form.[5] The President also thinks that developing nations such as India and China should do more to reduce greenhouse gases. The United States contributes 25 percent of the greenhouse gases responsible for global warming. An agreement without U.S. participation will certainly not achieve the objectives of the treaty. President Bush also sought exemptions for U.S. companies from the Ozone-Layer Protection Treaty, which calls for a ban on methyl bromide by 2005, a popular pesticide that damages the environment.[6]

At a review conference of the Kyoto Protocol held in Montreal in December 2005, the Bush administration fought hard to undermine the talks by opposing effort to hold a review conference to adopt more stringent measures for reducing carbon dioxide when the Kyoto Protocol expires in 2012. The United States subsequently relented on its position to oppose the treaty outright by agreeing to participate in future talks. The U.S. Undersecretary for Global Affairs, Paula Dobriansky, said the Bush administration would oppose any formalized discussions that called for "a one size fits all approach" to climate change. President Bush has resisted efforts to imposed benchmarks on reduction in greenhouse gases. Instead, the President advocates a market approach that would provide for trading in pollution and for the development of new technologies to reduce global warming. Most of the delegates at the Montreal Conference rejected that approach as inadequate.[7] Prior to commencement of the G8 summit in Germany, and in response to pressure from the German Chancellor, Angela Merkel and then British Prime Minister, Tony Blair, President Bush proposed a September 26 international conference of all the major producers of greenhouse gases to begin immediately after the United Nations conference in New York to discuss a new treaty after the Kyoto Protocol expires in 2012. The United States did not participate in the United Nations conference, nor did President Bush mention the issue of global climate change in his address before the General Assembly. The U.S. conference of major polluters seems designed to undermine the United Nations conference, which calls for the international community to take more drastic mandatory measures to reduce greenhouse gases. The Bush administration favors voluntary cuts in greenhouse gases, a strategy most experts believe is unworkable. The administration also took a similar position at the follow-up conference in Bali, Indonesia, which was intended to begin negotiations for a post-Kyoto climate change framework convention. After much pressure from delegates from developing countries, the Bush administration accepted a proposal to include mandatory benchmarks for reducing greenhouse gases in a future treaty.[8]

The President's position is untenable. American states and corporations have taken the lead in opposing the policies of the administration on climate change. Many states have adopted more stringent measures, consistent with the Kyoto Protocol, and exceed what the Bush administration is proposing. Several states also sued the Bush administration to force the Environmental Protection Agency (EPA) to adhere to provisions of the Clean Air Act that the Bush administration had deemed outside the authority of the EPA. The Supreme Court ruled in favor of the states.[9]

Long before Bush was elected President of the United States, members of his Republican Party were vehemently hostile to the Rome Statute for the establishment of the International Criminal Court (ICC), and they campaigned vigorously to undermine the treaty. Bush made no effort to renegotiate provisions of the treaty his administration found incompatible with U.S. law. Prior to the treaty entering into force on July 1, 2002, the Bush administration notified the United Nations of its intention to withdraw from the treaty. In a letter to Secretary General Kofi Anan, as depositary of the treaty, John Bolton informed him that the United States would not become a party to the treaty and that the United States has no legal obligations arising from its signature on December 31, 2000.[10] The State Department thereafter gave the reasons why the United States would not join the ICC:

1. it undermined the role of the UN Security Council in maintaining international peace and security;
2. it created a prosecutorial system that is an unchecked power;
3. it purports to assert jurisdiction over nationals of states that have not ratified the treaty; and
4. it is therefore built on a "flawed foundation."[11]

The president's action was unprecedented in the history of the United States, as it was the first time a seating president withdrew the signature of his predecessor from a treaty.

President Clinton was a strong advocate for the creation of the *ad hoc* International Criminal Tribunal for the Former Yugoslavia (ICTY) and the International Criminal Tribunal for Rwanda (ICTR) following U.S. refusal to directly intervene in the conflicts in Bosnia and Rwanda to stop the killing of civilians. The Clinton administration subsequently made significant financial contributions and provided technical support for the operation of the tribunals. Clinton created a new post of Ambassador-at-Large for War Crimes within the State Department to work closely with the two tribunals. He also established reward programs of $5 million each for the capture of fugitive war criminals indicted by the ICTY and ICTR.[12] Clinton signed an Executive Agreement with the ICTR to surrender suspected indicted war criminals to the tribunal. The Justice Department vigorously defended that agreement in a challenge to the extradition of Elizaphan Ntakirutimana to the ICTR.[13]

Like Clinton, President Bush continued U.S. cooperation with the *ad hoc* tribunals. He renewed the rewards for the capture of fugitive war criminals indicted by the two tribunals, and he made aid to Serbia contingent on its cooperation with the ICTY. That requirement, coupled with a similar demand from the European Union for commencing accession talks with Serbia, led to the extradition of Slobodan Milošvić to the ICTY. However, President Bush was less enthusiastic about the whole idea of establishing international tribunals than his predecessor. Bush's Ambassador-at-Large for War Crimes, Pierre Prosper, was critical of the slow pace of the tribunal and called for them to expedite their caseload. Prosper further called for the tribunals to reach plea bargain agreements with low ranking war crimes suspects, and for the tribunals to wrap up their work by 2008. In 2003 the United States co-sponsored a Security Council resolution calling for the ICTY and ICTR to complete their work by 2008.[14] As an alternative the Bush administration favored the creation of mixed international tribunals, such as the Special Court for Sierra Leone, which the Security Council established at U.S. urging.[15] These tribunals would have limited jurisdiction based on national and international law and would include a combination of national and international judges. The U.S. also supported a tribunal for Cambodia to try former members of the Pol Pot regime. The U.S. did not support a United Nations tribunal for the trial of Saddam Hussein and members of the Ba'ath Party. Instead the Bush administration helped establish the Iraqi Special Tribunal under the new Iraqi constitution. Human rights organizations criticized that tribunal as fundamentally flawed and biased against the defendants.

The Clinton administration played a key role in the negotiations leading to the adoption of the Rome Statute for the establishment of the International Criminal Court (ICC), and it remained committed to international justice. Most United States concerns were addressed and settled before the treaty was signed, with the exception of two issues: an exemption for American citizens and a Security Council veto over referrals to the court.[16] The majority of delegates were not willing to exempt U.S. citizens or soldiers from prosecution. A substantial number also felt granting the Security Council a veto over what crimes the court should investigate would compromise the integrity and independence of the ICC.[17] Sensing opposition in Congress and the Pentagon, President Clinton delayed signing the treaty until his final days in office and only days before the deadline to sign the treaty was to expire.[18] Upon signing the treaty, Clinton issued a statement in which he said:

> The United States is today signing the 1998 Rome Treaty on the International Criminal Court. In taking this action, we join more than 130 other countries that have signed by the December 31, 2000, deadline established in the treaty. We do so to reaffirm our strong support for international accountability and for bringing to justice perpetrators of genocide, war crimes, and crimes against humanity. We do so as well because we wish to remain engaged in making the ICC an instrument of impartial and effective justice in the years to come.
>
> The United States has a long history of commitment to the principle of accountability, from our involvement in the Nuremberg tribunals that brought Nazi war criminals to justice, to our leadership in the effort to establish the international criminal tribunals for the Former Yugoslavia and Rwanda. Our action today sustains that tradition of moral leadership.
>
> Under the Rome Treaty, the International Criminal Court (ICC) will come into being with the ratification of 60 governments and will have jurisdiction over the most heinous abuses that result from international conflict, such as war crimes, crimes against humanity, and genocide. The treaty requires that the ICC not supersede or interfere with functioning national judicial systems; that is, the ICC prosecutor is authorized to take action against a suspect only if the country or nationality is unwilling or unable to investigate allegations of egregious crimes by their national. The U.S. delegation to the Rome Conference worked hard to achieve these limitations, which we believe are essential to the international credibility and success of the ICC.
>
> In signing, however, we are not abandoning our concerns about significant flaws in the treaty. In particular, we are concerned that when the court comes into existence it will not only exercise authority over personnel of states that

> have ratified the treaty but also claim jurisdiction over personnel of states that have not. With signature, however, we will be in a position to influence the evolution of the court. Without signature, we will not.
>
> Signature will enhance our ability to further protect U.S. officials from unfounded charges and to achieve the human rights and accountability objectives of the ICC. In fact, in negotiations following the Rome Conference, we have worked effectively to develop procedures that limit the likelihood of politicized prosecutions. For example, U.S. civilian and military negotiators helped to ensure greater precision in the definitions of crimes within the court's jurisdiction.
>
> But more must be done. Court jurisdiction over U.S. personnel should come only with U.S. ratification of the treaty. The United States should have the chance to observe and assess the function of the court, over time, before choosing to become a subject to its jurisdiction. Given these concerns, I will not, and do not recommend that my successor, submit the treaty to the Senate for advice and consent until our fundamental concerns are satisfied."[19]

The message to the international community was that the United States wanted to establish a dual system of justice, one for American citizens and another for the rest of the world. Clinton's statement placed the future of the treaty in jeopardy and the prospect that the Senate would never ratify it.

President Bush's vehement opposition to the ICC gave ammunition to opponents in Congress to pass legislation to restrict U.S. cooperation with the new court. Congress subsequently passed the American Service Members Protection Act (ASPA), sometimes referred to as (the Hague Invasion Act), to prevent the President from cooperating with the ICC.[20] The Act prohibits

1. any U.S. court and any state or local government from responding to a request for cooperation from, or supporting the ICC;
2. U.S. agencies from transferring a letter rogatory or any other ICC request for cooperation to the U.S. entity to whom it is addressed;
3. the federal government, any state or local government from extraditing a person from the United States to the ICC; and
4. ICC investigative activities on U.S. territory.

In addition, the ASPA prohibits the deployment of U.S. troops with United Nations peacekeeping missions unless they are protected from the ICC.[21] The law calls for the U.S. to seek a permanent exemption from the ICC as a precondition for U.S. participation in United Nations operations. Furthermore, section 2007 of ASPA prohibits military assistance to any state that is party to the Rome Statute, with the exception of NATO countries, a major non-NATO ally, Taiwan or countries the President grants a waiver to upon signing an Article 98 agreement with the United States. The President may waive the restriction imposed by section 2007 of the Act if he determines and notifies Congress that the waiver "is important to the national interest of the United States." President Bush exercised such authority in over a dozen cases. However, in October 2006 the President signed a memorandum in which he permanently waived the prohibition of section 2007 (a) of the Act with respect to a number of Caribbean, Latin American and African countries.[22] Congress later included an earmark into the Defense Authorization Act for fiscal year 2007 to permanently repeal the prohibition on assistance under the Foreign Assistance Act of 1961.[23]

In signing the Act into law on August 22, 2002, President Bush sided with his conservative allies in Congress and vowed not to cooperate with the ICC unless he received an exemption for American citizens.[24] Bush also threatened to withhold U.S. funding or to veto future United Nations peacekeeping missions unless the Security Council explicitly exempts American servicemen from criminal prosecution before the ICC.[25] President Bush made an exemption from the ICC for U.S. military personnel serving in United Nations peacekeeping missions a top priority of his administration, and he pressured a number of nations into signing an Article 98 bilateral agreement with the United States to forbid them from extraditing American citizens to the ICC.[26] The Bush administration threatened to cut off military aid to any country that did not sign such an agreement with the United States.[27] So far, over a hundred countries have signed such agreements under threat of losing U.S. foreign assistance.[28] However, some key U.S. allies in Europe and Latin American refused to sign an Article 98 agreement and became ineligible for military training and assistance.[29]

Under pressure from the Bush administration, the Security Council voted twice to grant one-year exemptions to American servicemen serving in United Nations peacekeeping missions from the reach of the Court in exchange for continued U.S. participation in United Nations peacekeeping operations.[30] However, on the recommendation of the Secretary General, several members of the Security Council opposed renewing the agreement for a third time.[31] The United States subsequently withdrew the resolution, requesting a further exemption.[32] It is not clear how this will affect future U.S. participation in United Nations peacekeeping activities, especially in places like Darfur, Sudan. The issue has become a major point of contention between the United States and its European allies.

President Bush opposed the United Nations Convention on Illicit Trade in Small Arms and Light Weapons in All Its Aspects. The intention of the treaty is to ban the sale of small arms to war-torn nations such as Liberia, Sierra Leone, Burundi and the Democratic Republic of the Congo (DRC). The United States is a leading exporter of small arms and sells over $1 billion worth of such weapons to developing countries. Most of these weapons end up in Africa and Asia and are responsible for fueling the civil wars in countries in those two regions.[33] Many of these weapons are used to commit atrocities against civilians, particularly women and children.

The Bush Administration did not revisit the Ottawa Landmines Convention with the intention of signing it. Bush later shifted his administration's policy on the use of land mines but did not call for a complete ban, as the Ottawa Treaty requires.[34] Bush initially supported a review of the United Nations Biological Weapons Convention but abandoned the review process over objections to the monitoring mechanism, which the administration deemed too intrusive.[35] The Senate ratified the Chemical Weapons Convention, but critics challenged its inspection regime as incompatible with the Fourth Amendment of the U.S. Constitution. Congress subsequently passed legislation to implement the treaty, but it limited the authority of the inspection regime, which requires intrusive onsite inspection of all chemical weapons facilities.[36] President Bush opposed the Comprehensive Test Ban Treaty (CTBT) and has taken steps to withdraw the U.S.'s signature from that treaty. Although the United States has the technical capabilities to conduct computer simulated nuclear testing, it continues to insist on the right to conduct underground testing.

In December 2001, President Bush carried out his campaign pledge to withdraw from the Anti-Ballistic Missile Treaty (ABM) by notifying Russia of his administration's intention to withdraw from the treaty after the six-month notification requirement expires.[37] The President opted out of the treaty in order to pursue development of a space-based missile defense system to protect the United States mainland from incoming missiles from rogue nations. President Bush claimed that the treaty was no longer relevant given the threats posed by terrorist organizations and the vulnerability of the United States to incoming missiles launched by such organizations. The President was also concerned about the proliferation of weapons of mass destruction by *rogue* nations like North Korea, Iran and Iraq, which he labeled the "axis of evil" in his 2002 State of the Union Address.[38] The President's decision to withdraw from the ABM treaty destroyed what many considered the cornerstone of arms control agreements between the United States and the Soviet Union for the past four decades. A group of thirty-two Congressmen later filed suit in U.S. District Court to stop the President from withdrawing from the ABM Treaty without Senate advice and consent. But the court ruled that the plaintiffs lack standing and that the issue was political.[39]

President Bush followed his decision to withdraw from the ABM Treaty with an announcement in September 2002 of his new National Security Strategy (NSS). The doctrine departed sharply from previous national security doctrines by emphasizing preemptive strikes against nations suspected of possessing weapons of mass destruction or nuclear weapons capabilities.[40] Previous U.S. doctrines had emphasized a strong second-strike capability and Mutual Assured Destruction (MAD). The Bush doctrine made reference to an evolving right under international law for nations to use preemptive military force against rogue nations possessing weapons of mass destruction.[41] However, if implemented, the administration's new National Security Strategy would violate Article 51 of the United Nations Charter, which limits states' right to self-defense only "if an armed attack occurs." The Charter regime does not permit anticipatory self-defense or preemptive strikes.[42]

President Bush's second National Security Strategy, announced in March 2005, abandoned his doctrine of preemption and concentrated instead on the more immediate threats and challenges facing the United States. President Bush singled out the Iranian regime and extremist enemies with weapons of mass destruction as the greatest threat facing the United States. The new strategy called for strengthening alliances and building partnerships in order to secure strategic access and retain global freedom of action.[43]

President Bush has pursued a non-proliferation policy that targets selected countries and ignores others. Bush's non-proliferation policy calls for stopping the spread of nuclear weapons among *rogue regimes,* such as Iran, North Korea and Syria. However, the administration has said little about countries such as Pakistan, India and Israel, which knowingly possess nuclear weapons and the means of delivering them. In fact, President Bush rewarded Pakistan for its cooperation on the war on terror by lifting the U.S. ban on the sale of F-16 warplanes to Pakistan, which previous administrations had maintained due to Pakistan's nuclear weapons program and its failure to open its facilities to IAEA on-site inspection.[44] The Bush administration did not impose sanctions on Pakistan for its sale of nuclear weapons technology to North Korea and Libya. Instead, the administration accepted Pakistan's explanation that a *rogue* scientist sold the material to these countries without the knowledge of President Musharraf. President Musharraf subsequently received an invitation to the White House.

In an effort to improve relations with India and to build a counterweight to China's growing military and economic power in Asia, President Bush visited India in March 2006 and signed a Nuclear Cooperation Agreement with the Indian Government. The agreement requires the United States to share civilian nuclear technology with India in exchange for India's commitment to open its civilian nuclear facilities to IAEA inspection. But India will continue to keep its military facilities closed to international inspection. The agreement undermines the nuclear Non-Proliferation regime by rewarding India despite its refusal to sign the NPT and open its facilities to international inspection. The agreement will also complicate diplomatic efforts to persuade Iran and North Korea to give up their nuclear ambition. In December 2006 Congress tentatively approved the U.S.-India nuclear agreement, and President Bush signed it into law. The Indian Parliament delayed approval of the agreement for fear it may constrain India's ability to continue developing its nuclear weapons program. However, in July the Indian Parliament approved the accord, which paved the way for Prime Minister Manmohan Singh to ratify the agreement. The U.S. House of Representatives approved the agreement on September 27, and the Senate gave its approval on October 2. President Bush signed into law the United States-India Nuclear Cooperation Approval and Nonproliferation Enhancement Act on October 8, and Secretary of State Rice and her India counterpart formally exchanged instruments of ratification of the agreement on October 11. The agreement will allow the United States to begin export of civilian nuclear material to India. However, before the United States can begin nuclear trade with India, India must sign a safeguard agreement with the IAEA and a convention with the Nuclear Suppliers Group, which approved the U.S.-India accord in September. The U.S.-India nuclear agreement reversed a three-decade policy of the United States to deny nuclear material to states that are not signatories to the NPT.[45]

The Bush administration strongly opposes Iran's development of uranium enrichment program, which it believes Iran is using to manufacture a nuclear bomb. Bush continues to pressure the Iranian regime to cancel the program or face international sanctions. Iran claims that its nuclear program is for civilian purposes and that no one has a right to prevent it from developing such a program. The United States and its European allies believe Iran is developing a nuclear weapons program and want Iran to terminate the program. Bush rejects direct talks with Iran but supports negotiations by Britain, France and Germany (EU-3) with Iran.

On the insistence of the United States, France, Britain and Germany, the IAEA Board of Governors, voted to refer Iran to the Security Council.[46] However, the likelihood of a successful Security Council resolution of the Iranian nuclear crisis seems remote. Instead of a resolution invoking Chapter VII, the Security Council agreed to a vaguely worded Presidential Statement in which it said:

> The Security Council notes with serious concern Iran's decision to resume enrichment-related activities, including research and development, and to suspend cooperation with the IAEA under the Additional Protocol.
>
> The Security Council calls upon Iran to take the steps required by the IAEA Board of Governors, notably in the first operative paragraph of its resolution GOV/2006/14, which are essential to build confidence in the exclusively peaceful purpose of its nuclear program and to resolve outstanding questions, and underlines, in this regards, the particular importance of re-establishing full and sustained suspension of all enrichment-related and reprocessing activities, including research and development, to be verified by the IAEA.
>
> The Security Council expresses the conviction that such suspension and full, verified Iranian compliance with the requirements set out by the IAEA Board of Governors would contribute to a diplomatic, negotiated solution that guarantees Iran's nuclear program is for exclusively peaceful purposes, and underlines the willingness of the international community to work positively for such a solution which will also benefit nuclear non-proliferation elsewhere.
>
> The Security Council requests in 30 days a report from the Director General of the IAEA on the process of Iranian compliance with the steps required by the IAEA Board, to the IAEA Board of Governor and in parallel to the Security Council for its consideration."[47] Given China and Russia's opposition to the imposition of sanctions on Iran, the options for the Security Council seem limited.[48] Given the Bush administration's limited options in Iran, it must rely on surrogates to persuade Iran to cooperate with the international community.

In an attempt to persuade Iran to terminate its nuclear weapons program, the five permanent members of the Security Council plus Germany offered Iran a package of incentives, which if rejected would result in "serious consequences."[49] So far, Iran has not responded to the offer but previously rejected as insulting a thirty-one-page proposal presented by the EU-3. President Bush has repeatedly threatened Iran with sanctions if it does not accept the EU-3 proposal. Iranian officials welcomed the proposal but have maintained that they have a sovereign right to develop a nuclear program. Following weeks of diplomatic wrangling between the permanent members of the Security Council over the appropriate sanction measures to impose on Iran, the Security Council voted unanimously on December 23, 2006 to sanction Iran for its failure to suspend its nuclear program. Acting under Chapter Article 41 of Chapter VII, the Security Council called on Iran to suspend its proliferation-sensitive nuclear activities along with all enrichment-related and processing activities, including research and development, which the IAEA must verify. In addition, it required that the IAEA also verify work on all heavy water-related projects, including the construction of a research reactor moderated by heavy water. The resolution also called on the state to prevent the sale of nuclear-related technology, which would contribute to Iran's enrichment-related reprocessing or heavy water-related activities, or the development of nuclear weapon delivery systems.[50]

Following the expiration of the time given to Iran to comply with the demands of the Security Council under resolution 1737 (2006), the Security Council adopted resolution 1747 (2007) to impose additional sanctions on Iran. Resolution 1747 (2007) reaffirmed the demands of the Security Council specified in resolutions 1696 (2006) and 1737 (2006), which called on Iran to discontinue its nuclear weapons program and to cooperate with the IAEA to meet the requirements of the IAEA Bard of Governors. Acting under Article 41 of Chapter VII of the Charter of the United Nations, the Security Council banned the sale or procurement of nuclear weapons technology to or from Iran. The Security Council also imposed a ban on financial transactions with the Government of Iran, and it froze the assets of some targeted individuals, institutions and Iranian Revolutionary Guard Corps entities, as well as members of the Iranian Revolutionary Guards.[51] This new sanctions regime may have an adverse effect on Iran's effort to develop its natural gas fields. Foreign oil companies are at risk of being penalized by the United States if they enter joint ventures with Iran.

Iran denounced the sanctions and vowed not to cooperate or discontinue its nuclear development program. Iran continued to maintain that its nuclear program was for peaceful purposes and that it would not halt the project. Iran also claimed that it was being treated unfairly, and that the Security Council was opposed to Iran's development of nuclear enrichment for civilian use but would not condemn Israel, Pakistan and India for possessing nuclear weapons. Iran further claimed that the United States and Britain were using the Security Council to bring about regime change in Iran. The Bush administration continues to pressure Iran to abandon its nuclear program and to accept the EU proposal for resolving the dispute, but Iran has rejected that proposal. President Bush accused Iran of meddling in Iraq and supplying explosive devices to insurgents in Iraq. The Bush administration has also deployed two naval destroyers in the Persian Gulf and conducted war games off the coast of Iran to intimidate Iran.

Following the release of new reports by the IAEA and the European Commission, the United States called for new United Nations sanctions against Iran.

However, both Russia and China were reluctant to go along with the U.S. proposal and called for Iran to receive more time to declare its nuclear program. The release by the CIA of a new National Intelligence Estimate (NIE), which said Iran had halted its nuclear weapons program in 2003, has cast doubt on the likelihood of passage of any new sanctions against Iran.

The Bush administration has had similar difficulty persuading North Korea to give up its nuclear weapons program. President Bush initially opposed direct talks with North Korea over dismantling its nuclear weapons program, and he criticized the Agreed Framework the Clinton administration negotiated with Pyongyang, which provided billions of dollars in energy aid and political concessions to North Korea in exchange for cancellation of its nuclear weapons program. However, after years of making no progress with North Korea, the Bush administration shifted its position and agreed to participate in the Six-Party Talks, which includes Japan, China, Russia, South Korea and the United States.[52] In September 2004 the parties reached an agreement that calls for North Korea to discontinue its nuclear weapons program in exchange for normalization of diplomatic relations with the U.S. and a series of financial and energy incentives from the other participating countries. The parties agreed to finalize the details of that agreement at a fifth round of talks in late November 2006, but North Korea reneged on the agreement.[53]

The Bush administration has had little leverage over the North Korean regime and continues to change its policy to meet North Korea's demands. The Bush administrative was surprised when North Korea tested a nuclear device in October 2006. The administration condemned North Korea's behavior and threatened to take the matter to the Security Council. The Bush administration's response to North Korea's nuclear test underscores its limited policy options against Pyongyang. Given the Bush administration's difficulties in Iraq and Afghanistan, a military strike against North Korea is inconceivable. A military attack would certainly lead North Korea to retaliate by attacking Seoul or Tokyo, which would cause millions of civilian casualties. For this reason the Bush administration turned to the United Nations for help. However, the options for the United Nations Security Council are equally limited.

The United States sponsored a draft resolution in the Security Council calling for comprehensive sanctions against North Korea. However, against opposition from China, the Security Council adopted a watered-down version of the resolution in which it called on North Korea to reconsider its withdrawal from the Nuclear Non-Proliferation Treaty (NPT) and to abandon all its activities related to nuclear weapons. The resolution also imposed sanctions on the sale of battle tanks, armored combat vehicles, large caliber artillery systems, combat aircraft, attack helicopters, warships and missiles or missile systems as defined for the purpose of the United Nations Register on Conventional Arms. The resolution also banned the sale of luxury goods to North Korea.[54]

The sanctions the Security Council imposed on North Korea will have little or no impact on North Korea's behavior. North Korea is already under U.S. sanctions and is one of the most closed societies in the world. The new sanctions will not force the regime to negotiate an end to its nuclear program. The nuclear test will increase the regime's bargaining power at future Six-Party talks and improve North Korea's chances of getting a better deal from the U.S. than previously offered.

In June North Korea formally signed the Six Party agreement, which called for Pyongyang to dismantle its nuclear weapons program and to open its nuclear facilities to international inspectors. The Bush administration hailed the agreement as a diplomatic success in spite of criticism from the opponents of that agreement. In November North Korea submitted a report on its nuclear program. In exchange for North Korea's acceptance of the agreement the Bush administration agreed to lift the freeze on North Korea's assets in Banco Delta Asia (BDA) in Macau and to transfer millions of dollars of North Korean assets via Moscow. The United States also agreed to remove North Korea from the list of state sponsors of terrorism after North Korea turned over a report detailing its nuclear program.[55] The Bush administration was to remove North Korea from the terrorism list within forty-five days after formally notifying Congress. However, opposition in Congress toward the deal made it difficult for Mr. Bush to keep his promise. In September North Korea reneged on the agreement and resumed its nuclear program. The U.S. negotiator, Christopher Hill, flew to Pyongyang to meet with North Korean officials in an attempt to salvage the agreement. On October 12 North Korea agreed to resume compliance with the agreement and to allow international inspectors access to its nuclear sites. In response the Bush administration, in a desperate move to save one of its few foreign policy achievements, formally removed North Korea from the list of terrorist nations.[56]

Similarly, the Bush administration was opposed to negotiating with Libya because of Libya's status as a state sponsor of terrorism. Libya had been implicated in the terrorist bombing of Pan Am flight 103 and was also accused of supporting various terrorist organizations in the Middle East. Libya subsequently accepted a United Nations brokered agreement for a specially constituted Scottish court in The Hague to try the two Libyan intelligence agents suspected of involvement in the Pan Am bombing. After months of testimony one Libyan was convicted and the other was acquitted.[57] However, in June 2007 the Scottish Criminal Cases Review Commission granted Al Megrahi the right to appeal his conviction out of concern for a possible miscarriage of justice.[58] Libya also agreed to pay compensation to the victims of the bombing. In March 2003, Libyan officials held secret talks with U.S. and UK government officials and agreed to dismantle its nuclear weapons program.[59] In December 2003, Libya's Foreign Minister issued a statement that his government was ending its Weapons of Mass Destruction (WMD) program.[60] In exchange for Libya agreeing to give up its nuclear program the United States agreed to normalize diplomatic relations with Tripoli and lifted sanctions against Libya.[61] On May 15, 2006, the Bush administration re-established full diplomatic relations with Libya and removed that country from the list of nations that are state sponsors of terrorism.[62]

The Bush administration supported efforts in the General Assembly to strengthen the Nuclear Non-Proliferation Treaty (NPT). In 2002 President Bush transmitted to the Senate for ratification the Additional Protocol to the safeguards agreements of the NPT, which President Clinton signed in 1998. Contrary to the NPT, which requires nuclear states to pursue negotiations in good faith to bring about nuclear disarmament, the Bush administration's policy places greater emphasis on the non-proliferation of nuclear weapons while completely ignoring its disarmament obligations under Article VI of the treaty.[63]

During the 2004 NPT review conference the Bush administration made a strong push to prevent the proliferation of nuclear weapons among certain states such as Iran, Syria and North Korea, but it made no mention of disarmament. Many observers criticized the administration for its failure to begin negotiations on nuclear disarmament. The Bush administration has begun development of new generations of nuclear weapons, and Russia has indicated that it will do the same. The Bush administration supported the new General Assembly measure to suppress the spread of nuclear weapons to terrorist organizations by signing the International Convention for the Suppression of Acts of Nuclear Terrorism, which was adopted by consensus on April 13, 2005.[64]

In 2003, President Bush launched a new multilateral initiative to contain the transportation of weapons of mass destruction (WMD). The new Proliferation Security Initiative (PSI) allows the United States and its close allies to search planes and ships carrying suspected cargo and to seize illegal weapons or missile technologies.[65] The administration has signed such agreements with more than a dozen countries, including Australia, Panama and Liberia.[66] The PSI allows member states to board suspicious vessels flying their own flags, to consent to the boarding of flag vessels by other states, to stop and search suspicious vessels in their territorial waters or contiguous zones, to require suspicious aircraft in their airspace to land for inspection, to carry out rigorous inspections at their ports and airfields and not to transport WMD cargoes to or from states of concern.[67]

Endnotes

1. Cronin, Bruce. 2001. The paradox of hegemony: America's ambiguous relationship with the United Nations, *EJIL* 7:104.
2. Gerson, Allan. 2000. Multilateralism a la carte: The consequences of unilateral 'pick and pay' approaches, *EJIL* 11:61.
3. Memorandum on Restoration of the Mexico City Policy. 2001. 37 *Weekly Comp. Pres. Doc.*, Jan. 22, 216.
4. Sanger, David. 2001. Bush will continue to oppose Kyoto Pact on global warming. *New York Times*, June 12, 2001, A1; Sean Murphy, 2001, Contemporary practice of the United States relating to international law, *AJIL* 95:649.
5. Wirth, David A. 2002. The sixth session (part two) and seventh session of the Conference of the Parties to the Framework Convention on Climate Change, *AJIL* 96:657.
6. Revkin, Andrew C. 2004. U.S. requests exemptions to Zone Pact for Chemical. *New York Times*, Mar. 4, A20.
7. Harvey, Fiona Harvey. 2005. U.S. agreement paves the way for fresh climate change talks. *Fin. Times*, Dec. 12, 3.
8. Harvey, Fiona, John Aglionby, and Krishna Guha. 2007. White House seeks to reassure on climate deal. *Fin. Times*, Dec. 17, 3.
9. *Massachusetts et al v. Environmental Protection Agency*, S.Ct. No. 05-1120 (April 2, 2007).
10. Letter from John Bolton, Under Secretary of State for Arms Control and International Security, to the UN Secretary General Kofi Annan (May 6, 2002), at *http://www.state.gov/r/pa/prs/2002/9968.htm*. See Neil A. Lewis, 2002, U.S. rejects all support for new court on atrocities. *New York Times*, May 7, A9.
11. U.S. Under Secretary of State for Political Affairs Marc Grossman, American Foreign Policy and the International Criminal Court, Remarks to the Center for Strategic and International Studies (May 6, 2002), at *http://www.state.gov/p/9949pf.htm*.
12. §2202 of Foreign Affairs Reform and Restructuring Act of 1998, contained in the Omnibus Consolidated and Emergency Supplemental Appropriations Act of 1999, Pub. L. No. 105-77, 112 Stat. 2681, & Pub. L. No. 105-323, 112 Stat. 3029 (1998); Pub. L. No. 106-277, §1, 114 Stat. 813 (2000), Department of Sate Press Release (Jan. 5, 2001), at *http://www.state.gov*.
13. *In re Surrender of Elizaphan Ntakirutimana*, N. L-98-43, 1998, U.S. Dist. LEXIS 22173, at *100 (S.D. Tex., Aug. 6, 1998); *Ntakirutimana v. Reno*, 184 F. 3d 419,430 (5th Cir., 1999), *cert. Denial*, 528 U.S. 1135 (2000).

14. Senate Res. 1503. 2003. Adopted unanimously on August 28, 2003.
15. Senate Res. 1315. 2000. Adopted on August 14, 2000.
16. Scheffer, David J. 1999. The United States and the International Criminal Court. *AJIL* 93:12, 18.
17. Roth, Kenneth. 2008. The court the U.S. doesn't want. In *International human rights in context,* ed. Henry J. Steiner, Philip Alston and Ryan Goodman, 1300.
18. See Statement by President Clinton authorizing the United States to sign the Treaty on the International Criminal Court, reprinted in Sean Murphy, "Contemporary Practice of the United States in International Law." 1999. *AJIL* 93:387, 399.
19. Statement on the Rome Treaty on the International Criminal Court. 2000. 37 *Weekly Comp. Pres. Doc.,* Dec. 31, 4.
20. 2002 Supplemental Appropriations Act for Further Recovery from and Response to Terrorist Attacks on the United States, Pub. L. No. 107-206, §§2001-2015, 116 Stat. 820 (2002).
21. 2002 Supplemental Appropriations Act for Further Recovery from and Response to Terrorist Attacks on the United States, Pub. L. No. 107-2006 §§2001-2015, 116 Stat. 820 (2002).
22. President George W. Bush, Memorandum for the Secretary of State (Oct. 2, 2006), at *http://www.whitehouse.gov/news/releases/2006/10/20061002-7.http.*
23. Pub. L. No. 109-364, §1222, 120 Stat. 2083, 2423 9 approved Oct. 17, 2006.
24. See Georg Nolte. 2003. The United States and the International Criminal Court. In *Unilateralism & U.S Foreign Policy,* ed. David Malone and Yuen Foong Khong, 71. Lynne Rienner Publishers, Boulder, CO.
25. See Serge Schmemann. 2002. Sovereignty debate with the U.S. limits U.N. support for Bosnia force, *New York Times,* June 22, A6.
26. See Serge Schmemann. 2002. U.S. links peacekeeping to immunity from new court, *New York Times,* June 19, A3.
27. Forero, Juan. 2005. Bush's aid cuts on court issue roil neighbors, *New York Times,* Aug. 19, A1.
28. Dept. of State Press Statement, U.S. Signs 100th Article 98 Agreement, May 3, 2005, at *http://www.state.gov/r/pa/prs/ps/p05.*
29. Forero, Bush's aid cuts, A1.
30. Senate Res. 1422. 2002. Adopted July 12; and Senate Res. 1487, 2003, adopted June 12; See Sean Murphy, 2002, Contemporary practice of the United States relating to international law, *AJIL* 96:727–728; and 2003, 97:710; Serge Schmemann, 2002, U.S. peacekeepers given year's immunity from new court. *New York Times,* July 13, A3; Colum Lynch, 2002, U.S. wins 1-year shield from war crimes court. *Wash. Post,* July 13, A16.
31. Hodge, Warren. 2004. Annan rebukes U.S. for move to give its troops immunity. *New York Times,* June 18, A13.

32. See Warren Hodge. 2004. U.S. drops plan to exempt G.I.'s from U.N. court. *New York Times*, June 24, A1.
33. See Barbara Crossette. 2001. Effort by U.N. to cut traffic in arms meets U.S. rebuff. *New York Times*, July 10, A6.
34. See Bradley Graham. 2004. Bush shifts U.S. stance on use of land mines. *Wash. Post*, Feb. 27, A1; Lincoln Bloomfield, America's promise on landmines, *Fin. Times*, Feb. 27, 13.
35. Murphy, Sean D. 2001. Contemporary practice of the United States relating to international law, *AJIL* 95:873, 899.
36. Deller, N., A. Makhijani, and J. Burroughs, eds. 2002. *Rule of power or rule of law? An assessment of U.S. policies and actions regarding security-related treaties*, 57; Amy E. Smithson, 2002, The chemical weapons convention. In *Multilateralism and U.S. foreign policy*, ed. Stewart Patrick and Shepard Forman, 247, 257.
37. President Bush's Remarks Announcing the United States Withdrawal from the Anti-Ballistic Missile Treaty, 37 *Weekly. Comp. Pres. Doc.* 1783; See Dana Milbank, 2002, U.S. withdraws from missile treaty. *Wash. Post*, June 14, A28.
38. State of the Union Address, Jan. 29, 2002, at *http://www.whitehouse.gov/news/releases/2002/01/20020129-11.html.*
39. See *Kucinich v. Bush* 236 F. Supp. 2d 1 (D.D.C., 2002).
40. See National Security Strategy of the United States of America (Sept. 17, 2002), at *http://www.whitehouse.gov/nsc/nss.pdf.*
41. Sean Murphy. 2003. Contemporary practice of the United States relating to international law, *AJIL* 97:203.
42. Article 51 of the Charter of the United Nations; see Ian Brownlie, 1963, *International law and the use of force by states*, 250–7, 281–301.
43. *http://www.globalsecurity.org/military/library/policy/dod/nds-usa_mar2005_sum.htm.*
44. President Waives Sanctions on India and Pakistan (Sept. 22, 2001), Presidential Determination No. 2001-28.
45. Daniel, Caroline. 2006. Bush signs nuclear energy pact with India. *Fin. Times*, Dec. 19, 6.
46. IAEA Staff Report, Report on Iran's nuclear programme sent to UN Security Council. *http://www.iaea.org/NewsCenter/Transcripts/2006/transcr08032006.html.*
47. Statement by the President of the Security Council, UN Doc. S/PRST/2006/15 (Mar. 29, 2006).
48. Hoge, Warren. 2006. U.N. council urges Iran to halt atom activity. *New York Times*, Mar. 30, A6.
49. Sciolino, Elaine, and William J. Broad. 2006. Iran quietly learns of penalties in a nuclear incentive deal. *New York Times*, June 15, A3.
50. Senate Res. 1737. 2006.
51. Senate Res. 1747. 2007.
52. Ward, Andrew. 2004. Dealing with North Korea: Fears of proliferation and secret nuclear programme set a stiff test for the U.S. *Fin. Times*, Feb. 25, 11.

53. Khan, Joseph, and David Sanger. 2005. U.S.-Korean deal on arms leaves key points open. *New York Times,* Sept. 20, A1.
54. Senate Res. 1718. 2006. Adopted on Oct. 14, 2006.
55. Harden, Blaine, and Robin Wright. 2008. U.S. to delist North Korea as sponsor of terrorism. *Wash. Post,* June 27, A1.
56. Richter, Paul. 2008. North Korea removed from terrorism list after nuclear agreement. *Los Angeles Times,* Oct. 12, A1.
57. Finn, Peter. 2001. Libyan convicted of Lockerbie bombing. *Wash. Post,* Feb. 1, A1.
58. Sengupta, Kim. 2007. Libyan convicted over Lockerbie bombing given leave to appeal. *The Independent* (UK), June 29.
59. Murphy, Sean. 2004. Contemporary practice of the United States relating to international law, *AJIL* 98:195.
60. Communiqué of the Libyan Arab Jamahiriya, *appended to* Letter Dated 19 December 2003 from the Permanent Representative of the Libyan Arab Jamahiriya to the United Nations Addressed to the President of the Security Council, UN Doc. S/2003/1196 (Dec. 29, 2003).
61. Executive Order 13357. 2004. 40 *Weekly Comp. Pres. Doc.* Sept. 20, 2067; George Gedda, Bush lifts sanctions against Libya, *Wash. Post,* Sept. 21, A17; Peter Slevin, U.S. resumes ties with Libya, *Wash. Post,* June 29, A15.
62. Brinkley, Joel. 2006. U.S. will restore diplomatic links with the Libyans. *New York Times,* May 16, A1.
63. Deller, Nicole, Arjun Makhijani, and John Burroughs, eds. 2003. *Rule of power or rule of law?* 17.
64. GA Res. 59/290, annex (April 13, 2005).
65. See President's Remarks to the People of Krakow, Poland. 2003. 39 *Weekly Comp. Pres. Doc.* May 31, 700, 702.
66. See Pact with Liberia allows U.S. to board ships. 2004. *Wash. Post,* Feb. 14, 2004, A26.
67. White House Office of the Press Secretary, Fact Sheet on Proliferation Security Initiative: Statement of Interdiction Principles (Sept. 4, 2003), at *http://whitehouse.gov.*

chapter V

THE UNITED STATES' ATTITUDE TOWARD THE USE OF FORCE PRE- AND POST-SEPTEMBER 11, 2001

The United States has never fully subscribed to the United Nations' ban on the use of force, which it helped to negotiate in the Charter. In fact, the United States expected other states to comply with the principle of the non-use of force enshrined in the United Nations Charter, but it did not feel it had to comply with the U.N. regime. Since 1945 the United States has resorted to the unauthorized unilateral use of force in a number of cases; including Guatemala in 1954, Cuba in 1961, the Dominican Republic in 1967, Vietnam in 1968, Libya in 1982, Grenada in 1983, Nicaragua in 1985, Panama in 1989, Iraq in 1993, the Sudan and Afghanistan in 1998, Afghanistan in 2001 and Iraq in 2003. The United States never admitted to violating international law in any of the above instances. Instead, it invoked international law to justify its invasion in all of the above situations. In addition to intervening unilaterally, the United States also encouraged or funded proxy wars against Soviet-backed regimes in Angola, Afghanistan and Nicaragua and supported brutal regimes fighting civil wars in Central America.

There are only two instances in which the United States relied on United Nations Security Council authorization to use force: in Korea in 1950 and in Iraq in 1991. In Korea the United States received United Nations backing while the Soviet Union was boycotting the Security Council to protest the U.N. refusal to admit Communist China as the legitimate representation of China instead of Taiwan. Support for an invasion of Iraq in 1991 came in the wake of a change in the attitude of the new Soviet leadership toward multilateral intervention. Iraq's invasion of Kuwait was also viewed as a blatant violation of international law and the evolving post-Cold War political consensus between the U.S. and the USSR.

By the time President Bush took office there was a well-established tradition in American foreign policy for the President of the United States to disregard international law and the United Nations Charter ban on the use of force when it was in the U.S. national interest to do so. The invasion of Afghanistan in response to the September 11 terrorist attacks was no exception. This focus of this chapter is on the U.S.-led invasion of Afghanistan in the wake of the September 11 terrorist attacks on the World Trade Center in New York and the Pentagon in Washington, and the precedent it established for states to resort to military force against real or imaginary threats to international peace and security. But first we will look at previous instances of the U.S.'s unilateral use of force.

THE SEPTEMBER 11 TERRORIST ATTACKS

On September 11, 2001, nineteen individuals with ties to Osama bin Laden and his Al Qaeda terrorist network hijacked three American planes and crashed them into the World Trade Center in New York, the Pentagon in Washington, D.C. and in a field in southern Pennsylvania, respectively. Officials believe the last plane was en route to crash into a government building in Washington but that a struggle on board between passengers and the hijackers diverted the plane and forced it to land in Pennsylvania. The three incidents resulted in the death of approximately three thousand civilians and caused billions of dollars in damages.[1] President Bush, who was away from the White House at the time, was informed of the terrorist attacks as the situation was unfolding. Later that day Mr. Bush issued a statement in which he said that terrorists had declared war on the United States and that the United States would hunt down those responsible and punish them. President Bush equated the September 11 attacks as equivalent to an armed attack carried out by one state against another state. A few days later the President declared a national emergency and called to active duty the reserves of the United States armed forces.[2]

There is no disputing that the terrorist attacks of September 11 were heinous criminal acts and that the domestic courts of the United States or the courts of other nations should criminally prosecute those responsible. Alternatively they should be brought before an international tribunal and tried for violating international humanitarian law. However, to call the terrorist attacks an act of war is to use the word "war" rhetorically rather than in the traditional legal context. On the issue of an appropriate response, there is broad disagreement among legal scholars as to whether the United States had a right to self-defense or even the right to retaliate with limited military force. However, given the magnitude of the September 11 attacks and the huge number of civilian casualties, the Bush administration saw the invasion of Afghanistan as a necessary response. Domestic public opinion and the call for revenge greatly influenced the administration's decision to invade Afghanistan. The September 11 attacks also helped to convince many nations that terrorism was a serious threat to international peace and security that required more than just economic sanctions to combat it.

Domestic Reaction

In the wake of the September 11 attacks the Congress of the United States gave unprecedented bipartisan support to the President, and it said the country was united against those who perpetrated this heinous act against innocent civilians. In the weeks following the attacks, Congress passed a series of legislations granting the President sweeping powers to curtail civil liberties, to conduct surveillance of suspected terrorist organizations and to detain indefinitely anyone suspected of links to international terrorism.[3] The President also received greater latitude in foreign affairs to defend the national security of the United States against future terrorist threats. The American public rallied around the President as commander-in-chief, and public support for military strikes against those responsible for the attacks was overwhelming. On September 18 Congress passed a joint resolution by which it authorized the President to use "all necessary and appropriate force against those nations, organizations, or persons he determines planned, authorized, commanded, or aided the terrorist attacks that occurred on September 11, 2001, or harbored such organizations or persons, in order to prevent any future acts of international terrorism against the United States by such nations, organizations or persons."[4]

The joint resolution reads as follows:

> WHEREAS, on September 11, 2001, acts of treacherous violence were committed against the United States and its citizens; and
>
> WHEREAS, such acts render it both necessary and appropriate that the United States exercise its right of self defense and to protect United States citizens both at home and abroad; and

WHEREAS, in light of the threat to the national security and foreign policy of the United States posed by these grave acts of violence; and

WHEREAS, such acts continue to pose an unusual and extraordinary threat to the national security and foreign policy of the United States; and

WHEREAS, the President has authority under the Constitution to take action to deter and prevent acts of international terrorism against the United States: Now, therefore, be it

Resolved by the Senate and the House of Representatives of the United States of America in Congress assembled.

Section 2 Authorization for Use of United States Armed Forces

a. IN GENERAL.—That the President is authorized to use all necessary and appropriate force against those nations, organizations, or persons he determines planned, authorized, committed, or aided the terrorist attacks that occurred on September 11, 2001, or harbored such organizations or persons, in order to prevent any future acts of international terrorism against the United States by such nations, organizations or persons.
b. War Powers Resolution Requirements—
    1. SPECIFIC STATUTORY AUTHORIZATION.—Consistent with Section 8 (a)(1) of the War Powers Resolution, the Congress declares that this section is intended to constitute specific statutory authorization within the meaning of Section 5(b) of the War Powers Resolution.
    2. APPLICABILITY OF OTHER REQUIREMENTS.—Nothing in this resolution supersedes any requirement of the War Powers Resolution.[5]

President Bush signed the resolution into law but he acknowledged that: "the President has authority under the Constitution to take action to deter and prevent acts of international terrorism against the United States."

In a nationally televised speech to Congress on September 20, President Bush declared: "On September 11th, enemies of freedom committed an act of war against our country."[6] President Bush vowed to punish those responsible for the attacks on the United States, and he called for Afghanistan to turn over Osama bin Laden or face a military attack. The President also put all nations on guard when he said that in the war against terrorism countries were either "with us or against us." President Bush demanded that the Taliban "deliver to United States authorities all the leaders of Al Qaida who hide in your land. Release all foreign nationals, including American citizens, you have unjustly imprisoned. Protect foreign journalists, diplomats, and aid workers in your country. Close immediately and permanently, every terrorist training camp in Afghanistan, and hand over every terrorist and every person in their support structure to appropriate authorities. Give the United

States full access to terrorist training camps, so we can make sure they are no longer operating. These demands are not open to negotiation or discussion. The Taliban must act and act immediately. They will hand over the terrorists, or they will share their fate."[7] The President said he would establish an Office of Homeland Security, as well as a Homeland Security Council, to develop and coordinate the implementation of a comprehensive national strategy to secure the United States from terrorist threats or attacks.[8]

On September 24 President Bush invoked his presidential authority, including his power under the International Emergency Economic Powers Act (IEEPA), to issue an executive order that expended the U.S. Treasury Department's power to target financial support for terrorist organizations worldwide. The executive order froze the assets of twenty-seven persons (including bin Laden) and groups, and it blocked the U.S. transactions of those persons and others who support them.[9] In addition, the executive order increased the ability of the Treasury Department to block U.S. assets of, and to deny access to U.S. markets by, foreign banks that refused to cooperate with U.S. authorities in identifying and freezing terrorist assets abroad. Finally, the order authorized the Secretary of State and the Secretary of the Treasury to make additional designations from time to time.[10] By early October the Treasury Department had frozen over $100 million of suspected terrorist assets worldwide.[11]

The International Response

An overwhelming majority of states, friends and foes alike, condemned the terrorist attacks on the United States. A majority of states supported the United States' view that those responsible should be brought to justice. However, not all states that condemned the attacks supported a United States military operation against Afghanistan. Many states wanted to see the evidence that bin Laden was behind the attacks before they supported air strikes against Afghanistan. Traditional United States allies were quick to condemn the attacks and to support President Bush's stance. The North Atlantic Council of the North Atlantic Treaty Organization (NATO) decided that if it was determined that the incidents were directed from abroad against the United States, "it shall be regarded as an action covered by Article 5 of the Washington Treaty, which states that an armed attack against one or more of the Allies in Europe or North America shall be considered an attack against them all."[12] On October 2, after a briefing from U.S. officials, the council determined that the facts were "clear and compelling" and that "the attack against the United States on 11 September was directed from abroad and shall therefore be regarded as an action covered by Article 5 of the Washington Treaty."[13] NATO called on its members to join the United States in defending against future attacks. NATO warplanes also patrolled the air space of the eastern United States.

On September 21 the Organization of American States (OAS) gave its unconditional support to the United States. At the twenty-fourth meeting of the Consultation of the OAS Ministers of Foreign Affairs acting as the organ of consultation in the application of the Inter-American Treaty of Reciprocal Assistance, it resolved that "these terrorist attacks against the United States of America are attacks against all American states" and that "all states parties to the Rio Treaty shall provide effective reciprocal assistance to address such attacks and threat of any similar attacks against any American state and to maintain the peace and security of the continent."[14] The resolution further provides that "the states parties shall render additional assistance and support to the United States and each other, as appropriate, to address the September 11 attacks and also to prevent future terrorist acts."[15]

Following the commencement of United States military action against Afghanistan, the OAS Ministers of Foreign Affairs met again on October 16 to reaffirm support for the United States. The Ministers resolved: "That the measures being applied by the United States of America and other states in the exercise of their inherent right of individual and collective self-defense have the full support of the states parties to the Rio Treaty." "That states parties to the Rio Treaty reiterate their willingness to provide additional assistance and support to the United States and to one another, as appropriate, taking into consideration all the provisions of the Rio Treaty, in connection with the attacks of September 11 and to prevent future armed attacks by terrorists."[16]

The Role of the United Nations

Following the September 11 attacks, the Security Council adopted resolution 1368 (2001) by which it determined to combat by all means threats to international peace and security caused by terrorist acts. In its preamble to resolution 1368 (2001), the Security Council said it "recognizes the inherent right of individual or collective self-defense in accordance with the Charter," but it made no determination with respect to the existence of a threat to the peace or a breach of the peace brought about by the September 11 attacks on the United States.[17] Nor did the Security Council recognize the attacks as an "armed attack."[18] The Security Council unequivocally condemned in the strongest term as "horrifying" the terrorist attacks that took place on September 11 in New York, Washington and Pennsylvania and regarded such acts, like any act of terrorism, as a threat to international peace and security. The Security Council called on states to work together urgently to bring to justice the perpetrators, organizers and sponsors of these terrorist attacks and stressed that those responsible for aiding, supporting or harboring the perpetrators, organizers and sponsors of these acts would be held accountable.[19] The Security Council further called on member states to redouble their efforts to prevent and suppress terrorist acts, including increased cooperation of the relevant international anti-terrorist conventions and Security Council resolutions and in particular resolution 1269 (1999).[20] Finally, the Security Council expressed its readiness to take all necessary steps to respond to the terrorist attacks of September 11, and to combat all forms of terrorism, in accordance with its responsibilities under the Charter of the United Nations.[21]

Security Council resolution 1368 (2001) recognized the inherent right of individual or collective self-defense of all states in general, but it did not specifically affirm the right of the United States to self-defense.[22] The Security Council called for the perpetrators of these terrorist acts to be held accountable, and it expressed its readiness to take all necessary steps to respond to the terrorist attacks of September 11, but it did not authorize states to use force to combat terrorism. The Security Council did not recognize the terrorist attacks on the United States as an armed attack.[23]

On September 28 the Security Council adopted resolution 1373 (2001) by which it reaffirmed the inherent right of individual or collective self-defense as recognized by the Charter of United Nations and as reiterated in resolution 1368 (2001).[24] The crafting of the language of Security Council resolution 1368 (2001) left open the possibility of the United States invading Afghanistan. Acting under Chapter VII of the Charter of the United Nations, the Security Council called on all states to freeze the assets of persons who commit, or who attempt to commit, terrorist acts or who participate in or facilitate the commission of terrorist acts.[25] The Security Council further called on all states to refrain from providing any form of support to entities or persons involved in terrorist acts. The Security Council expressed its determination to take all necessary steps in order to ensure the full implementation of this resolution, in accordance with its responsibilities under the Charter.

Within two weeks of the adoption of resolution 1373 (2001), the United States began an air campaign against targets in Afghanistan. The United States informed the Security Council of its military activities in Afghanistan and said its actions were consistent with its right to self-defense under Article 51 of the Charter.[26] The Security Council debated the United States' military operation in Afghanistan but took no further action. The President of the Security Council later issued a statement affirming the United States' right to self-defense. The Security Council did not revisit the United States' military operation in Afghanistan until November 14. Following the debate, the Security Council adopted resolution 1378 (2001) in which it said "it supports international efforts to root out terrorism, in keeping with the Charter of the United Nations, and reaffirmed also its resolutions 1368 (2001) and 1373 (2001)".[27] The Security Council condemned the Taliban for allowing Afghanistan to be used as a base for the export of terrorism by the Al Qaeda network and other terrorist groups and for providing safe haven to Osama bin Laden, Al Qaeda and others associated with them. The Security Council endorsed the "efforts of the Afghan people to replace the Taliban regime."[28] The Security Council did not specifically endorse the United States military operation in Afghanistan, but by saying that it was "supporting international efforts to root out terrorism," the Security Council was giving its tacit approval to the United States-led military operation.[29]

On December 6 the Security Council adopted resolution 1383 (2001) by which it endorsed the December 5 Agreement signed in Bonn on provisional arrangements in Afghanistan pending the re-establishment of permanent government institutions, as reported in the Secretary General's letter of December 5.[30] On December 20 the Security Council adopted resolution 1386 (2001) by which it established the International Security Assistance Force. Acting under Chapter VII of the Charter of the United Nations, the Security Council authorized the establishment for six months of an International Assistance Force to assist the Afghan Interim Authority in the maintenance of security in Kabul and its surrounding areas. Its purpose was to enable the Afghan Interim Authority as well as the personnel of United Nations to operate in a secure environment.[31] The Security Council called upon member states to contribute personnel, equipment and other resources to the International Security Assistance Force, and it invited those member states to inform the leadership of the Force and the Secretary General. The Security Council also authorized the member states participating in the International Security Assistance Force to take all necessary measures to fulfill its mandate.[32]

The International Security Assistance Force was established before the cessation of the United States military campaign and without the participation of the United States. The United States refused to join the peacekeeping operation and decided to continue its anti-terrorist campaign until it had accomplished its military objectives. The Security Council did not insist on an end to the United States' military campaign, nor did it press for the United States to participate in the peacekeeping operation. The International Security Assistance Force had a limited mandate to provide security only for the Kabul area.[33] Despite the obvious security situation in the outer provinces, the Security Council refused to extend the mandate of the International Security Assistance Force throughout the entire country. The failure of the international community to assist the interim government to extend its control over all of Afghanistan has left much of Afghanistan under the control of warlords, a situation that existed before the Taliban seized control. The United Nations' cautious approach to dealing with the situation in Afghanistan will make it more difficult to accomplish a permanent peace in that country.

On May 23 the Security Council held a meeting to review the situation in Afghanistan. The Security Council adopted resolution 1413 (2002) by which it extended the authorization of the International Security Assistance Force, as defined in resolution 1386 (2001) for an additional six months beyond June 20.[34] Acting under Chapter VII of the Charter of the United Nations, the Security Council authorized the member states participating in the International Security Assistance Force to take all necessary measures to fulfill the mandate of the International Security Assistance Force. It called upon member states to contribute personnel, equipment and other resources to the International Security Assistance Force, and to make contributions to the Trust Fund established pursuant to resolution 1386 (2001).[35] Resolution 1413 (2002) said that the Security Council was in support of efforts to root out terrorism, but it did not address specifically the United States' military campaign in Afghanistan.[36] The resolution did not call on the United States and other states with concerns about international terrorism to find a peaceful solution to the situation in Afghanistan. To the contrary, the resolution seems to have implicitly endorsed the military operation in Afghanistan, and it said nothing about the violation of international humanitarian laws. It would be accurate to say that the Security Council did not adequately exercise its responsibility in the war on terror. The Security Council gave the United States a blank check to violate international law and the United Nations Charter in this respect.

The General Assembly also weighed in on the issue. On September 12 the General Assembly adopted resolution 56/1 (2001) by which it strongly condemned "the heinous acts of terrorism against the United States, which resulted in the enormous loss of human life, destruction and damage in the cities of New York, and Washington, D.C., and in Pennsylvania."[37] The United Nations General Assembly also urgently called for international cooperation to prevent and eradicate acts of terrorism, and it stressed that those responsible be brought to justice and be held accountable for aiding, supporting or harboring the perpetrators, organizers and sponsors of such acts.[38] The Taliban regime ignored the demands of the international community and continued to ask for evidence that bin Laden was involved in the attacks. The Taliban asked for negotiation over the surrender of bin Laden to a third country, but the United States rejected the offer.[39]

THE INVASION OF AFGHANISTAN

On October 7 President Bush ordered the United States military to begin a bombing campaign against selected targets in Afghanistan.[40] That same day the United States Representative to the United Nations, Ambassador John Negroponte, informed the Security Council that the United States was a victim of "massive and brutal attacks" and that it was exercising its right of individual self-defense in taking actions in Afghanistan against Al Qaeda terrorist training camps and Taliban military installations.[41] The letter went on to say that the United States had acted in accordance with Article 51 and that, together with other states, it had initiated actions in the exercise of its inherent right of individual and collective self-defense following the armed attacks carried out against the United States on September 11.[42] The letter further stated that:

> The attacks on 11 September 2001 and the ongoing threat to the security to the United States and its nationals posed by the al-Qaeda organization has been made possible by the decision of the Taliban regime to allow the parts of Afghanistan that it controls to be used by this organization as a base of operation. Despite every effort by the United States and the international community, the Taliban regime has refused to change its policy. From the territory of Afghanistan, the al-Qaeda organization continues to train and support agents of terror who attack innocent people throughout the world and target United States nationals and interest in the United States and abroad.[43]

The Security Council met for several hours to hear the justifications of the United States and Britain for acting in self-defense. The Security Council ended its meeting without adopting a resolution in support of or against the United

States-led invasion of Afghanistan. The Security Council subsequently issued a Presidential Statement in which it said that the unanimity of support expressed in the Security Council's two prior resolutions "is absolutely maintained."[44] The Security Council gave no indication that it was willing to oppose the United States-led invasion.

Two weeks after the bombing campaign began the United States gained air superiority over Afghanistan. Meanwhile, the Northern Alliance, which controlled the Northeastern Province of Afghanistan, intensified its military offensive against the Taliban regime to coincide with the U.S. ground operation. With American air support, the Northern Alliance quickly captured areas previously held by the Taliban, including the capital, Kabul, and formed an interim government.[45] The international community withheld immediate recognition of the Northern Alliance. Instead it called for the creation of a broad-based consensus transitional government to be agreed upon at a German-sponsored international conference in Bonn.

The Bonn conference brought together the various Afghan factions to negotiate, and, together with the U.S., the EU and the United Nations, they agreed to establish a transitional administration headed by Hamid Karzi as the interim president.[46] The Karzi administration was to rule Afghanistan for six months, after which time a *Loya Jirga,* comprising representatives of all of Afghanistan's main ethnic and political groups, would convene to select a new president. The former Afghan king was expected to play a key role in the new government. The transition government would rule for two years, after which time an elected government would assume power. A new constitution was to be drafted during the transition period, followed by national elections to elect a democratic parliament and president.[47]

The Right to Resort to Force Under International Law

Prior to the creation of the United Nations, customary international law governed the right of states to use force. However, the assumption now exists that the United Nations Charter ban on the use of force invalidated customary international law and that it is now the primary rule governing armed conflicts between states.[48] Prior to the Charter ban states claimed to have legal rights to use force in self-defense and self-preservation, to protect their nationals abroad, to protect foreign owned property, to enforce international judgments, and to protect the nationals of other states who were abused by their governments. These claims were very controversial, and smaller states rejected them. They therefore never became fully accepted as legitimate customary international law. Following World War I attempts took place to impose limits on states' discretionary right to go to war. The League of Nations Covenant imposed a six-month waiting period before states could resort to war, and the Kellog-Briand Pact banned war as an instrument of national policy. Both treaties had flaws and did not deter states from going to war.

The Charter of the United Nations attempted to fill the loopholes in both agreements. Article 2 (4) of the Charter calls on all member states "to refrain in their international relations from the threat or use of force against the territorial integrity or political independence of any state, or in any other manner inconsistent with the Purposes of the United Nations."[49] There are only two exceptions to this ban: Chapter VII of the Charter, which grants the Security Council the authority to maintain international peace and security, and Article 51, which recognizes a state's inherent right to self-defense if an armed attack occurs.

Under Chapter VII of the Charter of the United Nations the Security Council is granted exclusive responsibility for determining the existence of a threat to the peace, a breach of the peace or an act of aggression, and to take the necessary measures to restore or to maintain international peace and security.[50] The Security Council can authorize collective enforcement measures under Articles 41 and 42 against any state that threatens a breach of international peace and security. However, in order for the Security Council to authorize collective enforcement measures a consensus must exist among the five permanent members of the Council that a particular situation constitutes a threat or a breach of international peace and security.[51] The Security Council can carry out the enforcement measures or delegate its authority to an individual state or to a group of states to carry out the measures.

The second exception to the United Nations ban on the use of force in Article 2 (4) is Article 51, which recognizes a state's inherent right to individual or collective self-defense if an armed attack occurs against the state, and up until the Security Council has taken the measures necessary to maintain international peace and security.[52] A state acting in self-defense under Article 51 must inform the Security Council of its action and provide the evidence for international review. To claim self-defense a state must demonstrate that there was "a necessity of self-defence, instant, overwhelming, leaving no choice of means and no moment of deliberation."[53] To be considered legal, a right of self-defense must be exercised in a timely fashion, in response to a previous armed attack. The Charter, however, does not define what constitutes an armed attack, nor does it specify who must be responsible for the armed attack in order to give rise to self-defense.

In the immediate post-World War II era states retained the monopoly over the use and means of warfare, and the intention of Article 51 was to address relations between states. However, in the post-Cold War era non-state actors exercise as much control over the means of warfare as states, and a majority of the post Cold War conflicts have been intra-state instead of inter-state. Since the United Nations Charter is a compact between states, the framers of the Charter did not anticipate non-state actors posing a grave threat to international peace and security, and therefore it did not include threats from non-state actors in the definition of threats to the peace.[54] In order to justify a military response to terrorism under Article 51 a state would have to provide a broad interpretation of the right to self-defense to include not only an armed attack from another state but an attack from non-state actors as well. The alternative is for a state to resort to reprisal to prevent a future violation of international law.

THE UNITED STATES' RIGHT TO SELF-DEFENSE

The events of September 11, which resulted in the deaths of over three thousand civilians and caused billions of dollars in damages, was a unique event in international relations. Never before have non-state actors carried out such massive acts of destruction against a state, particularly a major military power. This incident raises some troubling questions with regards to the laws governing armed conflict and a state's right to self-defense. It begs the questions of what constitutes an armed attack and whether a terrorist attack gives rise to the right of self-defense under Article 51 of the Charter of the United Nations.

Article 51 of the Charter of the United Nations recognizes a state's inherent right to individual and collective self-defense if an armed attack occurs and up until the Security Council has taken the measures necessary for maintaining international peace and security.[55] However, the Charter does not specify what constitutes an armed attack and whether, in order to give rise to the right of self-defense, one state must carry out an armed attack against another state. State practice since the adoption of the Charter has assumed that a state's right to self-defense under Article 51 is only legal if one state carries out the armed attack against the territory of another state.[56] All other attacks, real or anticipatory, were not considered exceptions to the ban on the use of force in Article 2 (4) of the Charter and did not give rise to the right of self-defense under Article 51. In the past the United States has made claims of self-defense in response to terrorist attacks on its nationals, but a majority of states rejected many of these claims as a violation of the Charter of the United Nations.[57] However, unlike previous terrorist attacks, the September 11 attacks took place on American soil and resulted in a huge number of civilian casualties and billions of dollars in damages.

The right of the United States to retaliate against those responsible for the September 11 attacks came up in Security Council debates, as a majority of Council members felt the United States would launch a military attack once it had identified the targets in Afghanistan, mobilized its military and assembled an international coalition. However, the Security Council did not recognize the September 11 events as an armed attack in the context of Article 51, nor did it explicitly say that the United States had a right of self-defense in this particular situation. In the two resolutions it adopted after the September 11 attacks, the Security Council reaffirmed a state's inherent right of self-defense, but the references to self-defense in the resolutions gave no indication as to whether the Security Council felt the United States had a right to self-defense in that particular instance.

Before the September 11 attacks the general assumption was that the concept of "armed attack" in Article 51 meant a military attack carried out by one state against another. There is no indication the framers intended to include bombings by terrorist groups or, for that matter, the use of civilian planes by terrorists to carry out deadly operations as constituting an armed attack. If this reading of Article 51 is accurate, then the United States could not claim a right of self-defense. The United States also could not claim self-defense because of the time period that had lapsed between the time of the attacks and the date the United States initiated military measures against Afghanistan. More importantly, the United States failed to make available for international scrutiny the evidentiary information to implicate Afghanistan in the attacks. Finally, the Security Council had taken the measures necessary for maintaining international peace and security by imposing mandatory sanctions on the Taliban and Al Qaeda. Hence the criteria for a legitimate claim of self-defense did not exist. The United States basically confused the law of state responsibility with the right to self-defense.

Justifying the U.S. War Against Terrorism

The U.S. military invasion of Afghanistan is unprecedented in its scale and duration. However, that is not the first time states have resorted to military force to retaliate against terrorists. In 1976 Israel stormed an airline at the Entebbe airport in Uganda to free Israeli citizens held hostage by Palestinian terrorists. Israel claimed self-defense of its nationals but also offered a new interpretation of Article 2 (4). The Security Council did not condemn Israel because the United States exercised its veto to shield the Israeli action, but several states rejected the Israeli argument.[58] The General Assembly later condemned the Israeli incursion into Ugandan territory as a violation of the Charter. In 1979 President Carter authorized a military rescue mission of American diplomats held hostage at the American Embassy in Teheran. Neither the Security Council nor the International Court of Justice ICJ) condemned the United States' action.[59] In1986 President Reagan used military force against Libya in response to alleged Libyan involvement in the bombing of a Berlin nightclub that left several American servicemen injured.[60] In 1985 Reagan commandeered an Egyptian airline in mid air and forced it to land in Italy in order to arrest the Palestinian hijackers on board who were responsible for killing an American citizen, Leon Klinghoffer, on the *Achille Laro* cruise ship in the Mediterranean.[61] In 1993 President Clinton authorized military strikes against Iraq for President Hussein's suspected involvement in a plot to assassinate former President Bush.[62] In 1998 President Clinton authorized the bombing of targets in Sudan and Afghanistan in response to the bombing of United States embassies in Nairobi and Dar-es-Salaam.[63] In all of the cases cited above the United States said it was exercising its right of self-defense.

THE USE OF FORCE POST-SEPTEMBER 11, 2001

The nature of armed conflicts and the participants who engage in them are very different today than in the period prior to World War II. These new developments have led to revisiting calls for the Charter ban on the use of force to reflect the above changes. However, a majority of states have resisted such calls, including the Permanent Members of the Security Council, for fear that they may weaken the ban on the use of force. Since the September 11 attacks, states are more willing to make an exception to the Charter ban on the use of force and are more inclined to use force against terrorists. The United States and a number of other nations have supported Israel's right to use force against Hamas and Hezbollah, as well as Ethiopia's invasion of Somalia against the Islamic Court, which the United States labeled a terrorist organization. Although states remain the dominant actors in international relations, they no longer have the monopoly over the use of violence.

Non-state actors are increasingly becoming the principal culprits of international conflicts and are capable of launching major military attacks against states. Hamas's military victory in the Gaza Strip, Hezbollah's resistance to Israel's military invasion of Lebanon in 2006 and the Iraqi insurgents' ability to resist U.S. occupation and to inflict heavy casualties upon U.S. forces are three examples of the growing military capabilities of non-state actors. The September 11 attacks underscore the emergence of a new security paradigm, and the Charter norms should change to reflect such a paradigm.

The post-September 11 world requires a re-conceptualization of the ban on the use of force and how to deal with threats posed by non-state actors. The framers of the Charter did not anticipate attacks of such magnitude carried out by terrorist organizations. Article 51 makes no provisions for self-defense against attacks perpetrated by non-state actors.[64] In order to consider the United States-led invasion of Afghanistan legal, the Security Council had to determine that the September 11 attacks were a threat to international peace and security and authorize enforcement measures against Afghanistan. The failure of the Security Council to make such a determination left the United States the freedom to act on its own behalf. The United States did not seek Security Council endorsement for its invasion of Afghanistan because it wanted to keep all its options open.

International Humanitarian Law and the War Against Terrorism

In the wake of the terrorist attacks on the United States, President Bush froze the assets of suspected terrorist organizations and detained hundreds of men of Middle Eastern descent living in the United States.[65] The President called on foreign governments to crack down on terrorist organizations in their countries. Bush designated a number of groups as terrorist organizations and placed them on a State Department list of banned organizations. Congress passed tough new immigration laws to tighten visa requirements for entry into the U.S., and it increased border security. Congress also created the new Department of Homeland Security.[66] Some of the President's anti-terrorist policies were quite controversial and seem to contradict international law. The President's decision not to recognize the Geneva Conventions as applicable in the Afghanistan conflict, and to detain members of Al Qaeda and the Taliban indefinitely without charge, violate international humanitarian law.

International humanitarian laws (the laws governing conduct in war) have more specific definition than the laws governing states' right to go to war. A number of international conventions elaborate international humanitarian laws, including the 1899 and 1907 Hague Conventions on the Laws and Customs of War on Land and annexed to the 1907 Hague Convention IV Respecting the Laws and Customs of War on Land; the Geneva Protocol for the Prohibition of the Use in War of Asphyxiating, Poisonous or Other Gases and the Bacteriological Methods of Warfare of 1925; the Geneva Convention of 1949 for the Amelioration of the Conditions of the Wounded and Sick in Armed Forces in the Field (GC I); the Geneva Convention of 1949 for the Amelioration of the Condition of the Wounded, Sick and Shipwrecked Members of Armed Forces at Sea (GC II); the Geneva Convention of 1949 Relative to the Treatment of Prisoners of War (GC III); and the Geneva Convention of 1949 Relative to the Protection of Civilian Persons in Time of War (GC IV). [67]

Two additional protocols amended the Geneva Conventions in 1977: Additional Protocol I, Relating to the Protection of Victims of International Armed Conflicts of 1977 (AP I); and the Additional Protocol II, Relating to the Protection of Victims of Non-International Armed Conflicts of 1977 (AP II).[68] AP I treats guerrilla warfare in the exercise of self-determination against alien domination as an international armed conflict entitled to the protection accorded by AP I. AP I also widens the scope of protection accorded to victims of international armed conflicts under the four Geneva Conventions.[69] Article 3, common to the four Geneva Conventions, provides a minimum protection for victims of armed conflict not of an international character. Additional Protocol II supplements this requirement. The United States is not a signatory to AP II. However, provisions of the Geneva Conventions are now recognized as customary international law.

The manual of the International Committee of the Red Cross (ICRC) spells out the essence of international humanitarian law applicable in armed conflicts as follows:

1. Persons *hors de combat* and those who do not take a direct part in hostilities are entitled to respect for their lives and their moral, and physical integrity. They shall in all circumstances be protected and treated humanely without any adverse distinction.
2. It is forbidden to kill or injure an enemy who surrenders or who is *hors de combat.*
3. The wounded and sick shall be collected and cared for by the party to the conflict, which has them in its power. Protection also covers medical

personnel, establishments, transports, and equipment. The emblem of the Red Cross or the Red Crescent is the sign of such protection and must be respected.

4. Captured combatants and civilians under the authority of an adverse party are entitled to respect for their lives, dignity, personal rights, and convictions. They shall be protected against all acts of violence and reprisals. They shall have the right to correspond with their families and to receive relief.
5. Everyone shall be entitled to benefit from fundamental judicial guarantees. No one shall be held responsible for an act he has not committed. No one shall be subjected to physical or mental torture, corporal punishment, or cruel or degrading treatment.
6. Parties to a conflict and members of their armed forces do not have an unlimited choice of methods of warfare of a nature to cause unnecessary losses or excessive suffering.
7. Parties to a conflict shall at all times distinguish between the civilian population and combatants in order to spare civilian population and property. Neither the civilian population as such nor civilian persons shall be the objects of attack. Attacks shall be directed solely against military objectives.[70]

International humanitarian laws state the manner in which states should conduct warfare and the responsibilities of states and individuals in armed conflicts. The laws of war protect both soldiers and civilians and provide for holding individuals criminally responsible for war crimes, crimes against humanity and genocide.[71] International humanitarian law mandates that military strategy must be carried out in conformity with the principle of necessity and proportionality. International humanitarian law also bans the use of certain types of weapons that would prolong the suffering of the wounded; it protects prisoners of war, whether legitimate or illegitimate combatants, and protects works of art, monuments and churches.[72] New conventions have been adopted in recent years to protect the global environment, to ban the use of anti-personnel mines (Ottawa Convention) and to protect internationally protected persons, such as United Nations employees and humanitarian aid workers.

International humanitarian law takes effect from the beginning of an armed conflict and extends beyond the cessation of hostilities, until the signing of a peace agreement. The Geneva Conventions are applicable in the Afghanistan operation, whether or not the United States recognizes the captured Taliban and Al Qaeda forces as legitimate combatants. In fact, the manner in which the United States treats the captured Taliban and Al Qaeda detainees raises serious questions about the Bush administration's compliance with international humanitarian law. The administration is holding captured Taliban and Al Qaeda prisoners in Guant·namo Bay, Cuba, and does not recognize them as POWs.

United States Compliance with International Humanitarian Laws

The United States' compliance with international humanitarian laws is questionable to say the least. The United States initially conducted an air campaign in which it used weapons that did not discriminate between Al Qaeda forces and the civilian population. Several bombs missed their targets and hit civilian facilities, including a hospital, a Red Cross site and residential apartment buildings. The bombing campaign killed hundreds of civilians. Heavy bombs from B52 bombers dropped on suspected Taliban and Al Qaeda hideouts would have killed anyone occupying these areas. The United States military also used two thousand pound cluster bombs to flush out caves occupied by suspected Al Qaeda forces.[73] Many of these bombs were left behind as unexploded ordnances.

The treatment meted out to captured Taliban and Al Qaeda forces also raises questions about the United States' compliance with international humanitarian law. The United States has not fulfilled the basic requirements stipulated in the Geneva Conventions for captured combatants. Prisoners held in Afghanistan exist in extreme inhumane conditions, without food, water and other basic necessities. Those transferred to Guantánamo Bay, Cuba, are held without charges and are prevented from contacting their relatives. Their captors subject these detainees to interrogation and deny them basic POW status under the Geneva Conventions of 1949.[74] The United States plans to try some of these detainees before military tribunals and will continue to hold them in detention even if it finds them not guilty of the charges against them. Convicted detainees will have no right to appeal in civilian court.[75]

The United States' European allies have protested the treatment of the Afghan detainees at Guantánamo Bay and called on President Bush to recognize the detainees as POWs. Our European allies also contested the plan by the Bush administration to establish military tribunals to try some of the detainees. Some European allies are refusing to turn over to U.S. authorities Taliban and Al Qaeda forces they have captured in Afghanistan, or suspected Al Qaeda members arrested on their territory. The OAS's Inter-American Commission on Human Rights has also called on the United States to clarify the status of the Afghan detainees.[76] The International Committee of the Red Cross has also criticized the Bush administration's decision not to grant POW status to the Afghan detainees.[77]

There is a real question whether Al Qaeda fighters should receive POW status, given the fact that they are considered terrorists and not legitimate combatants. However, the question remains how to distinguish between an Al Qaeda that is a terrorist and one that was in Afghanistan fighting on behalf of the Taliban in its war against the Northern Alliance. Also, there is the question of whether all captured foreign nationals in Afghanistan are members of Al Qaeda. The Bush Administration bowed to international pressure and granted rights under the Geneva Conventions to Taliban fighters, but so far it has refused to grant similar rights to Al Qaeda fighters. President Bush continues to deny POW status to the detainees.

Some have also attacked the Bush administration's policy of detaining Al Qaeda and Taliban suspects indefinitely, without charge or trial, or even the right to see an attorney, as violating basic principles of human rights and humanitarian law. President Bush declared the four hundred plus detainees at Guantánamo Bay, Cuba, "enemy combatants" and refused to grant them prisoner of war status, in violation of the Geneva Conventions of 1949.[78] These detainees are to be tried by military commissions established pursuant to a Presidential Military Order entitled "Detention, Treatment, and Trial of Certain Non-Citizens in the War Against Terrorism."[79]

The President's Order states:

> By the authority vested in me as President and Commander in Chief of the Armed Forces of the United States by the Constitution and the laws of the United States of America, including the authorization for Use of Military Force Joint Resolution (Public Law 107-40, 115 Stat. 224) and sections 821 and 836 of title 10, United States Code, it is hereby ordered as follows:

Section 2. Definition and Policy

a. The term "individual subject to this order" shall mean any individual who is not a United States citizen with respect to whom I determine from time to time in writing that:
   1. there is no reason to believe that such individual, at the relevant times,
      i. is or was a member of the organization known as al Qaeda;
      ii. has engaged in, aided or abetted, or conspired to commit, have caused, threaten to cause, or have as their aim to cause, injury to or adverse effects on the United States, its citizens, national security, foreign policy, or economy; or

iii. has knowingly harbored one or more individuals described in subparagraphs (i) or (ii) of subsection 2(a)(1) of this order; and

2. it is in the interest of the United States that such individual be subject to this order. . . .

Section 4. Authority of the Secretary of Defense Regarding Trials of Individuals Subject to this Order.

a. Any individual subject to this order shall, when tried, be tried by military commission for any and all offenses triable by military commission that such individual is alleged to have committed, and may be punished in accordance with the penalties provided under applicable law, including life imprisonment or death.
b. As a military function and in light of the findings [above] . . . , the Secretary of Defense shall issue such orders and regulations, including orders for the appointment of one or more military commissions, as may be necessary to carry out subsection (a) of this section.
c. Orders and regulations issued under subsection (b) of this section shall include, but not be limited to, rules for the conduct of the proceedings of military commissions, including pretrial, trial, and post-trial procedures, modes of proof, issuance of process, and qualifications of attorneys, which shall at a minimum provide for—
    1. military commissions to sit at any time and any place, consistent with such guidance regarding time and place as the Secretary of Defense may provide;
    2. a full and fair trial, with the military commission sitting as the triers of both fact and
    3. admission of such evidence as would, in the opinion of the presiding officer of the military commission . . . have probative value to a reasonable person;
    4. in a manner consistent with the protection of [classified information],
        A. the handing of, admission into evidence of, and access to materials and information, and
        B. the conduct, closure of, and access to proceedings;
    5. conduct of prosecution by one or more attorneys designated by the Secretary of Defense and conduct of the defense by attorneys for the individual subject to this order;
    6. conviction only upon the concurrence of two-thirds of the members of the commission present at the time of the vote, a majority being present;
    7. sentencing only upon the concurrence of two-thirds of the members of the commission present at the time of the vote, a majority being present; and
    8. submission of the record of the trial, including any conviction or sentence, for review and final decision by me or by the secretary of defense if so designated by me for that purpose. . . .

Section 6. Additional Authorities of the Secretary of Defense,

a. As a military function and in light of the findings [above], the Secretary of Defense shall issue such orders and regulations as may be necessary to carry out any of the provisions of this order. . . .

Section 7. Relationship to Other Law and Forums. . . .

b. With respect to any individual subject to this order—
   1. military tribunals shall have exclusive jurisdiction with respect to offenses by the individual; and
   2. the individual shall not be privileged to seek any remedy or maintain any proceedings, directly, or to have any such remedy or proceeding sought on the individual's behalf, in
      i. any court of the United States, or any State thereof
      ii. any court of any foreign nation, or
      iii. any international tribunal.[80]

Under the Military Order detainees will be prosecuted for violations of the laws of war and other applicable laws. Detainees will have limited rights under these commissions and no access to the evidence against them. Furthermore, the burden of proof against them will be lower than that generally reserved for detainees in civilian courts. Detainees could also face the death penalty if found guilty.[81] Numerous allegations exist of detainee mistreatment by the U.S. military. Several detainees have gone on hunger strikes, and some have attempted suicide. Three detainees at Guantánamo Bay committed suicide in June 2006.[82] The International Committee of the Red Cross (ICRC) and other human rights organizations cited the use of sleep deprivation, having detainees sitting for long hours in an uncomfortable position, long periods of isolation and other painful interrogation techniques as inhumane treatment and as a violation of U.S. and international law.[83] The indefinite detention of suspected terrorists without trial violates internationally recognized standards of human decency. It is also a violation of the Universal Declaration of Human Rights and the International Covenant on Civil and Political Rights.[84]

President Bush has also detained American citizens as "enemy combatants" and denied them basic constitutional rights guaranteed under the United States Constitution.[85] Yaser Esam Hamdi was picked up in Afghanistan and detained at Guant·namo Bay as an unlawful combatant. American interrogators subsequently discovered that Hamdi was born in the United States of Saudi Arabian parents. He was moved to a naval brig in South Carolina and held in solitary confinement for three years as an enemy combatant. Lawyers acting on Hamdi's behalf petitioned the D.C. Circuit Court for relief for their client. The court granted the motion, but later the Fourth Circuit Court of Appeals reversed it. The Supreme Court later reversed the decision of the Fourth Circuit and awarded Hamdi the right to challenge his detention. In the wake of the Supreme Court ruling, the Bush administration negotiated a plea agreement with Hamdi's attorneys that stripped him of his American citizenship and deported him to Saudi Arabia.[86]

A second American citizen, Jose Padilla, was arrested in May 2002 at Chicago O'Hare International Airport on his way to New York and detained as a material witness in the September 11 investigation. On June 10 Attorney General John Ashcroft charged him with plotting to detonate a radioactive dirty bomb. Ashcroft also stated that Padilla was in association with Al Qaeda and that he had met with Khalid Sheik Mohammed in Afghanistan where he received training and instruction on detonating a dirty bomb.[87]

The Justice Department initially denied Padilla the right to see an attorney. But a federal judge in New York rejected the Bush administration's claim that Padilla's right to meet with his attorney would compromise national security. Judge Michael Mukasey (now attorney general) ruled that the government had a right to hold Padilla without charge until the end of hostilities, but he upheld Padilla's right to counsel.[88] The Justice Department appealed the judge's decision to the Supreme Court on the grounds that the District Court in New York lacked jurisdiction, as the government had moved Padilla had to a naval brig in South Carolina. In June 2004, the Supreme Court avoided the issues of Padilla's right to challenge his detention by voting to send the case to the federal court in South Carolina. The federal court in South Carolina subsequently ruled that the Bush administration had the authority as commander-in-chief to detain U.S. citizens indefinitely. The case was later appealed to the Fourth Circuit, which upheld the authority of the President to detain U.S. citizens as enemy combatants and to deny them the right to review by a civilian court.[89] Padilla's attorneys subsequently appealed that decision to the Supreme Court. However, prior to the Supreme Court actually hearing oral arguments in the case, the Justice Department announced that the President had ordered the Department of Defense to turn over Padilla to the jurisdiction of the Justice Department.

On November 22, 2006 Attorney General Alberto Gonzales announced a new indictment against Padilla with a set of charges different from those under which he was previously detained for three and a half years as an enemy combatant. The charge against Padilla was multiple counts of conspiracy to commit acts of terrorism abroad, and he was ordered transferred from the naval brig in South Carolina to a prison in Miami.[90] The Attorney General said in his news conference that the previous charges against Padilla were "legally irrelevant" and that the pending case before the Supreme Court brought by Padilla's attorneys to challenge the President's authority to detain American citizens indefinitely was "moot."[91] Jose Padilla went on trial in June and received conviction on August 16 of charges different from the ones against him when originally detained as an enemy combatant.[92] Padilla subsequently received a sentence of seventeen years in prison, a lighter sentence than the prosecutor had requested. In sentencing Padilla to a lighter sentence, Judge Marcia Cook indicated that Padilla had not killed anyone, nor had he carried out any acts of terrorism on American soil.[93]

The Bush administration's sudden decision to charge Padilla with a different set of charges may have been intended to preempt the Supreme Court review of the Fourth Circuit Court of Appeals's decision granting the President far-reaching powers to detain American citizens. The Bush administration was fearful that a Supreme Court ruling to reverse that decision would impact greatly his authority to conduct his war on terror. Lawyers for Padilla asked the Supreme Court to hear their challenge because the issue is still relevant, and the administration can restore Padilla's enemy combatant status if he is found not guilty in the criminal case.

Following the Attorney General's announcement, the Fourth Circuit Court of Appeals asked the Bush administration to explain its decision to charge Padilla under a different set of charges than the ones under which it had previously detained him. The Bush administration responded by asking the court to vacate that judgment. The Fourth Circuit Court of Appeals subsequently rejected the Bush administration's reasoning for transferring Padilla to civilian court and called on the Supreme Court to render a decision in the case. However, after several closed-door sessions the justices decided against hearing Padilla's appeal for relief. The Supreme Court did not rule on the Bush administration's argument that it had the authority under the Constitution to detain American citizens as enemy combatants without review. In its *Hamdi* decision the Supreme Court majority had previously ruled that Congress authorized the President to use all necessary means to pursue the terrorists who attacked the United States and that they granted President Bush the authority to detain American citizens. However, Justice O'Connor cautioned that, given the indefinite nature of the war on terror, the administration had to provide American citizens the opportunity to challenge their indefinite detention. The administration was seeking to overturn that ruling. Three justices who voted with the majority warned the government against reclassifying Padilla as an enemy combatant if the civilian court found him not guilty.[94]

FBI agents arrested a non-resident alien, Ali Saleh Kahlah al Marri of Qatar, in Illinois on December 12, 2001, and held as a material witness in the government investigation of the September 11 attacks. Al Marri came under suspicion as he arrived in the United States on September 10 from Qatar to pursue graduate studies in Computer Science at Bradley University in Peoria, Illinois. Officials later transferred al-Marri to New York, charging him with credit card fraud in 2002. In January 2003, they charged him with a second six-count indictment, with two counts of making false statements to the FBI, three counts of making a false statement on a bank application and one count of using another person's identification for the purpose of influencing the action of a federally insured financial institution. Al-Marri pleaded not guilty to all the charges. In May 2003, the federal court in New York dismissed all the charges against al Marri for lack of venue. Al Marri was subsequently returned to Peoria where he was re-indicted in the Central District of Illinois on the same counts. Al-Marri pleaded not guilty, and a trial date was set for July 21, 2003. On June 23, the government sought a dismissal of the indictment based on an order signed by President Bush that same morning.

The President's order determined that al Marri is an enemy combatant; is closely associated with Al Qaeda; engaged in conduct that constituted hostile and war-like acts, including conduct in preparation for acts of international terrorism; possesses intelligence that would aid U.S. efforts to prevent attacks by Al Qaeda; and represents a continuing, present, and grave danger to the national security of the United States. The President ordered the Attorney General to transfer al Marri to the Secretary of Defense to be detained as an enemy combatant. Officials later moved al-Marri to a naval brig in South Carolina. They kept al Marri in isolation for sixteen months before allowing him to meet with an attorney. He alleged they abused him with harsh interrogation techniques and sleep deprivation. The district court in Central Illinois and the Seventh Circuit denied al Marri's petition for writ of habeas corpus. The Supreme Court also denied certiorari.[95] A The District Court of South Carolina denied a similar petition for failure to rebut allegations in the government's motion. A subsequent appeal was filed on Al Marri's behalf, but the government requested a dismissal of the appeal for lack of jurisdiction. The administration cited the newly enacted Military Commissions Act of 2006, which stripped detainees at Guant·namo of the right to petition for habeas corpus in federal court. On that basis al Marri's habeas petition was denied. That decision was then appealed to the Fourth Circuit Court of Appeals. The decision of the Fourth Circuit in this case was a setback for the Bush administration's claim of extraordinary executive power to detain anyone as an enemy combatant, including

American citizens or foreign nationals legally residing in the United States, without granting them the right to counsel or the opportunity to challenge their detention.

In a ruling from a three-judge panel of the Fourth Circuit Court of Appeals, the majority chastised the Bush administration for its broad interpretation of executive authority. The court's majority ruled that: "The President cannot eliminate constitutional protections with the stroke of a pen by proclaiming a civilian, even a criminal civilian, an enemy combatant subject to indefinite military detention. Put simply, the Constitution does not allow the President to order the military to seize civilians residing within the United States and detain them indefinitely without criminal process, and this so even if he calls them 'enemy combatants.'"[96] The court reversed the judgment of the district court dismissing al Marri's petition for writ of habeas corpus and remanded the case to the lower court with instructions to issue a writ of habeas corpus directing the Secretary of Defense to release al Marri from military custody within a reasonable time set by the district court. The court further stated that the government can transfer al Marri to civilian authorities to face criminal charges, initiate deportation proceedings against him, hold him as a material witness in connection with grand jury proceedings or detain him for a limited time pursuant to the Patriot Act. The Appeals Court called for the termination of al Marri's military detention.[97] The Bush administration appealed the ruling to the full court, further delaying al Marri's release or transfer from military detention.

The Fourth Circuit Court of Appeals, which is one of the most conservative in the federal system, rendered its decision in the case on July 14. In its decision the court split 5-4 in favor of the President's authority to detain a U.S. citizen or a permanent resident indefinitely. However, the majority agreed that the executive branch must give al Marri an additional opportunity to challenge his detention in federal court. The court concluded that the evidence holding al Marri was flimsy and that he should receive access to more than the hearsay evidence the administration presented to the lower court to hold al Marri as an enemy combatant.98 However, the court asserted the President's authority granted to him by Congress under the Authorization for Use of Military Force (AUMF). The Supreme Court may have to resolve the split decisions.

Endnotes

1. See Dead and mission. 2002. *New York Times*, Jan. 28, A6.
2. Proclamation 7463, 66 Fed Reg. 48, 1999 (Sept. 18, 2001).
3. See USA Patriot Act, H.R. 3162 (2001).

4. Joint Resolution to Authorize the Use of United States Armed Forces Against Those Responsible for the Recent Attacks Launched Against the United States, Sept. 18, 2001, Pub. L. No. 107-40, 115 Stat 224, *reprinted in* 40 *ILM* 1282 (2001).
5. Joint Resolution to Authorize the Use of United States Forces Against Those Responsible for the Recent Attacks Launched Against the United States, Sept. 18, 2001, Pub. Law No. 107-40 Stat. 224.
6. See Address Before Joint Session of the Congress on the United States Response to the Terrorist Attacks of September 11. 2001. 37 *Weekly Comp. Pres. Doc.*, Sept. 20, 1347.
7. *Id.*
8. Exec. Order No. 13,228, 66 Fed. Reg. 51812 (Oct. 10, 2001)
9. Exec. Order No. 13, 224, 66 Fed. Reg. 49,079 (2001); See Mike Allen and Paul Blustein, 2001, Bush moves to cut terrorists' support, *Wash. Post,* Sept. 25, A1.
10. Ibid.
11. See Karen DeYoung and Dan Eggen, 2001, $100 million in terrorists' assets frozen, U.S. says. *Wash. Post,* Oct. 3, A9.
12. North Atlantic Treaty Organization (NATO) Press Release No. 124, Statement by the North Atlantic Council (Sept. 12, 2001), at *http://www.nato.int.*
13. Secretary General Lord Robertson, Statement at NATO headquarters (Oct. 2, 2001), at *http://www.nato.int.*
14. OAS Doc. OEA/Ser.F/II.24/RC.24/RES.1/01 (Sept. 21, 2001), at *http://www.oas.org.*
15. Ibid.
16. OAS Doc. OEA/Ser.F/II.24/CS/TIAR/RES.1/01 (Oct. 16, 2001), at *http://www.oas.org.*
17. Senate Res/1368 (2001), at http://www.un.org/Sec.Doc.
18. In order for the United States to claim a right of self-defense under Article 51 of the Charter of the United Nations, it would have to have been the subject of an armed attack. The fact that the Security Council did not mention "armed attack" in its resolution is an indication that it did not recognize that such an attack had occurred.
19. Ibid.
20. Senate Res/1269 (1999) unequivocally condemns all acts, methods and practices of terrorism as criminal and unjustifiable, regardless of their motivation, in all their forms and manifestations, wherever and by whomever committed, in particular those which could threaten international peace and security.
21. Senate Res/1368 (2001), at *http://www.un.org/Sec.Doc.*
22. Ibid.
23. Ibid.
24. Senate Res/1373 (2001), at *http:// www.un.org.Sec.Doc.*
25. Ibid.
26. Letter dated 7 October from the Permanent Representative of the United States of America to the United Nations Addressed to the President of the Security Council, UN Doc. S/2001/946 (Oct. 7, 2001), at *http://www.un.int./usa/s-2001-946.htm.*

27. Senate Res/1378 (2001), at *http://www.un.org/Sec.Doc.*
28. Ibid.
29. Ibid.
30. Senate Res/1383 (2001), at *http://www.un.org/Sec.Doc.*
31. Ibid.
32. Ibid.
33. Senate/Res/1386 (2001), at *http://www.un.org/Sec.Doc.*
34. Senate/Res/1386 (2001), at *http://www.un.org/Sec.Doc.*
35. Ibid.
36. Senate/Res/1413 (2002), at *http://www.un.org/Sec.Doc.*
37. A/RES/56/1, at *http://ww.un.org/GA.Doc.*
38. Ibid.
39. See Elisabeth Bumiller, 2001, President rejects offer by Taliban for negotiations. *New York Times,* Oct. 15, A1.
40. Address to the Nation Announcing Strikes Against Al Qaida Training Camps and Taliban Military Installations. 2001. 37 *Weekly Comp. Pres. Doc.,* Oct. 7, 1432, 1432; See Patrick E. Tyler, 2001, U.S. and Britain strike Afghanistan, aiming at bases and terrorist camps; Bush warns "Taliban will pay a price." *New York Times,* Oct. 8, A1.
41. Letter dated 7 October 2001 from Permanent Representative of the United States of America to the United Nations Addressed to the President of the Security Council, UN Doc. S/2001/946, at *http://www.un.org.int'lusa/s-2001-946.htm.* The United Kingdom provided a similar notification.
42. Ibid.
43. Ibid.
44. See Christopher S. Wren, 2001, U.S. advises U.N. council more strikes could come, *New York Times,* Oct. 9, B5.
45. See William Branigin and Richburg, 2001, Alliance surges across north. *Wash. Post,* Oct. 25, A1.
46. See Letter of the Secretary General to the President of the Security Council, UN Doc.S/2001/1154 (2001); Steven Erlanger, 2001, After arm-twisting, Afghan factions pick interim government and leader, *New York Times,* Dec. 6, B1
47. Ibid.
48. See Ian Brownlie, 1983, *International law and the use of force by states.*
49. Bruno Simma, ed. 1995. The Charter of the United Nations, 111.
50. Ibid., 608–613.
51. Ibid.
52. Ibid., 668–69.
53. Jennings, Robert. 1938. The Caroline and McLeod cases, *AJIL,* 32:82.
54. Ibid., 105.
55. Bruno Simma, ed. 1995. The Charter of the United Nations, 668–69.

56. Brownlie, Ian. 1983. *International law and the use of force by states,* 278.
57. Higgins, Rosalyn. 1994. *Problems and process,* 243.
58. SC 194 2nd meeting, para. 102 (1976), UNYB, 315.
59. Senate Res/461 (1979), at *http://www.un.org/Sec.Doc.*; ICJ Reports (1980). P.3 at *http://www.icj-cij.org.*
60. Greenwood, Christopher. 1987. International law and the United States' air operation against Libya, *West Virginia Law Review,* 89:933.
61. For a comprehensive legal analysis of the *Achille Lauro* affairs, see Antonio Cassese, *Terrorism, politics and law: The Achille Lauro affair,* 1989.
62. Ratner, Michael, and Jules Lobel. 1993. Bombing Baghdad: Illegal reprisal or self-defense? *Legal Times,* July 5, 24; W. Michael Reisman, 1994, Self-defence or reprisal? The raid on Baghdad: Some reflections on its lawfulness and implications, *Eur. J. Int'l L.,* 120.
63. Lobel, Jules. 1999. The use of force to respond to terrorist attacks: The bombing of Sudan and Afghanistan, *Yale J. Int'l L.,* 24:537.
64. Sofaer, Abram. 1986. Terrorism and the law, *Foreign Affairs,* 64:901, 919.
65. Murphy, Sean. 2002. Contemporary practice of the United States relating to international law, *AJIL* 96:251.
66. Hastedt, Glen. 2005. Creation of the Department of Homeland Security. In *Contemporary cases in U.S. foreign policy,* ed. Ralph G. Carter, 172.
67. See in general, Ingrid Detter, 2001, *The law of war.*
68. Ibid.
69. Ibid.
70. See the *Manual of the International Committee of the Red Cross.*
71. For an analysis of international humanitarian law, see Adam Roberts and Richard Guelf, eds., 2001, *Document on the laws of war.*
72. Ibid.
73. See Eric Schmitt and Steven Lee Myers, U.S. escalating efforts to bomb Taliban caves, 2001. *New York Times,* Nov. 6, A1.
74. DeYoung, Karen. 2002. Group criticizes U.S. on detainee policy. *Wash. Post,* May 28, A4.
75. Shanker, Thom, and Katharine Q. Seelye. 2002. Behind-the-scenes clash led Bush to reverse himself on applying Geneva Conventions. *New York Times,* Feb. 22, A12.
76. Mintz, John. 2002. U.S. told to rule on detainees' status. *Wash. Post,* Mar. 14, A12.
77. Robinson, Gwen. 2002. Red Cross concern over 5,000 Afghan prisoners. *Fin. Times,* Jan. 30, 8.
78. Mundis, Daryl A. 2002. The use of military commissions to prosecute individuals accused of terrorist acts, *AJIL* 96:320, 325; Also see Linda Cornett and Mark Gibney, 2005, The rights of detainees: Determining the limits of law. In *Contemporary cases in U.S. foreign policy,* ed. Ralph G. Carter, 427.

79. "Detention, Treatment, and Trial of Certain Non-Citizens in the War Against Terrorism," issued Nov. 13, 2001, 66 FED. Reg. 57,883.
80. Ibid.
81. Daryl A. Mundis, *supra* note 160, 322.
82. Alden, Edward. 2006. EU to press for Guantánamo closure. *Fin. Times,* June 13, 4.
83. Lewis, Neil A. 2004. Red Cross find detainee abuse in Guantánamo. *New York Times,* Nov. 30, A1; Josh White and John Mintz, 2004, Red Cross cites 'inhumane' treatment at Guantánamo. *Wash. Post,* Dec. 1, A10.
84. See Article 9 of the International Covenant on Civil and Political Rights (Freedom from Arbitrary Detention); also, Sarah Joseph, Jenny Schultz and Melissa Castan, eds., 2005, *The international covenant on civil and political rights,* 303.
85. Cornett and Gibney, *supra* note 160, 430–434; See also Edward Alden and Patti Waldmeir, 2005, Court allows Bush to detain U.S. 'enemy combatant' indefinitely without civilian trial, *Fin. Times,* Sept. 10–11, 2.
86. Crook, James. 2005. Contemporary practice of the United States relating to international law, *AJIL* 99:262; Jerry Markon, 2004, U.S. to free Hamdi, send him home, *Wash. Post,* Sept. 23, A1.
87. Cornett and Gibney, 431.
88. Lewis, Neil A., and William Glaberson. 2003. U.S. courts reject detention policy in 2 terror. *New York Times,* Dec. 19, A1; Michael Powell and Michelle Garcia, 2003, Padilla ordered released. *Wash. Post,* Dec. 19, A1.
89. Patti, Edward Alden. 2005. Court allows Bush to detain U.S. 'enemy combatant' indefinitely without civilian trial. *Fin. Times,* Sept. 10/11, 2.
90. Lichblau, Eric. 2005. In legal shift, U.S. charges detainee in terrorism case. *New York Times,* Nov. 23, A1.
91. Kirchgaessner, Stephanie. 2005. Criminal charges against 'dirty bomber' hit a snag. *Fin. Times,* Dec. 1, 10.
92. Sevastopulo, Demetri. 2007. U.S. convicts former "enemy combatant' on terror charges. *Fin. Times,* Aug. 17, 2.
93. Waldmeir, Patti. 2008. Padilla jailed for 17 years over terrorism support. *Fin. Times,* Jan. 23, 6.
94. Greenhouse, Linda. 2006. Justices decline terrorism case of a U.S. citizen. *New York Times,* April 4, A1.
95. See complaint, *al Marri v. Bush,* 274 F. Supp. 2d 1003 (C.D. Ill., 2003); Seven Circuit affirmed, *al Marri v. Rumsfeld,* 360 F. 3d 707 (7th Cir., 2004); and Supreme Court denied certiorari, *al Marri v. Rumsfeld,* 543 U.S. 809 (2004).
96. *Ali Saleh Al-Marri v. Commander S. L. Wright,* 4th Cir. Ct., No. 06-7427 (June 11, 2007).
97. Liptak, Adam. 2007. Judges say U.S. can't hold man as 'combatant'. *New York Times,* June 12, A1.
98. Liptak, Adam. 2008. Court ruling favors Bush on detainees, *New York Times,* Jul. 16, A11.

chapter VI

INTERNATIONAL LAW AND U.S. ECONOMIC AND TRADE POLICY

The United States has always championed free trade and has ripped the benefits of an open trading system. The United States played a leadership role in the creation of the post-war trade regime, the GATT and the various trade rounds that led to the elimination of tariffs and other trade barriers in a number of sectors and to the massive growth in world trade. The shift in the U.S. attitude toward free trade came as the EU and Japan were emerging as major trade competitors that did not play by the rules. The United States has since pushed for fair trade instead of for free trade.

President Bush has pursued a similar unilateralist international economic and trade policy that conflicts with U.S. international treaty obligations. In 2002, President Bush imposed tariffs on steel imports into the United States from certain nations in order to protect the steel sector in key electoral battleground states such as Ohio, Pennsylvania and West Virginia, which he considered crucial for his reelection bid.[1] The President acted in response to the Steel Revitalization Act passed by Congress in March 2001, which called for quotas to limit imports of unfinished steel into the United States.[2] The President also signed into law the largest farm subsidy bill in U.S. history, which provides billions of dollars in direct payment to American farmers.[3] The steel tariff was later ruled a violation of World Trade Organization (WTO) law governing unfair trade practices after the EU challenged the steel tariffs and won.[4] The Bush administration delayed complying with the WTO ruling but subsequently lifted the tariffs.[5] By then the steel sector in the United States had improved its performance and the administration could justify the fact that the measure was no longer necessary.[6] The farm subsidy bill threatened to undermine the ongoing Doha trade negotiations, which focuses on eliminating farm subsidies that the U.S. and EU pay to their farmers. These subsidies adversely affect prices for agricultural goods on the world market and in turn hurt producers from developing countries.

The EU also requested a ruling from the WTO against the United States Foreign Sales Corporation Tax provision, which provides $400 billion in tax incentives to American IT companies with foreign subsidiaries. The WTO considered the measure a violation of international trade rules, as it gives an unfair competitive advantage to U.S. firms over their foreign competitors. The WTO ruling called for the U.S. to lift the measure, and it authorized the EU to retaliate by imposing a dollar amount in tariff on U.S. goods equal to the damage suffered by the EU.[7] The Bush administration was slow to implement the WTO ruling and did not call for Congress to repeal the measure immediately. Many in Congress considered the measure too politically sensitive to repeal it before the 2004 election.

The EU initially planned to impose the equivalent amount in tariff against the United States but delayed the measure to give Congress time to pass the necessary legislation to repeal the act. In October 2004, Congress passed the American Jobs Creation Act to replace the Foreign Sales Corporation Tax (FSC), which granted tax breaks to six thousand exporters, such as Boeing, General Electric and Microsoft. The legislation contained transition periods that would basically extend the illegal tax incentives to 2006.[8] In July 2005, the WTO ruled that the United States had failed to comply with its January 2002 ruling, which outlawed the tax break to exporters.[9] The WTO then authorized the EU to resume the sanctions suspended in 2004, starting on January 1, 2006, or 60 days after a final decision in the case, whichever came later. The United States appealed that decision, but the WTO rejected that appeal and ruled that the FSC amounted to unfair trade subsidies.[10]

The United States has had a number of longstanding trade disputes with the EU that are hurting multilateral trade liberalization. Disputes over *Beef Hormones* and Genetically Modified Organisms (GMOs) have not reached a settlement in spite of a WTO ruling against the EU.[11] The EU regulation prohibits the import of GMO products into the EU because of inconclusive scientific evidence about possible health complications.[12] In 2003, the U.S., along with Canada and Argentina, filed a complaint with the WTO on the grounds that the EU ban violated the trade rules on Sanitary and PhytoSanitary Measures (SPS). After a three-year investigation the WTO ruled that the EU ban breached international trade rules and called for it to be lifted.[13]

The United States and the EU have also been at odds over EU preferential treatment given to banana imports from EU former colonies in Africa, the Caribbean and the Pacific (ACP) under the Lomé Convention. The WTO initially ruled that the preferential treatment violated international trade rules. The EU subsequently appealed the decision and lost. In 2001, President Bush suspended retaliatory measures against the EU for five years. However, in a final ruling in December 2005 the WTO declared the preferences illegal and a violation of WTO rules. President Bush has threatened to impose sanctions on the EU in all three cases unless it complies with the WTO rulings.

The EU also challenged the United States over the Continued Dumping and Subsidy Offset Act, which Congress passed in 2000. Known as the Byrd Amendment, the law requires the government to impose anti-dumping duties on foreign steel products and to use the proceeds collected on the import duties to compensate U.S. companies affected by such imports.[14] President Bush has acted slowly to get Congress to repeal the measure in spite of a WTO ruling that found the act a violation of trade rules.

In May 2004, President Bush asked the WTO to rule on the legality of the EU aid to Airbus in excess of $3.7 billion, after both sides failed to reach an agreement to settle the issue. In response, the EU counter-sued by claiming that the indirect support by the United States of $20 billion for Boeing since 1992 similarly violates WTO rules.[15] Efforts to reach a negotiated settlement failed, leaving both sides to proceed with their separate claims before the WTO. This case is the biggest and one of the most complex cases ever brought before the WTO. Its outcome will have enormous implications for the WTO and the future of the airline industry in Europe and the United States.

In spite of his public opposition to international law and his lack of enthusiasm for multilateral diplomacy, President Bush has relied on the WTO dispute settlement machinery to decide on a number of critical trade disputes between the U.S. and its trading partners. The Bush administration has shown a willingness to comply with decisions by both the WTO Dispute Settlement Board (DSB) and NAFTA.[16] However, with the present Trade Promotion Authorization about to expire in June, and strong opposition in Congress against a renewal, the President does not have the domestic political support that would allow him to implement any new decisions from the WTO.

The WTO decided on a number of other trade disputes between the United States and other nations. Among them is a dispute with Canada over the U.S. imposition of tariff on *softwood lumber* imports from Canada. Canada filed complaints both under NAFTA Chapters 11 and 19, and with the WTO. The outcomes of the proceedings have been mixed. In April 2006, the WTO DSB rejected Canada's claim that U.S. antidumping duties were inconsistent with a prior ruling of the DSB. Soon thereafter Canada's new Prime Minister, Stephen Harper, and President Bush agreed to terminate all litigation over softwood lumber.[17] Under the new agreement Canadian softwood lumber will receive free access to the U.S. market at a guaranteed price of $355 or above per thousand board feet.[18]

The twin island nation of Antigua and Barbuda filed a complaint with the WTO against the United States over the U.S. restriction on Internet gambling. Antigua deemed the measure a violation of the General Agreement in Trade in Services agreement (GATS). The WTO initially ruled the measure was illegal, but the United States did not comply.[19] Antigua and Barbuda filed an appeal with the WTO regarding the U.S. noncompliance. In October 2006, President Bush signed into law the Unlawful Internet Gambling Enforcement Act to ban American financial institutions from transmitting payments for online gambling for American citizens.[20] However, in March 2007, the WTO ruled that the new American legislation unfairly discriminates against foreign online gambling companies. The panel said that the United States was protecting American companies operating interstate horse-race gambling while at the same time prosecuting United States-based operators that used foreign gambling services.[21] In June 2007, Antigua launched a second complaint with the WTO in which it accused the United States of failing to comply with the WTO previous ruling. Antigua is seeking WTO authorization to impose $3.4 billion per year in retaliatory compensation against the United States. The measure would come in the form of an exemption for Antigua from complying with U.S. copyright and patent laws, which would deprive American companies of royalties.[22] The WTO also ruled in favor of Brazil in a dispute with the U.S. over cotton subsidies. However, the Bush administration did not comply.[23]

President Bush has not made multilateral trade negotiations a top priority of his administration. He has not provided the leadership necessary for a successful completion of the Doha Development Round. Instead, the Bush administration has chosen to negotiate bilateral trade agreements with as many developing countries as possible. The failure of the U.S. and the EU to reach an agreement over the reduction of farm subsidies has delayed progress on the successful completion of the WTO Doha Development Round.[24]

The Bush administration has negotiated bilateral trade agreements with Australia, Singapore, Chile, Morocco, Bahrain, Jordan, the Dominican Republic and five Central American countries (DR-CAFTA).[25] The administration has also concluded trade agreements with Colombia, Panama, Peru and South Korea. These agreements are currently before Congress where they face an uphill battle. The Democratic majority in Congress has insisted that the Bush administration must secure commitments from these countries that they will respect the workers' right to organize and improve labor and environmental standards before Congress can approve these trade agreements.

The agreement with South Korea is by far the most important for the Bush administration. Signed on April 2, 2007, the agreement calls for the elimination of tariffs on a wide range of goods traded between the two countries. The Bush administration sees this agreement as a milestone, as South Korea has the eleventh largest economy in the world and an estimated $78 billion in trade with the United States.[26] However, many observers see such agreements as an attempt to manage trade in particular sectors of the economy, instead of advancing the global trade agenda of the WTO.[27] The administration is also negotiating similar agreements with South Africa, Egypt and Israel. President Bush called for a hemispheric-wide free trade agreement with the nations of Latin America and the Caribbean, but many nations in the region oppose such an agreement.[28] The goal of the Bush administration is to negotiate these bilateral trade agreements ahead of completion of the Doha Round, which would give the United States greater leverage to set trade policies with these countries. These U.S. bilateral agreements have made completion of the Doha Round a lot more difficult to achieve.[29]

Trade Ministers have failed to complete the Doha Round due to differences between the United States and the EU over farm subsidies.[30] Although the Bush administration has said repeatedly that it wants a trade agreement, the administration has not demonstrated flexibility on farm subsidies to persuade Brazil, India and the EU that it is serious about a multilateral trade agreement. The outcome of the midterm election has complicated the President's negotiating ability and made it more difficult for him to reach a compromise with the EU on farm subsidies in time to complete the Doha Round before his Trade Promotion Authority runs out. President Bush faces a Democratic majority in Congress that is more protectionist than the previous Republican Congress and less willing to accept trade agreements that do not take into consideration safeguard measures to protect workers' rights and provisions and existing environmental standards.

Endnotes

1. Allen, Mike, and Jonathan Weisman. 2003. Steel tariffs appear to have backfired on Bush. *Wash. Post*, Sept. 19, A1.

2. The Steel Revitalization Act of 2001 (H.R. 8708 and S. 957).
3. Remarks by President Upon Signing farm Bill, at *www.whitehouse.gov/news/releases/2002/05/20020513-2.html.*
4. Becker, Elizabeth. 2003. U.S. tariffs on steel are illegal, World Trade Organization says. *New York Times,* Nov. 11, A1.
5. Stevenson, Richard W. 2003. Bush set to lift tariffs on steel, *New York Times,* Dec. 4, A1.
6. Becker, Robert A. 2005. U.S. steel import tariffs: The politics of global markets. In *Contemporary cases in U.S. foreign policy,* ed. Ralph G. Carter, P. 250.
7. United States-tax treatment for "foreign sales corporation" (EU DS 108); See WTO Ruling, Jan. 14, 2002, at *http://wto.org/english/tratop_e/dispu_e/ds108-ehtm.*
8. Minder, Raphael, and Edward Alden. 2005. WTO setback for U.S. tax break. *Fin.Times,* Oct. 1–2, 3.
9. 2005. WTO backs EU complaints over U.S. tax breaks. *Fin. Times,* July 25, 4.
10. Meller, Paul. 2006. World trade group rules tax benefits by U.S. illegal. *New York Times,* Feb. 14, C6.
11. See P. C. Mavroidis. 2003. The trade disputes concerning health policy between the EC and the US. In *Transatlantic economic disputes,* ed. Ernst-Ulrich Petersmann and Mark A. Pollack, 234.
12. Lowenfeld, Andreas F. 2002. *International economic law,* 323.
13. Pollack, Andrew. 2006. World Trade Agency rules for U.S. in biotech dispute. *New York Times,* Feb. 8, C6; Raphael Minder and Edward Alden, 2006, EU shrugs off modified foods censure. *Fin. Times,* Feb. 9, 6.
14. The Continuing Dumping and Subsidy Offset Act. 2001. See Lewis E. Leibowitz, *Safety valve or flash point? The worsening conflict between U.S. trade laws and WTO Rules,* Cato Institute Trade Policy Brief No. 17. Nov.
15. See Separate Complaints by the U.S. and EU: *Measures Affecting Trade in Large Civil Aircraft,* US DS316, EU DS317 (Oct. 6, 2004), at *http://www.wto.org/english/tratop_e/dispu_e/ds316_ehtm. (e/ds317_ehtm).*
16. Wijkman, Per Magnus. 2003. U.S trade policy: Alternative tracks or parallel tracks? In *Unilateralism and U.S. policy,* ed. David M. Malone and Yuen Foong Khong, 271; Phillippe Sands, 2005, *Lawless World,* 21.
17. Simon, Bernard. 2006. Canada and U.S. end long dispute over lumber. *Fin. Times,* April 28, 6.
18. USTR Press Release. 2006. U.S., Canada Reach Agreement on Lumber Dispute, Apr. 27, at *http://www.ustr.gov/document_Library/Press_Releases/Section_Index.html.*
19. 2006. Antigua hits back at U.S. gaming law. *Fin. Times,* June 114, 3.
20. This measure was attached to the Security and Accountability for Every Port Act of 2006, PL 109-347, 120 Stat. 1884 (Oct. 13).
21. Beattie, Alan. 2007. WTO rules against U.S. over online gaming. *Fin. Times,* Mar. 31/Apr. 1, 3.

22. Bounds, Andrew, and Eoin Callan. 2007. WTO to hear online gambling complaint. *Fin. Times,* June 21, 4.
23. *http://networkideas.org/news/mar2005/news31_Cotton_Dispute.htm*
24. Bradsher, Keith. Farm goods impasse stalls trade talks in Hong Kong. *New York Times,* Dec. 16, C3.
25. See Sean Murphy. 2004. Contemporary practice of the United States relating to international law, AJIL 98:820, 835 for detail of Bahrain and Morocco Trade Agreements.
26. Sang-Hun, Choe. 2007. U.S. and South Korea agree to sweeping trade deal. *New York Times,* Apr. 3, C1.
27. Wolf, Martin. 2007. A Korean-American strand enters trade's spaghetti bowl. *Fin. Times,* Mar. 4, 11.
28. Murphy, Sean. 2001. Contemporary practice of the United States relating to international law, *AJIL* 95:646.
29. 2005. Undermining the Doha Round. *Fin. Times,* Sept. 16, 14; Victor Fung, 2005, Bilateral deals destroy global trade. *Fin. Times,* Nov. 4, 15.
30. Wright, Tom, and Steven R. Weisman. 2006. Trade talks fail over an impasse on farm subsidies. *New York Times,* July 25, A1.

chapter VII

INTERNATIONAL LAW AND U.S. HUMAN RIGHTS AND GLOBAL PUBLIC HEALTH POLICY

Human Rights Policy

The promotion of human rights has existed as a core pillar of American foreign policy since the end of World War II. Indeed, the United States played a leadership role in the negotiations and adoption of many of the international human rights conventions. Practically all of the conventions contain language quite similar to what is in the American Bill of Rights and that reflects American constitutionalism.[1] International human rights would not have attained the status they now enjoy were it not for the Government of the United States, which pushed strongly for the elevation of human rights to a status almost equal to that of state sovereignty. Although different administrations deviated from the doctrine of the Rights of Man upon which the Republic was founded, it remains an important value that represents the U.S. in international affairs. During the Cold War era ideological and geopolitical considerations took precedence over human rights, as the U.S. tried to contain Soviet influence around the world. The United States engaged in the selective enforcement of human rights and in some instances turned a blind eye to violations of human rights by regimes that were close allies of the United States in its struggle against the Soviet communism. The Carter administration reversed that policy and made human rights a top priority of its foreign policy. Carter's emphasis on human rights led to the collapse of several pro-American dictatorial regimes. President Reagan reversed that trend by embracing regimes that were anti-communist and supportive of U.S. foreign policy. President Reagan predicated his foreign policy upon stopping the spread of Soviet communism and reestablishing U.S. strategic influence around the world. Reagan therefore ignored human rights violations of key U.S. allies, such as Pinochet of Chile, Suharto of Indonesia, Mobutu of Zaire, Rios Mont of Guatemala and Marcos of the Philippines. Reagan also financed and supported death squads in Central America, which led to the killing of thousands of innocent civilians and the opponents of these regimes.[2] Although Reagan is credited for ending communism, his record on promoting respect for human rights is less than stellar.

The United States co-sponsored many of the human rights conventions adopted in the post-World War II era. The Universal Declaration of Human Rights, the Genocide Convention and the Convention Against Torture and Other Cruel, Inhuman or Degrading Treatment or Punishment were all negotiated and adopted with full U.S. support. While a strong proponent of human rights conventions, the United States has had a very poor record ratifying human rights treaties.[3] In many instances the United States would sign the conventions but would not submit them for Senate ratification in a timely manner. In other cases the President submitted the treaties to the Senate for ratification, but the Senate would delay the ratification process. When the Senate did ratify the treaties, it attached a number of reservations, declarations and understandings to the treaties that make them inoperable under U.S. law.[4] The Genocide Convention, the Convention Against Torture, and Other Cruel, Inhuman or Degrading Treatment or Punishment, the Convention on the Elimination of Racial Discrimination and the International Covenant on Civil and Political Rights (ICCPR) are examples of human rights treaties the United States played a pivotal role in negotiating but that took years to ratify. Senate reservations to the above conventions made them difficult for individuals to invoke their provisions in domestic law. The reservations also undermined the spirit and intent of the treaties.[5] For example, in ratifying the Convention Against Torture (CAT), the Senate indicated that its advice and consent is subject to the following reservations:

1. That the United States considers itself bound by obligations under Article 16 to prevent "cruel, inhuman or degrading treatment or punishment" to the cruel, unusual and inhumane treatment or punishment prohibited by the Fifth, Eight, and/or Fourth Amendments to the Constitution of the United States.

2. That pursuant to Article 30 (2) the United States declares that it does not consider itself bound by Article 30 (1), but reserves the right specifically to agree to follow this or any other procedure for arbitration in a particular case.

Secondly, the Senate said its advice and consent is subject to the following understanding, which shall apply to the obligations of the United States under this Convention:

1. **a.** That with reference to Article 1, the United States understands that, in order to constitute torture, an act must be specifically intended to inflict physical or mental pain or suffering and that mental pain or suffering refers to prolonged mental harm caused by or resulting from: (1) the intentional infliction or threatened infliction of severe physical pain or suffering; (2) the administration or application, or threatened administration or application, of mind altering substances or other procedures calculated to disrupt profoundly the senses or personality; (3) the threat of imminent death; or (4) the threat that another person will imminently be subjected to death, severe physical pain or suffering, or the administration or application of mind altering substances or other procedures calculated to disrupt profoundly the senses or personality.
2. That the United States understands that the definition of torture in Article 1 is intended to apply only to acts directed against persons in the offender's custody or physical control.
   a. That with reference to Article 1 of the Convention, the United States understands that "sanctions" includes judicially imposed sanctions and other enforcement actions authorized by United States law or by judicial interpretation of such law. Nonetheless, the United States understands that a Party could not through its domestic sanctions defeat the object and purpose of the Convention to prohibit torture.
   b. That with reference to Article 1 of the Convention, the United States understands that the term "acquiescence" requires that the public official, prior to the activity constituting torture, have awareness of such activity and therefore breach his legal responsibility to intervene to prevent such activity.
   c. That with reference to Article 1 of the Convention, the United States understands that noncompliance with applicable legal procedural standards does not *per se* constitute torture.

3. That the United States understands the phrase, "where there are substantial grounds for believing that he would be in danger of being subjected to torture," as used in Article 3 of the Convention, to mean "if it is more likely than not that he would be tortured."
4. That it is the understanding of the United States that Article 1 requires a State Party to provide a private right of action for damages only for acts of torture committed in territory under the jurisdiction of that State Party.
5. That the United States understands that international law does not prohibit the death penalty, and does not consider this Convention to restrict or prohibit the United States from applying the death penalty consistent with the Fifth, Eight and/or Fourteenth Amendments to the Constitution of United States, including any constitutional period of confinement prior to the imposition of the death penalty.
6. That the United States understands that this Convention shall be implemented by the United States Government to the extent that it exercises legislative and jurisdiction over the matters covered by the Convention and otherwise by the state and local governments. Accordingly, in implementing Articles 10–14 and 16, the United States Government shall take measures appropriate to the Federal system to the end that the competent authorities of the constituent units of the United States of America may take appropriate measures for the fulfillment of the Convention.

Thirdly, the Senate maintained that its advice and consent is subject to the following declarations:

1. That the United States declares that provisions of Articles 1 through 16 of the Convention are not self-executing.
2. That the United States declares, pursuant to Article 21, paragraph 1, of the Convention, that it recognizes the competence of the Committee against Torture to receive and consider communications to the effect that a State Party claims that another State Party is not fulfilling its obligations under the Convention. It is the understanding of the United States that, pursuant to the above mentioned article, such communications shall be accepted and processed only if they come from a State Party which has made a similar declaration.

Fourthly, the Senate stated that its advice and consent is subject to the following proviso, which the instrument of ratification to be deposited by the President shall not include:

> The President of the United States shall not deposit the instrument of ratification until such time as he has notified all present and prospective ratifying parties to this Convention that nothing in this Convention requires or authorizes legislation, or other action, by the United States of America prohibited by the Constitution of the United States as interpreted by the United States.[6]

The Senate ratification of the Genocide Convention was also subject to reservations, understandings and declarations. These measures made the Genocide Convention unenforceable under U.S. law. Attached to the Senate instrument of ratification was the following:

I. The Senate's advice and consent is subject to the following reservations:

1. That with reference to Article IX of the Convention, before any dispute to which the United States is a party may be submitted to the jurisdiction of the International Court of Justice under this article, the specific consent of the United States is required in each case.
2. That nothing in the Convention requires or authorizes legislation or other action by the United States of America prohibited by the Constitution of the United States as interpreted by the United States.

II. The Senate advice and consent is subject to the following understandings, which shall apply to the obligations of the United States under this Convention:

1. That the term "intent to destroy, in whole or in part, a national, ethnical, racial, or religious group as such" appearing in Article II means the specific intent to destroy, in whole or in substantial part, a national, ethnical, racial or religious group as such by the facts specified in Article II.
2. That the term "mental harm" in Article II (b) means permanent impairment of mental facilities through drugs, torture or similar techniques.
3. That the pledge to grant extradition in accordance with a state's laws and treaties in force found in Article VII extends only to acts which are criminal under the laws of both the requesting and requested state and nothing in Article VI affects the right of any state to bring to trial before its own tribunals any of its nationals for acts committed outside a state.
4. That acts in the course of armed conflicts committed without the specific intent required by Article II are not sufficient to constitute genocide as defined by this Convention.

5. That with regard to the reference to an international penal tribunal in Article VI of the Convention, the United States declares that it reserves the right to effect its participation in any such tribunal only by a treaty entered into specifically for that purpose with the advice and consent of the Senate.

III. The Senate's advice and consent is subject to the following declaration:

That the President will not deposit the instrument of ratification until after the implementing legislation referred to in Article V has been enacted.[7]

In ratifying the International Covenant on Civil and Political Rights (ICCPR) the Senate attached an unprecedented number of reservations, understandings and declarations contrary to the object and purpose of the convention. These reservations are as follow:

I. The Senate's advice and consent is subject to the following reservations:

1. That Article 20 does not authorize or require legislation or other action by the United States that would restrict the right of free speech and association protected by the Constitution and laws of the United States.
2. That the United States reserves the right, subject to its Constitutional constraints, to impose capital punishment on any person (other than a pregnant woman) duly convicted under existing or future laws permitting the imposition of capital punishment, including such punishment for crimes committed by persons below eighteen years of age.
3. That the United States considers itself bound by Article 7 to the extent that "cruel, inhuman or degrading treatment or punishment" means the cruel and unusual treatment or punishment prohibited by the Fifth, Eighth and/or Fourteenth Amendments to the Constitution of the United States.
4. That because U.S. law generally applies to an offender the penalty in force at the time the offense was committed, the United States does not adhere to the third clause of paragraph 1 of Article 15.
5. That the policy and practice of the United States are generally in compliance with and supportive of the Covenant's provisions regarding treatment of juveniles in the criminal justice system. Nevertheless, the United States reserves the right, in exceptional circumstances, to treat juveniles as adults, notwithstanding paragraphs 2(b) and 3 of Article 10 and paragraph 4 of Article 14. The United States further reserves to these provisions with respect to individuals who volunteer for military service prior to age 18.

II. The Senate's advice and consent is subject to the following understandings, which shall apply to the obligations of the United States under this Covenant:

1. That the Constitution and laws of the United States guarantee all persons equal protection of the law and provide extensive protections against discrimination. The United States understands distinctions based upon race, color, sex, language, religion, political or other opinion, national or social origin, property, birth or any other status—as those terms are used in Article 2, paragraph 1 and Article 26—to be permitted when such distinctions are, at minimum, rationally related to a legitimate governmental objective. The United States further understands the prohibition in paragraph 1 of Article 4 upon discrimination, in time of public emergency, based "solely" on the status of race, color, sex, language, religion or social origin not to bar distinctions that may have a disproportionate effect upon persons of a particular status.
2. That the United States understands the right to compensation referred to in Articles 9(5) and 14(6) to require the provision of effective and enforceable mechanisms by which a victim of an unlawful arrest or detention or a miscarriage of justice may seek and, where justified, obtain compensation from either the responsible individual or the appropriate governmental entity. Entitlement to compensation may be subject of the reasonable requirements of domestic law.
3. That the United States understands the reference to "exceptional circumstance" in paragraph 2(a) of Article 10 to permit the imprisonment of an accused person with convicted persons where appropriate in light of an individual's overall dangerousness, and to permit accused persons to waive their right to segregation from convicted persons. The United States further understands that paragraph 3 of Article 10 does not diminish the goals of punishment, deterrence, and incapacitation as additional legitimate purposes for a penitentiary system.
4. That the United States understands that subparagraphs 3(b) and (d) of Article 14 do not require the provision of a criminal defendant's counsel of choice when the defendant is provided with court-appointed counsel on grounds of indigence, when the defendant is financially able to retain alternative counsel, or when imprisonment is not imposed. The United States further understands that paragraph 3(e) does not prohibit a requirement that the defendant make a showing that any witness whose attendance he seeks to compel is necessary for his defense. The United States

understands the prohibition upon double jeopardy in paragraph 7 to apply only when the judgment of acquittal has been rendered by a court of the same governmental unit, whether the Federal Government or a constituent unit, as is seeking a new trial for the same cause.

5. That the United States understands that this Covenant shall be implemented by the Federal Government to the extent that it exercises legislative and judicial jurisdiction over the matters covered therein, and otherwise by the state and local governments; to the extent that state and local governments exercise jurisdiction over such matters, the Federal Government shall take measures appropriate to the Federal system to the end that the competent authorities of the state or local governments may take appropriate measures for the fulfillment of the Covenant.

III. The Senate's advice and consent is subject to the following declarations:

1. That the United States declares that the provisions of Articles 1 through 27 of the Covenant are not self-executing.
2. That it is the view of the United States that States Party to the Covenant should wherever possible refrain from imposing any restrictions or limitations on the exercise of the rights recognized and protected by the Covenant, even when such restrictions and limitations are permissible under the terms of the Covenant. For the United States, Article 5, paragraph 2, which provides that fundamental human rights existing in any State Party may not be diminished on the pretext that the Covenant recognizes them to a lesser extent, has particular relevance to Article 19, paragraph 3, which would permit certain restrictions on the freedom of expression. The United States declares that it will continue to adhere to the requirements and constraints of its Constitution in respect to all such restrictions and limitations.
3. That the United States declares that it accepts the competence of the Human Rights Committee to receive and consider communications under Article 41 in which a State Party claims that another State Party is not fulfilling its obligations under the Covenant.
4. That the United States declares that the right referred to in Article 47 may be exercised only in accordance with international law.

IV. The Senate's advice and consent is subject to the following proviso, which shall not be included in the instrument of ratification to be deposited by the President:

Nothing in this Covenant requires or authorizes legislation, or other action, by the United States of America prohibited by the Constitution of the United States as interpreted by the United States.[8]

The United States remains the lone holdout on a number of international human rights treaties that an overwhelming majority of states have ratified. The United States is one of only two countries that did not sign the Convention on the Rights of the Child.[9] The United States signed but has not ratified the International Covenant on Economic, Social and Cultural Rights (ICESCR) and the Convention on the Elimination of Discrimination Against Women (CEDAW).[10] The United States signed CEDAW in July 1980, and President Carter transmitted it to the Senate for advice and consent. The Senate Foreign Relations Committee debated the treaty for two days but took no action. In 1994, the Senate Foreign Relations Committee recommended the treaty to the full Senate for its advice and consent, subject to certain reservations, but the Senate did not act. In 2002 the Senate Foreign Relations Committee held a series of hearings on CEDAW with the hope of giving its advice and consent. But the Bush administration notified the Senate that it was opposed to ratifying CEDAW at the present time.[11] The Bush administration also tried to block effort by the United Nations Economic and Social Council (ECOSOC) to adopt a protocol to the Torture Convention.[12] The Optional Protocol to the Convention Against Torture, and Other Cruel, Inhuman, or Degrading Treatment or Punishment (OPCAT) came into force in 2006, following the required number of ratifications. It calls for the establishment of a global system of independent inspection of detention facilities in signatory countries. The United States is one of five countries that did not sign or ratify the Protocol. The remaining states are Australia, China, Iran and Iraq.[13]

In September 2007 the United States was one of only four states to vote against the United Nations General Assembly Declaration on the Rights of Indigenous Peoples.[14] The United States opposed the declaration on the grounds that it was not transparent and worthy of implementation. The Bush administration further condemned the text as fundamentally flawed and unacceptable to the government of the United States.[15] The Bush administration voiced concern over language in the text dealing with the right of indigenous people to self-determination and ownership rights over land and resources.[16]

Since the September 11 terrorist attacks President Bush has sought broad powers from Congress to expand his authority to suspend the civil liberties of those suspected of terrorism and to limit Congressional and judicial oversight of his administration's handling of the war on terror and allegations of human rights abuse. In the wake of 9/11 the Bush administration carried out a massive sweep of Muslim and Arab immigrants in the United States and held them indefinitely as material witnesses or suspected terrorists. Many of these detainees were denied basic rights, and some showed signs of physical abuse by guards at the detention center in Brooklyn.[17] The Justice Department Inspector General subsequently confirmed that guards indeed abused some detainees.[18] The government has since deported several of the detainees for violating U.S. immigration law. Lawsuits by the detainees against guards at the detention center are pending. The administration also required all nationals from Muslim and Arab nations between the ages of eighteen and forty-nine to register with U.S. Immigration authorities. The government later used that list to detain or expel a number of immigrants who had violated immigration law or had previously been convicted of a felony.[19] Under the USA PATRIOT Act, passed by Congress after September 11, federal law enforcement authorities received broad powers to conduct wiretaps of international telephone calls, to search the bank records of Americans and foreign nationals and to detain suspected terrorists without charge.[20]

The Bush administration has had an abysmal human rights record both at home and abroad. The President has attempted to expand the federal death penalty statute to include juveniles, criminals with low IQ and those deemed mentally retarded. The administration has also restricted the *habeas corpus* right of death row inmates by limiting the number of appeals they can make to federal courts. The Bush administration has dismissed challenges from opponents of the death penalty that the disproportionate number of minorities currently on death row, or of those executed since 1977, are evidence of racial discrimination in the application of the death penalty.[21] Although the Supreme Court has refused to entertain legal challenges to the disparity in the application of the death penalty as unlawful, it decided in March 2005 that the execution of juveniles who committed crimes before they were eighteen was cruel and unusual punishment and therefore unconstitutional. The court's majority relied on international human rights conventions and the practices of states to show an evolving attitude against the execution of minors.[22] Prior to the Supreme Court's decision in *Roper v. Simmons,* the United States was the only industrialized country, and one of a few nations in the world, to continue executing juveniles.[23] The practice of executing minors under the age of eighteen violates both Article 5 of the International Covenant on Civil and Political Rights and Article 37 of the Convention on the Rights of the Child.[24]

The Bush administration has paid lip service to the Vienna Convention on Consular Relations (VCCR), despite two rulings by the International Court of Justice (ICJ) against the United States for its failure to enforce the convention.[25] The Convention requires signatory states to notify foreign nationals arrested in their territory of their right to contact their consular officer. In January 2003 the government of Mexico sought relief for fifty-one Mexican nationals on death row in the United States by instituting proceedings against the United States before the International Court of Justice. Mexico contended that the United States had breached its Article 36 obligation under the Vienna Convention on Consular Relations by denying the fifty-one Mexican nationals their right to contact the Mexican Consulate to seek legal assistance.[26]

The United States first objected to the ICJ jurisdiction, but it subsequently maintained that the failure to notify the Mexicans of their consular right had no impact on the outcome of the cases.[27] The ICJ ruled that the United States had indeed violated its obligations under Article 36 of the Vienna Convention on Consular Relations, and it ordered the United States to give some form of judicial relief to the Mexican nationals on death row.[28] Oklahoma agreed to comply with the court's ruling and immediately commuted the death penalty of Torres, the one Mexican national on its death row, to life in prison.[29]

Jose Ernesto Medellin, another Mexican national on death row in Texas, and one whom Mexico cited in the Avena case, challenged his conviction in the Court of Appeals for the Fifth Circuit on the grounds that his Vienna Convention rights were denied. The Fifth Circuit Court denied Medellin's request for federal *habeas corpus* relief.[30] Medellin subsequently filed an appeal before the Supreme Court. In December 2004, the Supreme Court granted certiorari to Medellin and set a date of Mach 28, 2005 for oral argument. In the case of *Medellin v. Dretke* the Supreme Court had to decide the following:

1. In a case brought by a Mexican national whose rights the *Avena* judgment adjudicated, must a court in the United States apply as the rule of decision, notwithstanding any inconsistent United States precedent, the *Avena* holding that the United States courts must review and consider the national's conviction and sentence, without resort to procedural default doctrines?
2. In a case brought by a foreign national of a state party to the Vienna Convention, should a court in the United States give effect to the *LaGrand* and *Avena* judgments as a matter of international judicial comity and in the interest of uniform treaty interpretation?[31]

President Bush, reacting to the ICJ decision in the *Avena* case and the Supreme Court decision to hear Medellin's appeal sent a memorandum to the Attorney General in February 2005 ordering him to inform state courts that they must give effect to the judgment of the ICJ in *Avena* as a matter of comity. The President's memorandum stated:

> The United States is a party to the Vienna Convention on Consular Relations (the "Convention") and the Convention's Optional Protocol Concerning the Compulsory Settlement of Disputes (Optional Protocol), which gives the International Court of Justice (ICJ) jurisdiction to decide disputes concerning "the interpretation and application" of the Convention.
>
> I have determined, pursuant to the authority vested in me as President by the Constitution and laws of the United States of America, that the United States will discharge its international obligations under the decision of the Inter- national Court of Justice in the Case Concerning Avena and Other Mexican Nationals (*Mexico v. United States of America*) (*Avena*), 2004 ICJ 128 (Mar. 31), by having State courts give effect to the decision in accordance with general principles of comity in cases filed by the 51 Mexican nationals addressed in that decision.[32]

Shortly thereafter the Department of State informed the Secretary General of the United Nations, as depositary for the Optional Protocol of the Vienna Convention on Consular Relations, of the U.S. intention to withdraw from the Protocol.[33]

The Supreme Court heard oral arguments in the Medellin case in March 2005, and in May it issued a decision dismissing, as improvidently granted, its order granting certiorari in *Medellin v. Dretke.*[34] The Supreme Court took into consideration the changed circumstances in light of the President's memorandum requiring state courts to give effect to the ruling of the International Court of Justice in the *Avena* case. The Supreme Court did not rule on the legality of the President's action, on which the State of Texas initially based its opposition for granting effect to the decision of the ICJ. Nor did it rule on the merits of Medellin's claims. Instead, the Supreme Court cited the changed situation caused by the President's action, Medellin's decision to file a state application for a writ of habeas corpus and the procedural hurdles under U.S. law that precluded review of the merits in Medellin's claims at that time. In conclusion, the court's majority said: "In light of the possibility that the Texas courts will provide Medellin with the review he seeks pursuant to the *Avena* judgment and the President's memorandum, and potential for review in this Court once the Texas courts have heard and decided Medellin's pending action, we think it would be unwise to reach and resolve the multiple hindrances to dispositive answers to the questions here presented. Accordingly, we dismissed the writ as improvidently granted."[35]

The Texas Court of Criminal Appeals issued its ruling in Medellin's appeal on November 15, which unanimously upheld the death sentence the lower court imposed on Medellin. The court said that Medellin could not rely on the Vienna Convention to save him from execution. The court reasoned that President Bush exceeded his constitutional authority by intruding into the independent powers of the judiciary. Presiding Judge Sharon Keller wrote in a concurring opinion that the President's "unprecedented, unnecessary and intrusive exercise of power over the Texas court system cannot be supported by foreign policy authority conferred on him by the United States Constitution."[36] In light of this ruling, Medellin's lawyers filed a new appeal with the U.S. Supreme Court. On April 30 the Supreme Court agreed to Medellin's request for relief and held hearings in October. The Bush administration took the unusual position of siding with Medellin, by arguing that the failure of the Texas court to reverse the previous ruling would leave the United States in breach of its international treaty obligation.[37]

The Justice Department articulated the administration's views in the Medellin case in an *amicus curiae* brief submitted to the Supreme Court, which says that the United States has a legal obligation under international law to provide review and reconsideration through a judicial process in the cases of each individual defendant referred to in the ICJ decision in the *Avena* case. The brief goes on to say that by invalidating the President's decision, the Texas Court of Criminal Appeals has intruded on the Executive's authority to conduct foreign affairs and to implement the treaty obligation of the United States. The brief provides the Constitutional justifications for the President's action.[38] The Supreme Court disagreed. In a 6 to 3 opinion, the majority ruled that President Bush did not have the authority under the Constitution to enforce a non-self executing treaty against the states. Therefore, his order requesting the states to grant review and consideration to Medellin and other Mexican nationals on death row, as required by the International Court of Justice, violated state law.[39]

Writing for the majority, Chief Justice Roberts said that the Vienna Convention on Consular Relations was not "self-executing," meaning it did not become binding domestic law when ratified by the Senate in 1969. Justice Roberts argued that the President could not act alone in making the treaty enforceable against the states, but had to work with Congress.[40] According to Roberts, "The President has an array of political and diplomatic means available to enforce international obligations, but unilaterally converting a non-self-executing treaty into a self-executing one is not among them. The responsibility for transforming an international obligation arising from a non-self-executing treaty into domestic law falls with Congress."[41] Roberts further stated that "[t]he President's statutory authorization to represent the United States before the U.N., the ICJ, and the U.N. Security Council speaks to his *international* responsibilities, not any unilateral authority to create domestic law."[42] A more controversial part of the ruling is Roberts' interpretation of Article 94 (1) of the Charter of the United Nations, which says: "Each Member State of the United Nations undertakes to comply with the decision of the International Court of Justice in any case to which it is a party." According to Roberts the phrase "undertakes to comply" is a promise for states to do their best and that one cannot interpret it as legally binding.[43] Roberts argued that the language of Article 94 "does not provide that the United States 'shall' or 'must' comply with an ICJ decision."[44] Roberts further referenced Article 94 (2) as proof that ICJ decisions are not binding: " If any party to a case fails to perform the obligations incumbent upon it under a judgment rendered by the Court, the other party may have recourse to the Security Council, which may, if it deems necessary, make recommendations or decide upon measures to be taken to give effect to the judgment." Roberts noted that with the United States holding a veto on the Security Council, it could effectively prevent the Security Council from enforcing an ICJ judgment against it.[45] Finally, Roberts suggested that since ICJ proceedings are between states, and ICJ decisions have "no binding force except between the parties and in respect of that particular case," it provides no relief to individuals.[46] Chief Justice Roberts's interpretation contradicts the principle of *Pacta sunt Servanda* contained in Article 26 of the Vienna Convention on the Law of Treaties, which requires states to negotiate treaties in good faith. Roberts's interpretation of the historical evidence regarding U.S. treaty obligation contradicts the Supreme Court decision in Belmont.[47] The decision raises questions about U.S. compliance with a number of its international treaty obligations. Roberts also fails to take into consideration Article 27 of the Convention, which forbids states from invoking national law to avoid compliance with their obligations under a treaty.[48]

As Governor of the state of Texas, President Bush presided over the largest number of executions. His position in the Medellin case was a surprise to many observers. The President's strong views on state rights, his withdrawal from the Optional Protocol to the Vienna Convention on Consular Relations, his staunch support for the death penalty and his refusal to recognize the legitimacy of international law made it extremely difficult to comprehend his position in this case. According to his press secretary, "the administration was trying to assert the president's power to make states comply with international agreements."[49] However, given the President's position on the death penalty, it is ironic he chose this case with which to assert his presidential authority.

Following the decision in the U.S. Supreme Court, Mexico filed a new case before the International Court of Justice in which it asked the ICJ to clarify the interpretation of its judgment in the Medellin case, which it said that the United States failed to implement fully. The government of Mexico asserts that the United States has not exhausted all available options in complying with the decision of the ICJ, and that referring the matter to the Supreme Court was just one of many options the President of the United States had at his disposal. Mexico further maintains that the President has not done all that is necessary to save the lives of Mexican nationals on death row whose rights were violated as a result of the failure of U.S. authorities to notify them of their right under the Vienna Convention on Consular Relations. Mexico further asked the ICJ to issue an order of interim measure to prevent authorities in the state of Texas from executing Medellin on August 5 and five other Mexicans scheduled to die within ninety days. The execution of Medellin took place as scheduled after the Supreme Court refused to grant him a stay pending the outcome of the ICJ decision.

Germany filed a similar case against the United States before the International Court of Justice in 1999, concerning U.S. failure to comply with its obligations under Article 36 of the Vienna Convention on Consular Relations (VCCR). Although it filed the case during the tenure of President Clinton, and it was partly complete by the time President Bush took office, the position taken by the Clinton administration mirrored that taken by the Bush administration in the Avena case. The dispute stems from U.S failure to notify two German nationals on death row in Arizona, the LaGrand brothers, of their consular rights.[50] One brother was executed prior to Germany referring the matter to the ICJ. On March 3 the ICJ issued an order prohibiting the parties from taking any action that would prejudice the case.[51] Notwithstanding issuance of the ICJ Order the state of Arizona proceeded to execute the second LaGrand brother. President Clinton did not try to persuade Arizona authorities to delay the execution pending a settlement in the dispute between Germany and the United States. Germany contended that the breach of Article 36 of the VCCR by the U.S. not only infringed upon the rights of Germany as a state party to the Vienna Convention but also entailed a violation of the individual rights of the LaGrand brothers. Germany sought relief on grounds of diplomatic protection and maintained that the right to be informed of the rights under Article 36 of the Vienna Convention is an individual right of every national of a state party to the Convention who enters the territory of another state party.[52]

The United States questioned Germany's claim of additional diplomatic protection and argued that there are no parallels between the present case and cases of diplomatic protection involving the espousal by a state of economic claims of its nationals. The United States maintained that the right of a state to provide consular assistance to nationals detained in another country, and the right of a state to espouse the claims of its nationals through diplomatic protection, are different legal concepts.[53] The United States further argued that rights of consular notification and access under the Vienna Convention are rights of states and not of individuals. It maintained that the treatment due to individuals under the Convention is inextricably linked to and derived from the rights of the state, acting through its consular officer, to communicate with its nationals, and does not constitute a fundamental right or a human right. The U.S. also contended that Article 36 by its terms recognizes the rights or the remedies required under the Vienna Convention for breaches of the Article.[54]

In its ruling the ICJ ruled that by not informing Karl and Walter LaGrand without delay following their arrest of their rights under Article 36, paragraph 2 (b), of the Vienna Convention, and by thereby depriving Germany of the possibility, in timely fashion, to render the assistance provided for by the Convention to the individuals concerned, the United States breached its obligations to Germany and to the LaGrand brothers under Article 36, paragraph 1. The court also said that by failing to take all measures at its disposal to ensure that Walter LaGrand was not executed pending the final decision of the court in the case, the United States breached the obligation incumbent upon it under the order indicating provisional measures issued by the court on March 3, 1999.[55] The court took note of the commitment of the United States to ensure implementation of the specific measures adopted in performance of its obligations under Article 36, paragraph 1 (b) of the Convention; and it said this commitment must be regarded as meeting Germany's request for a general assurance of non-repetition. Finally, the court ruled that should nationals of Germany nonetheless receive sentences with severe penalties, without respect shown for their rights under Article 36, paragraph 1 (b) of the Convention, the United States, by means of its own choosing, shall allow the review and consideration of the conviction and sentence by taking account of the violation of the rights set forth in the Convention.[56]

In spite of the Bush administration's strong opposition to the Vienna Convention on Consular Relations, foreign nationals continue to bring claims in federal court challenging their convictions on the ground that the government violated their consular rights. Since the *Avena* judgment two Consular Notification cases have been referred to the U.S. Supreme Court for review. The court agreed to hear the appeals of Mario Bustillo, a Honduran national, who was convicted in Virginia of gang-related murder and sentenced to thirty years of imprisonment, and Moises Sanchez-Llamas, a Mexican national, who was convicted of attempted murder of a police officer in Oregon and sentenced to life imprisonment. Both Bustillo and Sanchez-Llamas challenged their conviction on the ground that they were not notified of their rights to contact their consular officers as is required under Article 36 of the Vienna Convention on Consular Relations.[57] Bustillo and Sanchez-Llamas maintained that the failure of local law enforcement officials to notify them of their Vienna Convention notification rights deprived them of a fair trial.

The Bustillo case posed the question of whether the Vienna Convention creates individually enforceable rights and whether claims of Convention violations not raised during the state trial can be barred. The Supreme Court's order specified the following questions:

Whether, contrary to the International Court of Justice's interpretation of the Vienna Convention on Consular Relations, April 24, 1963, U.S. T. 77, 100–101, state courts may refuse to consider violations of Article 36 of that treaty because of a procedural bar or because the treaty does not create individual enforceable rights.[58]

In the Moises Sanchez-Llamas case the Supreme Court faced the issue of whether the failure to inform a foreign national of his consular notification rights would lead to a suppression of incriminating statements given to the police. The Supreme Court granted certiorari on the following questions in the case:

1. Does the Vienna Convention convey individual rights of consular notification and access to a foreign detainee enforceable in the courts of the United States?
2. Does the state's failure to notify a foreign detainee of his rights under the Vienna Convention result in the suppression of his statements to police?

In oral arguments in the two cases, a majority of the justices raised questions about the validity of the claims of Sanchez-Llamas and Bustillo. The justices were skeptical of the individual enforceable rights to which the defendants claimed entitlement.[59] Previously, the International Court of Justice had affirmed such a right in the *Avena* and *LaGrand* cases. The issue is one of increasing concern for the Bush administration, which feels that no such individual right exists under the Vienna Convention on Consular Relations.

In a 6 to 3 decision, the Supreme Court ruled that foreign criminal defendants were not entitled to any such rights from courts in the United States. Chief Justice

Roberts held that the decisions of the ICJ were "entitled only the respectful consideration due an interpretation of international agreement by an international court," but were not binding as precedent on American court.[60] The Supreme Court said that it was not necessary to answer the question of whether the Vienna Convention conveys rights enforceable by individuals, as opposed to nation-to-nation diplomacy, as neither defendant had a valid claim.

In carrying out its war on terror the Bush administration has committed a number of egregious human rights violations. The administration has ignored or refused to condemn human rights violations in states that support its war on terror. Whereas it singled out Iran, Cuba, Syria and North Korea for criticism of their human rights violations, allies such as Egypt, Saudi Arabia, Pakistan and Uzbekistan have received mild condemnation or none at all.[61] Even after the Uzbek government killed hundreds of innocent civilians in a demonstration in the city of Andijan, the Bush administration delayed issuing a strong condemnation of the regime for fear of jeopardizing the close military alliance with the regime of Islam Karimov. The United States subsequently condemned the violence against peaceful demonstrators and called for an international inquiry, but the Uzbek regime resisted. The United States has used the military base in Uzbekistan to carry out operations against the Taliban and Al Qaeda forces in Afghanistan.

The Bush administration has captured hundreds of so-called terrorists in Afghanistan and elsewhere around the world and detained them at Guantánamo Bay, Cuba, and at other undisclosed locations in what Amnesty International calls "an archipelago of prisons."[62] In what many saw as a gross miscarriage of justice, U.S. authorities picked up six Algerian Muslims in Bosnia and took them to Guantánamo Bay. They released the six defendants after the Bosnian Supreme Court found them not guilty of terrorism charges. The Council of Europe later criticized Bosnia for its complicity in the transfer of these prisoners.[63] The government has held these suspects since 2001 without charge, and they have denied many of them access to attorneys or the right to challenge their detention in federal court. Following a wave of international criticism of the Bush administration's detention policy, the Pentagon decided to establish a penal panel to provide annual review for the detainees.[64] The government repatriated some suspected terrorists to other countries for interrogation under a policy known as "extraordinary rendition." Under that policy detainees are sent to countries with questionable human rights records that knowingly practice torture or harsh methods of interrogation.[65] Three instances of extraordinary renditions in which the victims alleged that national authorities tortured them have raised questions about the practice and led to lawsuits against U.S. officials. U.S. authorities arrested Maher Arar, a Canadian national of Syrian ancestry, at JFK airport in New York on his way back to Canada from Tunisia. They detained and interrogated him for several days and later deported him to Syria where Syrian authorities tortured him and held him in seclusion for almost one year before they released him and he returned to Canada. Authorities arrested Khaled El-Masri, a German citizen of Lebanese ancestry, while he was on vacation in Macedonia and sent him to Afghanistan where he alleged he was tortured, beaten and held in solitary confinement for several months. They later released him and dropped him off on a roadside in Albania. CIA agents kidnapped a third suspect in Milan, Sheik Abu Omar, an Islamic cleric, and sent him to Egypt where authorities have held him for the past three years without charge. He alleged that Egyptian authorities tortured and beat him with the complicity of the CIA. Italian authorities charged the head of Italy's intelligence agency and indicted several CIA agents in the scheme. The Bush administration neither acknowledged nor denied U.S. complicity in the scheme, and it refused to cooperate with the Italian prosecutor in the case. The CIA agents were being tried in absentia because the U.S. refused to extradite them.

Authorities have transferred some detainees to their home countries for further interrogation and detention. Many of them have been released upon arrival due to lack of evidence linking them with acts of terrorism, or the evidence against them was obtained through torture and is therefore inadmissible in civilian court. Both El-Masri and Arar filed separate lawsuits in federal courts in Washington and New York respectively against Bush administration officials. The plaintiffs sought punitive and compensatory damages for their illegal detention and the violation of their human rights. The lawsuits were dismissed on the grounds that they would lead to the revelation of state secrets. Attorneys for El-Masri and Arar appealed these decisions. However, in March 2007, the U.S. Court of Appeals for the Fourth Circuit unanimously affirmed the lower court's dismissal of El-Masri's lawsuit against the United States on the ground that to go forward with the case would lead the government to reveal state secrets.[66] The Second Circuit dismissed Arar's lawsuit on the ground that federal courts lack jurisdiction to hear Arar's complaint. The court said Arar was never in the United States. However, on August 14, 2008, the Second Circuit notified lawyers for Arar that the full court would rehear the plaintiff's complaint.[67]

The Bush administration initially denied El-Masri entry into the United States to argue his case. The administration subsequently reversed itself and granted El-Masri permission to enter the United States. Similarly, they denied entry to Arar, even after Canadian authorities cleared him of any terrorist connection. They kept his name on the U.S. terrorist watch list, which makes him ineligible for entry into the U.S. Canada recently apologized to Arar and compensated him for the ordeal he and his family suffered.[68] Canada also protested to U.S. authorities the decision to keep Arar on the U.S.'s terrorist list.

A court in Munich, Germany recently issued warrants for the arrest of thirteen CIA agents for their involvement in the abduction and torture of El-Masri.[69] The German Parliament is also investigating the complicity of German agents in the abduction and torture of El-Masri. The Bush administration has not commented on the German arrest warrants except to say that the United States works closely with its allies and friends in combating terrorism and has not violated the sovereignty of any nation.

Several reports exist of detainee mistreatment at Guantánamo Bay, including sexually suggestive tactics by female interrogators to break the morale of Muslim detainees. Some detainees have attempted suicide, and many have gone on hunger strikes to protest their indefinite confinement.[70] Serious violations of human rights have also occurred in Iraq where the notorious Abu Ghraib photos that surfaced in 2005 showed U.S. soldiers abusing Iraqi detainees. A number of detainees have also died in U.S. custody in Afghanistan and Iraq under suspicious circumstances.[71] U.S. troops have carried out raids on insurgent strongholds and in the process destroyed whole villages and killed or wounded hundreds of civilians.[72] The Bush administration has shown a total disregard for the Geneva Conventions and international human rights and humanitarian law treaties in its conduct of its so-called war on terror.

The United States military has refused to allow an independent investigation into the conduct of its troops in Afghanistan and Iraq, and it has granted limited access to the International Committee of the Red Cross (ICRC) to visit the detention centers and to interview prisoners. The Bush administration would neither confirm nor deny whether it is holding certain prisoners, and it has refused to disclose their whereabouts. Revelations of ghost detainees in secret prisons in Europe and the use of European airspace and airports to transfer detainees to secret locations where they could be tortured stirred controversy in Europe and led to investigations by individual governments and the Council of Europe.[73] The controversy led to a temporary rapture in transatlantic relations, forcing Secretary Rice to visit Europe in December 2005 to defend administration policy on allegations of torture of suspected terrorists, secret prisons in Europe and ghost detainees.[74] In its report on the CIA extraordinary rendition, the Council of Europe concluded that certain European governments, including Britain, Italy, Spain, Poland and Romania had colluded with the United States in violating the rights of suspected terrorists by knowingly allowing the use of their airspace to transfer prisoners to locations where torture would occur. The report also mentioned a few countries that allowed the CIA to operate secret prisons on their soil.[75]

Legal challenges to the Bush administration's treatment of detainees have had limited success. The administration initially argued that the detainees did not have constitutional rights to challenge their detention before U.S. federal courts because Guantánamo Bay was outside the jurisdiction of the United States.[76] Attorneys for President Bush maintain that the President's commander-in-chief power gives him exclusive authority to designate someone captured on the "battlefield" as an "enemy combatant" and to hold him indefinitely.[77] Justice Department lawyers have also stretched the definition of torture, inhumane and degrading treatment to exempt the President from his Constitutional and treaty obligations under the United Nations Convention Against Torture and Other Cruel, Inhumane and Degrading Treatment or Punishment (CAT) in order to permit U.S. interrogators to apply harsh interrogation methods against detainees.[78] After human rights organizations criticized the administration's interrogation techniques as a violation of CAT, the Justice Department issued new guidelines that repudiated the August 2002 memorandum.[79] Under pressure from some Senators and former military officials during his Senate Judiciary Committee confirmation hearing, Alberto Gonzales retracted his previous position on the Bush administration's compliance with the Geneva Conventions and the Convention Against Torture.[80]

In June 2004, the Supreme Court ruled in *Hamdi v. Rumsfeld* and in *Rasul et al. v. Bush* that federal courts have jurisdiction to consider alien detainees' habeas corpus petitions contesting their detention as enemy combatants.[81] In response to the Supreme Court ruling, the Bush administration established Combat Status Review Tribunals (CSRT). Their purpose is to review the status of detainees to determine whether they have the proper classification as unlawful combatants and should continue being held and tried by a military tribunal or whether they are wrongly held need repatriation.[82] However, the procedure falls far short of what human rights lawyers say the Supreme Court intended. Under the CSRT, detainees have limited rights and have no authorization to see the evidence against them or to cross-examine witnesses. Human rights lawyers have petitioned the Supreme Court to clarify its ruling in the above cases and to rule on the administration's constitutional authority to establish military commissions.

On July 3, 2004, the government formally charged Salim Ahmed Hamdan, a former driver for Osama bin Laden, with conspiracy to commit terrorism, attacking civilians, attacking civilian objects and murder by an unprivileged belligerent. Lawyers for Hamdan filed suit on his behalf in the Circuit Court of the District of Columbia, challenging his denial of a speedy trial in violation of Article 10 of the Uniform Code of Military Justice (UMCJ), the nature and length of Hamdan's pre-trial detention as a violation of the Geneva Conventions and the legitimacy of the order establishing the Military Commissions as a violation of the separation of powers doctrine. They also argued that the authority granted to the Military Commission exceeds the law of war. Hamdan's lawyers further argued that the Military Commission violated Common Article 3 of the Geneva Conventions, which calls for a regularly constituted court to try all persons captured in a non-international armed conflict, thus affording them all the judicial guarantees recognized as indispensable by civilized peoples.

The Bush administration argued that Hamdan was a terrorist captured in a separate conflict against Al Qaeda as opposed to the war against the Taliban, hence he was not entitled to protection under the Geneva Conventions. The government further contended that the "war on terror" is a global conflict and does not fall under Common Article 3 of the Geneva Conventions. Finally, the government argued that members of Al Qaeda such as Hamdan are not entitled to POW status because they do not meet the requirements established by Article 4(2) of the Third Geneva Convention: to carry arms openly and operate under the laws and customs of war. In November 2004, the District Court ruled that the Guantánamo detainees were entitled to habeas corpus writs and called on the government to justify their detentions before a court of law. The court further ruled that the military commission could not try Hamdan unless a competent tribunal first determined that he was a prisoner of war protected by the Third Geneva Convention of 1949.[83] According to the court the President's designation of Hamdan as an unlawful combatant violated the Geneva Conventions. The judge ordered a halt to future hearings by the military commissions.[84]

On appeal, the D.C. Circuit Court of Appeals unanimously reversed the District Court's ruling. It opined that the President's authority to establish military commissions to try the Guantánamo detainees was consistent with the President's constitutional authority as commander-in-chief and the authority granted to him in a joint resolution passed by Congress after September 11 that authorized the president "to use all necessary and appropriate force against those nations, organizations, or persons he determines planned, authorized, committed, or aided the attacks."[85] The court also rejected Hamdan's claim that his rights under the Third Geneva Convention were denied, saying that such individual claims based on the Convention do not provide for judicially enforceable individual rights. Lawyers for Hamdan appealed the ruling to the Supreme Court, and the court granted certiorari. The questions the Supreme Court faced in Hamdan were:

1. Whether the military commission established by the President to try the petitioner and others similarly situated for alleged war crimes in the "war on terror" is duly authorized under Congress's Authorization for the Use of Military Force (AUMF), Pub. L. No. 107-40, 115 Stat. 224; the Uniform Code of Military Justice (UCMJ); or the inherent powers of the President?
2. Whether the petitioner and others similarly situated can obtain judicial enforcement from an Article III court of rights protected under the 1949 Geneva Convention in an action for writ of habeas corpus challenging the legality of their detention by the executive branch?[86]

On December 30, 2005, President Bush signed into law the Detainee Treatment Act of 2005, which the House and Senate passed as part of the Department of Defense Appropriations Act of 2006. The measure incorporated the McCain Amendment and the Graham-Levin Amendment on detainees. Section 1003 of the Act prohibits "cruel and inhuman or degrading treatment or punishment of persons under the custody or control of the United States Government."[87] Section 2214 of title 28, United States Code, was amended by adding the following at the end:

e. Except as provided in section 1005 of the Detainee Treatment Act 2005, no court, justice, or judge shall have jurisdiction to hear or consider:
   1. an application for a writ of habeas corpus filed by or on behalf of an alien detained by the Department of Defense at Guantánamo Bay, Cuba; or
   2. any other action against the United States or its agents relating to any aspect of the detention by the Department of Defense of an alien at Guantánamo Bay, Cuba, who—
      A. is currently in military custody; or
      B. has been determined by the United States Court of Appeals for the District of Columbia Circuit in accordance with the procedures set have been properly detained as an enemy combatant.[88]

The Supreme Court heard oral arguments in *Hamdan v. Rumsfeld* on March 27 at which time the Solicitor General presented the President's case for denying the Supreme Court the right to review the status of detainees at Guantánamo Bay and to deny the detainees the right to challenge the legality of the military commission established by the President. A majority of the justices were skeptical of the Bush administration's argument that the President has the constitutional authority in times of war to detain enemy combatants indefinitely without granting them access to civilian court. The Bush administration contended that the Guantánamo detainees were unlawful combatants and were not entitled to protection under Article 3 of the Geneva Conventions. The Bush administration also maintained that the Authorization for Use of Military Force (AUMF) passed by Congress in 2001 granted him authority to establish the military commission to try these detainees. Finally, the Bush administration argued that the laws of war allow the United States to hold "enemy combatants" without charge or access to counsel for the duration of hostilities for security and military necessity.[89]

In a 5 to 3 decision, the Supreme Court ruled on June 29 that President Bush overstepped his authority in establishing the military commission to try the Guantánamo detainees. The court said that the military commission lacks the power to proceed because its structure and procedures violated both the Union Code of Military Justice (UCMJ) and the Geneva Conventions.[90] The court said Common Article 3 of the Geneva Conventions affords some minimal protection to individuals associated with neither a signatory nor even a non-signatory who are involved in a conflict in the territory of a signatory. The court went on to say that "[e]ven assuming that Hamdan is a dangerous individual who would cause great harm or death to innocent civilians given the opportunity, the Executive nevertheless must comply with the prevailing rule of law in undertaking to try him and subject him to criminal punishment."[91]

The Supreme Court Hamdan decision, coupled with international criticism of the administration's detention policy, forced the Bush administration to reverse its policy on the treatment of detainees and to consult Congress regarding new rules governing war crimes trials for all detainees.[92] In a major policy shift, the administration announced in July 2006 that terror suspects in U.S. custody had rights under the Geneva Conventions. Although the administration maintained that it always treated its detainees humanely and that there was no change in policy, it is clear that it was reacting to the decision of the Supreme Court.[93] The statement from the White House was in sharp contrast to the administration February 2002 statement, at which time President Bush said that neither Taliban fighters nor Al Qaeda personnel were entitled to POW protection under the Geneva Conventions.[94]

In a series of hearings in July 2006 before both the Senate and House Armed Services Committees, administration lawyers called on Congress to simply ratify the existing rules for its current military commission and not to create new rules that would complicate the President's ability to conduct the war on terror. The administration continued to hold that the country should not treat the Guantánamo detainees as POWs and that they should have fewer rights than those stipulated in the Geneva Conventions and in the Union Code of Military Justice (UCMJ).[95] There was a division of senators over whether to grant the Guantánamo detainees full Geneva Convention rights or rights under the court martial system of the UCMJ.[96]

Congress took up the issue of military tribunals in September 2006 in an attempt to establish guidelines for the administration to try suspected terrorists. In a surprise statement on September 6, President Bush announced that fourteen high profile terrorist suspects held by the CIA in secret prisons until now were transferred to Guantánamo Bay for possible trial by military commissions. Bush acknowledged that the CIA had used "alternative interrogation techniques" to extract information from these detainees that forestalled future attacks on the United States. The President called on Congress to allow him to continue these interrogation techniques and to grant him the authority to establish military commissions under standards different from what Common Article 3 of the Geneva Conventions stipulate.[97]

Republicans on the Senate Armed Services Committee opposed the President's proposal, which would technically allow him to continue to use harsh interrogation techniques that many in the international community say violate the Geneva Conventions and are tantamount to torture. These Republicans have sponsored their own bill that would prohibit torture and grant more rights to detainees than the Bush administration proposes. The administration proposal would allow for the use of secret evidence against the detainees; they could be absent when there is a presentation of secret evidence against them, and information extracted through torture could be admissible at trial. The Republican version would prohibit evidence obtained under torture, require that detainees have access to all secret evidence against them and that they should be present at all times during the introduction of evidence against them at their trial.[98]

On September 28 Congress passed the Military Commissions Act (MCA), which President Bush signed into law on October 17.[99] The new law establishes for the first time since World War II a system of military commissions to try terror suspects.[100] The law gives the President the authority to designate any citizen or non-citizen an unlawful combatant. The law prohibits alien enemy unlawful combatants from invoking the Geneva Conventions as a source of rights during their trial before a military commission, and it takes away their right to petition for writ of habeas corpus in federal court.[101] This would apply to all pending cases at the time the Act was enacted, as well as all future cases. This provision of the Act violates both the U.S. Constitution and international human rights norms. However, a vote of 51 to 48 defeated an amendment by Senators Specter and Leahy to preserve habeas corpus. In 2007 the Democratic majority in the Senate attempted to adopt new legislation to grant Guantánamo detainees the right to seek *habeas corpus* review, which Republicans also blocked.[102]

The MCA allows for the use against them of evidence extracted from suspects through unconventional means. It allows for the admission of hearsay evidence and evidence obtained without a warrant at a detainee's trial. The Act makes no provision for repatriating or compensating detainees found not guilty. The Act protects the CIA and other law enforcement officials from prosecution for violating the War Crimes Act. The law gives a narrower definition of War Crimes Offenses under federal criminal code by eliminating certain offenses from the current definition of the term "war crimes." A number of civil liberties groups and lawyers representing the detainees have filed suit challenging the constitutionality of the Act. One such lawsuit was filed on behalf of Hamdan in the D.C. Circuit, but Judge Robertson dismissed the lawsuit on the grounds that the new Military Commissions Act strips detainees of their habeas corpus right, which allows them to challenge their detention in civilian court.[103] The judge held that it is highly unlikely the Supreme Court will sustain the new Act.

Lawyers for several detainees filed suit in Federal District Court in Washington challenging the Military Commissions Act of 2006. On February 20 a divided panel of the U.S. Court of Appeals for the D.C. Circuit ruled against the detainees and upheld the MCA restriction over habeas corpus petitions for detainees. The majority reasoned that it was the intention of Congress when it passed the Military Commissions Act to bar detainees from the right to file habeas corpus petition claims in U.S. civilian courts. The majority also argued that the MCA did not contradict the Suspension Clause of the U.S. Constitution.[104] The lawyers called for an expedited appeal before the Supreme Court. On April 2 the Supreme Court issued a statement refusing to hear the case at this time until the detainees had exhausted all remedies before the military tribunals. The Supreme Court left open the possibility of hearing the appeals in the future.[105]

In June the Supreme Court reversed itself and agreed to hear the Guantánamo detainees' appeal of their right to challenge their detention in federal courts. The decision was unusual for the Supreme Court, which seldom votes to hear an appeal that it had previously declined to hear. The case would require the Supreme Court to answer the following questions: (1) Should the Military Commissions Act of 2006 be interpreted to strip federal courts of jurisdiction over habeas petitions filed by foreign citizens detained at Guantánamo Bay? (2) If so, is the Military Commissions Act of 2006 a violation of the Suspension Clause of the Constitution? (3) Are the detainees at Guantánamo Bay entitled to the protection of the Fifth Amendment right not to be deprived of liberty without due process of law and the Geneva Conventions? (4) Can the detainees challenge the adequacy of judicial review provisions of the MCA before they have sought to invoke that review?[106]

In a major blow to the President, the Supreme Court answered in the affirmative all five questions. On June 12 the court's 5 to 4 majority reversed the ruling of the D.C. Circuit and found in favor of the detainees.[107] The five justices stated that the procedures laid out in the Detainee Treatment Act are not an adequate and effective substitute for habeas corpus, and that the Military Commissions Act (MCA) operates as an unconstitutional suspension of the writ. The Supreme Court further ruled that the detainees at Guantánamo Bay were entitled to habeas relief, not withstanding their designation as enemy combatants, and that the Suspension Clause of the Constitution applies to the detainees. Therefore, the detainees could petition for habeas relief directly in the District of Columbia Circuit Court without first having to seek review of the Combatant Status Review Tribunals' determinations.[108] The court's majority, however, acknowledged that under the Authorization for Use of Military Force (AUMF) the President has the authority to detain for the duration of the conflict those who planned, authorized, committed or aided the terrorist attacks of September 11, 2001, in order to prevent future acts of terrorism against the United States.[109]

Despite these legal challenges in federal court, the trial of David Hicks of Australia proceeded before a military commission as established by the Military Commissions Act of 2006. The charge against David Hicks was providing material support to a terrorist organization. His initial charges were dropped after the Supreme Court voided the first military commissions. Hicks was later charged with conspiracy to commit terrorism, but that charge became reduced to a single count of providing material support to terrorism. Hicks initially pleaded not guilty to the charge on advice of his civilian attorney. But his civilian attorney was suddenly removed from the case after he protested the lack of standard criminal procedures in the trial. Hicks' newly appointed military attorney subsequently struck a plea deal with the tribunal judge that allowed Hicks to plead guilty to the lesser charge in exchange for a lighter sentence he would serve in Australia.[110]

Hicks pleaded guilty because it was the best option available to him under the circumstances. The plea deal allows Hicks to serve a sentence of seven years with six years and three months suspended. The agreement allows Hicks to serve his sentence in Australia. As part of the plea deal, Hicks is prohibited from discussing the case with the media for two years and is forbidden from saying that he was tortured. A not guilty plea would have kept Hicks in detention at Guantánamo indefinitely. As an unlawful enemy combatant, Hicks risked being held in detention for the duration of the war on terror or whenever President Bush determines he is no longer a threat to U.S. national security. The Hicks plea was a gesture to Prime Minister John Howard of Australia, where the Hicks case has become a major campaign issue in his bid for re-election battle later this year. The Bush administration saw the Hicks plea as a validation of its military tribunal. However, human rights organizations saw it differently. Amnesty International said the proceedings underscored the urgent need to close Guantánamo. The Center for Constitutional Rights cautioned against using the Hicks plea to affirm the legitimacy of the military commission.[111] The commission proceeding in the Hicks case was flawed and cannot be seen as establishing a precedent for future trials.

Following the Hicks plea deal two separate Military Commissions held hearings for Salim Ahmed Hamdan and Omar Ahmed Khadr. The judges in both cases initially dismissed the charges on the grounds that the defendants did not have proper classification as "unlawful enemy combatants" under the Military Commissions Act passed by Congress in 2006.[112] The Bush administration appealed that decision. On September 24 a three judge panel of a special military appeals court overturned the decision of the military tribunal and authorized the government to present evidence to reconcile the flaws in the MCA. The appeals panel said the trial judge had abused his discretion in deciding on the critical jurisdictional matter without full consideration of the government's evidence.[113] Hamdan's attorneys later appealed that ruling to the Federal District Court in Washington. On June 17 the District Court ruled that Hamdan could contest in civilian court the constitutionality of his military tribunal trial until that trial had concluded.[114] The military tribunal resumed Hamdan's trial in July, and after a month of hearings he was found guilty of aiding terrorism but not guilty on the conspiracy to commit terrorism. Hamdan received a sentence of sixty-six months, but with time already served he can obtain a release by the end of the year.[115] There will likely be an appeal of the verdict to the federal courts on the grounds that the trial was flawed and some of the evidence was inadmissible because investigators obtained it through torture and other coercive techniques.

The President's view of expansive executive authority would allow him to exercise broad unchecked powers without Congressional or judicial scrutiny. The Supreme Court decision in the Boumediene case sends a clear message to President Bush that his powers are not unlimited and that he cannot circumvent the rule even in times of war. A victory for the President would have allowed him to continue his indefinite detention, rendition and torture policy without judicial intervention. This decision limits what the President can do, and it gives rights to Guantánamo detainees that authorities deemed them not to possess because of the suspicion that he had engaged in terrorist activities. The Supreme Court decision may ultimately lead to an end of the military tribunal system and the restoration of the rule of law in the President's so-called war on terror.

The issue of what to do with some of the Guantánamo detainees that are no longer of intelligence value to the administration or that were wrongly detained has created a dilemma for the administration. What to do with detainees who are stateless, unwilling to accept repatriation to their home countries or whom other countries are unwilling to accept continues to hinder the administration's effort to close Guantánamo. The Bush administration held talks with a number of Muslim nations in an effort to persuade them to accept their nationals, but few agreed to the request.[116] Some detainees have refused repatriation for fear that they might experience persecution upon their return to their home countries.[117] The Bush administration also faced a dilemma of what to do with the remaining *Uighurs*, a group of Chinese Muslims captured in Pakistan in 2001 and sent to Guantánamo. A military commission determined they were not enemy combatants, but officials has kept them in detention until the administration finds a country willing to accept them. The *Uighurs* cannot be repatriated to China for fear that the Chinese government may execute them for their insurgent activities against it. Several European allies rejected requests from the Bush administration to grant the *Uighurs* asylum. Finally, the administration persuaded Albania to accept five of them after legal challenges by a group of ethnic *Uighurs* living in the United States to have them released in their custody failed.[118] Officials continue to hold the seventeen remaining *Uighurs* at Guantánamo in isolation under very harsh conditions. Following the Supreme Court's decision in *Boumediene,* which granted habeas corpus rights to Guantánamo detainees to sue in U.S. federal court, attorneys for the seventeen *Uighurs* petitioned the U.S. District Court in Washington for their release. Judge Richardo Urbino ruled that the United States must release the seventeen Chinese Muslims and bring them to the United States mainland. However, President Bush convinced the Appeals Court to delay the reparation of the seventeen *Uighurs* to give the administration time to make its case against their release in the United States.

In the wake of the *Boumediene* decision Congress is debating a new act to grant additional rights to the detainees. Some members of Congress want to restore the writ of habeas corpus while others would like to close Guantánamo Bay and move the detainees to the mainland United States. The Bush administration has continued to repatriate detainees who are no longer of intelligence value and whose governments are willing to accept them. So far it has repatriated over three hundred detainees to their home countries, the majority of whom were Saudis or Afghanis. However, a number of detainees cleared for release remain at Guantánamo because no country is willing to accept them.

U.S. Policy Regarding the Situation in Darfur

After reports of atrocities committed against civilians by the Sudanese-backed *Janjaweed* militia surfaced, the Bush administration delayed releasing a statement of condemnation. In September 2004 Secretary Powell and the Secretary General of the United Nations, Kofi Annan, visited Darfur to assess the situation. On his return to the U.S. Secretary Powell characterized the situation in Darfur as genocide, and he deplored the violence against civilians.[119] President Bush later supported the creation of a high-level United Nations Commission of Inquiry to investigate the atrocities in Darfur. The Bush administration co-sponsored several resolutions in the Security Council to threaten Sudan with sanctions unless it stops the *Janjaweed* from committing further violence.[120] Sudan promised to act but did little to stop the killing. The United States later concluded that acts of genocide had been committed in Darfur, but it stopped short of taking any action against Sudan as required by the Genocide Convention.[121]

In September 2004 the Security Council called on the Secretary General to establish an international commission of inquiry to investigate reports of violations of international humanitarian law and human rights law in Darfur.[122] In January 2005 the International Commission of Inquiry on Darfur submitted its report to the Secretary General in which it concluded that crimes against humanity had occurred but that it found no evidence of genocide.[123] The violence against civilians has continued while the Security Council remains divided on how to respond to Sudan's intransigence.

On March 31, 2005, the Security Council adopted resolution 1593 (2005) to refer the situation in Darfur to the International Criminal Court (ICC). Despite its opposition to the ICC the United States abstained on the resolution instead of exercising its veto.[124] The United States insists that Sudan is a valuable ally in the war on terror and that it needs the cooperation of Sudanese officials. As an alternative the United States proposed the establishment of a regional court to try those responsible for the crimes committed in Darfur.[125] It later accepted the European compromise and agreed to abstain on the resolution. The United States and the European Union continue to support the African Union peacekeeping mission in Darfur, and some European troops are currently serving as advisers to the AU mission. However, the Bush administration has refused to deploy troops to Darfur as part of a United Nations peacekeeping mission.

With the humanitarian situation in Darfur continuing to deteriorate, the Security Council on April 25, 2006 adopted resolution 1672 (2006) by which it imposed sanctions on four Sudanese: one commander from the Sudanese Armed Forces and three high ranking officials from the various rebel organizations.[126]

The government of Sudan opposed the deployment of a United Nations peacekeeping force in Darfur to replace the AU force. Sudan also refused to cooperate with the United Nations in the delivery of humanitarian aid to the Darfur. The various factions attending peace talks in Abuja, Nigeria reached a tentative agreement to end the violence in Darfur; however, the Sudanese government is unable or unwilling to stop the *Janjaweed* from committing further atrocities against civilians in Darfur. Meanwhile, a lack of troop contribution from member states has caused a delay in the deployment of the United Nations force to enhance the AU force. A new indictment handed down against Sudan's president, Omar Hasan al-Bashir, by the International Criminal Court is likely to complicate Sudan's effort to cooperate with the United Nations.

On July 15 the Chief Prosecutor for the International Criminal Court (ICC) formally requested an arrest warrant for President Omar Hasan al-Bashir on charges of genocide, crimes against humanity and war crimes, holding him personally responsible for the atrocities committed in Darfur over the past five years. President Bashir is the only seated president charged with such high crimes. He is accused of masterminding and implementing a plan to destroy three main ethnic groups in Darfur. The arrest warrant further charged President al-Bashir with deliberately targeting civilians and ordering the killing of at least 35,000 members of the Fur, Masalit and Zaghawa ethnic groups.[127] Russia, China and the African Union have called for the Security Council to invoke its authority under the Rome Statute and to delay the indictment of al-Bashir to avoid a complete collapse of the peace process in southern Sudan and to ensure Sudan's continuing cooperation with the international community.

It is not clear where the Bush administration stands on the ICC indictment of al-Bashir. The United States initially abstained on the Security Council resolution referring the situation in Darfur to the ICC, and it has not shown a willingness to support the ICC's investigation of those suspected of committing genocide in Darfur. The Bush administration remained silent on the issuance of an arrest warrant for President al-Bashir by the ICC prosecutor. The administration later abstained on a Security Council resolution to extend the mandate of the United Nations peacekeeping mission in Sudan (UNAMID). In a statement issued after the vote in the Security Council, the U.S. representative to the Security Council said the U.S. did so because of disagreement over language in the resolution, which it said sends the wrong message to President al-Bashir and undermines efforts to bring him to justice. The Bush administration is willing to sacrifice justice in Darfur for preserving peace in southern Sudan, which it helped negotiate. The Bush administration, like Sudan, is not a member of the ICC, and it has been highly critical of the ICC. The Bush administration fears that any U.S. support for the ICC indictment of al-Bashir would set a dangerous precedent that could lead to possible indictments against President Bush and members of his administration after they leave office. The Bush administration is concerned that the ICC could one day issue indictments against high-ranking Bush administration officials for war crimes committed in Iraq and Afghanistan. The Security Council did adopt resolution 1828 (2008), which extended the mandate of UNAMID. However, there was division among members of the Council over the issue of whether the Security Council should delay the indictment of al-Bashir in exchange for extending the mandate of UNAMID. South Africa, Libya, China and Russia favored a delay of the indictment, whereas Britain and France wanted to keep the ICC indictment separate from the extension of UNAMID's mandate.[128]

Security Council resolution 1769 (2007) established the AU/UN Hybrid operation in Darfurto replace the African Union Mission in Sudan (AMIS), which has been underfunded, underequipped and understaffed. However, UNAMID has not received the necessary equipment and personnel to bring it to capacity to implement its mandate. Many nations are either unwilling or unable to provide helicopters and other heavy equipments needed to make UNAMID the force the Secretary General envisioned in his peace plan for Darfur.

U.S. Asylum and Refugee Policy

The United States has long offered its shores to those fleeing persecution from repressive regimes, particularly during the communist era. As an immigrant nation, the United States has maintained an open door policy for those who are victims of human rights abuse at the hands of their governments. During the Cold War the United States granted automatic asylum to those fleeing communism. However, with the collapse of the Soviet empire and the liberation of Eastern Europe the faces of those seeking asylum changed and so did U.S. policy. Successive administrations have not been consistent in their refugee and asylum policy. For example, Cuban refugees and asylum seekers have received more favorable treatment than Haitian refugees, even though both groups are fleeing what the State Department has documented as gross violations of human rights at the hands of repressive regimes. The end of the Cold War, the rise in ethnic conflicts in the Balkans and Africa, civil wars in Central American, economic hardship in developing countries and globalization have led to a dramatic increase in the number of poor people from Africa, Asia, the Caribbean and Latin America seeking asylum in the United States. The United States has also tightened its asylum and refugee policy to make sure that those who are not genuine refugees do not enter the country.

In 1980 Congress passed the Refugee Act to codify the United Nations Refugee Protocol's definition of a refugee The Act defines a refugee as someone displaced abroad and unable or unwilling to return based on a well-founded fear of persecution on account of race, religion, nationality, membership in a particular social group or political opinion.[129] The Act limits the number of refugees and asylumees whom the United States will admit, and it gives broad discretionary powers to the Attorney General to determine whom the United States should admit and who not.

In 1996 the United States revised its asylum policy to establish procedures by which asylum seekers entering the United States without proper documentation can petition an immigration judge for a hearing to determine their eligibility for asylum. Those found not genuine asylum seekers can request an administrative and judicial hearing before expulsion. The Illegal Immigration Reform and Immigrant Responsibility Act of 1996 (IIRIRA, P.L. 104-208) made major changes in the asylum process. It instituted expedited removal proceedings, codified many regulatory changes, added time limits of filing claims and limited judicial review in certain situations. The revised Act also provided for mandatory detention for asylum seekers who arrived in the United States without proper documentation and have their petition pending. The revised Act further denied asylum to those whom the United States can return to a "safe-third country." Finally, the revised Act established various categories of asylum seekers and gave preference to those who meet the criteria in each separate category. For example, someone who seeks asylum because he or she is a victim of torture receives different treatment under legislations implementing the United Nations Convention Against Torture and Other Cruel, Inhuman or Degrading Treatment or Punishment. Article 3 of the Convention Against Torture prohibits the return of any person to a country where substantial grounds exist to believe he or she would be in danger of torture. The foreign national must satisfy the three elements necessary to demonstrate torture: (1) The torture must involve the infliction of severe pain or suffering, either physical or mental; (2) the torture must be intentionally inflicted; and (3) the torture must be committed by or at the acquiescence of a public official or person acting in an official capacity.[130]

The Bush Administration's Policy on Asylum

Following the September 11 attacks the Bush administration adopted a new policy toward refugees and asylum seekers. The policy tightened entry into the United States and implemented stringent security measures to prevent terrorists from infiltrating the U.S.'s generous asylum program for genuine refugees. The Bush administration put in place new national security measures that required background checks on all refugees and asylum seekers. It also negotiated an immigration accord with Cuba that allowed the U.S. Coast Guard to return all Cubans caught at sea to Cuba. However, those who successfully reach the shore of the United States are allowed to remain and receive asylum the following year under the Cuban Adjustment Act. On the other hand, Haitians intercepted at sea are immediately repatriated to Haiti without a proper hearing to determine whether they have a genuine fear of persecution.[131] Critics maintain that this policy violates the spirit and letter of the 1951 United Nations Convention on Refugees.

Since 9/11 the Bush administration has increased border patrol, enforced immigration laws, tightened entry into the United States and taken measures to identify all passengers bound for the United States before flights arrive. The administration has also cracked down on criminal illegal aliens and illegal aliens in general. The Bush administration has expedited deportation procedures for all illegal aliens. Asylum seekers are subjected to thorough background checks before the processing of their petitions. Those found to be economic migrants or posing a threat to national security are subject to removal. Officials at U.S. airports have turned back many legitimate asylum seekers and visitors and denied them entry for fear that they pose a security risk to the United States. Muslim asylum seekers or those coming from countries of "special concern" (Saudi Arabia, Syria, Iran Pakistan, Egypt, China, North Korea, Lebanon, Jordan, Afghanistan, Yemen and Somalia) are deemed potential national security risks and subjected to more stringent screening than others. Some in the administration argue that national security should take precedent over humanitarian considerations, and that the United States should restrict asylum relief and provide judicial review of asylum cases limited to only a few.

Whereas the number of foreign nationals seeking asylum has increased in recent years, the number granted asylum in the United States has declined considerably. The nationalities of those seeking asylum or granted asylum have also changed. The majority of those granted asylum come from countries in Central America and the Caribbean, Africa and Asia. The number of asylum seekers from the Middle East has increased due to the war in Iraq and Afghanistan. However, due to the extensive security check required for nationals of those countries, many find themselves waiting for years before resettling in the United States. When compared to previous administrations, we can define the Bush administration's record on granting asylum as abysmal. Foreign nationals no longer feel welcome to the United States. The security barriers erected on the U.S.-Mexican border and the anti-immigrant rhetoric of the Republican Party convey the wrong message to foreigners that the United States is no longer a safe haven for those fleeing persecution.

U.S. Policy Against Human Trafficking

Although the Bush administration has an overall unfavorable record on human rights, many have highly rated the President's policy against human trafficking. President Bush has made enforcement against trafficking in persons (TIP) a top priority of his administration's human rights agenda. In his National Security Strategy President Bush listed trafficking in persons as a form of modern-day slavery and made a commitment to eliminate it. Human trafficking is the greatest national security threat to the United States, second only to terrorism. In its annual report the State Department noted that approximately 600,000 to 800,000 people, mostly women and children, are illegally trafficked across state borders annually. More than 50,000 of these victims end up in the United States as sex slaves or as illegal migrant workers.[132] This global criminal enterprise generates an income of more than $10 billion for the traffickers.

Similarly President Clinton made trafficking in persons a top priority of his administration human rights agenda. In 2000 he signed into law the Victims of Trafficking and Violence Protection Act. P.L. 106-386, which:

i. Directed the Secretary of State to provide an annual report by June 1, listing countries that do and do not comply with minimum standards for the elimination of trafficking and to provide in his annual report on human rights information on a country-by-country basis describing the nature and extent of severe forms of trafficking in persons in each country and an assessment of the efforts by governments to combat trafficking;
ii. Called for establishing an Interagency Task Force to Monitor and Combat Trafficking, chaired by the Secretary of State, and authorized the Secretary to establish within the Department of State and Office to Monitor and Combat Trafficking to assist the Task Force;
iii. Called for measures to enhance economic opportunity for potential victims of trafficking as a method to deter trafficking, to increase public awareness, particularly among potential victims, of the dangers of trafficking and the protections that are available for victims, and for the government to work with NGOs to combat trafficking;
iv. Established programs and initiatives in foreign countries to assist in the safe integration, reintegration, or resettlement of victims of trafficking and their children, as well as programs to provide assistance to victims of severe forms of trafficking in persons within the United States, without regard to such victims' immigration status and to make such victims eligible, without regard to their immigration status, for any benefits that are otherwise available under the Crime Victims Funds;
v. Provided protection and assistance for victims of severe forms of trafficking while in the United States;
vi. Amended the code to make funds derived from the sale of assets seized from and forfeited by trafficking available for victims assistance programs under this act;
vii. Amended the Immigration and Nationality Act to allow the Attorney General to grant up to 5000 non-immigrant visas per year to certain victims of severe forms of trafficking who are in the United States and who would face a significant possibility of retribution or other harm if they were removed from the United States. In addition, amended the act to adjust to lawful permanent residents the status of up to 5000 victims per year who have been in the United States continuously for three years since admission, who have remained of good moral character, who have not unreasonably refused to assist in trafficking investigations or prosecutions, and who would face a significant possibility of redistribution or other harm if removed from the United States.[133] In 2005 Congress reauthorized the Act by authorizing appropriations for FY 2006 and FY 2007. The Act also amended previous laws to further strengthen anti-trafficking policies.[134]

The Bush administration continued the Clinton administration's strong anti-trafficking measures. The President took several steps to combat trafficking in persons. The administration designated a high-level diplomat to oversee U.S. anti-trafficking policy, to coordinate global anti-trafficking rules and to monitor countries' compliance with anti-trafficking measures. The Bush administration appointed an officer at each U.S. embassy where human trafficking is a major problem. In January 2002 the administration announced the "T" visa for victims of trafficking in the U.S. who cooperate with law enforcement against their traffickers. In February 2002 President Bush signed an Executive Order establishing an Interagency Task Force to Monitor and Combat Trafficking in Persons. The Task Force was charged with strengthening coordination among key agencies and identifying what more needs doing to protect potential victims, to punish traffickers and to prevent future trafficking. Through its annual Trafficking in Persons report, the State Department assesses the effectiveness of measures taken by national governments to combat human trafficking. The report divides countries into four tiers based on the efforts they have made to stop human trafficking. Countries identified as Tier Three for failing to cooperate with anti-trafficking efforts are subject to U.S. sanctions.[135]

U.S. Global Public Health Policy

The Bush administration has been equally objectionable on global public health issues, which many people increasingly are considering a basic human right. President Bush opposes women's rights to choose various forms of contraceptives, including the morning-after pill. Immediately after he was sworn into office in 2001, President Bush signed an Executive Order cutting off funding for the United Nations Funds for Population Activities (UNFPA) to prevent U.S. funds from being used for reproductive health counseling for women in developing countries. President Bush was reviving the so-called Mexico City policy instituted by President Reagan in 1984 but revoked by President Clinton. The Bush policy would require that foreign NGOs, in order to be eligible for family planning funds from USAID, not to use their own funds for abortion-related services or to engage in any advocacy aimed at liberalizing that country's abortion laws. The President also threatened to punish other organizations receiving U.S. funds that cooperate with UNFPA.

The Bush administration initially opposed the World Health Organization (WHO) Framework Convention on Tobacco Control (FCTC). The convention envisions taking a number of measures intended to reduce global tobacco sale and consumption.[136] Initially, the Bush administration opposed certain provisions of the treaty, but it succeeded in getting the conference delegates to change these provisions. The Bush administration also opposed provisions of the treaty dealing with tobacco advertising, the sale of tobacco products to minors, tobacco companies' sponsorship of sporting events and the size of warnings and the language in which warnings are written on cigarette boxes.[137] The Bush administration further claimed that the treaty ban on advertising of tobacco products would violate the free speech right of American tobacco companies, protected under the First Amendment of the U.S. Constitution.[138] Under pressure from its European allies, the Bush administration reluctantly reversed itself and signed the treaty without resolving the constitutional issue.[139]

Since signing the treaty the Bush administration has shown little enthusiasm for its implementation into law and has delayed submitting it to the Senate for ratification.[140] Similarly, Bush opposed a World Trade Organization (WTO) initiative under the Trade Related Intellectual Property Rights (TRIPS) Convention to allow countries such as India and Brazil to manufacture and export generic antiretroviral drugs at lower cost to developing countries plagued by the HIV/AIDS pandemic. The Bush administration later dropped its opposition to the TRIPS following a compromised agreement that satisfied its concerns.[141]

The Bush administration also opposed the distribution of condoms to developing countries with high HIV/AIDS infection rates to stem the flow of the virus. President Bush has used World AIDS Day to reaffirm his commitment to combating the AIDS pandemic by highlighting his administration's accomplishments. President Bush also endorsed Africa's ABC Aids prevention program (Abstinence, Be Faithful, Use Condom).[142] The ABC program has been successful in Senegal and Uganda, but the Bush administration has not supported some aspects of the program.

The Bush administration's AIDS program has not gone far enough in addressing the HIV/AIDS pandemic. The President's policy places greater emphasis on abstinence and being faithful over condom distribution. The fastest growing infected sector of the AIDS population is heterosexual women and pregnant mothers. The abstinence policy has done little to reverse the spread of the disease among these groups. The President's Emergency Plan for AIDS Relief (PEPFAR) has spent millions of dollars over the past five years to fund various anti-AIDS initiatives in Africa, Asia and the Caribbean. The program has been renewed for another five years as part of the President's 2009 budget request. However, the policy imposes unnecessary restrictions on the disbursement of the funds to at-risk groups. Foreign governments must make a pledge not to use the fund for purchasing condoms. Also, NGOs receiving funding had to make an anti-prostitution pledge. Consequently, PEPFAR has had great success in the distribution of AIDS medication to over a million patients but a limited effect on halting the spread of the virus.

President Bush opposed efforts by the WHO and FAO to curb the growing problem of obesity and its health consequences caused by the widespread use of sugar and other food additives. The U.S. Sugar Association, an industry lobby group, has called on the administration to oppose the WHO/FAO draft report on "Diet, Nutrition and the Prevention of Chronic Diseases." The report noted that, "obesity, heart disease and diabetes were becoming the biggest threats to health."[143] The administration said the treaty did not emphasize enough personal responsibility. However, a more accurate reason why the administration opposed the treaty was to satisfy sugar producers who make huge contributions to the campaigns of both the Republican and Democratic candidates.

Finally, the administration opposed efforts by some European countries to encourage stem cell research that could provide possible cures to countless terminally ill patients. The Bush administration banned federal funding for stem cell research in the United States and allows only for existing stem cells already in use for further development. The Bush administration joined a number of Catholic countries, including the Vatican, to vote in favor of a General Assembly resolution banning human cloning.[144] The measure fell short of the administration's initial effort to seek a binding treaty to completely ban any form of stem cell research, but it abandoned the effort in November 2004 after it failed to win support from a majority of countries.

Endnotes

1. Henkin, Louis. 1985. International human rights and rights in the United States. In *Human rights in international law,* ed. Theodor Meron, 39.
2. Forsythe, David P. 2006. *Human Rights in International Relations,* 8.
3. Wedgwell, Catherine. U.S. reservation to human rights treaties: All for one and one for all? In Michael Byer and Georg Nolte, eds., *supra* note 6, 394.
4. Ibid.
5. Tyagi, Yogeshi. 2000. The conflict of law and policy on reservations to human rights treaties, *Brit. yearbook of international law,* 71:188; William A. Schabas, 1995, Invalid reservations to the international covenant on civil and political rights: Is the United States still a party? *Brooklyn J. Int'l L.,* 21:277, 289.

6. U.S. Reservations, Declarations, and Understandings Convention Against Torture and Other Cruel, Inhuman or Degrading Treatment or Punishment, Cong. Rec. S 17486-01 (Oct. 27, 1990).
7. U.S. Reservations, Declarations, and Understandings, International Convention on the Prevention and Punishment of the Crime of Genocide, Cong. Rec. S 1355-01 (Feb. 1986).
8. U.S. Reservations, Declarations, and Understandings, International Covenant on Civil and Political Rights, 138 Cong. Rec. S 4781-01 (daily ed., April 2, 1992).
9. Somalia is the only other state that has not signed the Convention on the Rights of the Child.
10. Foot, Rosemary. 2003. Credibility at stake: Domestic supremacy in U.S. human rights policy. In *Unilateralism & U.S. foreign policy,* ed. David Malone and Yuen Foong Khong, 99.
11. Murphy, Sean. 2002. Contemporary practice of the United States relating to international law, *AJIL* 96:972; See Karen Young, Senate panel defy Bush, vote on women's treaty. *Wash. Post,* July 18, A21; James Dao, 2002, Senate panel approves treaty banning bias against women, *New York Times,* July 31, A8.
12. Crossette, Barbara. 2002. U.S. fails in effort to block vote on U.N. Convention on torture, *New York Times,* July 25, A5.
13. See, Optional Protocol to the Convention Against Torture, at *http://www.ohchr.org/english/bodies/cat/opcat/index.htm.*
14. The document was adopted by a vote of 143 to 4 (Australia, Canada and New Zealand and the United States), with 11 abstentions (Azerbaijan, Bangladesh, Bhutan, Burundi, Colombia, Georgia, Kenya, Nigeria, Russian Federation, Samoa and Ukraine).
15. USUN Press Release 204(07), Sept. 13, 2007.
16. Ibid.
17. See *Human Rights Watch,* Presumption of guilt: Human rights abuses of post-September 11 detainees, Aug. 2002, at *http://www.hrw.org/reports/2002/us911/Index.htm#TopOfPages.*
18. The September 11 Detainees: A Review of the Treatment of Aliens Held on Immigration Charges in Connection With the Investigation of the September 11 Attacks. 2002. U.S. Department of Justice, Office of the Inspector General, April, at *http://www.usdoj.gov/oig/special/0603/full.pdf.*
19. Murphy, Sean. 2002. Contemporary practice of the United States relating to international law, *AJIL* 96:461, 471.
20. Uniting and Strengthening America by Providing Appropriate Tools Required to Interpret and Obstruct Terrorism (USA PATRIOT) Act [of 2001, Pub. L. No. 107-56, 115 Stat. 272 (2001)]; *supra* note 122 at 252–253.

21. See Fact Sheet: The Death Penalty and Racial Bias, at *http://www.ncadp.org/fact sheet2.html.*
22. See, U.S. Supreme Court Decision in *Roper v. Simmons,* 125 S.Ct., 1183 (2005); John R. Crook, 2005, Contemporary practice of the United States relating to international law, *AJIL* 99:487.
23. Other countries that continue to execute minors are Iran, Nigeria, Pakistan, Saudi Arabia, the Democratic Republic of Congo, China and Yemen.
24. The Second Optional Protocol to the International Covenant on Civil and Political Rights, Aiming at the Abolition of the Death Penalty, concluded on Dec. 15, 1989 and entered into force on July 11, 1991, Annex to GA Res. 44/128, Dec. 15, 1989.
25. See LaGrand (*Germany v United States of America*), Judgment (June 27, 2001); and Summary of the Order of 9 April 1998, Case concerning the Vienna Convention on consular relations (*Paraguay v. United States of America*), at *http://www.icj-cij.org.*
26. Avena and other Mexican nationals *(Mexico v. United States of America)* (2003–2004), ICJ Press Release 2004/16.
27. Murphy, Sean. 2004. Contemporary practice of the United States relating to international law, *AJIL* 98:366.
28. Shelton, Dinah. 2004. Case concerning Avena and other Mexican nationals (*Mexico v. United States*), *AJIL* 98:560-61.
29. Office of Governor Brad Henry, Press Release: Governor Henry Grants Clemency to Death Row Inmate Torres (May 13, 2004), at *http://www.governor.state.ok.us/;* Sean Murphy, *supra* note 153, 582.
30. *Medellin v. Dretke,* 371 F. 3rd 270 (5th Cir., 2004), *cert. Granted,* 125 S.Ct. 686 (2004).
31. *Medellin v. Dretke,* No. 04-5928 (U.S.), at *http://www.supremecourtus.gov/docket/ 04-5928.htm.*
32. Memorandum from President George W. Bush to the Attorney General (Feb. 28, 2005), at *http://www.asil.org/inthenews/avenamemo050308.html.*
33. Ibid., 490.
34. Greenhouse, Linda. 2005. Supreme Court drops case ruled on by World Court. *New York Times,* May 24, A15.
35. *Medellin v. Dretke,* 125 S.Ct. 2092 (2005).
36. Liptak, Adam. 2006. Texas court ruling rebuffs Bush and World Court. *New York Times,* Nov. 16, A25.
37. Greenhouse, Linda. 2007. Supreme Court to hear appeal of Mexican death row inmate. *New York Times,* May 1, A18.
38. Amicus Curiae Brief Supporting Petitioner at 8-17, *Medellin v. Texas,* No. 06-984 (S.Ct., Mar. 2007).
39. Greenhouse, Linda. 2008. Justices block new hearing for Mexican. *New York Times,* Mar. 26, A19.
40. Ibid.

41. *Medellin v. Texas,* No. 06-984, S.Ct. (Mar. 25, 2008), 30.
42. Ibid., Syllabus, 5.
43. Ibid., 11–15.
44. *Medellin,* 128 S.Ct. at 1358.
45. Ibid.
46. *Medellin,* 128 S.Ct. at 1360.
47. See *United States v. Belmont,* 301 U.S. 324, 331 (1937).
48. Vienna Convention on the Law of Treaties, opened for signature May 23, 1969, 1155 UNTS 331.
49. White House Press Briefing (Mar. 25, 2008).
50. Murphy, Sean. 2001. Contemporary practice of the United States relating to international law, *AJIL* 95:650-54.
51. Request for the Indication of Provisional Measures, ICJ Order of March 3, 1999.
52. LaGrand Case (*Germany v. the United States of America*), ICJ Judgment (June 27, 2001), para. 75.
53. Ibid., para 76.
54. Ibid.
55. Ibid, para. 128.
56. Ibid.
57. Greenhouse, Linda. 2005. Two convicts from abroad win hearing by justices. *New York Times,* Nov. 8, A22.
58. Jackman, Tom. 2005. Supreme Court to review Fairfax case. *Wash. Post,* Nov. 8, A4.
59. Greenhouse, Linda. 2006. Justices hear arguments over whether foreigners have reciprocal rights in the U.S. *New York Times,* Mar. 30, A15.
60. Greenhouse, Linda. 2006. Treaty doesn't give foreign defendants special status in U.S. courts, justices rule. *New York Times,* June 29, A15.
61. See State Department Annual Human Rights Report, 2004 (Feb. 28, 2005), at *www.state.gov/g/dr/rls/hrrpt/2004/index.htm;* See Guy Dinmore, 2005, Bush targets tyrants in human rights report, *Fin. Times,* Mar. 1, 2.
62. At *www.http://web.amnesty.org/report2005/index-eng.*
63. See Report on the Alleged Use of European Countries by the CIA for the Transportation and Illegal Detention of Prisoners, EUR. PARL. DOC. A6-0020/2007 available at *http://www.europarl.europa.eu/recherche/ResultatsAbreges.cfm.*
64. Loeb, Vernon. 2002. Panel set up to hear pleas of detainees. *Wash. Post,* Feb. 14, A1.
65. Crook, John R. 2005. Contemporary practice of the United States relating to international law, *AJIL* 99:691, 706.
66. See John R. Crook, 2007, Contemporary practice of the United States relating to international law, *AJIL* 101:506.
67. Barron, James. 2008. U.S. Court to Revisit its Decision on Deportee. *New York Times,* Aug. 15, A17.

68. Lawrence, Diana. 2007. Wrongly deported Canadian is offered $8.9m. *Fin. Times,* Jan. 27/28, 3.
69. Landler, Mark. 2007. German court challenges C.I.A. over abduction. *New York Times,* Feb. 1, A1.
70. Lewis, Neil A. 2005. Fresh details emerge on harsh methods at Guantánamo. *New York Times,* Jan. 1, A11; Dan Eggen and R. Jeffrey Smith, 2004, FBI agents allege abuse of detainees at Guantánamo Bay. *Wash. Post,* Dec. 21, A1.
71. Constable, Pamela. 2004. Rights report accuses U.S. troops of abuses in Afghanistan. *Wash. Post,* Mar. 9, A16.
72. Crook, John R., *supra* note 248 at pp. 263, 484, 504.
73. Fisher, Ian. 2005. Reports of secret U.S. prisons in Europe drew ire and otherwise red faces. *New York Times,* Dec. 1, A14.
74. Brinkley, Joel. 2005. Rice is challenged in Europe over secret prisons, *New York Times,* Dec. 7, A1; Richard Berstein, 2005, Skepticism seems to erode Europeans' faith in Rice. *New York Times,* Dec. 7, A16.
75. Dombey, Daniel, and Frances Williams. 2006. Europe faces dilemma on human rights. *Fin. Times,* June 8, 4.
76. See *Rasul v. Bush,* 124 S.Ct. 2686 (2004); David L. Sloss, 2004, Case report: *Rasul v. Bush, AJIL* 98:788; Neil A. Lewis, Judge extends legal rights for Guantánamo detainees, *New York Times,* Feb. 1, A12; John Barry, Michael Hirsh and Michael Isikoff, 2004, The roots of torture, *Newsweek International,* May 24.
77. Yoo, John. 2005. *The powers of war and peace,* 164.
78. See Jay S. Bybee, "Memorandum for Alberto Gonzales: Re: Standards of Conduct and Interrogation Under 18 U.S.C. §§2340-2340A (Aug. 1, 2002), at *http://news.findlaw.com/wp/docs/doj/bybee80102memo.pdf;* See Sean Murphy, 2004, Contemporary practice of the United States relating to international law, *AJIL* 98:825.
79. Memorandum from Acting Assistant Attorney General Daniel Levin to Deputy Attorney General James B. Comfey (Dec. 30, 2004) ("Re: Legal Standards Applicable Under 18 U.S.C. §§2340-2340A"), at *http://www.usdoj.gov/olc/dagmemo.pdf;* See R. Jeffrey Smith and Dan Eggen. 2004, Justice expands 'torture' definition, *Wash. Post,* Dec. 31, A1.
80. See Sean Murphy. 2005, Contemporary practice of the United States relating to international law, *AJIL* 99:481.
81. *Rasul v. Bush,* 124 S.Ct 2686 (2004); See David L. Sloss, 2004, Case report: *Rasul v. Bush, AJIL* 98:788; See *Hamdi v. Rumsfeld,* 124 S.Ct 2633 (2004); See Jeremy S. Martinez, 2004, *Hamdi v. Rumsfeld, AJIL* 98:782.
82. Alden, Edward. 2004. Guantánamo detainees to get legal review. *Fin. Times,* July 8, 2.
83. Art. 5 of the Geneva Convention [No. 3] Relative to the Treatment of Prisoners of war, Aug. 12, 1949, 6 UST 3316, 75 UNTS 135.

84. Lewis, Neil A. 2005. Judge halts Guantánamo trial. *New York Times,* Nov. 16, A15; See John R. Cook, 2005, Contemporary practice of the United States, *AJIL* 99:898.
85. Lewis, Neil. 2005. Ruling lets U.S. restart trials at Guantánamo. *New York Times,* July 16, A1.
86. Hamdan v. Rumsfeld, No. 05-184, at *http://www.supremecourtus.gov/qp/05-00184qp.pdf.*
87. H.R. 2863, Title X (Dec. 30, 2005).
88. Ibid.
89. Greenhouse, Linda. 2006. Justices hint they'll rule on detainee's challenge. *New York Times,* Mar. 29, A1.
90. 2006. *New York Times,* June 30, A1.
91. 548 U.S. (2006), 7.
92. Sevastopulo, Demetri, and Holly Yeager. 2006. Detainees to be given rights by Pentagon. *Fin. Times,* July 12, 1.
93. Mazzetti, Mark, and Kate Zernike. 2006. White House says terror detainees hold basic rights. *New York Times,* July 12, A1.
94. Fleischer, Ari. 2002. Special White House Announcement Re: Application of Geneva Conventions in Afghanistan, Feb. 7, at *www.whitehouse.gov/news/releases/2002/02/.*
95. Zernike, Kate. 2006. Administration prods Congress to curb the rights of detainees. *New York Times,* July 13, A1.
96. Zernike, Kate. 2006. Military lawyers urge protections for detainees. *New York Times,* July 14, A16.
97. Stolberg, Sheryl Gay. 2006. President moves 14 held in secret to Guantánamo. *New York Times,* Sept. 7, A1.
98. Zernike, Kate. 2006. Rebuff for Bush on terror trials in a Senate test. *New York Times,* Sept. 15, A1.
99. Stolberg, Sheryl Gay. 2006. President signs new rules to prosecute terror suspects. *New York Times,* Oct. 18, A14.
100. The United States Military Commissions Act of 2006, Pub. L. No. 109-366, 120 Stat. 2600 (Oct. 17, 2006).
101. 2006. Court told it lacks power in detainee cases. *Wash. Post,* Oct. 19, A1.
102. Zeleney, Jeff. 2007. Democrats hope to expand rights at Guantánamo. *New York Times,* June 6, A16; Jonathan Weisman, 2007, GOP blocks bid on rights of detainees. *Wash. Post,* Sept. 20, A5.
103. Lewis, Neil A. 2006. Judge sets back Guantánamo detainees. *New York Times,* Dec. 14, A24.
104. *Boumediene v. Bush,* No. 05-5065 (D.C. Cir., Feb. 20, 2007); See Stephen Labaton, 2007, Court endorses curbs on appeal by U.S. detainees. *New York Times,* Feb. 21, A1.
105. See *Boumediene v. Bush,* No. 06-1195, and *Al Odah v. United States,* No. 06-1196, S.Ct. (2007); Linda Greenhouse, Supreme Court turns down detainees' *habeas corpus* case. *New York Times,* Apr. 3, A14.

106. Glaberson, William. 2007. In shift, justices agree to review detainees' case. *New York Times*, June 30, A1.
107. Sevastopulo, Demetri. 2008. Guantánamo inmates have right to fight detentions in U.S. courts. *Fin. Times*, June 13, 1.
108. *Boumediene, et al. v. Bush, President of the United States, et al.*, No. 06-2295, S.Ct. (June 12, 2008).
109. Ibid.
110. White, Josh. 2007. Australian to return home to serve shortened term. *Wash. Post*, Mar. 31, A12.
111. Dinmore, Guy, and Raphael Minder. 2008. Rights advocates condemn Guantánamo trial. *Fin. Times*, Mar. 28, 2.
112. Glaberson, William. 2007. Military judges dismiss charges for 2 detainees. *New York Times*, June 5, A1.
113. Glaberson, William. Court advances war crimes trials. *New York Times*, Sept. 25, A1.
114. Shane, Scott, and William Glaberson. 2008. Rulings clear military trial of a detainee. *New York Times*, July 18, A1.
115. Sevastopulo, Demetri. 2008. Bin Laden driver receives 66-month sentence. *Fin. Times*, Aug. 8, 5.
116. Sevastopulo, Demetri. 2005. Muslim nations asked to take inmates. *Fin. Times*, Aug. 10, 3.
117. McDonough, Siobhan. 2005. Judge blocks transfer from Cuba for 13 Yemeni detainees. *Wash. Post*, Mar. 14, A15; Scott Shane, 2005, Judge bars U.S. from moving some detainees. *New York Times*, Mar. 13, A17.
118. See *Qassim v. Bush*, No. 05-892, S.Ct. (2006).
119. See Secretary of State Colin Powell, *The Crisis in Darfur* (Sept. 9, 2004), at *http://www.state.gov/secretary/rm/36042.htm;* See Steven R. Weisman, 2004, Powell says rapes and killings in Sudan are genocide, *New York Times*, Sept. 10, A3; Guy Dinmore and Mark Turner, 2004, Sudanese killing is genocide, says U.S. *Fin. Times*, Sept. 10, 3.
120. Lynch, Colum. 2004. U.N. puts Sudan sanctions into play. *Wash. Post*, Sept. 19, A1.
121. President George W. Bush, Address to the U.N. General Assembly, Sept. 21, 2004, at *http://whitehouse.gov/newsreleases/2004/09/print/20020921-3.htm.*
122. Senate Res. 1564 (2004) adopted on Sept. 18, 2004, para. 12.
123. Report of the International Commission Inquiry on Darfur to the United Nations Secretary General at 5 (Jan. 25, 2005), at *http:// www.un.org/News/dh/sudan/com_inq_darfur.pdf;* Also see Colum Lynch, 2005, U.N. panel finds no genocide in Darfur but urges tribunals. *Wash. Post*, Feb. 1, A3.
124. Crook, John R. 2005. Contemporary practice of the United States relating to international law, *AJIL* 99:691; See Mark Turner, 2005, U.S. compromise allows Darfur to be referred to ICC. *Fin. Times*, Apr. 2, 3.
125. Crook, John R. 2005. Contemporary practice of the United States relating to international law, *AJIL* 99:479, 501.

126. Senate Res. 1672 (2006); See Mark Turner, 2006, Security Council sanctions agreed for Darfur war crimes. *Fin. Times,* April 26, 8.
127. Marlise Simons, Lydia Polgreen and Jeffrey Gettleman. 2008. Arrest is sought of Sudan leader in genocide case. *New York Times,* July 15, A1.
128. MacFarquhar, Neil. 2008. Fate of Sudan's president snarls U.N. vote on Darfur. *New York Times,* Aug. 1, A11.
129. §101(a)(42) of INA; 8 U.S.C. §1101.
130. See CRS Report No. RL 32276, Michael John Garcia. 2006. *The U.N. Convention Against Torture: Overview of U.S. Implementation Policy Concerning the Removal of Aliens.*
131. See CRS Report No. RL 32621, Ruth Ellen Wasem. 2005. *U.S. Immigration Policy on Asylum Seekers.*
132. *http://www.state.gov/g/tip/rls/tiprpt/2006/*
133. P.L. 106-386.
134. P.L. 109-164, Trafficking Victims Protection Reauthorization Act of 2005.
135. *http://www.state.gov/g/tip/rls/tiprpt/2006/*
136. Framework Convention on Tobacco Control, adopted on May 21, 2003, at *http://www.who.int/features/2003/08/en/;* reprinted in 42 ILM 518 (2003).
137. See United States, Textual Proposals Made at the second Meeting of Working Group 1, WHO Framework Convention on Tobacco Control, WHO Doc. A/FCTC/INB2/WG1/Conf. Paper No. 2 (May 1, 2001).
138. Kauffman, Marc. 2003. U.S. seeks to alter anti-tobacco treaty; "reservations" clause sought as way out of some provisions. *Wash. Post,* April 30, A1.
139. Stein, Rob, and Marc Kaufman. 2003. U.S. back pact curbing tobacco use worldwide. *Wash. Post,* May 19, A1.
140. Kaufman, Marc. Inaction on tobacco treaty threatens U.S. influence. *Wash. Post,* Jul. 6, A5.
141. Murphy, Sean. 2003. Contemporary practice of the United States relating to international law, *AJIL* 97:981; See Frances Williams, 2005, WTO eases rules on drugs for the poor. *Fin. Times,* Dec. 7, 6.
142. President and Mrs. Bush Discuss HIV/AIDS Initiatives on World Aids Day, at *www.whitehouse.gov/news/releases/2005/12/20051201.html.*
143. Alden, Edward, and Neil Buckley. 2004. Sweet deals: 'Big Sugar' fights threats from free trade and a global drive to limit consumption. *Fin. Times,* Feb. 27, 11.
144. GA Res. 59/280, annex, para. (b) (Mar. 8, 2005).

chapter VIII

INTERNATIONAL LAW, THE U.S. PROMOTION OF DEMOCRACY AND THE RULE OF LAW

President Bush has made promoting democracy and the rule of law abroad a major priority of his administration's second term foreign policy agenda. The administration is continuing a longstanding policy of the United States to advocate the promotion of democracy abroad. But a closer scrutiny of American foreign policy shows tremendous flaws in its commitment to democracy in general. Successive administrations also made democracy a major component of their foreign policy, particularly during the Cold War when the United States had to compete with the Soviet Union for allies in Europe and the Third World. However, when it was in its national interest to do so, the United States subverted democracy and based it on a perceived communist threat.

Following the demise of the Soviet empire the administration of George Bush Sr. made a strong push for democratization in Central and Eastern Europe. The administration also made democracy a criterion for its recognition of the new states that emerged from the collapse of the former Yugoslavia. Bush supported the Copenhagen Declaration of 1990, in which states pledged to adhere to the principle of participatory democracy.[1] The Paris Charter followed this declaration, establishing institutional structures for monitoring the implementation of the conduct of free elections in member states and other provisions of the Copenhagen Declaration.[2] In October 1991 the CSCE adopted the Moscow Document, which condemned those who seek to take power by force against the will of the people expressed in free and fair elections.[3] These declarations have certainly helped to transform the political systems in Eastern Europe. However, a resurgence of the former communism has occurred in some of Eastern European countries as they have found the transition to democracy more difficult than originally predicted. In the former Soviet Union the situation is even worse. Many of the states, including Russia, continue to operate under authoritarian rule.

The Bush administration also pushed for a commitment to democracy from Latin American states by signing the Santiago Commitment to Democracy and Renewal of the Inter-American System in 1991, which called for the promotion and consolidation of democracy in the Americas. This was followed the next day by the passage of Resolution 1080, which reiterated the principles of the OAS Charter as requiring the political representation of states to be predicated on the effective exercise of representative democracy.[4] The resolution gives the Secretary General the authority to

> call for the immediate convocation of a meeting of the Permanent Council in the event of any occurrences giving rise to the sudden or irregular interruption of the democratic political institutional process or of the legitimate exercise of power by the democratically elected government in any of the Organization's member states.[5]

A subsequent Protocol signed in 1992 in Washington calls for the non-recognition of a regime that comes to power through undemocratic means.[6] President Bush also redirected U.S. foreign assistance programs to help promote democratic institutions and the rule of law in the former communist countries. Finally, following the cancellation of democratic elections in Panama in 1989, President Bush used the restoration of democracy in that country as a pretext to launch a military invasion to overthrow the military regime of Manuel Noriega.

When President Clinton assumed the presidency in 2003 the world was experiencing a democratic renaissance. The number of democratic governments had increased significantly. Except for the Middle East, all regions around the world saw a proliferation of democratic regimes. President Clinton continued the policy of his predecessor by pushing for other countries to democratize. Clinton linked U.S. bilateral and multilateral aid to a country's commitment to democracy. Following the overthrow of the democratically elected government of President Aristide of Haiti in1993, the Clinton administration condemned the coup and refused to recognize the military junta. Clinton supported OAS sanctions against the military junta and later sponsored resolutions in the Security Council to impose a comprehensive embargo on Haiti and to grant the U.S. authorization to lead a multinational force into Haiti to reinstate President Aristide.[7] The Clinton administration also backed the intervention of a Nigerian-led West African force into

Sierra Leone to restore the government of President Kabbah, overthrown in a military coup. The Clinton administration endorsed a Security Council resolution that called for the restoration of democracy and that commended the work of the Economic Community of West African States (ECOWAS) force toward that goal.[8]

The Bush administration's renewed emphasis on promoting democracy is nothing new. However, what has changed is the administration's rhetoric on the issue with no substance to back it up. In fact, the administration's words do not match its deeds, and its actions seem to contradict its pronouncement. President Bush lacks the democratic legitimacy of previous Presidents to push through a democracy agenda. His standing in the world is extremely low because of his alliance with such undemocratic regimes as Mubarak of Egypt and Musharraf of Pakistan and his administration's involvement in the removal of the legitimately elected governments of President Aristide of Haiti and the failed coup in Venezuela against Hugo Chavez. Bush came to office in 2000 under questionable circumstances in which a divided Supreme Court selected him over Al Gore in the disputed Florida vote count. In 2004 Bush's reelection for a second term occurred under a cloud of suspicion surrounding irregularities in Ohio. President Bush remains very unpopular even in countries considered traditional allies of the United States. Few believe Bush's commitment to promoting democracy is genuine. Observers in the United States also dismiss the President's statement as too Wilsonian.

There are serious contradictions in the President's democracy initiative. President Bush calls for countries to democratize, but he has either overlooked the erosion of democratic institutions in some countries or acquiesced to the overthrow of democratically elected governments. The Bush administration did not condemn a coup in Venezuela against the elected government of Hugo Chavez. Instead, the President's advisers blamed Mr. Chavez for his predicaments, and the administration quickly recognized the short-lived military regime.[9] Similarly, when Haitian rebels invaded Haiti from the Dominican Republic and began a violent campaign to overthrow President Aristide, the Bush administration blamed Aristide for failing to adhere to democratic principles and for the violence that was engulfing the country. It pressured Aristide to accept several unrealistic demands but did nothing to halt the invasion. By not condemning the violence, the Bush administration encouraged the rebels to march on to Port-au-Prince and to seize power.

At the height of the military invasion of Haiti the United States joined France in calling for Aristide to leave the country, and it deployed fifty-five U.S. Marines to Haiti to augment the embassy security force. The Marines were later used to depose Aristide, and they took him against his will to the Central African Republic.[10] Upon his arrival in the Central African Republic, President Aristide accused the United States of kidnapping him and sending him into exile, a charge the State Department denied.[11] The same day of Aristide's removal from the country Bush persuaded Haiti's representative to the United Nations to request the deployment of a United Nations peacekeeping force in Haiti.[12]

On February 29, 2004 the Security Council adopted resolution 1529 (2004) to authorize the deployment of a Multinational Interim Force (MIF) to Haiti for a three-month period for the purpose of creating a "secure and stable environment."[13] Immediately after the vote the United States dispatched two hundred additional U.S. combat forces to Haiti to secure key facilities, to facilitate the continued repatriation of Haitian migrants and to help create conditions in the capital for the anticipated arrival of the MIF.[14] The MIF later replaced United States forces, comprised of troops from Brazil, Canada, Chile, France and the United States.[15] The Bush administration played a pivotal role in the selection of Gerard Latortue, a Haitian exile living in Florida, to head the interim government.

The role played by the Bush administration in Venezuela and Haiti underscores its skewed commitment to democracy. The administration ignored longstanding OAS norms against recognizing regimes that come to power through undemocratic means. The Santiago Commitment to Democracy and the Renewal of the Inter-American System established a mechanism for collective action in the event of a sudden or irregular interruption of the democratic political institutional process or of the legitimate exercise of power by the democratically elected government in any member state.[16] Secondly, the Inter-American Democratic Charter adopted in Lima on September 11, 2001 states that any unconstitutional alteration or interruption of the democratic order in a state of the hemisphere constitutes an insurmountable obstacle to the participation of that state's government in the Summits of the Americas process.[17]

In his second inaugural address President Bush called for a democratic renaissance in the Middle East and made Afghanistan and Iraq his models for such a democratic transformation. The President also made advancing freedom a top priority of his second term:

> Today, America speaks anew to the peoples of the world:
>
> All who live in tyranny and hopelessness can know: the United States will not ignore your oppression, or excuse your oppressors. When you stand for liberty, we will stand with you.

> Democratic reformers facing repression, prison, or exile can know: America sees you for who you are: the future leaders of your free country.
>
> Rulers of outlaw regimes can know that we still believe as Abraham Lincoln did: "Those who deny freedom to others deserve it not for themselves; and under the rule of a just God, cannot long retain it."
>
> The leaders of governments with long habits of control need to know: To serve your people you must learn to trust them. Start on this journey of progress and justice, and America will walk at your side.[18]

Condoleezza Rice also echoed the Bush administration's democratic agenda in her confirmation hearing before the Senate Foreign Relations Committee. She listed three diplomatic priorities the administration would pursue:

> First, we will unite the community of democracies in building an international system that is based on shared values and the rule of law. Second, we will strengthen the community of democracies to fight the threats to our common security and alleviate the hopelessness that feeds terror. And third, we will spread freedom and democracy throughout the globe. That is the mission that President Bush has set for America in the world and is the great mission of American diplomacy today.[19]

Secretary Rice also spoke of "transformational diplomacy" whose objective is to "work with our many partners around the world to build and sustain democratic, well-governed states that will respond to the needs of their people and conduct themselves responsibly in the international system."[20] President Bush also made foreign assistance to developing countries contingent on progress toward freedom and democracy. USAID has set four distinct goals for promoting the President's freedom and democracy agenda:

- ✦ Strengthen the rule of law and respect for human rights
- ✦ Promoting more genuine and competitive election and political processes
- ✦ Increased development of a politically active civil society
- ✦ More transparent and accountable governance[21]

The Bush administration supported popular revolts in Georgia, Ukraine and Lebanon, and it joined France in co-sponsoring a resolution in the Security Council calling for the withdrawal of Syrian troops from Lebanon and for a free and fair electoral process in Lebanon's upcoming presidential election.[22] President Bush also hailed elections in Afghanistan and Iraq as benchmarks of democracy in spite of the extraordinary circumstances under which the organization of these elections occurred. However, he has not made a similar push for democratic change in Pakistan, Egypt and Saudi Arabia or in the former Soviet republics of Central Asia, key U.S. allies in the war on terror. The Bush administration has also ignored the reversal of the democratic process in Russia, and it has said little about the lack of political liberalization in China.

Following a military coup in Thailand in October 2006, the Bush administration issued a mild condemnation of the coup, called for a restoration of democracy and suspended military aid to the new regime. The administration also suspended negotiations on a free trade agreement between the United States and Thailand that was in progress at the time of the coup. However, the administration did not sever diplomatic relations with Thailand or withhold recognition of the new government.[23] The Bush administration has maintained good relations with the Thai military junta and remained silent on the junta's new constitutional referendum, which major opposition parties and an overwhelming majority of voters boycotted.

Similarly, after General Musharraf declared martial law in Pakistan and suspended the constitution and the process toward the restoration of democracy, the Bush administration criticized General Musharraf but did not suspend aid to Pakistan or withdraw support for General Musharraf. Musharraf's emergency decree led to the arrest and detention of hundreds of lawyers, opposition politicians and members of civic societies; it also restricted press freedom. Musharraf dismissed all the existing members of the Supreme Court and appointed jurists loyal to him. The new Supreme Court subsequently validated the election of Musharraf as president for the next five years. Musharraf, who came to power in a coup d'etat in 1999, has skillfully exploited the Bush administration's war on terror to extend his authoritarian rule. President Bush has been complicit in Musharraf's stay in power because of the fear of Pakistan's nuclear weapons falling into the hands of terrorists. President Bush has also relied on Musharraf as an important ally in the war on terror. Musharraf's emergency decree was a last minute desperate effort to remain in power as a military dictator transformed into a civilian president, which Pakistani's Supreme Court was about to invalidate as a constitutional violation.

Musharraf's emergency decree created a policy dilemma for the Bush administration. President Bush had refrained from pushing for democratic reform in Pakistan as he considered Musharraf an important ally in the war on terror. President Bush actually invested tremendous resources in making sure Musharraf remained in power. However, Bush soon discovered that Musharraf was part of the problem instead of the solution. Bush began pushing Musarraf to implement democratic reform, but Musarraf saw the reform as undermining authority over Pakistani politics, which he has dominated since 1999. The Bush administration forced Musarraf to accept a power sharing arrangement with Benazi Bhutto, which led to Ms. Bhutto returning from exile to contest the scheduled election. Under the arrangement Musarraf would remain in office as the civilian president and relinquish his military position. With the declaration of emergency rule on November 4 the power sharing arrangement seems all but dead. Ms. Bhutto called for Musarraf to resign as president and head of the army and said she would not work with him. Authorities placed Bhutto under temporary house arrest and prevented her from holding a planned match to Islamabad. Meanwhile, former Prime Minister Nawaz Sharif, whom officials prevented from returning to Pakistan from exile in Saudi Arabia a few weeks prior to declaration of martial law, was allowed to return to Pakistan a few weeks later and granted authorization to contest the election. President Bush remained publicly committed to Musharraf but privately was looking at a post-Musharraf alternative.[24] The collapse of the Musharraf-Bhutto deal was a blow to the Bush administration's Pakistan policy. The administration had initially backed a power sharing arrangement as the best hope for the restoration of democracy in Pakistan. However, Musharraf's declaration of martial law dashed that hope.

The very tenuous political situation in Pakistan took a turn for the worse on December 27 with the assassination of Ms. Bhutto who had become the most vocal critic of General Musharraf.[25] Her sudden death created a political vacuum in Pakistan, one difficult to fill with the current slate of politicians. Her death was also a setback for the Bush administration's goal of bringing about the restoration of democracy in Pakistan. Suddenly the unholy alliance President Bush had tried to forge between Ms. Bhutto and General Musharraf had unraveled, and it left the administration in a quandary with very few options. The administration's Pakistan policy, centered on Musharraf remaining in office as a civilian president, was very unpopular among Pakistanis. Ms. Bhutto's decision to initially cooperate with Musharraf, even though she later backed down after his declaration of martial law, made her a target of those who saw General Musharraf as the source of Pakistan's political turmoil. In light of the uncertain political climate, Musharraf rescheduled the January 8 parliamentary elections for February. As expected, the two main opposition parties made huge gains in that election and were able to form the new government. Pakistan's new government moved immediately to curtail

Musharraf's power and restore democratic institutions. The new government declared a change in Pakistan's relationship with the U.S. and support of the Bush administration's convoluted war on terror. To avoid being impeached, Musharraf abruptly resigned the presidency, which paved the way for the election of Asif Ali Zardari, Mrs. Bhutto's widower. The Bush administration had to reassess its counter terrorism policy in the wake of Musharraf's demise. Musharraf's downfall was not a result of the Bush administration's quest to promote democracy in Pakistan but due to pressure from all sectors of the Pakistani population that saw Musharraf as the problem instead of a solution. Musharraf was also a victim of his own flawed policies.

The Bush administration has acted deliberately selective in its promotion of democracy abroad, and it has done so only in countries where this policy does not threat U.S. vital interest. Recent setbacks in elections in Egypt, Iraq and Palestine, where groups hostile to U.S. interest in the region made significant gains in the polls, pose a policy dilemma for the Bush administration. The outcomes of these elections have forced the administration to reassess its push for democracy worldwide.[26] In fact, the Bush administration has all but abandoned its democratic agenda. More recently the administration has taken a more subtle approach to promoting democracy and is less vocal in its opposition to undemocratic regimes.

As President Bush ends his eight-year tenure in office, the democratic scoreboard looks a lot like when he took office, or in some instances worse than the political map he inherited from President Clinton. A retreat from democracy has occurred as more countries have embraced some brand of authoritarian rule or halted their transition to democracy. More regimes have become more repressive, and the wave of democracy that spread after the collapse of communism has all but evaporated. The Economist Intelligence Index of Democracy for 2006 lists only twenty-five countries as functioning democracies out of a total of 167 countries. More than 50 percent of the states surveyed are either authoritarian regimes or flawed democracies. Similarly, Freedom House, which tracks democracy and freedom around the world, reports a sharp decline in both democratic regimes and in individual and press freedoms around the world.[27]

Endnotes

1. Document of the Copenhagen Meeting of the Conference on the Human Dimension of the Conference on Security and Cooperation in Europe, June 29, 1990, reprinted in 29 ILM 1308, 1307 (1990).

2. CSCE Charter of Paris for a Free Europe, Nov. 21, 1990, reprinted in 30 ILM 190, 193 (1990).
3. Conference on Security and Cooperation in Europe, Document of the Moscow Meeting on Human Dimension, Emphasizing Respect for Human Rights, Pluralistic Democracy, the Rule of Law, and Procedures for Fact-Finding, Oct. 3, 1991, reprinted in 30 ILM 1670 (1991).
4. OEA/Ser.P/AG/RES.1080 (XXI-0/91).
5. Ibid.
6. See Texts Approved by the General Assembly Special Sixteenth Session in Connection with the Amendments to the Charter of the Organization, OEA/Ser.P, OAS Doc. AG/doc.II (XVI-E/92) (1992) (Article 8 bis) (Article 9 of the amended Charter).
7. See Senate Res. 841 (1993) and Senate Res. 940 (1994).
8. See Senate Res. 1132 (1997) and S/PRST/1998/5 (February 26, 1998).
9. Vulliamy, Ed. 2002. Venezuela coup linked to Bush team, April 12, at *http://observer.guardian.co.uk/international/story/0,6903,688071.html*
10. See Richard Lapper, 2004, Turmoil returns to Haiti: Aristide goes into exile and the region rues its failure to build stronger democracy. *Fin. Times*, Mar. 3, p. 11.
11. See Guy Dinmore, 2004, Aristide accuses U.S. of forcing him into exile. *Fin. Times*, Mar. 2, 3; David E. Sanger and Christopher Marquis, 2004, State Dept. denies leader was forced out of office, *New York Times*, Mar. 2, A10.
12. Letter dated 29 February 2004 from the Permanent Representative of Haiti to the United Nations Addressed to the President of the Security Council, UN Doc. S/2004/163.
13. Senate Res. 1529 (2004), para. 2 (Feb. 29, 2004).
14. Edward Alden, Robert Graham, and Richard Lapper. 2004. Bush sends Marines into Haiti. *Fin. Times*, Mar.1, 1.
15. Report of the Secretary General on Haiti, UN Doc. S/2004/300, para. 25 (Apr. 16, 2004).
16. AG/Res. 1080 (XXI-0/91).
17. *http://www.oas.org/OASpage/eng/Documents/Democratic_Chater.htm*
18. President Bush's Second Inaugural Address, Jan. 20, 2005, at *www.whitehouse.gov./news/releases/2005/01/20050120-1.html.*
19. The Secretary of State's Nomination Hearing before the Senate Foreign Relations Committee, Jan. 18, 2005.
20. Remarks by Secretary of State Rice at the School of Foreign Service, Georgetown University, Jan. 18, 2006.
21. *www.usaid.gov/our_work/democracy_and_governance/*
22. Senate Res. 1559 (2004), adopted on September 2, 2004.
23. See Whitehouse Statement, at *www.whitehouse.gov/news/releases/2006/10/20061003-5.html.*

24. Helen Cooper, Mark Mazzetti, and David Rohde. 2007. U.S. looking past Musharraf in case he falls. *New York Times,* Nov. 15, A1.
25. Masood, Salman, and Carlotta Gall. 2007. Bhutto is killed, and Pakistan faces rage and more turmoil. *New York Times,* Dec. 28, A1.
26. Guy Gilmore. 2006. U.S. defends its record on the promotion of democracy. *Fin. Times,* April 6, P3.
27. See the 2008 Freedom in the World Report, Freedom House, at *www.freedomhouse.org*.

chapter IX

INTERNATIONAL LAW AND UNITED STATES–UNITED NATIONS RELATIONS

Under President Bush relations between the United States and the United Nations have been rancorous. The United States helped establish the United Nations, but it took exception to the restrictions on a state's right of self-defense. The United States has always maintained that its right to protect its national interest is not negotiable. The creation of the United Nations did not deprive the United States of that right. The United Nations was seen as a useful instrument for promoting U.S. foreign policy. However, when the United Nations could not fulfill that purpose the United States bypassed the United Nations and acted unilaterally. The United States used the United Nations machinery to advance its agenda in the Korean Peninsula by skillfully manipulating the U.N. Charter regime to authorize a U.S.-led force to repel North Korean aggression. Although the Security Council authorized the force and it carried the banner of the United Nations, U.S. General Douglas Macarthur commanded it and reported to the President of the United States and not to the Secretary General of the United Nations.

The United States shielded its invasion and conduct of Vietnam and the bombing of Cambodia and Laos from Security Council condemnation or United Nations scrutiny. Similarly, the United States impeded efforts by the United Nations to investigate allegations of the United States' covert military activities in Guatemala and Cuba and its invasion of the Dominican Republic. The U.S. maintained that these issues were regional by nature and that the Organization of American States (OAS) should handle them first before the victim states could take their case to the United Nations.[1] Given the United States' veto power in the Security Council, it was able to block efforts by Cuba and Guatemala to persuade the Security Council to intervene in their disputes with the United States.

In the 1970s the relationship between the United States and the United Nations declined as the United States lost its automatic Western majority in the General Assembly with the entry of a large number of Third World states into the United Nations. The Third World majority adopted several anti-Western resolutions that alienated the United States and led to an erosion in relations between the United States and the United Nations. The relationship further deteriorated after the General Assembly adopted its now infamous resolution entitled "Zionism is Racism" in which it condemned Israel's policy of Zionism as a form of racism and racial discrimination.[2] The measure infuriated supporters of Israel in Congress, some of whom called for the United States to leave the United Nations.

During the presidency of Ronald Reagan relations between the United States and the United Nations reached its lowest point. Reagan withheld the U.S.'s regular dues to the United Nations to protest what he perceived as an anti-Western bias in the United Nations. Reagan also withheld funds until the United Nations implemented structural reform of the organization's bureaucracy. Reagan disregarded the Charter ban on the use of force when he invaded Grenada, bombed Libya and funded and supported the *Contra* war against the government of Nicaragua. Reagan withdrew from the Compulsory Jurisdiction Clause of the International Court of Justice (ICJ) after Nicaragua sued the United States for mining its harbors. Reagan subsequently refused to participate in the proceedings and vowed not to comply with the court's decision. The ICJ later ruled against the United States. Reagan supported anticommunist insurgents in Afghanistan, Angola and Central America, and he frustrated United Nations efforts to resolve these conflicts.

Both U.S. allies and its adversaries strongly criticized the Grenada invasion. It came at a time when tension between the U.S. and the USSR was particularly high. The Reagan administration had made anticommunism a centerpiece of his foreign policy, and the presence of Cuban troops in Grenada and Grenada's close alliance with radical regimes angered both the Reagan administration and some Caribbean governments. However, given Grenada's size and its insignificance in world affairs, many viewed the U.S. invasion as a blatant disregard for the principles of the Charter. The United States vetoed a resolution in the Security Council condemning its invasion of Grenada. However, an overwhelming majority of states supported a similar resolution in the General Assembly condemning the U.S. invasion as a flagrant violation of international law.[3] Reagan also helped prolong the Iran-Iraq war by providing weapons to Iraq and by stationing naval vessels in the Persian Gulf to provoke Iran into a confrontation.

Upon taking office former President Bush took a much more conciliatory tone toward the United Nations. Bush supported the Secretary General's peace initiatives in Afghanistan, Central America and Iran/Iraq. President Bush also endorsed the creation of United Nations peacekeeping forces to implement peace agreements in Cambodia, Namibia, Angola, Mozambique and Central America. After Iraq invaded Kuwait, President Bush utilized the United Nations Security Council's multilateral framework to win collective legitimacy for the U.S.-led invasion of Iraq. The United States used the Security Council machinery effectively to advance its interests in the Persian Gulf. The Security Council went along in authorizing sanctions against Iraq and later approved the use of military force to eject Iraqi forces from Kuwait. The Security Council also endorsed a comprehensive sanctions regime imposed on Iraq by the coalition at the end of the war.[4] The sanctions called for the complete disarmament of Iraq and for placing the sale of Iraqi oil under United Nations supervision. Iraq had to pay reparation to Kuwait and to compensate those affected by the invasion.

Following the forcible removal of Iraqi forces from Kuwait, Kurds and Shiites began simultaneous uprisings against Saddam Hussein's regime. Iraq's military brutally crushed the rebellions. In response President Bush persuaded the Security Council to authorize the creation of safe havens for Kurdish refugees in northern Iraq. The U.S., Britain and France then invoked the resolution to impose no-fly zones in the airspace over northern and southern Iraq, even though the resolution did not authorize such measures.[5]

In the waning days of his administration President Bush spearheaded the diplomatic effort in the Security Council to authorize the deployment of a U.S.-led international peacekeeping force to Somalia to protect humanitarian aid convoys and to aid workers engaged in distributing humanitarian assistance to the civilian population. United States intervention helped alleviate the humanitarian crisis, but subsequent U.S. involvement in the hunt for war criminals led to a botched military operation resulting in the death of several American servicemen.

The Bush administration also supported the efforts of the United Nations Secretary General to settle several longstanding regional conflicts fueled in part by the ideological conflict between the U.S. and the USSR. During President Bush's term in office the number of United Nations peacekeeping operations increased significantly, and the mandates of these missions expanded to include nations-building, organizing and monitoring elections, resuscitating failed states, protecting human rights, demobilization of combatants and resettling refugees and internally displaced persons.

In spite of President Bush's conciliatory tone and willingness to work within the United Nations framework, he did not always comply with Charter principles. In 1989, President Bush invaded Panama and removed the government of General Manuel Noriega. Although many states quietly welcomed the removal of Noriega from power, they denounced the U.S. invasion on the grounds that it violated international law and the sovereignty and territorial integrity of Panama.[6] The invasion was particularly disturbing as it occurred at a time when relations between the U.S. and the Soviet Union were improving. Soviet domination of East Europe was on the decline, and President Gorbachev was calling for a new international order based on the rule of law and respect for the principles of the United Nations Charter. President Bush seized the opportunity and used the United Nations framework successfully to advance the U.S.'s post-Cold War foreign policy agenda. By the time President Bush left office relations between the U.S. and the United Nations had improved significantly.

In 1993, President Clinton succeeded President Bush and vowed to work with the United Nations to address some of the protracted global problems that he felt the United States could not solve by itself. Clinton's policy of "assertive multilateralism" called for more vigorous U.S. participation in United Nations peacekeeping activities. In his first year in office President Clinton supported the creation of six new peacekeeping missions. Clinton inherited the Somalia crisis from former President Bush, but by then the political and security situation in Somalia had deteriorated. Clinton sought and received a new and more robust mandate from the Security Council to augment the existing mandate of the United Nations Operation in Somalia (UNOSOM II), to give it greater authority to implement the political aspects of the mission and to pursue warlords who were not cooperating with the United Nations. It was this new role for UNOSOM II that led U.S. forces to clash with some of the warlords and to the fiasco that followed. The military debacle changed public opinion in the United States and public support for the U.N. mission. It also led to calls from members of Congress for an expedited U.S. withdrawal from Somalia.

In the wake of the U.S. operation to capture General Aideed, the Clinton administration drew up a series of recommendations for future U.S. participation in U.N. peacekeeping. Under Presidential Decision Directive 25 (PDD 25) the U.N. had to be more selective in authorizing the deployment of peacekeeping missions, and it needed an exit strategy. President Clinton signed legislation to unilaterally reduce the U.S.'s peacekeeping contribution from 31.7 percent to 25 percent. Clinton opposed the effort to deploy a more robust force to Rwanda to stop the genocide of Tutsi civilians and resisted calls for U.S. intervention in Bosnia to stop the massacre of Muslim civilians. However, the administration supported the establishment of the ad hoc war crimes tribunals for the former Yugoslavia and Rwanda to prosecute those responsible for the atrocities.

In 1993, the Clinton administration bombed Iraq in retaliation for Iraq's alleged involvement in the attempted assassination of former President Bush. That same year the United States, France and Britain carried out air strikes against Iraq for violating the 1991 ceasefire agreement.[7] After Iraq expelled U.N. weapons inspectors in 1998, the United States and Britain bombed targets in Iraq to force the Iraqi government to comply with its obligations under Security Council resolution 687 (1991).[8] In 1998 Clinton bombed targets in Sudan and Afghanistan following terrorist attacks on U.S. embassies in Nairobi and Dar-es-Salaam that killed 224 people and wounded 4,600.[9] A more controversial act occurred in 1999 with the invasion of Yugoslavia by the United States and its NATO allies in response to Yugoslavia's mistreatment of ethnic Albanians in Kosovo and its refusal to accept NATO's peace plan for the region.[10] Notwithstanding the pending humanitarian crisis in Kosovo and the failure of Yugoslavia to heed the demands of the Security Council, many observers criticized the U.S. and NATO for failing to secure authorization from the Security Council.[11]

President Clinton used the United Nations framework to isolate the Haitian military regime and to internationalize the economic sanctions the Organization of American States (OAS) had imposed on Haiti. After the junta refused to leave office as required by the Governors Island Accord, Clinton persuaded the Security Council to authorize a military invasion of Haiti to reinstate President Aristide.[12] Also, following the signing of the Dayton Accords to end the conflicts in the former Yugoslavia, Clinton sought United Nations approval for the accords. The Security Council subsequently authorized the deployment of a NATO force to implement the agreement.[13] Similarly, after NATO invaded Yugoslavia without Security Council authorization, Clinton secured Security Council approval for NATO to monitor the ceasefire agreement and for the United Nations to assume full administrative authority over Kosovo.

During Clinton's administration the Security Council authorized more sanctions against states and non-state actors than at any time in the history of the United Nations. The Security Council also authorized deployments of United Nations peacekeeping missions under Chapter VII to the Democratic Republic of the Congo (DRC) and to Sierra Leone. The United States did not participate in any of these missions except to provide logistical support.

President Clinton never fully recovered from the Somalia debacle, and it defined his relationship with the United Nations for the rest of his presidency. Clinton blamed Secretary General Boutros Ghali for the military fiasco in Somalia, an unfounded charge given the fact that U.S. Marines were under American command. Clinton's refusal to back Boutros Ghali for a second term led to a further deterioration in U.S.-UN relations, which did not improve until Kofi Annan became Secretary General.

By the time President Clinton left office in January 2001 relations between the United States and the United Nations were excellent. Clinton received a standing ovation and several rounds of applause in his final speech before the General Assembly. Clinton had persuaded the Republican-controlled Congress to resume payment of U.S. arrears to the United Nations. Clinton also signed the Rome Statute for the International Criminal Court (ICC).

When President Bush took office in 2001 relations between the White House and the United Nations were cordial. Secretary General Kofi Annan received his education in the United States and had great admiration for the U.S. Despite Bush's campaign rhetoric, Annan made every effort to reach out to him. During the presidential campaign Bush criticized Clinton's policy of assertive multilateralism and vowed to reduce U.S. involvement in U.N. peacekeeping. Bush saw the United Nations as hostile to U.S. strategic interests and was generally ambivalent about U.S. participation in multilateral institutions. Bush viewed the United Nations with a great deal of skepticism and downgraded the status of the United Nations in his administration.

The invasion of Iraq represents the Bush administration's greatest insult to the principles of the Charter of the United Nations. The invasion was one of the most egregious violations of international law and the Charter of the United Nations since Iraq invaded Kuwait in 1990. The invasion of Iraq underscored the difficulty the United States had trying to balance its individual interest with the interest of the international community. Although the United States is a founding member of the United Nations, the United States has not always lived up to the ideals of the organization.[14] Successive presidents have used the United Nations system as an instrument for advancing American foreign policy, and the current President Bush is no exception. When American interest conflicts with the principles of the Charter, U.S. Presidents will defy the principles of the Charter and act unilaterally. Indeed, the action of the Bush administration is consistent with the policies of his predecessors who have resorted to military force without authorization from the United Nations. However, after the first Gulf War many in the international community assumed that in the future the major powers would seek authorization from the Security Council before resorting to military force. The invasion of Iraq showed that the United States would continue to bypass the Security Council when necessary.[15]

President Bush came into office with little understanding of the way the United Nations works. His foreign policy emphasized a selected brand of multilateralism that called for picking and choosing what international activities to participate in.[16] During the 2000 presidential campaign Bush advisers criticized the Clinton administration for being too reliant on United Nations peacekeeping and too committed to multilateralism.[17] Bush vowed to reverse that trend if elected. Bush's foreign policy team showed little enthusiasm for the peacemaking and nations-building efforts of the United Nations.[18]

Bush's first act as President was to sign an Executive Order to cut off funding for the United Nations Fund for Population Activities (UNFPA). Bush did not select a U.S. Permanent Representative to the United Nations until after the September 11 terrorist attacks. He also did not press Congress to pay U.S. back dues to the United Nations until after the attacks.[19] Bush also did not push for Senate ratification of the various United Nation terrorism conventions until after the September 11 attacks on the United States.[20]

In his first address to the General Assembly on November 11, 2001, Bush received a sympathetic audience that was willing to work with the United States in its war against terrorism. He used the occasion to make a case for war against states that harbor terrorists.[21] The reception for his second address to the General Assembly in September 2002 was lukewarm. Bush was confrontational and defiant, and he used the occasion to challenge the United Nations to enforce its resolutions against Iraq or to risk becoming irrelevant.[22] Reaction to the president's speech was mixed. Bush was commended for choosing to work with the United Nations to resolve Iraq's outstanding disarmament obligations under Security Council resolutions. But many delegates took issue with President Bush's ultimatum to the United Nations and his desire to act unilaterally if the United Nations did not join him.

In his State of the Union Address in January 2002, President Bush labeled Iraq, Iran and North Korea the "Axis of Evil" and a threat to U.S. national security.[23] The United States Congress later adopted a joint resolution titled *Authorization for the Use of Force Against Iraq*, which authorized President Bush to use the armed forces of the United States as he determined necessary and appropriate in order to (1) defend the national security of the United States against the continuing threat posed by Iraq; and (2) enforce all relevant United Nations Security Council Resolutions regarding Iraq.[24] With the support of Congress behind him Bush began his diplomatic offensive to win international backing for invading Iraq.

In April 2003, President Bush carried out his much-anticipated plan to invade Iraq. Bush acted unilaterally after he failed to persuade a majority of member states in the Security Council to support a resolution authorizing a U.S. invasion of Iraq. Both traditional allies and adversaries alike opposed the United States' invasion of Iraq. They felt that the weapons inspectors should have had more time to fulfill their mandate. The U.S. invasion of Iraq is a classic act of aggression by one state against another, which undermines the authority and legitimacy of the United Nations Charter.

Initially the Bush administration complied with the rules of the Charter and referred Iraq's non-compliance to the Security Council. The administration co-sponsored a resolution in the Security Council to force Iraq to resume cooperation with the weapons inspectors and to fulfill its international obligations.[25] Following long and arduous negotiations over the language of the resolution between the United States and Britain on the one hand, and France and Russia on the other, the two sides reached an agreement on a draft resolution that satisfied the concerns of all parties.[26] On November 8 the Security Council adopted resolution 1441 (2002) by which it called on Iraq to comply with all Security Council resolutions or to face "serious consequences."[27] The resolution set a timetable for Iraq to comply with the demands of the Security Council, and it required Iraq to cooperate fully with UN weapons inspectors. The resolution also required Iraq to submit an interim report on its disarmament program to the Security Council by a certain date, which it did. The United States and Britain immediately dismissed the report as inaccurate.

The Director of the International Atomic Energy Agency (IAEA) and the head of UNSCOM submitted interim reports, which found no evidence that Iraq was building or concealing weapons of mass destruction.[28] Both men requested more time to complete their investigation of Iraq's weapons program and to carry out more intrusive searches of Saddam's palaces. But Secretary Powell argued otherwise, claiming that Iraq had the means of manufacturing nuclear, chemical and biological weapons and had to be stopped.[29]

Following Powell's address, the Bush administration began circulating a draft resolution calling for a military invasion of Iraq. France, Russia and Germany and a majority of developing countries on the Security Council strongly opposed the rush to war and called for more time for the inspectors. France, Russia and

Germany also disagreed with the United States and Britain over the interpretation of resolution 1441 (2002) and whether the Security Council had to adopt a second resolution explicitly authorizing the use of force before the United States and Britain began to use military force against Iraq. Realizing that it would not receive the required votes in the Security Council and due to their concern over a veto threat from France and Russia, the United States and Britain withdrew the draft resolution. President Bush later conferred with his staunchest allies, Blair of Britain and Anzar of Spain, and thereafter gave Saddam Hussein an ultimatum to leave Iraq within forty-eight hours or face a military invasion.[30]

On the evening of March 20 the United States and its "coalition of the willing" invaded Iraq on the grounds that Iraq had failed to comply with its obligations under relevant resolutions of the Security Council; hence the United States was enforcing the Council's demands.[31] In a letter to the President of the Security Council the United States gave its justification for invading Iraq:

> The actions being taken are authorized under existing Council resolutions, including its resolutions 678 (1990) and 687 (1991) imposed a series of obligations on Iraq, including, most importantly, extensive disarmament obligations, that were conditions of the ceasefire established under it. It has been long recognized and understood that a material breach of these obligations removes the basis of the ceasefire and revives the authority to use force under resolution 678 (1990). This has been the basis for coalition use of force in the past and has been accepted by the Council, as evidenced, for example, by the Secretary General's public announcement in January 1993 following Iraq's material breach of resolution 687 (1991) that coalition forces had received a mandate from the Council to use force according to resolution 678 (1990).
>
> Iraq continues to be in material breach of its disarmament obligations under resolution 687 (1991), as the Council affirmed in its resolution 1441 (2002). Acting under the authority of Chapter VII of the Charter of the United Nations, the Council unanimously decided that Iraq has been and remained in material of obligations and recalled its repeated warnings to Iraq that it will face serious consequences as a result of its continued violations of its obligations. The resolution then provided Iraq a "final opportunity" to comply, but stated specifically that violations by Iraq of its obligations under resolution 1441 (2002) to present a currently accurate, full and complete declaration of all aspects of its weapons of mass destruction programmes and to comply with and cooperate fully in the implementation of the resolution would constitute a further material breach.
>
> The Government of Iraq decided not to avail itself of its final opportunity under resolution 1441 (2002) and has clearly committed additional violations. In view of Iraq's material breaches, the basis of the ceasefire has been removed and use of force is authorized under resolution 678 (1990).[32]

Following the invasion and the failure to find any weapons of mass destruction, the Bush administration provided additional justifications for the invasion. The administration invoked Hussein's human rights record, the need to bring democracy to the Middle East and Hussein's use of poisonous gas against the Kurds as additional justifications for the U.S. invasion.[33] A number of administration officials continued to link Hussein to the 9/11 attacks, even though there was no evidence linking Hussein to the 9/11 terrorists.

The legal basis for the United States' justifications is questionable. Although resolution 678 (1990) did authorize the U.S.-led coalition to free Kuwait and to "restore peace and security in the area," that authorization is said to have expired with the adoption of resolution 687 (1991), which formally approved the ceasefire between Iraq and the allies.[34] The United States never made a persuasive argument about the survivability of resolution 678 (1990). The mere fact that the Bush administration pushed for the adoption of resolution 1441 (2002) and introduced a second draft resolution seeking authorization from the Security Council to invade Iraq was indicative that the administration did not believe that resolutions 678 (1990) and 1441(2002) provided the necessary legal authorization to use force against Iraq.

Resolution 1441 (2002) threatened Iraq with "serious consequences" if it did not comply with all Security Council resolutions, and it placed any future decision on how to proceed if Iraq failed to comply with its obligation in the hands of the Security Council.[35] The United States had no legal authority to act unilaterally without the authorization of the Security Council. On the issue of Iraq's possession of weapons of mass destruction, mere possession of such weapons does not give rise to self-defense. Consequently, the United States had no legal justification for invading Iraq. The U.S. invasion was a blatant violation of international law and the Charter of the United Nations.

Following the President's announcement of the end of major combat, President Bush returned to the United Nations to seek international support for stabilizing the post-war situation in Iraq and to seek assistance in Iraq's reconstruction.[36] Having invaded Iraq without authorization from the Security Council, President Bush was keenly aware that he needed the legitimacy of the Security Council in order to sustain a prolonged U.S. occupation of Iraq. President Bush sought a resolution from the Security Council granting the United States and Britain the authority to occupy Iraq indefinitely. The return of the Bush administration to the United Nations was a vindication for opponents of the war. Despite scorning the United Nations, President Bush realized the United States needed to legalize the post-war occupation regime in Iraq, which only the United Nations could do.[37]

On May 22 the Security Council adopted resolution 1483 (2003) by which it recognized the United States and the United Kingdom as the "occupying powers" under unified command as the "Authority." The Security Council appealed to all states and organizations to assist the people of Iraq in their efforts to reform their institutions and to rebuild their country, and to contribute to conditions of stability and security in Iraq in accordance with this resolution.[38] The resolution called on the Secretary General to appoint a Special Representative for Iraq with broad authority to coordinate the various activities of the United Nations and other international agencies engaged in humanitarian assistance and post-conflict reconstruction activities in Iraq.[39] Finally, the resolution terminated the economic sanctions imposed on Iraq under resolutions 661 (1990) and 778 (1992), but it maintained the arms embargo.[40]

The Security Council subsequently adopted a series of resolutions on the situation in Iraq. Among them is resolution 1500 (2003) by which the Security Council established the United Nations Assistance Mission for Iraq (UNAMI) to assist the Secretary General in fulfilling his mandate under resolution 1483 (2003). On October 16 the Security Council adopted resolution 1511 (2003) by which it authorized the multinational force under unified command to take all necessary measures to contribute to the maintenance of security and stability in Iraq. On June 8, 2008 the Security Council adopted 1546 (2004) to endorse the formation of a sovereign Interim Government of Iraq, and welcomed the end of the Coalition Provisional Authority (CPA) and the resumption of Iraq's sovereignty. The resolution strengthened the role of the Special Representative of the Secretary General and the United Nations Assistance for Mission for Iraq (UNAMI). The resolution acknowledged the presence of the multinational force in Iraq as being there at the request of the incoming Interim Government of Iraq and it reaffirmed the authorization for the multinational force under unified command established under resolution 1511 (2003). Furthermore, resolution 1546 (2004) "Decides that the multinational force shall have the authority to take all necessary measures to contribute to the maintenance of security and stability in Iraq in accordance with the letters annexed to this resolution expressing, *inter alia,* the Iraqi request for the continuing presence of the multinational force and setting out its tasks, including by preventing and deterring terrorism. . . ."[41] The resolution also lifted the arms embargo against the government of Iraq and the multinational force.[42]

On November 28, 2006 the Security Council adopted yet another resolution on Iraq by which it extended the mandate of the multinational force until December 31, 2007 in accordance with the wishes of the Iraqi Government.[43] A subsequent resolution terminated the mandate of UNMOVIC and the IAEA under the relevant resolutions.[44] On December 18, 2007 the Security Council adopted resolution 1790 (2007) by which it extended the mandate of the multinational force until December 31, 2008, or earlier if the government of Iraq so requested. None of the Security Council resolutions addressed the legality of the United States' invasion of Iraq. The Security Council's failure to issue a statement against the United States invasion has led some to assume that the Security Council had by default approved the United States' invasion *post facto*.

In spite of the Security Council's *post hoc* legitimization of the United States' invasion of Iraq, the invasion was nonetheless a violation of Articles 2(4) and 51 of the United Nations Charter, various resolutions of the General Assembly, including the Resolution on Friendly Relations [2625 (XXV) 1970], the Resolution on the Inadmissibility of Intervention in the Internal and External Affairs of States [2131 (XX) 1965], and the Resolution on the Definition of Aggression [3314 (XXIV) 1974].[45] The invasion of Iraq was also a violation of fundamental principles of international law and of the sovereignty and independence of Iraq. The invasion violated resolution 1514 (XV) of 1960, the right of self-determination of peoples.[46] The conduct of the war in Iraq, the post-war occupation of the country and the behavior of American forces in Iraq in quelling insurgent attacks against U.S. troops constitutes a gross violation of provisions of the Geneva Conventions of 1949 and other international humanitarian law.[47] The mistreatment of Iraqi civilians and detainees also violates Common Article III of the Geneva Conventions and the laws and customs of war.[48] Change of Iraq's laws and to the privatization of Iraq's economy by the Coalition Provisional Authority also violated provisions of the Geneva Conventions of 1949 and the obligations of the United States as an occupying power.

The Pentagon conducted several investigations into allegations of widespread abuses by U.S. forces, including the killing of civilians in U.S. custody and the mistreatment of detainees. But none of these investigations have found evidence of culpability on the part of senior Pentagon officials. The court martial of several low level military officers for their role in the abuse of Iraqi detainees has occurred, but no charges against high level officials in the Bush administration for dereliction of duties has taken place. Justice Department memoranda, which authorized torture and other harsh interrogation techniques to gain evidence from detainees, created a climate in which military officers felt they could violate international humanitarian law with impunity.[49] The reports did not recommend any disciplinary measures against high-ranking officials.

With the war in Iraq now in its sixth year and President Bush's tenure as President about to expire, the Bush administration has tried to expand the role of the United Nations in Iraq. A United Nations commission is working on resolving a potential ethnic conflict between Kurds and Arabs in the northern city of Kirkuk. It is also negotiating a formula for ownership over the vast oil deposits in the semi-autonomous northern region, which is under the control of the Kurdish majority. The United Nations has also reopened its office in Baghdad and is providing assistance to the Iraqi Government to organize municipal elections. At the same time the Bush administration has kept the United Nations out of the discussions over the continuing presence of U.S. troops in Iraq after the United Nations mandate expires on December 31, 2008. The Bush administration has negotiated a Status of Forces Agreement (SOFA) with Iraq that would allow U.S. troops to operate in Iraq with impunity. The agreement calls for the withdrawal of U.S. troops from major Iraqi cities in June 2009 and deployment only with the consent of the Iraqi Prime Minister. However, the agreement continues to shield U.S. forces from Iraqi law. The agreement also does not clarify when U.S. forces can act unilaterally without the consent of the Iraqi government. The agreement calls for U.S. troops to withdraw from Iraq by 2011. But the decision to withdraw is dependent on the security situation in Iraq, as determined by the United States. A major disagreement remains between Iraq and the United States over certain provisions of the agreement.[50] The Bush administration wants to finalize the agreement before it leaves office. However, the Shiite-dominated Iraqi government has concerns about the political implications of a continuing U.S. troop presence in Iraq.[51]

Under President Bush relations between the United States and the United Nations have not been held in high esteem, and the Iraq invasion made the relationship worse. The United Nations was a low priority for the administration until September 11 when President Bush needed the support of the international community to fight his war on terror. Bush skillfully manipulated the United Nations system to legitimize his war on terror but abandoned the organization when support for his war in Iraq evaporated.

Both President Bush and his allies in Congress criticized the United Nations for not supporting U.S. goals in Iraq. Many Congressional Republicans and Bush administration officials began a crusade to reform the United Nations.[52] As a result of calls from the United States for reforming the United Nations the Secretary General convened a High Level Panel on Threats, Challenges and Change to examine ways to improve the capacity of the United Nations to meet the challenges of the twenty-first century. In its report the Panel called for expanding the definition of security to include non-military threats, enhancing the collective security system to include conflict prevention and institutional reform within the United Nations.[53]

The Bush administration reacted positively to the Panel's report but stopped short of endorsing it. The administration has paid more attention to the Volcker investigation into the Oil-for-Food Program and a simultaneous Congressional investigation into corruption in the program. When preliminary findings implicated the Secretary General's son and members of the U.N., Senator Norm Coleman personally called for Annan's resignation. The Bush administration neither affirmed its support for Annan nor condemned Coleman for his comment.

In his second term President Bush nominated John Bolton as his Ambassador to the United Nations, but Bolton failed to win Senate confirmation because of his harsh criticism of the United Nations. President Bush used a recess appointment to circumvent the Senate filibuster and appointed Bolton to serve until the next Congress convenes in 2007.[54] Bolton opposed language in the Secretary General's recommendations for reforming the United Nations, and he also objected to language in the final document that the Summit of World Leaders in September 2005 was supposed to sign.[55] The Bush administration opposed expansion of the Security Council to twenty-five members, including five new permanent members. The administration also opposed the Secretary General's Millennium Development Goals and efforts to strengthen the capacity of the United Nations.

In testimony before the Senate Foreign Relations Committee in July 2005, the Undersecretary for Political Affairs, Nicholas Burns, articulated the administration's position on reforming the United Nations as follows:

> **Reforming Priority No. 1: Budget and Management Reforms**
>
> The United States has consistently pressed the United Nations to undertake meaningful management, administrative, and budgetary reforms to make it more efficient, effective, and responsive. Budgetary discipline, accountability, and program relevancy are critical to these goals . . . In particular, for accountability, we want to boost the resources and independence of the Office of Internal Oversight Services, and an expanding role for this Office in peacekeeping and small agencies. For effectiveness, we seek consolidation of UN Information Centers, and rationalization of conferences. To boost relevance, the Secretary General's authority to re-deploy positions should be used and expanded, and all ongoing UN programs should be reviewed for continued relevancy and effectiveness.
>
> **Reforming Priority No. 2: Effective Human Rights Mechanism**
>
> We must recognize the way the United Nations works to protect Human Rights throughout the world. The United States supports the creation of a UN mechanism

such as the Human Rights Council proposal by the Secretary General to address more effectively the most serious human rights situations. We also believe that the Council's mandate should be to take effective action to address the most egregious human rights violations such as systematic torture or wide-scale deprivation of freedom of expression and assembly.

In regard to structure, we support a standing, action-oriented Council that downplays thematic resolutions. We also believe the Council should be a General Assembly subsidiary, pending a decision whether to create a stand-alone Charter body, because it would be easier and faster to implement. The membership should be limited—20 is ideal—and exclude nations under Security Council sanctions. Seats would be filled through elections to two-year terms with regional allocations.

Members of the Council should have a solid human rights records and states would have to secure two-thirds vote to be elected. Countries subject to Security Council sanctions or [a UN Security Council]-authored Commission of Inquiry would be ineligible. Elected Council members should affirm they will live up to the standards of the Universal Declaration of Human Rights.

Reforming Priority No. 3: Creation of a Peacebuilding Commission

We need a Peacebuilding Commission to provide recommendations on post-conflict situations and on bridging between peacekeeping missions, reconstruction and stabilization efforts. A [Peacebuilding] Commission should be set up to work in an advisory capacity to the Security Council on specific conflict situations as requested by the Council. The Commission's tasks would also include serving as a focal point for donor coordination. We believe participation in the core Commission should be limited to about 20 members and should include the five permanent Security Council members, five major donor nations, three major troop contributors, five representatives of [the Economic and Social Council], the World Bank and [International Monetary Fund]; and a UN system representative selected by the Secretary General. The Commission would provide advice to the Security Council on a consensus basis.

Reforming Priority No. 4: Economic Development

Building on the 2002 Monterrey Conference on Financing for Development, our approach emphasizes national responsibility, rule of law, governments accountable to the people, and sound economic policies. Such an enabling framework for development provides the essential context necessary for countries to make effective use of all available resources, public and private, foreign and domestic.

Reforming Priority No. 5: Democracy Fund

At last year's General Assembly, President Bush called for the establishment of a UN Democracy Fund and we have worked diligently with the UN Secretariat and other interested member states to make this initiative a reality. The Democracy

Fund will provide grants and in-kind assistance for democracy promotion efforts to expand the reach of freedom around the world. Several other nations, including India, Hungary and South Korea have expressed support for the Fund. Allies such as the United Kingdom and France have signed on and intend to contribute. Secretary General Annan highlighted the idea in his report "In Larger Freedom," issued proposed Terms of Reference, and on July 4th at the African Union Summit announced its establishment. . . .

Reforming Priority No. 6: Counter-Terrorism

We are in agreement with the counter-terrorism strategy proposed by the Secretary General, but do not agree with all its elements. Regarding a definition of terrorism, the U.S. welcomes the position, contained in the Secretary General's report, that the right to resist occupation does not justify the targeting and killing of civilians. We do not, however, want the effort to come to agreement on a definition of terrorism to distract from the more important task of moving forward on completion of the Comprehensive Convention on International Terrorism.[56]

Burns concluded his testimony with the United States' views on the issue of enlargement of the Security Council. He said the United States strongly supports a permanent seat for Japan and would support two or more new permanent members and two or three non-permanent members. However, the United States was more interested in an effective Security Council. Additionally, he said that discussion about expansion of the Security Council should not divert attention from, and delay action on, other important UN reforms.

The administration's commitment to reforming the United Nations was tested when the General Assembly adopted a resolution to establish the new United Nations Human Rights Council to replace the United Nations Human Rights Commission, which the United States said made a mockery of human rights by allowing countries that knowingly violate human rights, such as Sudan, Zimbabwe and Cuba, to sit on the commission. The United States was the lone Western country to vote against the resolution. In opposing the resolution the United States ambassador, John Bolton, said the text had not improved sufficiently to warrant U.S. support.[57]

Membership on the new Council will be restricted to countries with a good record on human rights, and their performance will be monitored periodically. Countries will be elected to the Council on an individual basis, not through regional grouping, as is currently the case under the Commission. Council members will be elected by an absolute vote of ninety-six members to be appointed to the Council. The United States declined to seek a seat on the new Human Rights

Council in part because it could not get the ninety-six votes required to gain a seat on the Council.[58] The United States was also concerned that new revelations about its secret prisons, allegations of detainee abuse and extraordinary rendition of suspected terrorists to countries that knowingly practice torture would make it difficult to win the backing of a majority of countries.

Given setbacks in Iraq and Afghanistan, the Bush administration has looked to improve relations with the United Nations. The administration appointed Zalmay Khalilzad to succeed John Bolton, who did nothing to repair U.S. image in the organization. The Bush administration also pushed for the appointment of Ban Ki-moon as the successor to Kofi Annan as the next Secretary General of the United Nations. Ban Ki-moon has been less vocal in his criticism of Bush's policies than Kofi Annan was. In his final address to the General Assembly, President Bush called for a greater role for the United Nations in tackling global problems. Mr. Bush spoke passionately about the work of the United Nations and other multilateral institutions and praised them for their contributions to solving complex global problems. Mr. Bush spoke like someone who had recently discovered the United Nations, instead of the President who had defied the organization during the past seven years. Unfortunately, Mr. Bush's sudden change of heart toward the United Nations seems a bit disingenuous.[59]

Endnotes

1. Akehurst, Michael. 1967. Enforcement action by regional agencies, with special reference to the Organization of American States, *Brit. Y.B.I.L.*, 42: 175.
2. G.A. Res. 3379, adopted on Nov. 10, 1975, by a vote of 72 to 35 with 32 abstentions.
3. G.A. Res. A/RES/38/7 (1983). The vote was 108-9-29.
4. Senate Res. 687 (1991).
5. Senate Res. 688 (1991).
6. G.A. Res. A/RES/44/240 (1989). The vote was 75-20-40.
7. Gray, Christine. 2002. From unity to polarisation: International law and the use of force against Iraq, *Eur. J. Intl'L*, 13:11–12.
8. Ibid., 12–13.
9. Wedgwood, Ruth. Unilateral action in a multilateral world. In Patrick and Forman, eds., *supra.* note 198, 182.
10. Simma, Bruno. 1999. NATO, the UN and the use of force: Legal aspects, *Eur. J. Int'l L.*, 10:1.
11. Cassese, Antonio. 1999. Ex iniura ius oritur: Are we moving towards international legitimization of forcible humanitarian counter measures in the world community? *Eur. J.Int'l L*, 10:23.

12. Senate Res. 940 (1994).
13. Senate Res. 1244 (1999).
14. Patrick, Stewart. 2002. Multilateralism and its discontents: The causes and consequences of U.S. ambivalence. In *Multilateralism & U.S. foreign policy,* ed. Stewart Patrick and Shepard Forman, 33.
15. See Jules Lobel and Michael Ratner, 1999, Bypassing the Security Council: Ambiguous authorization to use force, cease-fires and the Iraq inspection regime, *AJIL* 93:124.
16. Patrick, Stewart. 2002. Multilateralism and its discontents: The causes and consequences of U.S. ambivalence. In *Multilateralism & U.S. foreign policy,* ed. Stewart Patrick and Shepard Forman, 3.
17. Rice, Condoleeza Rice. 2000. Campaign 200-Promoting the national interest, *For. Aff.*, Jan.–Feb., 79:47.
18. Zoellick, Robert. Campaign 200—Republican foreign policy, *For. Aff.*, Jan.–Feb., 79:69.
19. Mahbubani, Kishore. 2003. The United Nations and the United States: An indispensable partnership. In *Unilateralism and U.S. foreign policy,* ed. David M. Malone and Yuen Foong, 138, 143.
20. Deller, Nicole, Arjun Makhijani, and John Burroughs, eds. 2003, *Rule of power or rule of law?* 16; Sean Murphy, 2002, Contemporary practice of the United States relating to international law, *AJIL* 96:256.
21. President's Remarks at the United Nations General Assembly (Nov. 11, 2001), at *www.whitehouse.gov/news/releases/2001/11/20011110-3.html*
22. President's Remarks at the United Nations General Assembly (Sept. 9, 2002), at *www.whitehouse.gov/nws/releases/2002/09/20020912-1.html*
23. Bush State of the Union Address (Jan. 29, 2002), at *http://www.whitehouse.gov/news/releases/2002/01.*
24. Joint Resolution to Authorize the Use of United States Armed Forces Against Iraq, Pubic Law No. 107-40 (Sept. 18, 2002) and signed by President Bush on Oct. 2, 2002, at *http://www.whitehouse.gov/news/releases/2002/10/20021002-2.html;* See David E. Sanger and Eric Schmitt, 2002, House, in 296-133 vote, backs Bush on using force in Iraq, citing continuing threat. *New York Times,* Oct. 11, A1.
25. Preston, Julia. 2002. 'Big 5' at the United Nations still jockeying over Iraq text. *New York Times,* Oct. 22, A10.
26. Lynch, Colum. 2002. France and Russia raise new objections to Iraq plan. *Wash. Post,* Oct. 23, A1.
27. Senate Res. 1441 (2002), para. 13, adopted on Nov. 8, 2002; See Colum Lynch, 2002, U.N. orders Iraq to disarm, *Wash. Post,* Nov. 9, A1.
28. Blix, Han. 2003. An Update on Inspection, Jan. 27, at *http://www.un.org/Depts/unmovic/Bx27.htm;* Mohamed ElBaradei, 2003, The Status of Nuclear Inspections in Iraq, Jan.27, at *http://www.iaea.org/worldatom/Press/Statements/2003/ebsp2003n003.shtml.*

29. Secretary of State Colin Powell's Address Before the Security Council (Feb. 5, 2003), at *http://www.un.org/pubs/chronicle/2003/issue1/01003p70.html.*
30. Stevenson, Richard W. Bush gives Hussein 48 hours and vows to act. *New York Times,* Mar. 18, A1.
31. See Congressional Research Service, U.S. Use Of Preemptive Military Force (CRS Order Code RS21311, updated Apr. 11, 2003).
32. Letter dated 20 March 2003 from the Permanent Representative of the United States of America to the United Nations Addressed to the President of the Security Council, UN Doc. S/2003/351 (Mar. 31, 2003).
33. Dobbs, Michael. 2003. Wolfowitz shifts rationales on Iraq war. *Wash. Post,* Sept. 30, A23; Rajiv Chandrasekaran, 2003, Powell says gas attack on Kurds justified war. *Wash. Post,* Sept. 16, A14.
34. Gray, Christine Gray. 1994. After the ceasefire: Iraq, the Security Council and the use of force, *Brit. Y.B.I.L.,* 45:143.
35. Hofmann, Rainer, *supra.* note 140, 25.
36. Harding, James. 2003. Defiant Bush seeks aid on Iraq. *Fin. Times,* Sept. 24, 1.
37. Allen, Mike, and Vernon Loeb. 2003. U.S. Wants Larger U.N. Role in Iraq. *Wash. Post,* Sept. 3, A1.
38. Senate Res. 1483 (2003), adopted on May 22, 2003.
39. *Para. 8* of SC/Res. 1483 (2003).
40. *Para. 10* of SC/Res. 1483 (2003).
41. *Para. 10* of SC/Res. 1546 (2004).
42. *Para. 21* of SC/Res. 1546 (2004).
43. SC/Res. 1723 (2006).
44. SC/Res. 1762 (2007).
45. See ICJ Ruling in Military and Paramilitary Activities in and Against Nicaragua (*Nicaragua v. United States of America*), ICJ Report (1986).
46. These principles have been recognized by the international community as *jus cogens.*
47. Hensel, Howard. 2005. *The law of armed conflict,* 152.
48. Ibid.
49. Cornett, Lind, and Mark Gibney. 2005. The rights of detainees: Determining the limits of law. In *Contemporary cases in U.S. foreign policy,* ed. Ralph G. Carter, 434–35.
50. Rubin, Alissa J., and Katherine Zoepe. 2008. Iraqi cabinet wants proposed security agreement altered. *New York Times,* Oct. 22, A6.
51. Khalaf, Roula. 2008. Between Iraq's needs and dreams. *Fin. Times,* Oct. 28, 13.
52. See Rice urges changes at U.N., 2005, *Wash. Post,* April 16, A5.
53. A More Secure World: Our Shared Responsibility, Report of the High-Level Panel on Threats, Challenges and Change, UN Doc. A/59/565 (2004), 8.
54. Bumiller, Elisabeth, and Sheryl Gay Stolberg. 2005. President sends Bolton to U.N.; bypasses the Senate. *New York Times,* Aug. 2, A1.

55. Hodge, Warren. 2005. Bolton pushes UN on change as U.S. objects to draft plan. *New York Times,* Aug. 25, A6.
56. Burns, R. Nicholas on United Nations Reform, Testimony as Prepared Before the Senate Foreign Relations Committee (July 21, 2005), at *http://www.state.gov/p/us/rm/2005/49900.htm.*
57. Turner, Mark. 2006. UN human rights vote leaves U.S. isolated. *Fin. Times,* Mar. 16, 8; Warren Hodge, 2006, As U.S. dissents, UN approves a new council on rights abuse. *New York Times,* Mar. 16, A3.
58. Hodge, Warren. 2006. U.S. won't seek a seat on the UN rights council. *New York Times,* April 7, A6.
59. President Bush Addresses the United Nations General Assembly, at *www.whitehouse.gov/news/releases/2008/09/20080923-5.html.*

chapter X

CONCLUSION

The attitude of the Bush administration toward international law and institutions has adversely affected the credibility of the United States abroad and undermined compliance with international law by other nations. The actions of the United States have alienated traditional U.S. allies, emboldened U.S. enemies and created a climate of lawlessness in the international system. More states are now willing to skirt their international legal obligations as a result of following the example of the United States. The Bush administration's selective compliance with international law to advance a very narrowly defined foreign policy objective has undermined the rule-based legal order established after World War II. The failure of the Bush administration to provide global leadership on key international legal issues is a sharp departure from the practices of the United States in international affairs.

The Bush administration has adopted a very hostile attitude toward international law and institutions. Although not new in U.S. foreign policy, the Bush administration has taken that attitude to a new level. The policy of the Bush administration has significantly undermined respect for the rule of law in international affairs and created a climate of lawlessness in the international community unprecedented in the history of modern diplomacy.

The Bush administration's war on terror has severely diminished the reputation of the United States abroad and complicated its long-term effort to combat terrorism. The United States can no longer be relied upon to provide the kind of moral leadership in the world that it is best known for. Under President Bush the United States has become the great outlaw nation that is incapable of providing global leadership on key international issues. It will take decades to repair the damage this administration has done to the U.S. image abroad.

The United States played a leadership role in the development of a rule-based post-war international legal order and has long held a tradition of respect for human rights and the rule of law in international relations. But under President Bush that tradition has become significantly compromised. The United States is now in the same category as such nations as Iran, Sudan and North Korea, countries it once criticized as evil and undemocratic. The failure of the Bush administration to comply with international law and fundamental principles of human rights and humanitarian law has done irreparable harm to America's standing in the world.

The next President will inherit a number of outstanding international law issues that this President deliberately left unresolved. The most critical is how to bring to an end the so-called war on terror and the war in Iraq and what to do with the thousands of detainees at Guantánamo Bay and in Iraq and Afghanistan, as well as in prisons around the world. Secondly, the next President has to decide whether the United States resigns the Rome Statute for an International Criminal Court, signs the Kyoto Protocol or negotiates a new climate accord, as well as whether to revive the Doha trade round and revise pending bilateral free trade agreements between the United States and several nations that Congress is currently holding up. The next President must pursue the Senate to ratify the Law of the Sea Treaty, various human rights conventions and conventions to amend the Convention on Conventional Weapons. The next President will also have to repair the damage done to U.S. reputation in the wake of the Iraq invasion and the allegations of torture of detainees in U.S. custody. Furthermore, the next President must find a less confrontational diplomatic approach to Iran and North Korea's nuclear weapons programs. The next President will also have to contemplate the establishment of a new global regulatory regime to deal with the current financial crisis. Finally, the next President will need to reevaluate U.S. global leadership in multilateral institutions in light of the decline of U.S. economic and political influence in the world. The emerging new world order will require the United States to play by the rules like every other nation, instead of making the rules and taking exception to complying with the rules.

appendix I

GENEVA CONVENTION III (1949)

Convention (III) relative to the Treatment of Prisoners of War. Geneva, 12 August 1949.

PREAMBLE

The undersigned Plenipotentiaries of the Governments represented at the Diplomatic Conference held at Geneva from April 21 to August 12, 1949, for the purpose of revising the Convention concluded at Geneva on July 27, 1929, relative to the Treatment of Prisoners of War, have agreed as follows:

PART I. GENERAL PROVISIONS

ART. 1. The High Contracting Parties undertake to respect and to ensure respect for the present Convention in all circumstances.

ART. 2. In addition to the provisions which shall be implemented in peace time, the present Convention shall apply to all cases of declared war or of any other armed conflict which may arise between two or more of the High Contracting Parties, even if the state of war is not recognized by one of them.

The Convention shall also apply to all cases of partial or total occupation of the territory of a High Contracting Party, even if the said occupation meets with no armed resistance.

Although one of the Powers in conflict may not be a party to the present Convention, the Powers who are parties thereto shall remain bound by it in their mutual relations. They shall furthermore be bound by the Convention in relation to the said Power, if the latter accepts and applies the provisions thereof.

ART. 3. In the case of armed conflict not of an international character occurring in the territory of one of the High Contracting Parties, each Party to the conflict shall be bound to apply, as a minimum, the following provisions:

1. Persons taking no active part in the hostilities, including members of armed forces who have laid down their arms and those placed hors de combat by sickness, wounds, detention, or any other cause, shall in all circumstances be treated humanely, without any adverse distinction founded on race, colour, religion or faith, sex, birth or wealth, or any other similar criteria. To this end the following acts are and shall remain prohibited at any time and in any place whatsoever with respect to the above-mentioned persons:
   - **a.** violence to life and person, in particular murder of all kinds, mutilation, cruel treatment and torture;
   - **b.** taking of hostages;
   - **c.** outrages upon personal dignity, in particular, humiliating and degrading treatment;
   - **d.** the passing of sentences and the carrying out of executions without previous judgment pronounced by a regularly constituted court affording all the judicial guarantees which are recognized as indispensable by civilized peoples.
2. The wounded and sick shall be collected and cared for.

An impartial humanitarian body, such as the International Committee of the Red Cross, may offer its services to the Parties to the conflict.

The Parties to the conflict should further endeavour to bring into force, by means of special agreements, all or part of the other provisions of the present Convention.

The application of the preceding provisions shall not affect the legal status of the Parties to the conflict.

Art. 4

A. Prisoners of war, in the sense of the present Convention, are persons belonging to one of the following categories, who have fallen into the power of the enemy:

1. Members of the armed forces of a Party to the conflict, as well as members of militias or volunteer corps forming part of such armed forces.
2. Members of other militias and members of other volunteer corps, including those of organized resistance movements, belonging to a Party to the conflict and operating in or outside their own territory, even if this territory is occupied, provided that such militias or volunteer corps, including such organized resistance movements, fulfill the following conditions:
   - **a.** that of being commanded by a person responsible for his subordinates;
   - **b.** that of having a fixed distinctive sign recognizable at a distance;
   - **c.** that of carrying arms openly;
   - **d.** that of conducting their operations in accordance with the laws and customs of war.
3. Members of regular armed forces who profess allegiance to a government or an authority not recognized by the Detaining Power.
4. Persons who accompany the armed forces without actually being members thereof, such as civilian members of military aircraft crews, war correspondents, supply contractors, members of labour units or of services responsible for the welfare of the armed forces, provided that they have received authorization, from the armed forces which they accompany, who shall provide them for that purpose with an identity card similar to the annexed model.
5. Members of crews, including masters, pilots and apprentices, of the merchant marine and the crews of civil aircraft of the Parties to the conflict, who do not benefit by more favourable treatment under any other provisions of international law.
6. Inhabitants of a non-occupied territory, who on the approach of the enemy spontaneously take up arms to resist the invading forces, without having had time to form themselves into regular armed units, provided they carry arms openly and respect the laws and customs of war.

B. The following shall likewise be treated as prisoners of war under the present Convention:

1. Persons belonging, or having belonged, to the armed forces of the occupied country, if the occupying Power considers it necessary by reason of such allegiance to intern them, even though it has originally liberated them while hostilities were going on outside the territory it occupies, in particular where such persons have made an unsuccessful attempt to rejoin the armed forces to which they belong and which are engaged in combat, or where they fail to comply with a summons made to them with a view to internment.
2. The persons belonging to one of the categories enumerated in the present Article, who have been received by neutral or non-belligerent Powers on their territory and whom these Powers are required to intern under international law, without prejudice to any more favourable treatment which these Powers may choose to give and with the exception of Articles 8, 10, 15, 30, fifth paragraph, 58–67, 92, 126 and, where diplomatic relations exist between the Parties to the conflict and the neutral or non-belligerent Power concerned, those Articles concerning the Protecting Power. Where such diplomatic relations exist, the Parties to a conflict on whom these persons depend shall be allowed to perform towards them the functions of a Protecting Power as provided in the present Convention, without prejudice to the functions which these Parties normally exercise in conformity with diplomatic and consular usage and treaties.

C. This Article shall in no way affect the status of medical personnel and chaplains as provided for in Article 33 of the present Convention.

ART. 5. The present Convention shall apply to the persons referred to in Article 4 from the time they fall into the power of the enemy and until their final release and repatriation.

Should any doubt arise as to whether persons, having committed a belligerent act and having fallen into the hands of the enemy, belong to any of the categories enumerated in Article 4, such persons shall enjoy the protection of the present Convention until such time as their status has been determined by a competent tribunal.

ART. 6. In addition to the agreements expressly provided for in Articles 10, 23, 28, 33, 60, 65, 66, 67, 72, 73, 75, 109, 110, 118, 119, 122 and 132, the High Contracting Parties may conclude other special agreements for all matters concerning which they may deem it suitable to make separate provision. No special agreement shall adversely affect the situation of prisoners of war, as defined by the present Convention, nor restrict the rights, which it confers upon them.

Prisoners of war shall continue to have the benefit of such agreements as long as the Convention is applicable to them, except where express provisions to the contrary are contained in the aforesaid or in subsequent agreements, or where more favourable measures have been taken with regard to them by one or other of the Parties to the conflict.

ART. 7. Prisoners of war may in no circumstances renounce in part or in entirety the rights secured to them by the present Convention, and by the special agreements referred to in the foregoing Article, if such there be.

ART. 8. The present Convention shall be applied with the cooperation and under the scrutiny of the Protecting Powers whose duty it is to safeguard the interests of the Parties to the conflict. For this purpose, the Protecting Powers may appoint, apart from their diplomatic or consular staff, delegates from amongst their own nationals or the nationals of other neutral Powers. The said delegates shall be subject to the approval of the Power with which they are to carry out their duties.

The Parties to the conflict shall facilitate to the greatest extent possible the task of the representatives or delegates of the Protecting Powers.

The representatives or delegates of the Protecting Powers shall not in any case exceed their mission under the present Convention. They shall, in particular, take account of the imperative necessities of security of the State wherein they carry out their duties.

ART. 9. The provisions of the present Convention constitute no obstacle to the humanitarian activities which the International Committee of the Red Cross or any other impartial humanitarian organization may, subject to the consent of the Parties to the conflict concerned, undertake for the protection of prisoners of war and for their relief.

ART. 10. The High Contracting Parties may at any time agree to entrust to an organization, which offers all guarantees of impartiality and efficacy the duties incumbent on the Protecting Powers by virtue of the present Convention.

When prisoners of war do not benefit or cease to benefit, no matter for what reason, by the activities of a Protecting Power or of an organization provided for in the first paragraph above, the Detaining Power shall request a neutral State, or such an organization, to undertake the functions performed under the present Convention by a Protecting Power designated by the Parties to a conflict.

If protection cannot be arranged accordingly, the Detaining Power shall request or shall accept, subject to the provisions of this Article, the offer of the services of a humanitarian organization, such as the International Committee of the Red Cross to assume the humanitarian functions performed by Protecting Powers under the present Convention.

Any neutral Power or any organization invited by the Power concerned or offering itself for these purposes, shall be required to act with a sense of responsibility towards the Party to the conflict on which persons protected by the present Convention depend, and shall be required to furnish sufficient assurances that it is in a position to undertake the appropriate functions and to discharge them impartially.

No derogation from the preceding provisions shall be made by special agreements between Powers one of which is restricted, even temporarily, in its freedom to negotiate with the other Power or its allies by reason of military events, more particularly where the whole, or a substantial part, of the territory of the said Power is occupied.

Whenever in the present Convention mention is made of a Protecting Power, such mention applies to substitute organizations in the sense of the present Article.

ART. 11. In cases where they deem it advisable in the interest of protected persons, particularly in cases of disagreement between the Parties to the conflict as to the application or interpretation of the provisions of the present Convention, the Protecting Powers shall lend their good offices with a view to settling the disagreement.

For this purpose, each of the Protecting Powers may, either at the invitation of one Party or on its own initiative, propose to the Parties to the conflict a meeting of their representatives, and in particular of the authorities responsible for prisoners of war, possibly on neutral territory suitably chosen. The Parties to the conflict shall be bound to give effect to the proposals made to them for this purpose. The Protecting Powers may, if necessary, propose for approval by the Parties to the conflict a person belonging to a neutral Power, or delegated by the International Committee of the Red Cross, who shall be invited to take part in such a meeting.

PART II. GENERAL PROTECTION OF PRISONERS OF WAR

ART. 12. Prisoners of war are in the hands of the enemy Power, but not of the individuals or military units who have captured them. Irrespective of the individual responsibilities that may exist, the Detaining Power is responsible for the treatment given them.

Prisoners of war may only be transferred by the Detaining Power to a Power which is a party to the Convention and after the Detaining Power has satisfied itself of the willingness and ability of such transferee Power to apply the Convention. When prisoners of war are transferred under such circumstances, responsibility for the application of the Convention rests on the Power accepting them while they are in its custody.

Nevertheless, if that Power fails to carry out the provisions of the Convention in any important respect, the Power by whom the prisoners of war were transferred shall, upon being notified by the Protecting Power, take effective measures to correct the situation or shall request the return of the prisoners of war. Such requests must be complied with.

Art. 13. Prisoners of war must at all times be humanely treated. Any unlawful act or omission by the Detaining Power causing death or seriously endangering the health of a prisoner of war in its custody is prohibited, and will be regarded as a serious breach of the present Convention. In particular, no prisoner of war may be subjected to physical mutilation or to medical or scientific experiments of any kind, which are not justified by the medical, dental, or hospital treatment of the prisoner concerned and carried out in his interest.

Likewise, prisoners of war must at all times be protected, particularly against acts of violence or intimidation and against insults and public curiosity.

Measures of reprisal against prisoners of war are prohibited.

Art. 14. Prisoners of war are entitled in all circumstances to respect for their persons and their honour.

Women shall be treated with all the regard due to their sex and shall in all cases benefit by treatment as favourable as that granted to men.

Prisoners of war shall retain the full civil capacity, which they enjoyed at the time of their capture. The Detaining Power may not restrict the exercise, either within or without its own territory, of the rights such capacity confers except in so far as the captivity requires.

Art. 15. The Power detaining prisoners of war shall be bound to provide free of charge for their maintenance and for the medical attention required by their state of health.

Art. 16. Taking into consideration the provisions of the present Convention relating to rank and sex, and subject to any privileged treatment which may be accorded to them by reason of their state of health, age or professional qualifications, all prisoners of war shall be treated alike by the Detaining Power, without any adverse distinction based on race, nationality, religious belief or political opinions, or any other distinction founded on similar criteria.

PART III. CAPTIVITY

Section 1. Beginning of Captivity

ART. 17. Every prisoner of war, when questioned on the subject, is bound to give only his surname, first names and rank, date of birth, and army, regimental, personal or serial number, or failing this, equivalent information.

If he willfully infringes this rule, he may render himself liable to a restriction of the privileges accorded to his rank or status.

Each Party to a conflict is required to furnish the persons under its jurisdiction who are liable to become prisoners of war, with an identity card showing the owner's surname, first names, rank, army, regimental, personal or serial number or equivalent information, and date of birth. The identity card may, furthermore, bear the signature or the fingerprints, or both, of the owner, and may bear, as well, any other information the Party to the conflict may wish to add concerning persons belonging to its armed forces. As far as possible the card shall measure 6.5 × 10 cm. and shall be issued in duplicate. The identity card shall be shown by the prisoner of war upon demand, but may in no case be taken away from him.

No physical or mental torture, nor any other form of coercion, may be inflicted on prisoners of war to secure from them information of any kind whatever. Prisoners of war who refuse to answer may not be threatened, insulted, or exposed to unpleasant or disadvantageous treatment of any kind.

Prisoners of war, who, owing to their physical or mental condition, are unable to state their identity, shall be handed over to the medical service. The identity of such prisoners shall be established by all possible means, subject to the provisions of the preceding paragraph.

The questioning of prisoners of war shall be carried out in a language, which they understand.

ART. 18. All effects and articles of personal use, except arms, horses, military equipment and military documents, shall remain in the possession of prisoners of war, likewise their metal helmets and gas masks and like articles issued for personal protection. Effects and articles used for their clothing or feeding shall likewise remain in their possession, even if such effects and articles belong to their regulation military equipment.

At no time should prisoners of war be without identity documents. The Detaining Power shall supply such documents to prisoners of war who possess none.

Badges of rank and nationality, decorations and articles having above all a personal or sentimental value may not be taken from prisoners of war.

Sums of money carried by prisoners of war may not be taken away from them except by order of an officer, and after the amount and particulars of the owner have been recorded in a special register and an itemized receipt has been given, legibly inscribed with the name, rank and unit of the person issuing the said receipt. Sums in the currency of the Detaining Power, or which are changed into such currency at the prisoner's request, shall be placed to the credit of the prisoner's account as provided in Article 64.

The Detaining Power may withdraw articles of value from prisoners of war only for reasons of security; when such articles are withdrawn, the procedure laid down for sums of money impounded shall apply.

Such objects, likewise sums taken away in any currency other than that of the Detaining Power and the conversion of which has not been asked for by the owners, shall be kept in the custody of the Detaining Power and shall be returned in their initial shape to prisoners of war at the end of their captivity.

ART. 19. Prisoners of war shall be evacuated, as soon as possible after their capture, to camps situated in an area far enough from the combat zone for them to be out of danger.

Only those prisoners of war who, owing to wounds or sickness, would run greater risks by being evacuated than by remaining where they are, may be temporarily kept back in a danger zone.

Prisoners of war shall not be unnecessarily exposed to danger while awaiting evacuation from a fighting zone.

ART. 20. The evacuation of prisoners of war shall always be effected humanely and in conditions similar to those for the forces of the Detaining Power in their changes of station.

The Detaining Power shall supply prisoners of war who are being evacuated with sufficient food and potable water, and with the necessary clothing and medical attention. The Detaining Power shall take all suitable precautions to ensure their safety during evacuation, and shall establish as soon as possible a list of the prisoners of war who are evacuated.

If prisoners of war must, during evacuation, pass through transit camps, their stay in such camps shall be as brief as possible.

Section II. Internment of Prisoners of War

Chapter I. General Observations

ART. 21. The Detaining Power may subject prisoners of war to internment. It may impose on them the obligation of not leaving, beyond certain limits, the camp where they are interned, or if the said camp is fenced in, of not going outside its perimeter. Subject to the provisions of the present Convention relative to penal and disciplinary sanctions, prisoners of war may not be held in close confinement except where necessary to safeguard their health and then only during the continuation of the circumstances which make such confinement necessary.

Prisoners of war may be partially or wholly released on parole or promise, in so far as is allowed by the laws of the Power on which they depend. Such measures shall be taken particularly in cases where this may contribute to the improvement of their state of health. No prisoner of war shall be compelled to accept liberty on parole or promise.

Upon the outbreak of hostilities, each Party to the conflict shall notify the adverse Party of the laws and regulations allowing or forbidding its own nationals to accept liberty on parole or promise. Prisoners of war who are paroled or who have given their promise in conformity with the laws and regulations so notified, are bound on their personal honour scrupulously to fulfill, both towards the Power on which they depend and towards the Power which has captured them, the engagements of their paroles or promises. In such cases, the Power on which they depend is bound neither to require nor to accept from them any service incompatible with the parole or promise given.

ART. 22. Prisoners of war may be interned only in premises located on land and affording every guarantee of hygiene and healthfulness. Except in particular cases, which are justified by the interest of the prisoners themselves, they shall not be interned in penitentiaries.

Prisoners of war interned in unhealthy areas, or where the climate is injurious for them, shall be removed as soon as possible to a more favourable climate.

The Detaining Power shall assemble prisoners of war in camps or camp compounds according to their nationality, language and customs, provided that such prisoners shall not be separated from prisoners of war belonging to the armed forces with which they were serving at the time of their capture, except with their consent.

ART. 23. No prisoner of war may at any time be sent to, or detained in areas where he may be exposed to the fire of the combat zone, nor may his presence be used to render certain points or areas immune from military operations.

Prisoners of war shall have shelters against air bombardment and other hazards of war, to the same extent as the local civilian population. With the exception of those engaged in the protection of their quarters against the aforesaid hazards, they may enter such shelters as soon as possible after the giving of the alarm. Any other protective measure taken in favour of the population shall also apply to them.

Detaining Powers shall give the Powers concerned, through the intermediary of the Protecting Powers, all useful information regarding the geographical location of prisoner of war camps.

Whenever military considerations permit, prisoner of war camps shall be indicated in the day-time by the letters PW or PG, placed so as to be clearly visible from the air. The Powers concerned may, however, agree upon any other system of marking. Only prisoner of war camps shall be marked as such.

ART. 24. Transit or screening camps of a permanent kind shall be fitted out under conditions similar to those described in the present Section, and the prisoners therein shall have the same treatment as in other camps.

Chapter II. Quarters, Food and Clothing of Prisoners of War

ART. 25. Prisoners of war shall be quartered under conditions as favourable as those for the forces of the Detaining Power who are billeted in the same area. The said conditions shall make allowance for the habits and customs of the prisoners and shall in no case be prejudicial to their health.

The foregoing provisions shall apply in particular to the dormitories of prisoners of war as regards both total surface and minimum cubic space, and the general installations, bedding and blankets.

The premises provided for the use of prisoners of war individually or collectively, shall be entirely protected from dampness and adequately heated and lighted, in particular between dusk and lights out. All precautions must be taken against the danger of fire.

In any camps in which women prisoners of war, as well as men, are accommodated, separate dormitories shall be provided for them.

ART. 26. The basic daily food rations shall be sufficient in quantity, quality and variety to keep prisoners of war in good health and to prevent loss of weight or the development of nutritional deficiencies. Account shall also be taken of the habitual diet of the prisoners.

The Detaining Power shall supply prisoners of war who work with such additional rations as are necessary for the labour on which they are employed.

Sufficient drinking water shall be supplied to prisoners of war. The use of tobacco shall be permitted.

Prisoners of war shall, as far as possible, be associated with the preparation of their meals; they may be employed for that purpose in the kitchens. Furthermore, they shall be given the means of preparing, themselves, the additional food in their possession.

Adequate premises shall be provided for messing.

Collective disciplinary measures affecting food are prohibited.

ART. 27. Clothing, underwear and footwear shall be supplied to prisoners of war in sufficient quantities by the Detaining Power, which shall make allowance for the climate of the region where the prisoners are detained. Uniforms of enemy armed forces captured by the Detaining Power should, if suitable for the climate, be made available to clothe prisoners of war.

The regular replacement and repair of the above articles shall be assured by the Detaining Power. In addition, prisoners of war who work shall receive appropriate clothing, wherever the nature of the work demands.

ART. 28. Canteens shall be installed in all camps, where prisoners of war may procure foodstuffs, soap and tobacco and ordinary articles in daily use. The tariff shall never be in excess of local market prices.

The profits made by camp canteens shall be used for the benefit of the prisoners; a special fund shall be created for this purpose. The prisoners' representative shall have the right to collaborate in the management of the canteen and of this fund.

When a camp is closed down, the credit balance of the special fund shall be handed to an international welfare organization, to be employed for the benefit of prisoners of war of the same nationality as those who have contributed to the fund. In case of a general repatriation, such profits shall be kept by the Detaining Power, subject to any agreement to the contrary between the Powers concerned.

Chapter III. Hygiene and Medical Attention

ART. 29. The Detaining Power shall be bound to take all sanitary measures necessary to ensure the cleanliness and healthfulness of camps and to prevent epidemics.

Prisoners of war shall have for their use, day and night, conveniences, which conform to the rules of hygiene and are maintained in a constant state of cleanliness. In any camps in which women prisoners of war are accommodated, separate conveniences shall be provided for them.

Also, apart from the baths and showers with which the camps shall be furnished prisoners of war shall be provided with sufficient water and soap for their personal toilet and for washing their personal laundry; the necessary installations, facilities and time shall be granted them for that purpose.

ART. 30. Every camp shall have an adequate infirmary where prisoners of war may have the attention they require, as well as appropriate diet. Isolation wards shall, if necessary, be set aside for cases of contagious or mental disease.

Prisoners of war suffering from serious disease, or whose condition necessitates special treatment, a surgical operation or hospital care, must be admitted to any military or civilian medical unit where such treatment can be given, even if their repatriation is contemplated in the near future. Special facilities shall be afforded for the care to be given to the disabled, in particular to the blind, and for their. rehabilitation, pending repatriation.

Prisoners of war shall have the attention, preferably, of medical personnel of the Power on which they depend and, if possible, of their nationality.

Prisoners of war may not be prevented from presenting themselves to the medical authorities for examination. The detaining authorities shall, upon request, issue to every prisoner who has undergone treatment, an official certificate indicating the nature of his illness or injury, and the duration and kind of treatment received. A duplicate of this certificate shall be forwarded to the Central Prisoners of War Agency.

The costs of treatment, including those of any apparatus necessary for the maintenance of prisoners of war in good health, particularly dentures and other artificial appliances, and spectacles, shall be borne by the Detaining Power.

ART. 31. Medical inspections of prisoners of war shall be held at least once a month. They shall include the checking and the recording of the weight of each prisoner of war.

Their purpose shall be, in particular, to supervise the general state of health, nutrition and cleanliness of prisoners and to detect contagious diseases, especially tuberculosis, malaria and venereal disease. For this purpose the most efficient methods available shall be employed, e.g. periodic mass miniature radiography for the early detection of tuberculosis.

Art. 32. Prisoners of war who, though not attached to the medical service of their armed forces, are physicians, surgeons, dentists, nurses or medical orderlies, may be required by the Detaining Power to exercise their medical functions in the interests of prisoners of war dependent on the same Power. In that case they shall continue to be prisoners of war, but shall receive the same treatment as corresponding medical personnel retained by the Detaining Power. They shall be exempted from any other work under Article 49.

Chapter IV. Medical Personnel and Chaplains Retained to Assist Prisoners of War

Art. 33. Members of the medical personnel and chaplains while retained by the Detaining Power with a view to assisting prisoners of war, shall not be considered as prisoners of war. They shall, however, receive as a minimum the benefits and protection of the present Convention, and shall also be granted all facilities necessary to provide for the medical care of, and religious ministration to prisoners of war.

They shall continue to exercise their medical and spiritual functions for the benefit of prisoners of war, preferably those belonging to the armed forces upon which they depend, within the scope of the military laws and regulations of the Detaining Power and under the control of its competent services, in accordance with their professional etiquette. They shall also benefit by the following facilities in the exercise of their medical or spiritual functions:

- **a.** They shall be authorized to visit periodically prisoners of war situated in working detachments or in hospitals outside the camp. For this purpose, the Detaining Power shall place at their disposal the necessary means of transport.
- **b.** The senior medical officer in each camp shall be responsible to the camp military authorities for everything connected with the activities of retained medical personnel. For this purpose, Parties to the conflict shall agree at the outbreak of hostilities on the subject of the corresponding ranks of the medical personnel, including that of societies mentioned in Article 26 of

the Geneva Convention for the Amelioration of the Condition of the Wounded and Sick in Armed Forces in the Field of August 12, 1949. This senior medical officer, as well as chaplains, shall have the right to deal with the competent authorities of the camp on all questions relating to their duties. Such authorities shall afford them all necessary facilities for correspondence relating to these questions.

c. Although they shall be subject to the internal discipline of the camp in which they are retained, such personnel may not be compelled to carry out any work other than that concerned with their medical or religious duties.

During hostilities, the Parties to the conflict shall agree concerning the possible relief of retained personnel and shall settle the procedure to be followed.

None of the preceding provisions shall relieve the Detaining Power of its obligations with regard to prisoners of war from the medical or spiritual point of view.

Chapter V. Religious, Intellectual and Physical Activities

ART. 34. Prisoners of war shall enjoy complete latitude in the exercise of their religious duties, including attendance at the service of their faith, on condition that they comply with the disciplinary routine prescribed by the military authorities.

Adequate premises shall be provided where religious services may be held.

ART. 35. Chaplains who fall into the hands of the enemy Power and who remain or are retained with a view to assisting prisoners of war, shall be allowed to minister to them and to exercise freely their ministry amongst prisoners of war of the same religion, in accordance with their religious conscience. They shall be allocated among the various camps and labour detachments containing prisoners of war belonging to the same forces, speaking the same language or practising the same religion. They shall enjoy the necessary facilities, including the means of transport provided for in Article 33, for visiting the prisoners of war outside their camp. They shall be free to correspond, subject to censorship, on matters concerning their religious duties with the ecclesiastical authorities in the country of detention and with international religious organizations. Letters and cards which they may send for this purpose shall be in addition to the quota provided for in Article 71.

ART. 36. Prisoners of war, who are ministers of religion, without having officiated as chaplains to their own forces, shall be at liberty, whatever their denomination, to minister freely to the members of their community. For this purpose, they shall receive the same treatment as the chaplains retained by the Detaining Power. They shall not be obliged to do any other work.

ART. 37. When prisoners of war have not the assistance of a retained chaplain or of a prisoner of war minister of their faith, a minister belonging to the prisoners' or a similar denomination, or in his absence a qualified layman, if such a course is feasible from a confessional point of view, shall be appointed, at the request of the prisoners concerned, to fill this office. This appointment, subject to the approval of the Detaining Power, shall take place with the agreement of the community of prisoners concerned and, wherever necessary, with the approval of the local religious authorities of the same faith. The person thus appointed shall comply with all regulations established by the Detaining Power in the interests of discipline and military security.

ART. 38. While respecting the individual preferences of every prisoner, the Detaining Power shall encourage the practice of intellectual, educational, and recreational pursuits, sports and games amongst prisoners, and shall take the measures necessary to ensure the exercise thereof by providing them with adequate premises and necessary equipment.

Prisoners shall have opportunities for taking physical exercise, including sports and games, and for being out of doors. Sufficient open spaces shall be provided for this purpose in all camps.

Chapter VI. Discipline

ART. 39. Every prisoner of war camp shall be put under the immediate authority of a responsible commissioned officer belonging to the regular armed forces of the Detaining Power. Such officer shall have in his possession a copy of the present Convention; he shall ensure that its provisions are known to the camp staff and the guard and shall be responsible, under the direction of his government, for its application.

Prisoners of war, with the exception of officers, must salute and show to all officers of the Detaining Power the external marks of respect provided for by the regulations applying in their own forces.

Officer prisoners of war are bound to salute only officers of a higher rank of the Detaining Power; they must, however, salute the camp commander regardless of his rank.

Art. 40. The wearing of badges of rank and nationality, as well as of decorations, shall be permitted.

Art. 41. In every camp the text of the present Convention and its Annexes and the contents of any special agreement provided for in Article 6, shall be posted, in the prisoners' own language, in places where all may read them. Copies shall be supplied, on request, to the prisoners who cannot have access to the copy, which has been posted.

Regulations, orders, notices and publications of every kind relating to the conduct of prisoners of war shall be issued to them in a language, which they understand. Such regulations, orders and publications shall be posted in the manner described above and copies shall be handed to the prisoners' representative. Every order and command addressed to prisoners of war individually must likewise be given in a language, which they understand.

Art. 42. The use of weapons against prisoners of war, especially against those who are escaping or attempting to escape, shall constitute an extreme measure, which shall always be preceded by warnings appropriate to the circumstances.

Chapter VII. Rank of Prisoners of War

Art. 43. Upon the outbreak of hostilities, the Parties to the conflict shall communicate to one another the titles and ranks of all the persons mentioned in Article 4 of the present Convention, in order to ensure equality of treatment between prisoners of equivalent rank. Titles and ranks, which are subsequently created, shall form the subject of similar communications.

The Detaining Power shall recognize promotions in rank which have been accorded to prisoners of war and which have been duly notified by the Power on which these prisoners depend.

Art. 44. Officers and prisoners of equivalent status shall be treated with the regard due to their rank and age.

In order to ensure service in officers' camps, other ranks of the same armed forces who, as far as possible, speak the same language, shall be assigned in sufficient numbers, account being taken of the rank of officers and prisoners of equivalent status. Such orderlies shall not be required to perform any other work.

Supervision of the mess by the officers themselves shall be facilitated in every way.

ART. 45. Prisoners of war other than officers and prisoners of equivalent status shall be treated with the regard due to their rank and age.

Supervision of the mess by the prisoners themselves shall be facilitated in every way.

Chapter VIII. Transfer of Prisoners of War after their Arrival in Camp

ART. 46. The Detaining Power, when deciding upon the transfer of prisoners of war, shall take into account the interests of the prisoners themselves, more especially so as not to increase the difficulty of their repatriation.

The transfer of prisoners of war shall always be effected humanely and in conditions not less favourable than those under which the forces of the Detaining Power are transferred. Account shall always be taken of the climatic conditions to which the prisoners of war are accustomed and the conditions of transfer shall in no case be prejudicial to their health.

The Detaining Power shall supply prisoners of war during transfer with sufficient food and drinking water to keep them in good health, likewise with the necessary clothing, shelter and medical attention. The Detaining Power shall take adequate precautions especially in case of transport by sea or by air, to ensure their safety during transfer, and shall draw up a complete list of all transferred prisoners before their departure.

ART. 47. Sick or wounded prisoners of war shall not be transferred as long as their recovery may be endangered by the journey, unless their safety imperatively demands it.

If the combat zone draws closer to a camp, the prisoners of war in the said camp shall not be transferred unless their transfer can be carried out in adequate conditions of safety, or unless they are exposed to greater risks by remaining on the spot than by being transferred.

ART. 48. In the event of transfer, prisoners of war shall be officially advised of their departure and of their new postal address. Such notifications shall be given in time for them to pack their luggage and inform their next of kin.

They shall be allowed to take with them their personal effects, and the correspondence and parcels, which have arrived for them. The weight of such baggage may be limited, if the conditions of transfer so require, to what each prisoner can reasonably carry, which shall in no case be more than twenty-five kilograms per head.

Mail and parcels addressed to their former camp shall be forwarded to them without delay. The camp commander shall take, in agreement with the prisoners' representative, any measures needed to ensure the transport of the prisoners' community property and of the luggage they are unable to take with them in consequence of restrictions imposed by virtue of the second paragraph of this Article.

The costs of transfers shall be borne by the Detaining Power.

Section III. Labour of Prisoners of War

ART. 49. The Detaining Power may utilize the labour of prisoners of war who are physically fit, taking into account their age, sex, rank and physical aptitude, and with a view particularly to maintaining them in a good state of physical and mental health.

Non-commissioned officers who are prisoners of war shall only be required to do supervisory work. Those not so required may ask for other suitable work, which shall, so far as possible, be found for them.

If officers or persons of equivalent status ask for suitable work, it shall be found for them, so far as possible, but they may in no circumstances be compelled to work.

ART. 50. Besides work connected with camp administration, installation or maintenance, prisoners of war may be compelled to do only such work as is included in the following classes:

- **a.** agriculture;
- **b.** industries connected with the production or the extraction of raw materials, and manufacturing industries, with the exception of metallurgical, machinery and chemical industries; public works and building operations which have no military character or purpose;
- **c.** transport and handling of stores which are not military in character or purpose;
- **d.** commercial business, and arts and crafts;
- **e.** domestic service;
- **f.** public utility services having no military character or purpose.

Should the above provisions be infringed, prisoners of war shall be allowed to exercise their right of complaint, in conformity with Article 78.

ART. 51. Prisoners of war must be granted suitable working conditions, especially as regards accommodation, food, clothing and equipment; such conditions shall not be inferior to those enjoyed by nationals of the Detaining Power employed in similar work; account shall also be taken of climatic conditions.

The Detaining Power, in utilizing the labour of prisoners of war, shall ensure that in areas in which such prisoners are employed, the national legislation concerning the protection of labour, and, more particularly, the regulations for the safety of workers, are duly applied.

Prisoners of war shall receive training and be provided with the means of protection suitable to the work they will have to do and similar to those accorded to the nationals of the Detaining Power. Subject to the provisions of Article 52, prisoners may be submitted to the normal risks run by these civilian workers.

Conditions of labour shall in no case be rendered more arduous by disciplinary measures.

Art. 52. Unless he is a volunteer, no prisoner of war may be employed on labour, which is of an unhealthy or dangerous nature.

No prisoner of war shall be assigned to labour which would be looked upon as humiliating for a member of the Detaining Power's own forces.

The removal of mines or similar devices shall be considered as dangerous labour.

Art. 53. The duration of the daily labour of prisoners of war, including the time of the journey to and fro, shall not be excessive, and must in no case exceed that permitted for civilian workers in the district, who are nationals of the Detaining Power and employed on the same work.

Prisoners of war must be allowed, in the middle of the day's work, a rest of not less than one hour. This rest will be the same as that to which workers of the Detaining Power are entitled, if the latter is of longer duration. They shall be allowed in addition a rest of twenty-four consecutive hours every week, preferably on Sunday or the day of rest in their country of origin. Furthermore, every prisoner who has worked for one year shall be granted a rest of eight consecutive days, during which his working pay shall be paid him.

If methods of labour such as piece work are employed, the length of the working period shall not be rendered excessive thereby.

Art. 54. The working pay due to prisoners of war shall be fixed in accordance with the provisions of Article 62 of the present Convention.

Prisoners of war who sustain accidents in connection with work, or who contract a disease in the course, or in consequence of their work, shall receive all the care their condition may require. The Detaining Power shall furthermore deliver to such prisoners of war a medical certificate enabling them to submit their claims to the Power on which they depend, and shall send a duplicate to the Central Prisoners of War Agency provided for in Article 123.

ART. 55. The fitness of prisoners of war for work shall be periodically verified by medical examinations at least once a month. The examinations shall have particular regard to the nature of the work which prisoners of war are required to do.

If any prisoner of war considers himself incapable of working, he shall be permitted to appear before the medical authorities of his camp. Physicians or surgeons may recommend that the prisoners who are, in their opinion, unfit for work, be exempted therefrom.

ART. 56. The organization and administration of labour detachments shall be similar to those of prisoner of war camps.

Every labour detachment shall remain under the control of and administratively part of a prisoner of war camp. The military authorities and the commander of the said camp shall be responsible, under the direction of their government, for the observance of the provisions of the present Convention in labour detachments.

The camp commander shall keep an up-to-date record of the labour detachments dependent on his camp, and shall communicate it to the delegates of the Protecting Power, of the International Committee of the Red Cross, or of other agencies giving relief to prisoners of war, who may visit the camp.

ART. 57. The treatment of prisoners of war who work for private persons, even if the latter are responsible for guarding and protecting them, shall not be inferior to that which is provided for by the present Convention. The Detaining Power, the military authorities and the commander of the camp to which such prisoners belong shall be entirely responsible for the maintenance, care, treatment, and payment of the working pay of such prisoners of war.

Such prisoners of war shall have the right to remain in communication with the prisoners' representatives in the camps on which they depend.

Section IV. Financial Resources of Prisoners of War

ART. 58. Upon the outbreak of hostilities, and pending an arrangement on this matter with the Protecting Power, the Detaining Power may determine the maximum amount of money in cash or in any similar form, that prisoners may have in their possession. Any amount in excess, which was properly in their possession and which has been taken or withheld from them, shall be placed to their account, together with any monies deposited by them, and shall not be converted into any other currency without their consent.

If prisoners of war are permitted to purchase services or commodities outside the camp against payment in cash, such payments shall be made by the prisoner himself or by the camp administration who will charge them to the accounts of the prisoners concerned. The Detaining Power will establish the necessary rules in this respect.

Art. 59. Cash which was taken from prisoners of war, in accordance with Article 18, at the time of their capture, and which is in the currency of the Detaining Power, shall be placed to their separate accounts, in accordance with the provisions of Article 64 of the present Section.

The amounts, in the currency of the Detaining Power, due to the conversion of sums in other currencies that are taken from the prisoners of war at the same time, shall also be credited to their separate accounts.

Art. 60. The Detaining Power shall grant all prisoners of war a monthly advance of pay, the amount of which shall be fixed by conversion, into the currency of the said Power, of the following amounts:

Category I: Prisoners ranking below sergeants: eight Swiss francs.

Category II: Sergeants and other non-commissioned officers, or prisoners of equivalent rank: twelve Swiss francs.

Category III: Warrant officers and commissioned officers below the rank of major or prisoners of equivalent rank: fifty Swiss francs.

Category IV: Majors, lieutenant-colonels, colonels or prisoners of equivalent rank: sixty Swiss francs.

Category V: General officers or prisoners of war of equivalent rank: seventy-five Swiss francs.

However, the Parties to the conflict concerned may by special agreement modify the amount of advances of pay due to prisoners of the preceding categories.

Furthermore, if the amounts indicated in the first paragraph above would be unduly high compared with the pay of the Detaining Power's armed forces or would, for any reason, seriously embarrass the Detaining Power, then, pending the conclusion of a special agreement with the Power on which the prisoners depend to vary the amounts indicated above, the Detaining Power:

a. shall continue to credit the accounts of the prisoners with the amounts indicated in the first paragraph above;

b. may temporarily limit the amount made available from these advances of pay to prisoners of war for their own use, to sums which are reasonable, but which, for Category I, shall never be inferior to the amount that the Detaining Power gives to the members of its own armed forces.

The reasons for any limitations will be given without delay to the Protecting Power.

ART. 61. The Detaining Power shall accept for distribution as supplementary pay to prisoners of war sums which the Power on which the prisoners depend may forward to them, on condition that the sums to be paid shall be the same for each prisoner of the same category, shall be payable to all prisoners of that category depending on that Power, and shall be placed in their separate accounts, at the earliest opportunity, in accordance with the provisions of Article 64. Such supplementary pay shall not relieve the Detaining Power of any obligation under this Convention.

ART. 62. Prisoners of war shall be paid a fair working rate of pay by the detaining authorities direct. The rate shall be fixed by the said authorities, but shall at no time be less than one-fourth of one Swiss franc for a full working day. The Detaining Power shall inform prisoners of war, as well as the Power on which they depend, through the intermediary of the Protecting Power, of the rate of daily working pay that it has fixed.

Working pay shall likewise be paid by the detaining authorities to prisoners of war permanently detailed to duties or to a skilled or semi-skilled occupation in connection with the administration, installation or maintenance of camps, and to the prisoners who are required to carry out spiritual or medical duties on behalf of their comrades.

The working pay of the prisoners' representative, of his advisers, if any, and of his assistants, shall be paid out of the fund maintained by canteen profits. The scale of this working pay shall be fixed by the prisoners' representative and approved by the camp commander. If there is no such fund, the detaining authorities shall pay these prisoners a fair working rate of pay.

ART. 63. Prisoners of war shall be permitted to receive remittances of money addressed to them individually or collectively.

Every prisoner of war shall have at his disposal the credit balance of his account as provided for in the following Article, within the limits fixed by the Detaining Power, which shall make such payments as are requested. Subject to financial or monetary restrictions which the Detaining Power regards as essential, prisoners of war may also have payments made abroad. In this case payments addressed by prisoners of war to dependents shall be given priority.

In any event, and subject to the consent of the Power on which they depend, prisoners may have payments made in their own country, as follows: the Detaining Power shall send to the aforesaid Power through the Protecting Power, a notification giving all the necessary particulars concerning the prisoners of war, the beneficiaries of the payments, and the amount of the sums to be paid, expressed in the Detaining Power's currency. The said notification shall be signed by the prisoners and countersigned by the camp commander. The Detaining Power shall debit the prisoners' account by a corresponding amount; the sums thus debited shall be placed by it to the credit of the Power on which the prisoners depend.

To apply the foregoing provisions, the Detaining Power may usefully consult the Model Regulations in Annex V of the present Convention.

ART. 64. The Detaining Power shall hold an account for each prisoner of war, showing at least the following:

1. The amounts due to the prisoner or received by him as advances of pay, as working pay or derived from any other source; the sums in the currency of the Detaining Power which were taken from him; the sums taken from him and converted at his request into the currency of the said Power.
2. The payments made to the prisoner in cash, or in any other similar form; the payments made on his behalf and at his request; the sums transferred under Article 63, third paragraph.

ART. 65. Every item entered in the account of a prisoner of war shall be countersigned or initialled by him, or by the prisoners' representative acting on his behalf.

Prisoners of war shall at all times be afforded reasonable facilities for consulting and obtaining copies of their accounts, which may likewise be inspected by the representatives of the Protecting Powers at the time of visits to the camp.

When prisoners of war are transferred from one camp to another, their personal accounts will follow them. In case of transfer from one Detaining Power to another, the monies which are their property and are not in the currency of the Detaining Power will follow them. They shall be given certificates for any other monies standing to the credit of their accounts.

The Parties to the conflict concerned may agree to notify to each other at specific intervals through the Protecting Power, the amount of the accounts of the prisoners of war.

Art. 66. On the termination of captivity, through the release of a prisoner of war or his repatriation, the Detaining Power shall give him a statement, signed by an authorized officer of that Power, showing the credit balance then due to him. The Detaining Power shall also send through the Protecting Power to the government upon which the prisoner of war depends, lists giving all appropriate particulars of all prisoners of war whose captivity has been terminated by repatriation, release, escape, death or any other means, and showing the amount of their credit balances. Such lists shall be certified on each sheet by an authorized representative of the Detaining Power.

Any of the above provisions of this Article may be varied by mutual agreement between any two Parties to the conflict.

The Power on which the prisoner of war depends shall be responsible for settling with him any credit balance due to him from the Detaining Power on the termination of his captivity.

Art. 67. Advances of pay, issued to prisoners of war in conformity with Article 60, shall be considered as made on behalf of the Power on which they depend. Such advances of pay, as well as all payments made by the said Power under Article 63, third paragraph, and Article 68, shall form the subject of arrangements between the Powers concerned, at the close of hostilities.

Art. 68. Any claim by a prisoner of war for compensation in respect of any injury or other disability arising out of work shall be referred to the Power on which he depends, through the Protecting Power. In accordance with Article 54, the Detaining Power will, in all cases, provide the prisoner of war concerned with a statement showing the nature of the injury or disability, the circumstances in which it arose and particulars of medical or hospital treatment given for it. This statement will be signed by a responsible officer of the Detaining Power and the medical particulars certified by a medical officer.

Any claim by a prisoner of war for compensation in respect of personal effects monies or valuables impounded by the Detaining Power under Article 18 and not forthcoming on his repatriation, or in respect of loss alleged to be due to the fault of the Detaining Power or any of its servants, shall likewise be referred to the Power on which he depends. Nevertheless, any such personal effects required for use by the prisoners of war whilst in captivity shall be replaced at the expense of the Detaining Power. The Detaining Power will, in all cases, provide the prisoner of war with a statement, signed by a responsible officer, showing all available information regarding the reasons why such effects, monies or valuables have not been restored to him. A copy of this statement will be forwarded to the Power on which he depends through the Central Prisoners of War Agency provided for in Article 123.

Section V. Relations of Prisoners of War With the Exterior

ART. 69. Immediately upon prisoners of war falling into its power, the Detaining Power shall inform them and the Powers on which they depend, through the Protecting Power, of the measures taken to carry out the provisions of the present Section. They shall likewise inform the parties concerned of any subsequent modifications of such measures.

ART. 70. Immediately upon capture, or not more than one week after arrival at a camp, even if it is a transit camp, likewise in case of sickness or transfer to hospital or to another camp, every prisoner of war shall be enabled to write direct to his family, on the one hand, and to the Central Prisoners of War Agency provided for in Article 123, on the other hand, a card similar, if possible, to the model annexed to the present Convention, informing his relatives of his capture, address and state of health. The said cards shall be forwarded as rapidly as possible and may not be delayed in any manner.

ART. 71. Prisoners of war shall be allowed to send and receive letters and cards. If the Detaining Power deems it necessary to limit the number of letters and cards sent by each prisoner of war, the said number shall not be less than two letters and four cards monthly, exclusive of the capture cards provided for in Article 70, and conforming as closely as possible to the models annexed to the present Convention. Further limitations may be imposed only if the Protecting Power is satisfied that it would be in the interests of the prisoners of war concerned to do so owing to difficulties of translation caused by the Detaining Power's inability to find sufficient qualified linguists to carry out the necessary censorship. If limitations must be placed on the correspondence addressed to prisoners of war, they may be ordered only by the Power on which the prisoners depend, possibly at the request of the Detaining Power. Such letters and cards must be conveyed by the most rapid method at the disposal of the Detaining Power; they may not be delayed or retained for disciplinary reasons.

Prisoners of war who have been without news for a long period, or who are unable to receive news from their next of kin or to give them news by the ordinary postal route, as well as those who are at a great distance from their homes, shall be permitted to send telegrams, the fees being charged against the prisoners of war's accounts with the Detaining Power or paid in the currency at their disposal. They shall likewise benefit by this measure in cases of urgency.

As a general rule, the correspondence of prisoners of war shall be written in their native language. The Parties to the conflict may allow correspondence in other languages.

Sacks containing prisoner of war mail must be securely sealed and labelled so as clearly to indicate their contents, and must be addressed to offices of destination.

Art. 72. Prisoners of war shall be allowed to receive by post or by any other means individual parcels or collective shipments containing, in particular, foodstuffs, clothing, medical supplies and articles of a religious, educational or recreational character which may meet their needs, including books, devotional articles, scientific equipment, examination papers, musical instruments, sports outfits and materials allowing prisoners of war to pursue their studies or their cultural activities.

Such shipments shall in no way free the Detaining Power from the obligations imposed upon it by virtue of the present Convention.

The only limits which may be placed on these shipments shall be those proposed by the Protecting Power in the interest of the prisoners themselves, or by the International Committee of the Red Cross or any other organization giving assistance to the prisoners, in respect of their own shipments only, on account of exceptional strain on transport or communications.

The conditions for the sending of individual parcels and collective relief shall, if necessary, be the subject of special agreements between the Powers concerned, which may in no case delay the receipt by the prisoners of relief supplies. Books may not be included in parcels of clothing and foodstuffs. Medical supplies shall, as a rule, be sent in collective parcels.

Art. 73. In the absence of special agreements between the Powers concerned on the conditions for the receipt and distribution of collective relief shipments, the rules and regulations concerning collective shipments, which are annexed to the present Convention, shall be applied.

The special agreements referred to above shall in no case restrict the right of prisoners' representatives to take possession of collective relief shipments intended for prisoners of war, to proceed to their distribution or to dispose of them in the interest of the prisoners.

Nor shall such agreements restrict the right of representatives of the Protecting Power, the International Committee of the Red Cross or any other organization giving assistance to prisoners of war and responsible for the forwarding of collective shipments, to supervise their distribution to the recipients.

Art. 74. All relief shipments for prisoners of war shall be exempt from import, customs and other dues.

Correspondence, relief shipments and authorized remittances of money addressed to prisoners of war or despatched by them through the post office, either direct or through the Information Bureaux provided for in Article 122 and the Central Prisoners of War Agency provided for in Article 123, shall be exempt from any postal dues, both in the countries of origin and destination, and in intermediate countries.

If relief shipments intended for prisoners of war cannot be sent through the post office by reason of weight or for any other cause, the cost of transportation shall be borne by the Detaining Power in all the territories under its control. The other Powers party to the Convention shall bear the cost of transport in their respective territories. In the absence of special agreements between the Parties concerned, the costs connected with transport of such shipments, other than costs covered by the above exemption, shall be charged to the senders.

The High Contracting Parties shall endeavour to reduce, so far as possible, the rates charged for telegrams sent by prisoners of war, or addressed to them.

Art. 75. Should military operations prevent the Powers concerned from fulfilling their obligation to assure the transport of the shipments referred to in Articles 70, 71, 72 and 77, the Protecting Powers concerned, the International Committee of the Red Cross or any other organization duly approved by the Parties to the conflict may undertake to ensure the conveyance of such shipments by suitable means (railway wagons, motor vehicles, vessels or aircraft, etc.). For this purpose, the High Contracting Parties shall endeavour to supply them with such transport and to allow its circulation, especially by granting the necessary safe-conducts.

Such transport may also be used to convey:

a. correspondence, lists and reports exchanged between the Central Information Agency referred to in Article 123 and the National Bureaux referred to in Article 122;

b. correspondence and reports relating to prisoners of war which the Protecting Powers, the International Committee of the Red Cross or any other body assisting the prisoners, exchange either with their own delegates or with the Parties to the conflict.

These provisions in no way detract from the right of any Party to the conflict to arrange other means of transport, if it should so prefer, nor preclude the granting of safe-conducts, under mutually agreed conditions, to such means of transport.

In the absence of special agreements, the costs occasioned by the use of such means of transport shall be borne proportionally by the Parties to the conflict whose nationals are benefited thereby.

ART. 76. The censoring of correspondence addressed to prisoners of war or despatched by them shall be done as quickly as possible. Mail shall be censored only by the despatching State and the receiving State, and once only by each.

The examination of consignments intended for prisoners of war shall not be carried out under conditions that will expose the goods contained in them to deterioration; except in the case of written or printed matter, it shall be done in the presence of the addressee, or of a fellow-prisoner duly delegated by him. The delivery to prisoners of individual or collective consignments shall not be delayed under the pretext of difficulties of censorship.

Any prohibition of correspondence ordered by Parties to the conflict, either for military or political reasons, shall be only temporary and its duration shall be as short as possible.

ART. 77. The Detaining Powers shall provide all facilities for the transmission, through the Protecting Power or the Central Prisoners of War Agency provided for in Article 123 of instruments, papers or documents intended for prisoners of war or despatched by them, especially powers of attorney and wills.

In all cases they shall facilitate the preparation and execution of such documents on behalf of prisoners of war; in particular, they shall allow them to consult a lawyer and shall take what measures are necessary for the authentication of their signatures.

Section VI. Relations Between Prisoners of War and the Authorities

Chapter I. Complaints of Prisoners of War Respecting the Conditions of Captivity

ART. 78. Prisoners of war shall have the right to make known to the military authorities in whose power they are, their requests regarding the conditions of captivity to which they are subjected.

They shall also have the unrestricted right to apply to the representatives of the Protecting Powers either through their prisoners' representative or, if they consider it necessary, direct, in order to draw their attention to any points on which they may have complaints to make regarding their conditions of captivity.

These requests and complaints shall not be limited nor considered to be a part of the correspondence quota referred to in Article 71. They must be transmitted immediately. Even if they are recognized to be unfounded, they may not give rise to any punishment.

Prisoners' representatives may send periodic reports on the situation in the camps and the needs of the prisoners of war to the representatives of the Protecting Powers.

Chapter II. Prisoner of War Representatives

ART. 79. In all places where there are prisoners of war, except in those where there are officers, the prisoners shall freely elect by secret ballot, every six months, and also in case of vacancies, prisoners' representatives entrusted with representing them before the military authorities, the Protecting Powers, the International Committee of the Red Cross and any other organization which may assist them. These prisoners' representatives shall be eligible for re-election.

In camps for officers and persons of equivalent status or in mixed camps, the senior officer among the prisoners of war shall be recognized as the camp prisoners' representative. In camps for officers, he shall be assisted by one or more advisers chosen by the officers; in mixed camps, his assistants shall be chosen from among the prisoners of war who are not officers and shall be elected by them.

Officer prisoners of war of the same nationality shall be stationed in labour camps for prisoners of war, for the purpose of carrying out the camp administration duties for which the prisoners of war are responsible. These officers may be elected as prisoners' representatives under the first paragraph of this Article. In such a case the assistants to the prisoners' representatives shall be chosen from among those prisoners of war who are not officers.

Every representative elected must be approved by the Detaining Power before he has the right to commence his duties. Where the Detaining Power refuses to approve a prisoner of war elected by his fellow prisoners of war, it must inform the Protecting Power of the reason for such refusal.

In all cases the prisoners' representative must have the same nationality, language and customs as the prisoners of war whom he represents. Thus, prisoners of war distributed in different sections of a camp, according to their nationality, language or customs, shall have for each section their own prisoners' representative, in accordance with the foregoing paragraphs.

Art. 80. Prisoners' representatives shall further the physical, spiritual and intellectual well-being of prisoners of war.

In particular, where the prisoners decide to organize amongst themselves a system of mutual assistance, this organization will be within the province of the prisoners' representative, in addition to the special duties entrusted to him by other provisions of the present Convention.

Prisoners' representatives shall not be held responsible, simply by reason of their duties, for any offences committed by prisoners of war.

Art. 81. Prisoners' representatives shall not be required to perform any other work, if the accomplishment of their duties is thereby made more difficult.

Prisoners' representatives may appoint from amongst the prisoners such assistants as they may require. All material facilities shall be granted them, particularly a certain freedom of movement necessary for the accomplishment of their duties (inspection of labour detachments, receipt of supplies, etc.).

Prisoners' representatives shall be permitted to visit premises where prisoners of war are detained, and every prisoner of war shall have the right to consult freely his prisoners' representative.

All facilities shall likewise be accorded to the prisoners' representatives for communication by post and telegraph with the detaining authorities, the Protecting Powers, the International Committee of the Red Cross and their delegates, the Mixed Medical Commissions and the bodies which give assistance to prisoners of war. Prisoners' representatives of labour detachments shall enjoy the same facilities for communication with the prisoners' representatives of the principal camp. Such communications shall not be restricted, nor considered as forming a part of the quota mentioned in Article 71.

Prisoners' representatives who are transferred shall be allowed a reasonable time to acquaint their successors with current affairs.

In case of dismissal, the reasons therefor shall be communicated to the Protecting Power.

Chapter III. Penal and Disciplinary Sanctions

I. General Provisions

ART. 82. A prisoner of war shall be subject to the laws, regulations and orders in force in the armed forces of the Detaining Power; the Detaining Power shall be justified in taking judicial or disciplinary measures in respect of any offence committed by a prisoner of war against such laws, regulations or orders. However, no proceedings or punishments contrary to the provisions of this Chapter shall be allowed.

If any law, regulation or order of the Detaining Power shall declare acts committed by a prisoner of war to be punishable, whereas the same acts would not be punishable if committed by a member of the forces of the Detaining Power, such acts shall entail disciplinary punishments only.

ART. 83. In deciding whether proceedings in respect of an offence alleged to have been committed by a prisoner of war shall be judicial or disciplinary, the Detaining Power shall ensure that the competent authorities exercise the greatest leniency and adopt, wherever possible, disciplinary rather than judicial measures.

ART. 84. A prisoner of war shall be tried only by a military court, unless the existing laws of the Detaining Power expressly permit the civil courts to try a member of the armed forces of the Detaining Power in respect of the particular offence alleged to have been committed by the prisoner of war.

In no circumstances whatever shall a prisoner of war be tried by a court of any kind which does not offer the essential guarantees of independence and impartiality as generally recognized, and, in particular, the procedure of which does not afford the accused the rights and means of defence provided for in Article 105.

ART. 85. Prisoners of war prosecuted under the laws of the Detaining Power for acts committed prior to capture shall retain, even if convicted, the benefits of the present Convention.

ART. 86. No prisoner of war may be punished more than once for the same act or on the same charge.

ART. 87. Prisoners of war may not be sentenced by the military authorities and courts of the Detaining Power to any penalties except those provided for in respect of members of the armed forces of the said Power who have committed the same acts.

When fixing the penalty, the courts or authorities of the Detaining Power shall take into consideration, to the widest extent possible, the fact that the accused, not being a national of the Detaining Power, is not bound to it by any duty of allegiance, and that he is in its power as the result of circumstances independent of his own will. The said courts or authorities shall be at liberty to reduce the penalty provided for the violation of which the prisoner of war is accused, and shall therefore not be bound to apply the minimum penalty prescribed.

Collective punishment for individual acts, corporal punishment, imprisonment in premises without daylight and, in general, any form of torture or cruelty, are forbidden.

No prisoner of war may be deprived of his rank by the Detaining Power, or prevented from wearing his badges.

Art. 88. Officers, non-commissioned officers and men who are prisoners of war undergoing a disciplinary or judicial punishment, shall not be subjected to more severe treatment than that applied in respect of the same punishment to members of the armed forces of the Detaining Power of equivalent rank.

A woman prisoner of war shall not be awarded or sentenced to a punishment more severe, or treated whilst undergoing punishment more severely, than a woman member of the armed forces of the Detaining Power dealt with for a similar offence.

In no case may a woman prisoner of war be awarded or sentenced to a punishment more severe, or treated whilst undergoing punishment more severely, than a male member of the armed forces of the Detaining Power dealt with for a similar offence.

Prisoners of war who have served disciplinary or judicial sentences may not be treated differently from other prisoners of war.

II. Disciplinary Sanctions

Art. 89. The disciplinary punishments applicable to prisoners of war are the following:

1. A fine which shall not exceed 50 per cent of the advances of pay and working pay which the prisoner of war would otherwise receive under the provisions of Articles 60 and 62 during a period of not more than thirty days.
2. Discontinuance of privileges granted over and above the treatment provided for by the present Convention.
3. Fatigue duties not exceeding two hours daily.
4. Confinement.

The punishment referred to under (3) shall not be applied to officers.

In no case shall disciplinary punishments be inhuman, brutal or dangerous to the health of prisoners of war.

Art. 90. The duration of any single punishment shall in no case exceed thirty days. Any period of confinement awaiting the hearing of a disciplinary offence or the award of disciplinary punishment shall be deducted from an award pronounced against a prisoner of war.

The maximum of thirty days provided above may not be exceeded, even if the prisoner of war is answerable for several acts at the same time when he is awarded punishment, whether such acts are related or not.

The period between the pronouncing of an award of disciplinary punishment and its execution shall not exceed one month.

When a prisoner of war is awarded a further disciplinary punishment, a period of at least three days shall elapse between the execution of any two of the punishments, if the duration of one of these is ten days or more.

Art. 91. The escape of a prisoner of war shall be deemed to have succeeded when:

1. he has joined the armed forces of the Power on which he depends, or those of an allied Power;
2. he has left the territory under the control of the Detaining Power, or of an ally of the said Power;
3. he has joined a ship flying the flag of the Power on which he depends, or of an allied Power, in the territorial waters of the Detaining Power, the said ship not being under the control of the last named Power.

Prisoners of war who have made good their escape in the sense of this Article and who are recaptured, shall not be liable to any punishment in respect of their previous escape.

Art. 92. A prisoner of war who attempts to escape and is recaptured before having made good his escape in the sense of Article 91 shall be liable only to a disciplinary punishment in respect of this act, even if it is a repeated offence.

A prisoner of war who is recaptured shall be handed over without delay to the competent military authority.

Article 88, fourth paragraph, notwithstanding, prisoners of war punished as a result of an unsuccessful escape may be subjected to special surveillance. Such surveillance must not affect the state of their health, must be undergone in a prisoner of war camp, and must not entail the suppression of any of the safeguards granted them by the present Convention.

ART. 93. Escape or attempt to escape, even if it is a repeated offence, shall not be deemed an aggravating circumstance if the prisoner of war is subjected to trial by judicial proceedings in respect of an offence committed during his escape or attempt to escape.

In conformity with the principle stated in Article 83, offences committed by prisoners of war with the sole intention of facilitating their escape and which do not entail any violence against life or limb, such as offences against public property, theft without intention of self-enrichment, the drawing up or use of false papers, or the wearing of civilian clothing, shall occasion disciplinary punishment only.

Prisoners of war who aid or abet an escape or an attempt to escape shall be liable on this count to disciplinary punishment only.

ART. 94. If an escaped prisoner of war is recaptured, the Power on which he depends shall be notified thereof in the manner defined in Article 122, provided notification of his escape has been made.

ART. 95. A prisoner of war accused of an offence against discipline shall not be kept in confinement pending the hearing unless a member of the armed forces of the Detaining Power would be so kept if he were accused of a similar offence, or if it is essential in the interests of camp order and discipline.

Any period spent by a prisoner of war in confinement awaiting the disposal of an offence against discipline shall be reduced to an absolute minimum and shall not exceed fourteen days.

The provisions of Articles 97 and 98 of this Chapter shall apply to prisoners of war who are in confinement awaiting the disposal of offences against discipline.

ART. 96. Acts which constitute offences against discipline shall be investigated immediately.

Without prejudice to the competence of courts and superior military authorities, disciplinary punishment may be ordered only by an officer having disciplinary powers in his capacity as camp commander, or by a responsible officer who replaces him or to whom he has delegated his disciplinary powers.

In no case may such powers be delegated to a prisoner of war or be exercised by a prisoner of war.

Before any disciplinary award is pronounced, the accused shall be given precise information regarding the offences of which he is accused, and given an opportunity of explaining his conduct and of defending himself. He shall be permitted, in particular, to call witnesses and to have recourse, if necessary, to the services of a qualified interpreter. The decision shall be announced to the accused prisoner of war and to the prisoners' representative.

A record of disciplinary punishments shall be maintained by the camp commander and shall be open to inspection by representatives of the Protecting Power.

Art. 97. Prisoners of war shall not in any case be transferred to penitentiary establishments (prisons, penitentiaries, convict prisons, etc.) to undergo disciplinary punishment therein.

All premises in which disciplinary punishments are undergone shall conform to the sanitary requirements set forth in Article 25. A prisoner of war undergoing punishment shall be enabled to keep himself in a state of cleanliness, in conformity with Article 29.

Officers and persons of equivalent status shall not be lodged in the same quarters as non-commissioned officers or men.

Women prisoners of war undergoing disciplinary punishment shall be confined in separate quarters from male prisoners of war and shall be under the immediate supervision of women.

Art. 98. A prisoner of war undergoing confinement as a disciplinary punishment, shall continue to enjoy the benefits of.the provisions of this Convention except in so far as these are necessarily rendered inapplicable by the mere fact that he is confined. In no case may he be deprived of the benefits of the provisions of Articles 78 and 126.

A prisoner of war awarded disciplinary punishment may not be deprived of the prerogatives attached to his rank.

Prisoners of war awarded disciplinary punishment shall be allowed to exercise and to stay in the open air at least two hours daily.

They shall be allowed, on their request, to be present at the daily medical inspections. They shall receive the attention which their state of health requires and, if necessary, shall be removed to the camp infirmary or to a hospital.

They shall have permission to read and write, likewise to send and receive letters. Parcels and remittances of money however, may be withheld from them until the completion of the punishment; they shall meanwhile be entrusted to the prisoners' representative, who-will hand over to the infirmary the perishable goods contained in such parcels.

III. Juridicial Proceedings

Art. 99. No prisoner of war may be tried or sentenced for an act which is not forbidden by the law of the Detaining Power or by international law, in force at the time the said act was committed.

No moral or physical coercion may be exerted on a prisoner of war in order to induce him to admit himself guilty of the act of which he is accused.

No prisoner of war may be convicted without having had an opportunity to present his defence and the assistance of a qualified advocate or counsel.

Art. 100. Prisoners of war and the Protecting Powers shall be informed as soon as possible of the offences which are punishable by the death sentence under the laws of the Detaining Power.

Other offences shall not thereafter be made punishable by the death penalty without the concurrence of the Power on which the prisoners of war depend.

The death sentence cannot be pronounced on a prisoner of war unless the attention of the court has, in accordance with Article 87, second paragraph, been particularly called to the fact that since the accused is not a national of the Detaining Power, he is not bound to it by any duty of allegiance, and that he is in its power as the result of circumstances independent of his own will.

Art. 101. If the death penalty is pronounced on a prisoner of war, the sentence shall not be executed before the expiration of a period of at least six months from the date when the Protecting Power receives, at an indicated address, the detailed communication provided for in Article 107.

Art. 102. A prisoner of war can be validly sentenced only if the sentence has been pronounced by the same courts according to the same procedure as in the case of members of the armed forces of the Detaining Power, and if, furthermore, the provisions of the present Chapter have been observed.

Art. 103. Judicial investigations relating to a prisoner of war shall be conducted as rapidly as circumstances permit and so that his trial shall take place as soon as possible. A prisoner of war shall not be confined while awaiting trial unless a member of the armed forces of the Detaining Power would be so confined if he were accused of a similar offence, or if it is essential to do so in the interests of national security. In no circumstances shall this confinement exceed three months.

Any period spent by a prisoner of war in confinement awaiting trial shall be deducted from any sentence of imprisonment passed upon him and taken into account in fixing any penalty.

The provisions of Articles 97 and 98 of this Chapter shall apply to a prisoner of war whilst in confinement awaiting trial.

ART. 104. In any case in which the Detaining Power has decided to institute judicial proceedings against a prisoner of war, it shall notify the Protecting Power as soon as possible and at least three weeks before the opening of the trial. This period of three weeks shall run as from the day on which such notification reaches the Protecting Power at the address previously indicated by the latter to the Detaining Power.

The said notification shall contain the following information:

1. Surname and first names of the prisoner of war, his rank, his army, regimental, personal or serial number, his date of birth, and his profession or trade, if any;
2. Place of internment or confinement;
3. Specification of the charge or charges on which the prisoner of war is to be arraigned, giving the legal provisions applicable;
4. Designation of the court which will try the case, likewise the date and place fixed for the opening of the trial.

The same communication shall be made by the Detaining Power to the prisoners' representative.

If no evidence is submitted, at the opening of a trial, that the notification referred to above was received by the Protecting Power, by the prisoner of war and by the prisoners' representative concerned, at least three weeks before the opening of the trial, then the latter cannot take place and must be adjourned.

ART. 105. The prisoner of war shall be entitled to assistance by one of his prisoner comrades, to defence by a qualified advocate or counsel of his own choice, to the calling of witnesses and, if he deems necessary, to the services of a competent interpreter. He shall be advised of these rights by the Detaining Power in due time before the trial.

Failing a choice by the prisoner of war, the Protecting Power shall find him an advocate or counsel, and shall have at least one week at its disposal for the purpose. The Detaining Power shall deliver to the said Power, on request, a list of persons qualified to present the defence. Failing a choice of an advocate or counsel by the prisoner of war or the Protecting Power, the Detaining Power shall appoint a competent advocate or counsel to conduct the defence.

The advocate or counsel conducting the defence on behalf of the prisoner of war shall have at his disposal a period of two weeks at least before the opening of the trial, as well as the necessary facilities to prepare the defence of the accused. He may, in particular, freely visit the accused and interview him in private. He may also confer with any witnesses for the defence, including prisoners of war. He shall have the benefit of these facilities until the term of appeal or petition has expired.

Particulars of the charge or charges on which the prisoner of war is to be arraigned, as well as the documents which are generally communicated to the accused by virtue of the laws in force in the armed forces of the Detaining Power, shall be communicated to the accused prisoner of war in a language which he understands, and in good time before the opening of the trial. The same communication in the same circumstances shall be made to the advocate or counsel conducting the defence on behalf of the prisoner of war.

The representatives of the Protecting Power shall be entitled to attend the trial of the case, unless, exceptionally, this is held in camera in the interest of State security. In such a case the Detaining Power shall advise the Protecting Power accordingly.

ART. 106. Every prisoner of war shall have, in the same manner as the members of the armed forces of the Detaining Power, the right of appeal or petition from any sentence pronounced upon him, with a view to the quashing or revising of the sentence or the reopening of the trial. He shall be fully informed of his right to appeal or petition and of the time limit within which he may do so.

ART. 107. Any judgment and sentence pronounced upon a prisoner of war shall be immediately reported to the Protecting Power in the form of a summary communication, which shall also indicate whether he has the right of appeal with a view to the quashing of the sentence or the reopening of the trial. This communication shall likewise be sent to the prisoners' representative concerned. It shall also be sent to the accused prisoner of war in a language he understands, if the sentence was not pronounced in his presence. The Detaining Power shall also immediately communicate to the Protecting Power the decision of the prisoner of war to use or to waive his right of appeal.

Furthermore, if a prisoner of war is finally convicted or if a sentence pronounced on a prisoner of war in the first instance is a death sentence, the Detaining Power shall as soon as possible address to the Protecting Power a detailed communication containing:

1. the precise wording of the finding and sentence;
2. a summarized report of any preliminary investigation and of the trial, emphasizing in particular the elements of the prosecution and the defence;
3. notification, where applicable, of the establishment where the sentence will be served.

The communications provided for in the foregoing sub-paragraphs shall be sent to the Protecting Power at the address previously made known to the Detaining Power.

ART. 108. Sentences pronounced on prisoners of war after a conviction has become duly enforceable, shall be served in the same establishments and under the same conditions as in the case of members of the armed forces of the Detaining Power. These conditions shall in all cases conform to the requirements of health and humanity.

A woman prisoner of war on whom such a sentence has been pronounced shall be confined in separate quarters and shall be under the supervision of women.

In any case, prisoners of war sentenced to a penalty depriving them of their liberty shall retain the benefit of the provisions of Articles 78 and 126 of the present Convention. Furthermore, they shall be entitled to receive and despatch correspondence, to receive at least one relief parcel monthly, to take regular exercise in the open air, to have the medical care required by their state of health, and the spiritual assistance they may desire. Penalties to which they may be subjected shall be in accordance with the provisions of Article 87, third paragraph.

PART IV. TERMINATION OF CAPTIVITY

Section I. Direct Repatriation and Accommodation in Neutral Countries

ART. 109. Subject to the provisions of the third paragraph of this Article, Parties to the conflict are bound to send back to their own country, regardless of number or rank, seriously wounded and seriously sick prisoners of war, after having cared for them until they are fit to travel, in accordance with the first paragraph of the following Article.

Throughout the duration of hostilities, Parties to the conflict shall endeavour, with the cooperation of the neutral Powers concerned, to make arrangements for the accommodation in neutral countries of the sick and wounded prisoners of war referred to in the second paragraph of the following Article. They may, in addition, conclude agreements with a view to the direct repatriation or internment in a neutral country of able-bodied prisoners of war who have undergone a long period of captivity.

No sick or injured prisoner of war who is eligible for repatriation under the first paragraph of this Article, may be repatriated against his will during hostilities.

Art. 110. The following shall be repatriated direct:

1. Incurably wounded and sick whose mental or physical fitness seems to have been gravely diminished.
2. Wounded and sick who, according to medical opinion, are not likely to recover within one year, whose condition requires treatment and whose mental or physical fitness seems to have been gravely diminished.
3. Wounded and sick who have recovered, but whose mental or physical fitness seems to have been gravely and permanently diminished.

The following may be accommodated in a neutral country:

1. Wounded and sick whose recovery may be expected within one year of the date of the wound or the beginning of the illness, if treatment in a neutral country might increase the prospects of a more certain and speedy recovery.
2. Prisoners of war whose mental or physical health, according to medical opinion, is seriously threatened by continued captivity, but whose accommodation in a neutral country might remove such a threat.

The conditions which prisoners of war accommodated in a neutral country must fulfil in order to permit their repatriation shall be fixed, as shall likewise their status, by agreement between the Powers concerned. In general, prisoners of war who have been accommodated in a neutral country, and who belong to the following categories, should be repatriated:

1. Those whose state of health has deteriorated so as to fulfil the condition laid down for direct repatriation;
2. Those whose mental or physical powers remain, even after treatment, considerably impaired.

If no special agreements are concluded between the Parties to the conflict concerned, to determine the cases of disablement or sickness entailing direct repatriation or accommodation in a neutral country, such cases shall be settled in accordance with the principles laid down in the Model Agreement concerning direct repatriation and accommodation in neutral countries of wounded and sick prisoners of war and in the Regulations concerning Mixed Medical Commissions annexed to the present Convention.

ART. 111. The Detaining Power, the Power on which the prisoners of war depend, and a neutral Power agreed upon by these two Powers, shall endeavour to conclude agreements which will enable prisoners of war to be interned in the territory of the said neutral Power until the close of hostilities.

ART. 112. Upon the outbreak of hostilities, Mixed Medical Commissions shall be appointed to examine sick and wounded prisoners of war, and to make all appropriate decisions regarding them. The appointment, duties and functioning of these Commissions shall be in conformity with the provisions of the Regulations annexed to the present Convention.

However, prisoners of war who, in the opinion of the medical authorities of the Detaining Power, are manifestly seriously injured or seriously sick, may be repatriated without having to be examined by a Mixed Medical Commission.

ART. 113. Besides those who are designated by the medical authorities of the Detaining Power, wounded or sick prisoners of war belonging to the categories listed below shall be entitled to present themselves for examination by the Mixed Medical Commissions provided for in the foregoing Article:

1. Wounded and sick proposed by a physician or surgeon who is of the same nationality, or a national of a Party to the conflict allied with the Power on which the said prisoners depend, and who exercises his functions in the camp.
2. Wounded and sick proposed by their prisoners' representative.
3. Wounded and sick proposed by the Power on which they depend, or by an organization duly recognized by the said Power and giving assistance to the prisoners.

Prisoners of war who do not belong to one of the three foregoing categories may nevertheless present themselves for examination by Mixed Medical Commissions, but shall be examined only after those belonging to the said categories.

The physician or surgeon of the same nationality as the prisoners who present themselves for examination by the Mixed Medical Commission, likewise the prisoners' representative of the said prisoners, shall have permission to be present at the examination.

Art. 114. Prisoners of war who meet with accidents shall, unless the injury is self-inflicted, have the benefit of the provisions of this Convention as regards repatriation or accommodation in a neutral country.

Art. 115. No prisoner of war on whom a disciplinary punishment has been imposed and who is eligible for repatriation or for accommodation in a neutral country, may be kept back on the plea that he has not undergone his punishment.

Prisoners of war detained in connection with a judicial prosecution or conviction, and who are designated for repatriation or accommodation in a neutral country, may benefit by such measures before the end of the proceedings or the completion of the punishment, if the Detaining Power consents.

Parties to the conflict shall communicate to each other the names of those who will be detained until the end of the proceedings or the completion of the punishment.

Art. 116. The cost of repatriating prisoners of war or of transporting them to a neutral country shall be borne, from the frontiers of the Detaining Power, by the Power on which the said prisoners depend.

Art. 117. No repatriated person may be employed on active military service.

Section II. Release and Repatriation of Prisoners of War at the Close of Hostilities

Art. 118. Prisoners of war shall be released and repatriated without delay after the cessation of active hostilities.

In the absence of stipulations to the above effect in any agreement concluded between the Parties to the conflict with a view to the cessation of hostilities, or failing any such agreement, each of the Detaining Powers shall itself establish and execute without delay a plan of repatriation in conformity with the principle laid down in the foregoing paragraph.

In either case, the measures adopted shall be brought to the knowledge of the prisoners of war.

The costs of repatriation of prisoners of war shall in all cases be equitably apportioned between the Detaining Power and the Power on which the prisoners depend. This apportionment shall be carried out on the following basis:

a. If the two Powers are contiguous, the Power on which the prisoners of war depend shall bear the costs of repatriation from the frontiers of the Detaining Power.

b. If the two Powers are not contiguous, the Detaining Power shall bear the costs of transport of prisoners of war over its own territory as far as its frontier or its port of embarkation nearest to the territory of the Power on which the prisoners of war depend. The Parties concerned shall agree between themselves as to the equitable apportionment of the remaining costs of the repatriation. The conclusion of this agreement shall in no circumstances justify any delay in the repatriation of the prisoners of war.

ART. 119. Repatriation shall be effected in conditions similar to those laid down in Articles 46 to 48 inclusive of the present Convention for the transfer of prisoners of war, having regard to the provisions of Article 118 and to those of the following paragraphs.

On repatriation, any articles of value impounded from prisoners of war under Article 18, and any foreign currency which has not been converted into the currency of the Detaining Power, shall be restored to them. Articles of value and foreign currency which, for any reason whatever, are not restored to prisoners of war on repatriation, shall be despatched to the Information Bureau set up under Article 122.

Prisoners of war shall be allowed to take with them their personal effects, and any correspondence and parcels which have arrived for them. The weight of such baggage may be limited, if the conditions of repatriation so require, to what each prisoner can reasonably carry. Each prisoner shall in all cases be authorized to carry at least twenty-five kilograms.

The other personal effects of the repatriated prisoner shall be left in the charge of the Detaining Power which shall have them forwarded to him as soon as it has concluded an agreement to this effect, regulating the conditions of transport and the payment of the costs involved, with the Power on which the prisoner depends.

Prisoners of war against whom criminal proceedings for an indictable offence are pending may be detained until the end of such proceedings, and, if necessary, until the completion of the punishment. The same shall apply to prisoners of war already convicted for an indictable offence.

Parties to the conflict shall communicate to each other the names of any prisoners of war who are detained until the end of the proceedings or until punishment has been completed.

By agreement between the Parties to the conflict, commissions shall be established for the purpose of searching for dispersed prisoners of war and of assuring their repatriation with the least possible delay.

Section III. Death of Prisoners of War

ART. 120. Wills of prisoners of war shall be drawn up so as to satisfy the conditions of validity required by the legislation of their country of origin, which will take steps to inform the Detaining Power of its requirements in this respect. At the request of the prisoner of war and, in all cases, after death, the will shall be transmitted without delay to the Protecting Power; a certified copy shall be sent to the Central Agency.

Death certificates, in the form annexed to the present Convention, or lists certified by a responsible officer, of all persons who die as prisoners of war shall be forwarded as rapidly as possible to the Prisoner of War Information Bureau established in accordance with Article 122. The death certificates or certified lists shall show particulars of identity as set out in the third paragraph of Article 17, and also the date and place of death, the cause of death, the date and place of burial and all particulars necessary to identify the graves.

The burial or cremation of a prisoner of war shall be preceded by a medical examination of the body with a view to confirming death and enabling a report to be made and, where necessary, establishing identity.

The detaining authorities shall ensure that prisoners of war who have died in captivity are honourably buried, if possible according to the rites of the religion to which they belonged, and that their graves are respected, suitably maintained and marked so as to be found at any time. Wherever possible, deceased prisoners of war who depended on the same Power shall be interred in the same place.

Deceased prisoners of war shall be buried in individual graves unless unavoidable circumstances require the use of collective graves. Bodies may be cremated only for imperative reasons of hygiene, on account of the religion of the deceased or in accordance with his express wish to this effect. In case of cremation, the fact shall be stated and the reasons given in the death certificate of the deceased.

In order that graves may always be found, all particulars of burials and graves shall be recorded with a Graves Registration Service established by the Detaining Power. Lists of graves and particulars of the prisoners of war interred in cemeteries and elsewhere shall be transmitted to the Power on which such prisoners of war depended. Responsibility for the care of these graves and for records of any subsequent moves of the bodies shall rest on the Power controlling the territory, if a Party to the present Convention. These provisions shall also apply to the ashes, which shall be kept by the Graves Registration Service until proper disposal thereof in accordance with the wishes of the home country.

ART. 121. Every death or serious injury of a prisoner of war caused or suspected to have been caused by a sentry, another prisoner of war, or any other person, as well as any death the cause of which is unknown, shall be immediately followed by an official enquiry by the Detaining Power.

A communication on this subject shall be sent immediately to the Protecting Power. Statements shall be taken from witnesses, especially from those who are prisoners of war, and a report including such statements shall be forwarded to the Protecting Power.

If the enquiry indicates the guilt of one or more persons, the Detaining Power shall take all measures for the prosecution of the person or persons responsible.

PART V. INFORMATION BUREAUX AND RELIEF SOCIETIES FOR PRISONERS OF WAR

ART. 122. Upon the outbreak of a conflict and in all cases of occupation, each of the Parties to the conflict shall institute an official Information Bureau for prisoners of war who are in its power. Neutral or non-belligerent Powers who may have received within their territory persons belonging to one of the categories referred to in Article 4, shall take the same action with respect to such persons. The Power concerned shall ensure that the Prisoners of War Information Bureau is provided with the necessary accommodation, equipment and staff to ensure its efficient working. It shall be at liberty to employ prisoners of war in such a Bureau under the conditions laid down in the Section of the present Convention dealing with work by prisoners of war.

Within the shortest possible period, each of the Parties to the conflict shall give its Bureau the information referred to in the fourth, fifth and sixth paragraphs of this Article regarding any enemy person belonging to one of the categories referred to in Article 4, who has fallen into its power. Neutral or non-belligerent Powers shall take the same action with regard to persons belonging to such categories whom they have received within their territory.

The Bureau shall immediately forward such information by the most rapid means to the Powers concerned, through the intermediary of the Protecting Powers and likewise of the Central Agency provided for in Article 123.

This information shall make it possible quickly to advise the next of kin concerned. Subject to the provisions of Article 17, the information shall include, in so far as available to the Information Bureau, in respect of each prisoner of war, his surname, first names, rank, army, regimental, personal or serial number, place and full date of birth, indication of the Power on which he depends, first name of the father and maiden name of the mother, name and address of the person to be informed and the address to which correspondence for the prisoner may be sent.

The Information Bureau shall receive from the various departments concerned information regarding transfers, releases, repatriations, escapes, admissions to hospital, and deaths, and shall transmit such information in the manner described in the third paragraph above.

Likewise, information regarding the state of health of prisoners of war who are seriously ill or seriously wounded shall be supplied regularly, every week if possible.

The Information Bureau shall also be responsible for replying to all enquiries sent to it concerning prisoners of war, including those who have died in captivity; it will make any enquiries necessary to obtain the information which is asked for if this is not in its possession.

All written communications made by the Bureau shall be authenticated by a signature or a seal.

The Information Bureau shall furthermore be charged with collecting all personal valuables, including sums in currencies other than that of the Detaining Power and documents of importance to the next of kin, left by prisoners of war who have been repatriated or released, or who have escaped or died, and shall forward the said valuables to the Powers concerned. Such articles shall be sent by the Bureau in sealed packets which shall be accompanied by statements giving clear and full particulars of the identity of the person to whom the articles belonged, and by a complete list of the contents of the parcel. Other personal effects of such prisoners of war shall be transmitted under arrangements agreed upon between the Parties to the conflict concerned.

Art. 123. A Central Prisoners of War Information Agency shall be created in a neutral country. The International Committee of the Red Cross shall, if it deems necessary, propose to the Powers concerned the organization of such an Agency.

The function of the Agency shall be to collect all the information it may obtain through official or private channels respecting prisoners of war, and to transmit it as rapidly as possible to the country of origin of the prisoners of war or to the Power on which they depend. It shall receive from the Parties to the conflict all facilities for effecting such transmissions.

The High Contracting Parties, and in particular those whose nationals benefit by the services of the Central Agency, are requested to give the said Agency the financial aid it may require.

The foregoing provisions shall in no way be interpreted as restricting the humanitarian activities of the International Committee of the Red Cross, or of the relief societies provided for in Article 125.

ART. 124. The national Information Bureaux and the Central Information Agency shall enjoy free postage for mail, likewise all the exemptions provided for in Article 74, and further, so far as possible, exemption from telegraphic charges or, at least, greatly reduced rates.

ART. 125. Subject to the measures which the Detaining Powers may consider essential to ensure their security or to meet any other reasonable need, the representatives of religious organizations, relief societies, or any other organization assisting prisoners of war, shall receive from the said Powers, for themselves and their duly accredited agents, all necessary facilities for visiting the prisoners, for distributing relief supplies and material, from any source, intended for religious, educational or recreative purposes, and for assisting them in organizing their leisure time within the camps. Such societies or organizations may be constituted in the territory of the Detaining Power or in any other country, or they may have an international character.

The Detaining Power may limit the number of societies and organizations whose delegates are allowed to carry out their activities in its territory and under its supervision, on condition, however, that such limitation shall not hinder the effective operation of adequate relief to all prisoners of war.

The special position of the International Committee of the Red Cross in this field shall be recognized and respected at all times.

As soon as relief supplies or material intended for the above-mentioned purposes are handed over to prisoners of war, or very shortly afterwards, receipts for each consignment, signed by the prisoners' representative, shall be forwarded to the relief society or organization making the shipment. At the same time, receipts for these consignments shall be supplied by the administrative authorities responsible for guarding the prisoners.

PART VI. EXECUTION OF THE CONVENTION

Section I. General Provisions

ART. 126. Representatives or delegates of the Protecting Powers shall have permission to go to all places where prisoners of war may be, particularly to places of internment, imprisonment and labour, and shall have access to all premises occupied by prisoners of war; they shall also be allowed to go to the places of departure, passage and arrival of prisoners who are being transferred. They shall be able to interview the prisoners, and in particular the prisoners' representatives, without witnesses, either personally or through an interpreter.

Representatives and delegates of the Protecting Powers shall have full liberty to select the places they wish to visit. The duration and frequency of these visits shall not be restricted. Visits may not be prohibited except for reasons of imperative military necessity, and then only as an exceptional and temporary measure.

The Detaining Power and the Power on which the said prisoners of war depend may agree, if necessary, that compatriots of these prisoners of war be permitted to participate in the visits.

The delegates of the International Committee of the Red Cross shall enjoy the same prerogatives. The appointment of such delegates shall be submitted to the approval of the Power detaining the prisoners of war to be visited.

ART. 127. The High Contracting Parties undertake, in time of peace as in time of war, to disseminate the text of the present Convention as widely as possible in their respective countries, and, in particular, to include the study thereof in their programmes of military and, if possible, civil instruction, so that the principles thereof may become known to all their armed forces and to the entire population.

Any military or other authorities, who in time of war assume responsibilities in respect of prisoners of war, must possess the text of the Convention and be specially instructed as to its provisions.

ART. 128. The High Contracting Parties shall communicate to one another through the Swiss Federal Council and, during hostilities, through the Protecting Powers, the official translations of the present Convention, as well as the laws and regulations which they may adopt to ensure the application thereof.

Art. 129. The High Contracting Parties undertake to enact any legislation necessary to provide effective penal sanctions for persons committing, or ordering to be committed, any of the grave breaches of the present Convention defined in the following Article.

Each High Contracting Party shall be under the obligation to search for persons alleged to have committed. or to have ordered to be committed, such grave breaches, and shall bring such persons, regardless of their nationality, before its own courts. It may also, if it prefers, and in accordance with the provisions of its own legislation, hand such persons over for trial to another High Contracting Party concerned, provided such High Contracting Party has made out a prima facie case.

Each High Contracting Party shall take measures necessary for the suppression of all acts contrary to the provisions of the present Convention other than the grave breaches defined in the following Article.

In all circumstances, the accused persons shall benefit by safeguards of proper trial and defence, which shall not be less favourable than those provided by Article 105 and those following of the present Convention.

Art. 130. Grave breaches to which the preceding Article relates shall be those involving any of the following acts, if committed against persons or property protected by the Convention: wilful killing, torture or inhuman treatment, including biological experiments, wilfully causing great suffering or serious injury to body or health, compelling a prisoner of war to serve in the forces of the hostile Power, or wilfully depriving a prisoner of war of the rights of fair and regular trial prescribed in this Convention.

Art. 131. No High Contracting Party shall be allowed to absolve itself or any other High Contracting Party of any liability incurred by itself or by another High Contracting Party in respect of breaches referred to in the preceding Article.

Art. 132. At the request of a Party to the conflict, an enquiry shall be instituted, in a manner to be decided between the interested Parties, concerning any alleged violation of the Convention.

If agreement has not been reached concerning the procedure for the enquiry, the Parties should agree on the choice of an umpire who will decide upon the procedure to be followed.

Once the violation has been established, the Parties to the conflict shall put an end to it and shall repress it with the least possible delay.

Section II. Final Provisions

Art. 133. The present Convention is established in English and in French. Both texts are equally authentic.

The Swiss Federal Council shall arrange for official translations of the Convention to be made in the Russian and Spanish languages.

Art. 134. The present Convention replaces the Convention of July 27, 1929, in relations between the High Contracting Parties.

Art. 135. In the relations between the Powers which are bound by the Hague Convention respecting the Laws and Customs of War on Land, whether that of July 29, 1899, or that of October 18, 1907, and which are parties to the present Convention, this last Convention shall be complementary to Chapter II of the Regulations annexed to th above-mentioned Conventions of the Hague.

Art. 136. The present Convention, which bears the date of this day, is open to signature until February 12, 1950, in the name of the Powers represented at the Conference which opened at Geneva on April 21, 1949; furthermore, by Powers not represented at that Conference, but which are parties to the Convention of July 27, 1929.

Art. 137. The present Convention shall be ratified as soon as possible and the ratifications shall be deposited at Berne.

A record shall be drawn up of the deposit of each instrument of ratification and certified copies of this record shall be transmitted by the Swiss Federal Council to all the Powers in whose name the Convention has been signed, or whose accession has been notified.

Art. 138. The present Convention shall come into force six months after not less than two instruments of ratification have been deposited.

Thereafter, it shall come into force for each High Contracting Party six months after the deposit of the instrument of ratification.

Art. 139. From the date of its coming into force, it shall be open to any Power in whose name the present Convention has not been signed, to accede to this Convention.

Art. 140. Accessions shall be notified in writing to the Swiss Federal Council, and shall take effect six months after the date on which they are received.

The Swiss Federal Council shall communicate the accessions to all the Powers in whose name the Convention has been signed, or whose accession has been notified.

Art. 141. The situations provided for in Articles 2 and 3 shall give immediate effect to ratifications deposited and accessions notified by the Parties to the conflict before or after the beginning of hostilities or occupation. The Swiss Federal Council shall communicate by the quickest method any ratifications or accessions received from Parties to the conflict.

Art. 142. Each of the High Contracting Parties shall be at liberty to denounce the present Convention.

The denunciation shall be notified in writing to the Swiss Federal Council, which shall transmit it to the Governments of all the High Contracting Parties.

The denunciation shall take effect one year after the notification thereof has been made to the Swiss Federal Council. However, a denunciation of which notification has been made at a time when the denouncing Power is involved in a conflict shall not take effect until peace has been concluded, and until after operations connected with release and repatriation of the persons protected by the present Convention have been terminated.

The denunciation shall have effect only in respect of the denouncing Power. It shall in no way impair the obligations which the Parties to the conflict shall remain bound to fulfil by virtue of the principles of the law of nations, as they result from the usages established among civilized peoples, from the laws of humanity and the dictates of the public conscience.

Art. 143. The Swiss Federal Council shall register the present Convention with the Secretariat of the United Nations. The Swiss Federal Council shall also inform the Secretariat of the United Nations of all ratifications, accessions and denunciations received by it with respect to the present Convention.

IN WITNESS WHEREOF the undersigned, having deposited their respective full powers, have signed the present Convention.

DONE at Geneva this twelfth day of August 1949, in the English and French languages. The original shall be deposited in the Archives of the Swiss Confederation. The Swiss Federal Council shall transmit certified copies thereof to each of the signatory and acceding States.

ANNEX I. Model Agreement Concerning Direct Repatriation and Accommodation in Neutral Countries of Wounded and Sick Prisoners of War (see Art. 110)

I. Principles for Direct Repatriation and Accommodation in Neutral Countries

A. DIRECT REPATRIATION

The following shall be repatriated direct:

1. All prisoners of war suffering from the following disabilities as the result of trauma: loss of a limb, paralysis, articular or other disabilities, when this disability is at least the loss of a hand or a foot, or the equivalent of the loss of a hand or a foot.

   Without prejudice to a more generous interpretation, the following shall be considered as equivalent to the loss of a hand or a foot:
   a. Loss of a hand or of all the fingers, or of the thumb and forefinger of one hand; loss of a foot, or of all the toes and metatarsals of one foot.
   b. Ankylosis, loss of osseous tissue, cicatricial contracture preventing the functioning of one of the large articulations or of all the digital joints of one hand.
   c. Pseudarthrosis of the long bones.
   d. Deformities due to fracture or other injury which seriously interfere with function and weight-bearing power.

2. All wounded prisoners of war whose condition has become chronic, to the extent that prognosis appears to exclude recovery—in spite of treatment—within one year from the date of the injury, as, for example, in case of:
   a. Projectile in the heart, even if the Mixed Medical Commission should fail, at the time of their examination, to detect any serious disorders.
   b. Metallic splinter in the brain or the lungs, even if the Mixed Medical Commission cannot, at the time of examination, detect any local or general reaction.
   c. Osteomyelitis, when recovery cannot be foreseen in the course of the year following the injury, and which seems likely to result in ankylosis of a joint, or other impairments equivalent to the loss of a hand or a foot.
   d. Perforating and suppurating injury to the large joints.
   e. Injury to the skull, with loss or shifting of bony tissue.
   f. Injury or burning of the face with loss of tissue and functional lesions.

g. Injury to the spinal cord.

h. Lesion of the peripheral nerves, the sequelae of which are equivalent to the loss of a hand or foot, and the cure of which requires more than a year from the date of injury, for.example: injury to the brachial or lumbosacral plexus median or sciatic nerves, likewise combined injury to the radial and cubital nerves or to the lateral popliteal nerve (N. peroneous communis) and medial popliteal nerve (N. tibialis); etc. The separate injury of the radial (musculo-spiral), cubital, lateral or medial popliteal nerves shall not, however, warrant repatriation except in case of contractures or of serious neurotrophic disturbance.

i. Injury to the urinary system, with incapacitating results.

3. All sick prisoners of war whose condition has become chronic to the extent that prognosis seems to exclude recovery—in, spite of treatment—within one year from the inception of the disease, as, for example, in case of:

a. Progressive tuberculosis of any organ which, according to medical prognosis, cannot be cured or at least considerably improved by treatment in a neutral country.

b. Exudate pleurisy.

c. Serious diseases of the respiratory organs of non-tubercular etiology, presumed incurable, for example: serious pulmonary emphysema, with or without bronchitis; chronic asthma*; chronic bronchitis* lasting more than one year in captivity; bronchiectasis*; etc.

d. Serious chronic affections of the circulatory system, for example: valvular lesions and myocarditis*, which have shown signs of circulatory failure during captivity, even though the Mixed Medical Commission cannot detect any such signs at the time of examination; affections of the pericardium and the vessels (Buerger's disease, aneurisms of the large vessels); etc.

e. Serious chronic affections of the digestive organs, for example: gastric or duodenal ulcer; sequelae of gastric operations performed in captivity; chronic gastritis, enteritis or colitis, having lasted more than one year and seriously affecting the general condition; cirrhosis of the liver; chronic cholecystopathy*; etc.

f. Serious chronic affections of the genito-urinary organs, for example: chronic diseases of the kidney with consequent disorders; nephrectomy because of a tubercular kidney; chronic pyelitis or chronic cystitis; hydronephrosis or pyonephrosis; chronic grave gynaecological conditions; normal pregnancy and obstetrical disorder, where it is impossible to accommodate in a neutral country; etc.

g. Serious chronic diseases of the central and peripheral nervous system, for example: all obvious psychoses and psychoneuroses, such as serious hysteria, serious captivity psychoneurosis, etc., duly verified by a specialist*; any epilepsy duly verified by the camp physician*; cerebral arteriosclerosis; chronic neuritis lasting more than one year; etc.

h. Serious chronic diseases of the neuro-vegetative system, with considerable diminution of mental or physical fitness, noticeable loss of weight and general asthenia.

i. Blindness of both eyes, or of one eye when the vision of the other is less than 1 in spite of the use of corrective glasses; diminution of visual acuity in cases where it is impossible to restore it by correction to an acuity of 1/2 in at least one eye*; other grave ocular affections, for example: glaucoma, iritis, choroiditis; trachoma; etc.

k. Auditive disorders, such as total unilateral deafness, if the other ear does not discern the ordinary spoken word at a distance of one metre*; etc.

l. Serious affections of metabolism, for example: diabetes mellitus requiring insulin treatment; etc.

m. Serious disorders of the endocrine glands, for example: thyrotoxicosis; hypothyrosis; Addison's disease; Simmonds' cachexia; tetany; etc.

n. Grave and chronic disorders of the blood-forming organs.

o. Serious cases of chronic intoxication, for example: lead poisoning, mercury poisoning, morphinism, cocainism, alcoholism; gas or radiation poisoning; etc.

p. Chronic affections of locomotion, with obvious functional disorders, for example: arthritis deformans; primary and secondary progressive chronic polyarthritis; rheumatism with serious clinical symptoms; etc.

q. Serious chronic skin diseases, not amenable to treatment.

r. Any malignant growth.

s. Serious chronic infectious diseases, persisting for one year after their inception, for example: malaria with decided organic impairment, amoebic or bacillary dysentery with grave disorders; tertiary visceral syphilis resistant to treatment; leprosy; etc.

t. Serious avitaminosis or serious inanition.

Note: *The decision of the Mixed Medical Commission shall be based to a great extent on the records kept by camp physicians and surgeons of the same nationality as the prisoners of war, or on an examination by medical specialists of the Detaining Power.

B. ACCOMMODATION IN NEUTRAL COUNTRIES

The following shall be eligible for accommodation in a neutral country:

1. All wounded prisoners of war who are not likely to recover in captivity, but who might be cured or whose condition might be considerably improved by accommodation in a neutral country.
2. Prisoners of war suffering from any form of tuberculosis, of whatever organ, and whose treatment in a neutral country would be likely to lead to recovery or at least to considerable improvement, with the exception of primary tuberculosis cured before captivity.
3. Prisoners of war suffering from affections requiring treatment of the respiratory, circulatory, digestive, nervous, sensory, genito-urinary, cutaneous, locomotive organs, etc., if such treatment would clearly have better results in a neutral country than in captivity.
4. Prisoners of war who have undergone a nephrectomy in captivity for a non-tubercular renal affection; cases of osteomyelitis, on the way to recovery or latent; diabetes mellitus not requiring insulin treatment; etc.
5. Prisoners of war suffering from war or captivity neuroses. Cases of captivity neurosis which are not cured after three months of accommodation in a neutral country, or which after that length of time are not clearly on the way to complete cure, shall be repatriated.
6. All prisoners of war suffering from chronic intoxication (gases, metals, alkaloids, etc.), for whom the prospects of cure in a neutral country are especially favourable.
7. All women prisoners of war who are pregnant or mothers with infants and small children.

The following cases shall not be eligible for accommodation in a neutral country:

1. All duly verified chronic psychoses.
2. All organic or functional nervous affections considered to be incurable.
3. All contagious diseases during the period in which they are transmissible, with the exception of tuberculosis.

II. General Observations

1. The conditions given shall, in a general way, be interpreted and applied in as broad a spirit as possible. Neuropathic and psychopathic conditions caused by war or captivity, as well as cases of tuberculosis in all stages, shall above all benefit by such liberal interpretation. Prisoners of war who have sustained several wounds, none of which, considered by itself, justifies repatriation, shall be examined in the same spirit, with due regard for the psychic traumatism due to the number of their wounds.
2. All unquestionable cases giving the right to direct repatriation (amputation, total blindness or deafness, open pulmonary tuberculosis, mental disorder, malignant growth, etc.) shall be examined and repatriated as soon as possible by the camp physicians or by military medical commissions appointed by the Detaining Power.
3. Injuries and diseases which existed before the war and which have not become worse, as well as war injuries which have not prevented subsequent military service, shall not entitle to direct repatriation.
4. The provisions of this Annex shall be interpreted and applied in a similar manner in all countries party to the conflict. The Powers and authorities concerned shall grant to Mixed Medical Commissions all the facilities necessary for the accomplishment of their task.
5. The examples quoted under (1) above represent only typical cases. Cases which do not correspond exactly to these provisions shall be judged in the spirit of the provisions of Article 110 of the present Convention, and of the principles embodied in the present Agreement.

ANNEX II. Regulations Concerning Mixed Medical Commissions (see Art. 112)

ART. 1. The Mixed Medical Commissions provided for in Article 112 of the Convention shall be composed of three members, two of whom shall belong to a neutral country, the third being appointed by the Detaining Power. One of the neutral members shall take the chair.

ART. 2. The two neutral members shall be appointed by the International Committee of the Red Cross, acting in agreement with the Protecting Power, at the request of the Detaining Power. They may be domiciled either in their country of origin, in any other neutral country, or in the territory of the Detaining Power.

Art. 3. The neutral members shall be approved by the Parties to the conflict concerned, who shall notify their approval to the International Committee of the Red Cross and to the Protecting Power. Upon such notification, the neutral members shall be considered as effectively appointed.

Art. 4. Deputy members shall also be appointed in sufficient number to replace the regular members in case of need. They shall be appointed at the same time as the regular members or, at least, as soon as possible.

Art. 5. If for any reason the International Committee of the Red Cross cannot arrange for the appointment of the neutral members, this shall be done by the Power protecting the interests of the prisoners of war to be examined.

Art. 6. So far as possible, one of the two neutral members shall be a surgeon and the other a physician.

Art. 7. The neutral members shall be entirely independent of the Parties to the conflict, which shall grant them all facilities in the accomplishment of their duties.

Art. 8. By agreement with the Detaining Power, the International Committee of the Red Cross, when making the appointments provided for in Articles 2 and 4 of the present Regulations, shall settle the terms of service of the nominees.

Art. 9. The Mixed Medical Commissions shall begin their work as soon as possible after the neutral members have been approved, and in any case within a period of three months from the date of such approval.

Art. 10. The Mixed Medical Commissions shall examine all the prisoners designated in Article 113 of the Convention. They shall propose repatriation, rejection, or reference to a later examination. Their decisions shall be made by a majority vote.

Art. 11. The decisions made by the Mixed Medical Commissions in each specific case shall be communicated, during the month following their visit, to the Detaining Power, the Protecting Power and the International Committee of the Red Cross. The Mixed Medical Commissions shall also inform each prisoner of war examined of the decision made, and shall issue to those whose repatriation has been proposed, certificates similar to the model appended to the present Convention.

ART. 12. The Detaining Power shall be required to carry out the decisions of the Mixed Medical Commissions within three months of the time when it receives due notification of such decisions.

ART. 13. If there is no neutral physician in a country where the services of a Mixed Medical Commission seem to be required, and if it is for any reason impossible to appoint neutral doctors who are resident in another country, the Detaining Power, acting in agreement with the Protecting Power, shall set up a Medical Commission which shall undertake the same duties as a Mixed Medical Commission, subject to the provisions of Articles 1, 2, 3, 4, 5 and 8 of the present Regulations.

ART. 14. Mixed Medical Commissions shall function permanently and shall visit each camp at intervals of not more than six months.

ANNEX III. Regulations Concerning Collective Relief (see Art. 73)

ART. 1. Prisoners' representatives shall be allowed to distribute collective relief shipments for which they are responsible, to all prisoners of war administered by their camp, including those who are in hospitals, or in prisons or other penal establishments.

ART. 2. The distribution of collective relief shipments shall be effected in accordance with the instructions of the donors and with a plan drawn up by the prisoners' representatives. The issue of medical stores shall, however, be made for preference in agreement with the senior medical officers, and the latter may, in hospitals and infirmaries, waive the said instructions, if the needs of their patients so demand. Within the limits thus defined, the distribution shall always be carried out equitably.

ART. 3. The said prisoners' representatives or their assistants shall be allowed to go to the points of arrival of relief supplies near their camps, so as to enable the prisoners' representatives or their assistants to verify the quality as well as the quantity of the goods received, and to make out detailed reports thereon for the donors.

ART. 4. Prisoners' representatives shall be given the facilities necessary for verifying whether the distribution of collective relief in all subdivisions and annexes of their camps has been carried out in accordance with their instructions.

Art. 5. Prisoners' representatives shall be allowed to fill up, and cause to be filled up by the prisoners' representatives of labour detachments or by the senior medical officers of infirmaries and hospitals, forms or questionnaires intended for the donors, relating to collective relief supplies (distribution, requirements, quantities, etc.). Such forms and questionnaires, duly completed, shall be forwarded to the donors without delay.

Art. 6. In order to secure the regular issue of collective relief to the prisoners of war in their camp, and to meet any needs that may arise from the arrival of new contingents of prisoners, prisoners' representatives shall be allowed to build up and maintain adequate reserve stocks of collective relief. For this purpose, they shall have suitable warehouses at their disposal; each warehouse shall be provided with two locks, the prisoners' representative holding the keys of one lock and the camp commander the keys of the other.

Art. 7. When collective consignments of clothing are available, each prisoner of war shall retain in his possession at least one complete set of clothes. If a prisoner has more than one set of clothes, the prisoners' representative shall be permitted to withdraw excess clothing from those with the largest number of sets, or particular articles in excess of one, if this is necessary in order to supply prisoners who are less well provided. He shall not, however, withdraw second sets of underclothing, socks or footwear, unless this is the only means of providing for prisoners of war with none.

Art. 8. The High Contracting Parties, and the Detaining Powers in particular, shall authorize, as far as possible and subject to the regulations governing the supply of the population, all purchases of goods made in their territories for the distribution of collective relief to prisoners of war. They shall similarly facilitate the transfer of funds and other financial measures of a technical or administrative nature taken for the purpose of making such purchases.

Art. 9. The foregoing provisions shall not constitute an obstacle to the right of prisoners of war to receive collective relief before their arrival in a camp or in the course of transfer, nor to the possibility of representatives of the Protecting Power, the International Committee of the Red Cross, or any other body giving assistance to prisoners which may be responsible for the forwarding of such supplies, ensuring the distribution thereof to the addressees by any other means that they may deem useful.

appendix

II

GENEVA CONVENTION IV (1949)

Convention (IV) relative to the Protection of Civilian Persons in Time of War. Geneva, 12 August 1949.

PREAMBLE

The undersigned Plenipotentiaries of the Governments represented at the Diplomatic Conference held at Geneva from April 21 to August 12, 1949, for the purpose of establishing a Convention for the Protection of Civilian Persons in Time of War, have agreed as follows:

PART I. GENERAL PROVISIONS

ART. 1. The High Contracting Parties undertake to respect and to ensure respect for the present Convention in all circumstances.

ART. 2. In addition to the provisions which shall be implemented in peace-time, the present Convention shall apply to all cases of declared war or of any other armed conflict which may arise between two or more of the High Contracting Parties, even if the state of war is not recognized by one of them.

The Convention shall also apply to all cases of partial or total occupation of the territory of a High Contracting Party, even if the said occupation meets with no armed resistance.

Although one of the Powers in conflict may not be a party to the present Convention, the Powers who are parties thereto shall remain bound by it in their mutual relations. They shall furthermore be bound by the Convention in relation to the said Power, if the latter accepts and applies the provisions thereof.

Art. 3. In the case of armed conflict not of an international character occurring in the territory of one of the High Contracting Parties, each Party to the conflict shall be bound to apply, as a minimum, the following provisions:

1. Persons taking no active part in the hostilities, including members of armed forces who have laid down their arms and those placed hors de combat by sickness, wounds, detention, or any other cause, shall in all circumstances be treated humanely, without any adverse distinction founded on race, colour, religion or faith, sex, birth or wealth, or any other similar criteria.

   To this end the following acts are and shall remain prohibited at any time and in any place whatsoever with respect to the above-mentioned persons:

   a. violence to life and person, in particular murder of all kinds, mutilation, cruel treatment and torture;
   b. taking of hostages;
   c. outrages upon personal dignity, in particular humiliating and degrading treatment;
   d. the passing of sentences and the carrying out of executions without previous judgment pronounced by a regularly constituted court, affording all the judicial guarantees which are recognized as indispensable by civilized peoples.
2. The wounded and sick shall be collected and cared for.

An impartial humanitarian body, such as the International Committee of the Red Cross, may offer its services to the Parties to the conflict.

The Parties to the conflict should further endeavour to bring into force, by means of special agreements, all or part of the other provisions of the present Convention.

The application of the preceding provisions shall not affect the legal status of the Parties to the conflict.

Art. 4. Persons protected by the Convention are those who, at a given moment and in any manner whatsoever, find themselves, in case of a conflict or occupation, in the hands of a Party to the conflict or Occupying Power of which they are not nationals.

Nationals of a State which is not bound by the Convention are not protected by it. Nationals of a neutral State who find themselves in the territory of a belligerent State, and nationals of a co-belligerent State, shall not be regarded as protected persons while the State of which they are nationals has normal diplomatic representation in the State in whose hands they are.

The provisions of Part II are, however, wider in application, as defined in Article 13.

Persons protected by the Geneva Convention for the Amelioration of the Condition of the Wounded and Sick in Armed Forces in the Field of 12 August 1949, or by the Geneva Convention for the Amelioration of the Condition of Wounded, Sick and Shipwrecked Members of Armed Forces at Sea of 12 August 1949, or by the Geneva Convention relative to the Treatment of Prisoners of War of 12 August 1949, shall not be considered as protected persons within the meaning of the present Convention.

Art. 5. Where in the territory of a Party to the conflict, the latter is satisfied that an individual protected person is definitely suspected of or engaged in activities hostile to the security of the State, such individual person shall not be entitled to claim such rights and privileges under the present Convention as would, if exercised in the favour of such individual person, be prejudicial to the security of such State.

Where in occupied territory an individual protected person is detained as a spy or saboteur, or as a person under definite suspicion of activity hostile to the security of the Occupying Power, such person shall, in those cases where absolute military security so requires, be regarded as having forfeited rights of communication under the present Convention.

In each case, such persons shall nevertheless be treated with humanity and, in case of trial, shall not be deprived of the rights of fair and regular trial prescribed by the present Convention. They shall also be granted the full rights and privileges of a protected person under the present Convention at the earliest date consistent with the security of the State or Occupying Power, as the case may be.

Art. 6. The present Convention shall apply from the outset of any conflict or occupation mentioned in Article 2.

In the territory of Parties to the conflict, the application of the present Convention shall cease on the general close of military operations.

In the case of occupied territory, the application of the present Convention shall cease one year after the general close of military operations; however, the Occupying Power shall be bound, for the duration of the occupation, to the extent that such Power exercises the functions of government in such territory, by the provisions of the following Articles of the present Convention: 1 to 12, 27, 29 to 34, 47, 49, 51, 52, 53, 59, 61 to 77, 143.

Protected persons whose release, repatriation or re-establishment may take place after such dates shall meanwhile continue to benefit by the present Convention.

Art. 7. In addition to the agreements expressly provided for in Articles 11, 14, 15, 17, 36, 108, 109, 132, 133 and 149, the High Contracting Parties may conclude other special agreements for all matters concerning which they may deem it suitable to make separate provision. No special agreement shall adversely affect the situation of protected persons, as defined by the present Convention, not restrict the rights which it confers upon them.

Protected persons shall continue to have the benefit of such agreements as long as the Convention is applicable to them, except where express provisions to the contrary are contained in the aforesaid or in subsequent agreements, or where more favourable measures have been taken with regard to them by one or other of the Parties to the conflict.

Art. 8. Protected persons may in no circumstances renounce in part or in entirety the rights secured to them by the present Convention, and by the special agreements referred to in the foregoing Article, if such there be.

Art. 9. The present Convention shall be applied with the cooperation and under the scrutiny of the Protecting Powers whose duty it is to safeguard the interests of the Parties to the conflict. For this purpose, the Protecting Powers may appoint, apart from their diplomatic or consular staff, delegates from amongst their own nationals or the nationals of other neutral Powers. The said delegates shall be subject to the approval of the Power with which they are to carry out their duties.

The Parties to the conflict shall facilitate to the greatest extent possible the task of the representatives or delegates of the Protecting Powers.

The representatives or delegates of the Protecting Powers shall not in any case exceed their mission under the present Convention.

They shall, in particular, take account of the imperative necessities of security of the State wherein they carry out their duties.

Art. 10. The provisions of the present Convention constitute no obstacle to the humanitarian activities which the International Committee of the Red Cross or any other impartial humanitarian organization may, subject to the consent of the Parties to the conflict concerned, undertake for the protection of civilian persons and for their relief.

Art. 11. The High Contracting Parties may at any time agree to entrust to an international organization which offers all guarantees of impartiality and efficacy the duties incumbent on the Protecting Powers by virtue of the present Convention.

When persons protected by the present Convention do not benefit or cease to benefit, no matter for what reason, by the activities of a Protecting Power or of an organization provided for in the first paragraph above, the Detaining Power shall request a neutral State, or such an organization, to undertake the functions performed under the present Convention by a Protecting Power designated by the Parties to a conflict.

If protection cannot be arranged accordingly, the Detaining Power shall request or shall accept, subject to the provisions of this Article, the offer of the services of a humanitarian organization, such as the International Committee of the Red Cross, to assume the humanitarian functions performed by Protecting Powers under the present Convention.

Any neutral Power or any organization invited by the Power concerned or offering itself for these purposes, shall be required to act with a sense of responsibility towards the Party to the conflict on which persons protected by the present Convention depend, and shall be required to furnish sufficient assurances that it is in a position to undertake the appropriate functions and to discharge them impartially.

No derogation from the preceding provisions shall be made by special agreements between Powers one of which is restricted, even temporarily, in its freedom to negotiate with the other Power or its allies by reason of military events, more particularly where the whole, or a substantial part, of the territory of the said Power is occupied.

Whenever in the present Convention mention is made of a Protecting Power, such mention applies to substitute organizations in the sense of the present Article.

The provisions of this Article shall extend and be adapted to cases of nationals of a neutral State who are in occupied territory or who find themselves in the territory of a belligerent State in which the State of which they are nationals has not normal diplomatic representation.

Art. 12. In cases where they deem it advisable in the interest of protected persons, particularly in cases of disagreement between the Parties to the conflict as to the application or interpretation of the provisions of the present Convention, the Protecting Powers shall lend their good offices with a view to settling the disagreement.

For this purpose, each of the Protecting Powers may, either at the invitation of one Party or on its own initiative, propose to the Parties to the conflict a meeting of their representatives, and in particular of the authorities responsible for protected persons, possibly on neutral territory suitably chosen. The Parties to the conflict shall be bound to give effect to the proposals made to them for this purpose. The Protecting Powers may, if necessary, propose for approval by the Parties to the conflict a person belonging to a neutral Power, or delegated by the International Committee of the Red Cross, who shall be invited to take part in such a meeting.

Part II. General Protection of Populations Against Certain Consequences of War

Art. 13. The provisions of Part II cover the whole of the populations of the countries in conflict, without any adverse distinction based, in particular, on race, nationality, religion or political opinion, and are intended to alleviate the sufferings caused by war.

Art. 14. In time of peace, the High Contracting Parties and, after the outbreak of hostilities, the Parties thereto, may establish in their own territory and, if the need arises, in occupied areas, hospital and safety zones and localities so organized as to protect from the effects of war, wounded, sick and aged persons, children under fifteen, expectant mothers and mothers of children under seven.

Upon the outbreak and during the course of hostilities, the Parties concerned may conclude agreements on mutual recognition of the zones and localities they have created. They may for this purpose implement the provisions of the Draft Agreement annexed to the present Convention, with such amendments as they may consider necessary.

The Protecting Powers and the International Committee of the Red Cross are invited to lend their good offices in order to facilitate the institution and recognition of these hospital and safety zones and localities.

Art. 15. Any Party to the conflict may, either direct or through a neutral State or some humanitarian organization, propose to the adverse Party to establish, in the regions where fighting is taking place, neutralized zones intended to shelter from the effects of war the following persons, without distinction:

- **a.** wounded and sick combatants or non-combatants;
- **b.** civilian persons who take no part in hostilities, and who, while they reside in the zones, perform no work of a military character.

When the Parties concerned have agreed upon the geographical position, administration, food supply and supervision of the proposed neutralized zone, a written agreement shall be concluded and signed by the representatives of the Parties to the conflict. The agreement shall fix the beginning and the duration of the neutralization of the zone.

Art. 16. The wounded and sick, as well as the infirm, and expectant mothers, shall be the object of particular protection and respect.

As far as military considerations allow, each Party to the conflict shall facilitate the steps taken to search for the killed and wounded, to assist the shipwrecked and other persons exposed to grave danger, and to protect them against pillage and ill-treatment.

Art. 17. The Parties to the conflict shall endeavour to conclude local agreements for the removal from besieged or encircled areas, of wounded, sick, infirm, and aged persons, children and maternity cases, and for the passage of ministers of all religions, medical personnel and medical equipment on their way to such areas.

Art. 18. Civilian hospitals organized to give care to the wounded and sick, the infirm and maternity cases, may in no circumstances be the object of attack but shall at all times be respected and protected by the Parties to the conflict.

States which are Parties to a conflict shall provide all civilian hospitals with certificates showing that they are civilian hospitals and that the buildings which they occupy are not used for any purpose which would deprive these hospitals of protection in accordance with Article 19.

Civilian hospitals shall be marked by means of the emblem provided for in Article 38 of the Geneva Convention for the Amelioration of the Condition of the Wounded and Sick in Armed Forces in the Field of 12 August 1949, but only if so authorized by the State.

The Parties to the conflict shall, in so far as military considerations permit, take the necessary steps to make the distinctive emblems indicating civilian hospitals clearly visible to the enemy land, air and naval forces in order to obviate the possibility of any hostile action.

In view of the dangers to which hospitals may be exposed by being close to military objectives, it is recommended that such hospitals be situated as far as possible from such objectives.

Art. 19. The protection to which civilian hospitals are entitled shall not cease unless they are used to commit, outside their humanitarian duties, acts harmful to the enemy. Protection may, however, cease only after due warning has been given, naming, in all appropriate cases, a reasonable time limit and after such warning has remained unheeded.

The fact that sick or wounded members of the armed forces are nursed in these hospitals, or the presence of small arms and ammunition taken from such combatants and not yet been handed to the proper service, shall not be considered to be acts harmful to the enemy.

Art. 20. Persons regularly and solely engaged in the operation and administration of civilian hospitals, including the personnel engaged in the search for, removal and transporting of and caring for wounded and sick civilians, the infirm and maternity cases shall be respected and protected.

In occupied territory and in zones of military operations, the above personnel shall be recognizable by means of an identity card certifying their status, bearing the photograph of the holder and embossed with the stamp of the responsible authority, and also by means of a stamped, water-resistant armlet which they shall wear on the left arm while carrying out their duties. This armlet shall be issued by the State and shall bear the emblem provided for in Article 38 of the Geneva Convention for the Amelioration of the Condition of the Wounded and Sick in Armed Forces in the Field of 12 August 1949.

Other personnel who are engaged in the operation and administration of civilian hospitals shall be entitled to respect and protection and to wear the armlet, as provided in and under the conditions prescribed in this Article, while they are employed on such duties. The identity card shall state the duties on which they are employed.

The management of each hospital shall at all times hold at the disposal of the competent national or occupying authorities an up-to-date list of such personnel.

Art. 21. Convoys of vehicles or hospital trains on land or specially provided vessels on sea, conveying wounded and sick civilians, the infirm and maternity cases, shall be respected and protected in the same manner as the hospitals provided for in Article 18, and shall be marked, with the consent of the State, by the display of the distinctive emblem provided for in Article 38 of the Geneva Convention for the Amelioration of the Condition of the Wounded and Sick in Armed Forces in the Field of 12 August 1949.

Art. 22. Aircraft exclusively employed for the removal of wounded and sick civilians, the infirm and maternity cases or for the transport of medical personnel and equipment, shall not be attacked, but shall be respected while flying at heights, times and on routes specifically agreed upon between all the Parties to the conflict concerned.

They may be marked with the distinctive emblem provided for in Article 38 of the Geneva Convention for the Amelioration of the Condition of the Wounded and Sick in Armed Forces in the Field of 12 August 1949.

Unless agreed otherwise, flights over enemy or enemy occupied territory are prohibited.

Such aircraft shall obey every summons to land. In the event of a landing thus imposed, the aircraft with its occupants may continue its flight after examination, if any.

Art. 23. Each High Contracting Party shall allow the free passage of all consignments of medical and hospital stores and objects necessary for religious worship intended only for civilians of another High Contracting Party, even if the latter is its adversary. It shall likewise permit the free passage of all consignments of essential foodstuffs, clothing and tonics intended for children under fifteen, expectant mothers and maternity cases.

The obligation of a High Contracting Party to allow the free passage of the consignments indicated in the preceding paragraph is subject to the condition that this Party is satisfied that there are no serious reasons for fearing:

- **a.** that the consignments may be diverted from their destination,
- **b.** that the control may not be effective, or
- **c.** that a definite advantage may accrue to the military efforts or economy of the enemy through the substitution of the above-mentioned consignments

for goods which would otherwise be provided or produced by the enemy or through the release of such material, services or facilities as would otherwise be required for the production of such goods.

The Power which allows the passage of the consignments indicated in the first paragraph of this Article may make such permission conditional on the distribution to the persons benefited thereby being made under the local supervision of the Protecting Powers.

Such consignments shall be forwarded as rapidly as possible, and the Power which permits their free passage shall have the right to prescribe the technical arrangements under which such passage is allowed.

Art. 24. The Parties to the conflict shall take the necessary measures to ensure that children under fifteen, who are orphaned or are separated from their families as a result of the war, are not left to their own resources, and that their maintenance, the exercise of their religion and their education are facilitated in all circumstances. Their education shall, as far as possible, be entrusted to persons of a similar cultural tradition.

The Parties to the conflict shall facilitate the reception of such children in a neutral country for the duration of the conflict with the consent of the Protecting Power, if any, and under due safeguards for the observance of the principles stated in the first paragraph.

They shall, furthermore, endeavour to arrange for all children under twelve to be identified by the wearing of identity discs, or by some other means.

Art. 25. All persons in the territory of a Party to the conflict, or in a territory occupied by it, shall be enabled to give news of a strictly personal nature to members of their families, wherever they may be, and to receive news from them. This correspondence shall be forwarded speedily and without undue delay.

If, as a result of circumstances, it becomes difficult or impossible to exchange family correspondence by the ordinary post, the Parties to the conflict concerned shall apply to a neutral intermediary, such as the Central Agency provided for in Article 140, and shall decide in consultation with it how to ensure the fulfilment of their obligations under the best possible conditions, in particular with the cooperation of the National Red Cross (Red Crescent, Red Lion and Sun) Societies.

If the Parties to the conflict deem it necessary to restrict family correspondence, such restrictions shall be confined to the compulsory use of standard forms containing twenty-five freely chosen words, and to the limitation of the number of these forms despatched to one each month.

ART. 26. Each Party to the conflict shall facilitate enquiries made by members of families dispersed owing to the war, with the object of renewing contact with one another and of meeting, if possible. It shall encourage, in particular, the work of organizations engaged on this task provided they are acceptable to it and conform to its security regulations.

PART III. STATUS AND TREATMENT OF PROTECTED PERSONS

Section I. Provisions Common to the Territories of the Parties to the Conflict and to Occupied Territories

ART. 27. Protected persons are entitled, in all circumstances, to respect for their persons, their honour, their family rights, their religious convictions and practices, and their manners and customs. They shall at all times be humanely treated, and shall be protected especially against all acts of violence or threats thereof and against insults and public curiosity.

Women shall be especially protected against any attack on their honour, in particular against rape, enforced prostitutiOn, or any form of indecent assault.

Without prejudice to the provisions relating to their state of health, age and sex, all protected persons shall be treated with the same consideration by the Party to the conflict in whose power they are, without any adverse distinction based, in particular, on race, religion or political opinion.

However, the Parties to the conflict may take such measures of control and security in regard to protected persons as may be necessary as a result of the war.

ART. 28. The presence of a protected person may not be used to render certain points or areas immune from military operations.

ART. 29. The Party to the conflict in whose hands protected persons may be, is responsible for the treatment accorded to them by its agents, irrespective of any individual responsibility which may be incurred.

ART. 30. Protected persons shall have every facility for making application to the Protecting Powers, the International Committee of the Red Cross, the National Red Cross (Red Crescent, Red Lion and Sun) Society of the country where they may be, as well as to any organization that might assist them.

These several organizations shall be granted all facilities for that purpose by the authorities, within the bounds set by military or security considerations.

Apart from the visits of the delegates of the Protecting Powers and of the International Committee of the Red Cross, provided for by Article 143, the Detaining or Occupying Powers shall facilitate, as much as possible, visits to protected persons by the representatives of other organizations whose object is to give spiritual aid or material relief to such persons.

Art. 31. No physical or moral coercion shall be exercised against protected persons, in particular to obtain information from them or from third parties.

Art. 32. The High Contracting Parties specifically agree that each of them is prohibited from taking any measure of such a character as to cause the physical suffering or extermination of protected persons in their hands. This prohibition applies not only to murder, torture, corporal punishments, mutilation and medical or scientific experiments not necessitated by the medical treatment of a protected person, but also to any other measures of brutality whether applied by civilian or military agents.

Art. 33. No protected person may be punished for an offence he or she has not personally committed. Collective penalties and likewise all measures of intimidation or of terrorism are prohibited.

Pillage is prohibited.

Reprisals against protected persons and their property are prohibited.

Art. 34. The taking of hostages is prohibited.

Section II. Aliens in the Territory of a Party to the Conflict

Art. 35. All protected persons who may desire to leave the territory at the outset of, or during a conflict, shall be entitled to do so, unless their departure is contrary to the national interests of the State. The applications of such persons to leave shall be decided in accordance with regularly established procedures and the decision shall be taken as rapidly as possible. Those persons permitted to leave may provide themselves with the necessary funds for their journey and take with them a reasonable amount of their effects and articles of personal use.

If any such person is refused permission to leave the territory, he shall be entitled to have refusal reconsidered, as soon as possible by an appropriate court or administrative board designated by the Detaining Power for that purpose.

Upon request, representatives of the Protecting Power shall, unless reasons of security prevent it, or the persons concerned object, be furnished with the reasons for refusal of any request for permission to leave the territory and be given, as expeditiously as possible, the names of all persons who have been denied permission to leave.

Art. 36. Departures permitted under the foregoing Article shall be carried out in satisfactory conditions as regards safety, hygiene, sanitation and food. All costs in connection therewith, from the point of exit in the territory of the Detaining Power, shall be borne by the country of destination, or, in the case of accommodation in a neutral country, by the Power whose nationals are benefited. The practical details of such movements may, if necessary, be settled by special agreements between the Powers concerned.

The foregoing shall not prejudice such special agreements as may be concluded between Parties to the conflict concerning the exchange and repatriation of their nationals in enemy hands.

Art. 37. Protected persons who are confined pending proceedings or serving a sentence involving loss of liberty, shall during their confinement be humanely treated.

As soon as they are released, they may ask to leave the territory in conformity with the foregoing Articles.

Art. 38. With the exception of special measures authorized by the present Convention, in particularly by Article 27 and 41 thereof, the situation of protected persons shall continue to be regulated, in principle, by the provisions concerning aliens in time of peace. In any case, the following rights shall be granted to them:

1. they shall be enabled to receive the individual or collective relief that may be sent to them.
2. they shall, if their state of health so requires, receive medical attention and hospital treatment to the same extent as the nationals of the State concerned.
3. they shall be allowed to practise their religion and to receive spiritual assistance from ministers of their faith.
4. if they reside in an area particularly exposed to the dangers of war, they shall be authorized to move from that area to the same extent as the nationals of the State concerned.
5. children under fifteen years, pregnant women and mothers of children under seven years shall benefit by any preferential treatment to the same extent as the nationals of the State concerned.

Art. 39. Protected persons who, as a result of the war, have lost their gainful employment, shall be granted the opportunity to find paid employment. That opportunity shall, subject to security considerations and to the provisions of Article 40, be equal to that enjoyed by the nationals of the Power in whose territory they are.

Where a Party to the conflict applies to a protected person methods of control which result in his being unable to support himself, and especially if such a person is prevented for reasons of security from finding paid employment on reasonable conditions, the said Party shall ensure his support and that of his dependents.

Protected persons may in any case receive allowances from their home country, the Protecting Power, or the relief societies referred to in Article 30.

Art. 40. Protected persons may be compelled to work only to the same extent as nationals of the Party to the conflict in whose territory they are.

If protected persons are of enemy nationality, they may only be compelled to do work which is normally necessary to ensure the feeding, sheltering, clothing, transport and health of human beings and which is not directly related to the conduct of military operations.

In the cases mentioned in the two preceding paragraphs, protected persons compelled to work shall have the benefit of the same working conditions and of the same safeguards as national workers in particular as regards wages, hours of labour, clothing and equipment, previous training and compensation for occupational accidents and diseases.

If the above provisions are infringed, protected persons shall be allowed to exercise their right of complaint in accordance with Article 30.

Art. 41. Should the Power, in whose hands protected persons may be, consider the measures of control mentioned in the present Convention to be inadequate, it may not have recourse to any other measure of control more severe than that of assigned residence or internment, in accordance with the provisions of Articles 42 and 43.

In applying the provisions of Article 39, second paragraph, to the cases of persons required to leave their usual places of residence by virtue of a decision placing them in assigned residence elsewhere, the Detaining Power shall be guided as closely as possible by the standards of welfare set forth in Part III, Section IV of this Convention.

Art. 42. The internment or placing in assigned residence of protected persons may be ordered only if the security of the Detaining Power makes it absolutely necessary.

If any person, acting through the representatives of the Protecting Power, voluntarily demands internment, and if his situation renders this step necessary, he shall be interned by the Power in whose hands he may be.

Art. 43. Any protected person who has been interned or placed in assigned residence shall be entitled to have such action reconsidered as soon as possible by an appropriate court or administrative board designated by the Detaining Power for that purpose. If the internment or placing in assigned residence is maintained, the court or administrative board shall periodically, and at least twice yearly, give consideration to his or her case, with a view to the favourable amendment of the initial decision, if circumstances permit.

Unless the protected persons concerned object, the Detaining Power shall, as rapidly as possible, give the Protecting Power the names of any protected persons who have been interned or subjected to assigned residence, or who have been released from internment or assigned residence. The decisions of the courts or boards mentioned in the first paragraph of the present Article shall also, subject to the same conditions, be notified as rapidly as possible to the Protecting Power.

Art. 44. In applying the measures of control mentioned in the present Convention, the Detaining Power shall not treat as enemy aliens exclusively on the basis of their nationality de jure of an enemy State, refugees who do not, in fact, enjoy the protection of any government.

Art. 45. Protected persons shall not be transferred to a Power which is not a party to the Convention.

This provision shall in no way constitute an obstacle to the repatriation of protected persons, or to their return to their country of residence after the cessation of hostilities.

Protected persons may be transferred by the Detaining Power only to a Power which is a party to the present Convention and after the Detaining Power has satisfied itself of the willingness and ability of such transferee Power to apply the present Convention. If protected persons are transferred under such circumstances, responsibility for the application of the present Convention rests on the

Power accepting them, while they are in its custody. Nevertheless, if that Power fails to carry out the provisions of the present Convention in any important respect, the Power by which the protected persons were transferred shall, upon being so notified by the Protecting Power, take effective measures to correct the situation or shall request the return of the protected persons. Such request must be complied with.

In no circumstances shall a protected person be transferred to a country where he or she may have reason to fear persecution for his or her political opinions or religious beliefs.

The provisions of this Article do not constitute an obstacle to the extradition, in pursuance of extradition treaties concluded before the outbreak of hostilities, of protected persons accused of offences against ordinary criminal law.

ART. 46. In so far as they have not been previously withdrawn, restrictive measures taken regarding protected persons shall be cancelled as soon as possible after the close of hostilities.

Restrictive measures affecting their property shall be cancelled, in accordance with the law of the Detaining Power, as soon as possible after the close of hostilities.

Section III. Occupied Territories

ART. 47. Protected persons who are in occupied territory shall not be deprived, in any case or in any manner whatsoever, of the benefits of the present Convention by any change introduced, as the result of the occupation of a territory, into the institutions or government of the said territory, nor by any agreement concluded between the authorities of the occupied territories and the Occupying Power, nor by any annexation by the latter of the whole or part of the occupied territory.

ART. 48. Protected persons who are not nationals of the Power whose territory is occupied, may avail themselves of the right to leave the territory subject to the provisions of Article 35, and decisions thereon shall be taken according to the procedure which the Occupying Power shall establish in accordance with the said Article.

ART. 49. Individual or mass forcible transfers, as well as deportations of protected persons from occupied territory to the territory of the Occupying Power or to that of any other country, occupied or not, are prohibited, regardless of their motive.

Nevertheless, the Occupying Power may undertake total or partial evacuation of a given area if the security of the population or imperative military reasons so demand. Such evacuations may not involve the displacement of protected persons outside the bounds of the occupied territory except when for material reasons it is impossible to avoid such displacement. Persons thus evacuated shall be transferred back to their homes as soon as hostilities in the area in question have ceased.

The Occupying Power undertaking such transfers or evacuations shall ensure, to the greatest practicable extent, that proper accommodation is provided to receive the protected persons, that the removals are effected in satisfactory conditions of hygiene, health, safety and nutrition, and that members of the same family are not separated.

The Protecting Power shall be informed of any transfers and evacuations as soon as they have taken place.

The Occupying Power shall not detain protected persons in an area particularly exposed to the dangers of war unless the security of the population or imperative military reasons so demand.

The Occupying Power shall not deport or transfer parts of its own civilian population into the territory it occupies.

Art. 50. The Occupying Power shall, with the cooperation of the national and local authorities, facilitate the proper working of all institutions devoted to the care and education of children.

The Occupying Power shall take all necessary steps to facilitate the identification of children and the registration of their parentage. It may not, in any case, change their personal status, nor enlist them in formations or organizations subordinate to it.

Should the local institutions be inadequate for the purpose, the Occupying Power shall make arrangements for the maintenance and education, if possible by persons of their own nationality, language and religion, of children who are orphaned or separated from their parents as a result of the war and who cannot be adequately cared for by a near relative or friend.

A special section of the Bureau set up in accordance with Article 136 shall be responsible for taking all necessary steps to identify children whose identity is in doubt. Particulars of their parents or other near relatives should always be recorded if available.

The Occupying Power shall not hinder the application of any preferential measures in regard to food, medical care and protection against the effects of war which may have been adopted prior to the occupation in favour of children under fifteen years, expectant mothers, and mothers of children under seven years.

ART. 51. The Occupying Power may not compel protected persons to serve in its armed or auxiliary forces. No pressure or propaganda which aims at securing voluntary enlistment is permitted.

The Occupying Power may not compel protected persons to work unless they are over eighteen years of age, and then only on work which is necessary either for the needs of the army of occupation, or for the public utility services, or for the feeding, sheltering, clothing, transportation or health of the population of the occupied country. Protected persons may not be compelled to undertake any work which would involve them in the obligation of taking part in military operations. The Occupying Power may not compel protected persons to employ forcible means to ensure the security of the installations where they are performing compulsory labour.

The work shall be carried out only in the occupied territory where the persons whose services have been requisitioned are. Every such person shall, so far as possible, be kept in his usual place of employment. Workers shall be paid a fair wage and the work shall be proportionate to their physical and intellectual capacities. The legislation in force in the occupied country concerning working conditions, and safeguards as regards, in particular, such matters as wages, hours of work, equipment, preliminary training and compensation for occupational accidents and diseases, shall be applicable to the protected persons assigned to the work referred to in this Article.

In no case shall requisition of labour lead to a mobilization of workers in an organization of a military or semi-military character.

ART. 52. No contract, agreement or regulation shall impair the right of any worker, whether voluntary or not and wherever he may be, to apply to the representatives of the Protecting Power in order to request the said Power's intervention.

All measures aiming at creating unemployment or at restricting the opportunities offered to workers in an occupied territory, in order to induce them to work for the Occupying Power, are prohibited.

ART. 53. Any destruction by the Occupying Power of real or personal property belonging individually or collectively to private persons, or to the State, or to other public authorities, or to social or cooperative organizations, is prohibited, except where such destruction is rendered absolutely necessary by military operations.

ART. 54. The Occupying Power may not alter the status of public officials or judges in the occupied territories, or in any way apply sanctions to or take any measures of coercion or discrimination against them, should they abstain from fulfilling their functions for reasons of conscience.

This prohibition does not prejudice the application of the second paragraph of Article 51. It does not affect the right of the Occupying Power to remove public officials from their posts.

Art. 55. To the fullest extent of the means available to it, the Occupying Power has the duty of ensuring the food and medical supplies of the population; it should, in particular, bring in the necessary foodstuffs, medical stores and other articles if the resources of the occupied territory are inadequate.

The Occupying Power may not requisition foodstuffs, articles or medical supplies available in the occupied territory, except for use by the occupation forces and administration personnel, and then only if the requirements of the civilian population have been taken into account. Subject to the provisions of other international Conventions, the Occupying Power shall make arrangements to ensure that fair value is paid for any requisitioned goods.

The Protecting Power shall, at any time, be at liberty to verify the state of the food and medical supplies in occupied territories, except where temporary restrictions are made necessary by imperative military requirements.

Art. 56. To the fullest extent of the means available to it, the Occupying Power has the duty of ensuring and maintaining, with the cooperation of national and local authorities, the medical and hospital establishments and services, public health and hygiene in the occupied territory, with particular reference to the adoption and application of the prophylactic and preventive measures necessary to combat the spread of contagious diseases and epidemics. Medical personnel of all categories shall be allowed to carry out their duties.

If new hospitals are set up in occupied territory and if the competent organs of the occupied State are not operating there, the occupying authorities shall, if necessary, grant them the recognition provided for in Article 18. In similar circumstances, the occupying authorities shall also grant recognition to hospital personnel and transport vehicles under the provisions of Articles 20 and 21.

In adopting measures of health and hygiene and in their implementation, the Occupying Power shall take into consideration the moral and ethical susceptibilities of the population of the occupied territory.

Art. 57. The Occupying Power may requisition civilian hospitals of hospitals only temporarily and only in cases of urgent necessity for the care of military wounded and sick, and then on condition that suitable arrangements are made in due time for the care and treatment of the patients and for the needs of the civilian population for hospital accommodation.

The material and stores of civilian hospitals cannot be requisitioned so long as they are necessary for the needs of the civilian population.

ART. 58. The Occupying Power shall permit ministers of religion to give spiritual assistance to the members of their religious communities.

The Occupying Power shall also accept consignments of books and articles required for religious needs and shall facilitate their distribution in occupied territory.

ART. 59. If the whole or part of the population of an occupied territory is inadequately supplied, the Occupying Power shall agree to relief schemes on behalf of the said population, and shall facilitate them by all the means at its disposal.

Such schemes, which may be undertaken either by States or by impartial humanitarian organizations such as the International Committee of the Red Cross, shall consist, in particular, of the provision of consignments of foodstuffs, medical supplies and clothing.

All Contracting Parties shall permit the free passage of these consignments and shall guarantee their protection.

A Power granting free passage to consignments on their way to territory occupied by an adverse Party to the conflict shall, however, have the right to search the consignments, to regulate their passage according to prescribed times and routes, and to be reasonably satisfied through the Protecting Power that these consignments are to be used for the relief of the needy population and are not to be used for the benefit of the Occupying Power.

ART. 60. Relief consignments shall in no way relieve the Occupying Power of any of its responsibilities under Articles 55, 56 and 59. The Occupying Power shall in no way whatsoever divert relief consignments from the purpose for which they are intended, except in cases of urgent necessity, in the interests of the population of the occupied territory and with the consent of the Protecting Power.

ART. 61. The distribution of the relief consignments referred to in the foregoing Articles shall be carried out with the cooperation and under the supervision of the Protecting Power. This duty may also be delegated, by agreement between the Occupying Power and the Protecting Power, to a neutral Power, to the International Committee of the Red Cross or to any other impartial humanitarian body.

Such consignments shall be exempt in occupied territory from all charges, taxes or customs duties unless these are necessary in the interests of the economy of the territory. The Occupying Power shall facilitate the rapid distribution of these consignments.

All Contracting Parties shall endeavour to permit the transit and transport, free of charge, of such relief consignments on their way to occupied territories.

ART. 62. Subject to imperative reasons of security, protected persons in occupied territories shall be permitted to receive the individual relief consignments sent to them.

ART. 63. Subject to temporary and exceptional measures imposed for urgent reasons of security by the Occupying Power:

- **a.** recognized National Red Cross (Red Crescent, Red Lion and Sun) Societies shall be able to pursue their activities in accordance with Red Cross principles, as defined by the International Red Cross Conferences. Other relief societies shall be permitted to continue their humanitarian activities under similar conditions;
- **b.** the Occupying Power may not require any changes in the personnel or structure of these societies, which would prejudice the aforesaid activities.

The same principles shall apply to the activities and personnel of special organizations of a non-military character, which already exist or which may be established, for the purpose of ensuring the living conditions of the civilian population by the maintenance of the essential public utility services, by the distribution of relief and by the organization of rescues.

ART. 64. The penal laws of the occupied territory shall remain in force, with the exception that they may be repealed or suspended by the Occupying Power in cases where they constitute a threat to its security or an obstacle to the application of the present Convention.

Subject to the latter consideration and to the necessity for ensuring the effective administration of justice, the tribunals of the occupied territory shall continue to function in respect of all offences covered by the said laws.

The Occupying Power may, however, subject the population of the occupied territory to provisions which are essential to enable the Occupying Power to fulfil its obligations under the present Convention, to maintain the orderly government of the territory, and to ensure the security of the Occupying Power, of the members and property of the occupying forces or administration, and likewise of the establishments and lines of communication used by them.

Art. 65. The penal provisions enacted by the Occupying Power shall not come into force before they have been published and brought to the knowledge of the inhabitants in their own language. The effect of these penal provisions shall not be retroactive.

Art. 66. In case of a breach of the penal provisions promulgated by it by virtue of the second paragraph of Article 64 the Occupying Power may hand over the accused to its properly constituted, non-political military courts, on condition that the said courts sit in the occupied country. Courts of appeal shall preferably sit in the occupied country.

Art. 67. The courts shall apply only those provisions of law which were applicable prior to the offence, and which are in accordance with general principles of law, in particular the principle that the penalty shall be proportionate to the offence. They shall take into consideration the fact the accused is not a national of the Occupying Power.

Art. 68. Protected persons who commit an offence which is solely intended to harm the Occupying Power, but which does not constitute an attempt on the life or limb of members of the occupying forces or administration, nor a grave collective danger, nor seriously damage the property of the occupying forces or administration or the installations used by them, shall be liable to internment or simple imprisonment, provided the duration of such internment or imprisonment is proportionate to the offence committed. Furthermore, internment or imprisonment shall, for such offences, be the only measure adopted for depriving protected persons of liberty. The courts provided for under Article 66 of the present Convention may at their discretion convert a sentence of imprisonment to one of internment for the same period.

The penal provisions promulgated by the Occupying Power in accordance with Articles 64 and 65 may impose the death penalty against a protected person only in cases where the person is guilty of espionage, of serious acts of sabotage against the military installations of the Occupying Power or of intentional offences which have caused the death of one or more persons, provided that such offences were punishable by death under the law of the occupied territory in force before the occupation began.

The death penalty may not be pronounced against a protected person unless the attention of the court has been particularly called to the fact that since the accused is not a national of the Occupying Power, he is not bound to it by any duty of allegiance.

In any case, the death penalty may not be pronounced on a protected person who was under eighteen years of age at the time of the offence.

ART. 69. In all cases the duration of the period during which a protected person accused of an offence is under arrest awaiting trial or punishment shall be deducted from any period of imprisonment of awarded.

ART. 70. Protected persons shall not be arrested, prosecuted or convicted by the Occupying Power for acts committed or for opinions expressed before the occupation, or during a temporary interruption thereof, with the exception of breaches of the laws and customs of war.

Nationals of the occupying Power who, before the outbreak of hostilities, have sought refuge in the territory of the occupied State, shall not be arrested, prosecuted, convicted or deported from the occupied territory, except for offences committed after the outbreak of hostilities, or for offences under common law committed before the outbreak of hostilities which, according to the law of the occupied State, would have justified extradition in time of peace.

ART. 71. No sentence shall be pronounced by the competent courts of the Occupying Power except after a regular trial.

Accused persons who are prosecuted by the Occupying Power shall be promptly informed, in writing, in a language which they understand, of the particulars of the charges preferred against them, and shall be brought to trial as rapidly as possible. The Protecting Power shall be informed of all proceedings instituted by the Occupying Power against protected persons in respect of charges involving the death penalty or imprisonment for two years or more; it shall be enabled, at any time, to obtain information regarding the state of such proceedings. Furthermore, the Protecting Power shall be entitled, on request, to be furnished with all particulars of these and of any other proceedings instituted by the Occupying Power against protected persons.

The notification to the Protecting Power, as provided for in the second paragraph above, shall be sent immediately, and shall in any case reach the Protecting Power three weeks before the date of the first hearing. Unless, at the opening of the trial, evidence is submitted that the provisions of this Article are fully complied with, the trial shall not proceed. The notification shall include the following particulars:

a. description of the accused;
b. place of residence or detention;
c. specification of the charge or charges (with mention of the penal provisions under which it is brought);
d. designation of the court which will hear the case;
e. place and date of the first hearing.

ART. 72. Accused persons shall have the right to present evidence necessary to their defence and may, in particular, call witnesses. They shall have the right to be assisted by a qualified advocate or counsel of their own choice, who shall be able to visit them freely and shall enjoy the necessary facilities for preparing the defence.

Failing a choice by the accused, the Protecting Power may provide him with an advocate or counsel. When an accused person has to meet a serious charge and the Protecting Power is not functioning, the Occupying Power, subject to the consent of the accused, shall provide an advocate or counsel.

Accused persons shall, unless they freely waive such assistance, be aided by an interpreter, both during preliminary investigation and during the hearing in court. They shall have the right at any time to object to the interpreter and to ask for his replacement.

ART. 73. A convicted person shall have the right of appeal provided for by the laws applied by the court. He shall be fully informed of his right to appeal or petition and of the time limit within which he may do so.

The penal procedure provided in the present Section shall apply, as far as it is applicable, to appeals. Where the laws applied by the Court make no provision for appeals, the convicted person shall have the right to petition against the finding and sentence to the competent authority of the Occupying Power.

ART. 74. Representatives of the Protecting Power shall have the right to attend the trial of any protected person, unless the hearing has, as an exceptional measure, to be held in camera in the interests of the security of the Occupying Power, which shall then notify the Protecting Power. A notification in respect of the date and place of trial shall be sent to the Protecting Power.

Any judgement involving a sentence of death, or imprisonment for two years or more, shall be communicated, with the relevant grounds, as rapidly as possible to the Protecting Power. The notification shall contain a reference to the notification made under Article 71 and, in the case of sentences of imprisonment, the name of the place where the sentence is to be served. A record of judgements other than those referred to above shall be kept by the court and shall be open to inspection by representatives of the Protecting Power. Any period allowed for appeal in the case of sentences involving the death penalty, or imprisonment of two years or more, shall not run until notification of judgement has been received by the Protecting Power.

ART. 75. In no case shall persons condemned to death be deprived of the right of petition for pardon or reprieve.

No death sentence shall be carried out before the expiration of a period of a least six months from the date of receipt by the Protecting Power of the notification of the final judgment confirming such death sentence, or of an order denying pardon or reprieve.

The six months period of suspension of the death sentence herein prescribed may be reduced in individual cases in circumstances of grave emergency involving an organized threat to the security of the Occupying Power or its forces, provided always that the Protecting Power is notified of such reduction and is given reasonable time and opportunity to make representations to the competent occupying authorities in respect of such death sentences.

ART. 76. Protected persons accused of offences shall be detained in the occupied country, and if convicted they shall serve their sentences therein. They shall, if possible, be separated from other detainees and shall enjoy conditions of food and hygiene which will be sufficient to keep them in good health, and which will be at least equal to those obtaining in prisons in the occupied country.

They shall receive the medical attention required by their state of health.

They shall also have the right to receive any spiritual assistance which they may require.

Women shall be confined in separate quarters and shall be under the direct supervision of women.

Proper regard shall be paid to the special treatment due to minors.

Protected persons who are detained shall have the right to be visited by delegates of the Protecting Power and of the International Committee of the Red Cross, in accordance with the provisions of Article 143.

Such persons shall have the right to receive at least one relief parcel monthly.

Art. 77. Protected persons who have been accused of offences or convicted by the courts in occupied territory, shall be handed over at the close of occupation, with the relevant records, to the authorities of the liberated territory.

Art. 78. If the Occupying Power considers it necessary, for imperative reasons of security, to take safety measures concerning protected persons, it may, at the most, subject them to assigned residence or to internment.

Decisions regarding such assigned residence or internment shall be made according to a regular procedure to be prescribed by the Occupying Power in accordance with the provisions of the present Convention. This procedure shall include the right of appeal for the parties concerned. Appeals shall be decided with the least possible delay. In the event of the decision being upheld, it shall be subject to periodical review, if possible every six months, by a competent body set up by the said Power.

Protected persons made subject to assigned residence and thus required to leave their homes shall enjoy the full benefit of Article 39 of the present Convention.

Section IV. Regulations for the Treatment of Internees

Chapter I. General Provisions

Art. 79. The Parties to the conflict shall not intern protected persons, except in accordance with the provisions of Articles 41, 42, 43, 68 and 78.

Art. 80. Internees shall retain their full civil capacity and shall exercise such attendant rights as may be compatible with their status.

Art. 81. Parties to the conflict who intern protected persons shall be bound to provide free of charge for their maintenance, and to grant them also the medical attention required by their state of health.

No deduction from the allowances, salaries or credits due to the internees shall be made for the repayment of these costs.

The Detaining Power shall provide for the support of those dependent on the internees, if such dependents are without adequate means of support or are unable to earn a living.

Art. 82. The Detaining Power shall, as far as possible, accommodate the internees according to their nationality, language and customs. Internees who are nationals of the same country shall not be separated merely because they have different languages.

Throughout the duration of their internment, members of the same family, and in particular parents and children, shall be lodged together in the same place of internment, except when separation of a temporary nature is necessitated for reasons of employment or health or for the purposes of enforcement of the provisions of Chapter IX of the present Section. Internees may request that their children who are left at liberty without parental care shall be interned with them.

Wherever possible, interned members of the same family shall be housed in the same premises and given separate accommodation from other internees, together with facilities for leading a proper family life.

Chapter II. Places of Internment

ART. 83. The Detaining Power shall not set up places of internment in areas particularly exposed to the dangers of war.

The Detaining Power shall give the enemy Powers, through the intermediary of the Protecting Powers, all useful information regarding the geographical location of places of internment.

Whenever military considerations permit, internment camps shall be indicated by the letters IC, placed so as to be clearly visible in the daytime from the air. The Powers concerned may, however, agree upon any other system of marking. No place other than an internment camp shall be marked as such.

ART. 84. Internees shall be accommodated and administered separately from prisoners of war and from persons deprived of liberty for any other reason.

ART. 85. The Detaining Power is bound to take all necessary and possible measures to ensure that protected persons shall, from the outset of their internment, be accommodated in buildings or quarters which afford every possible safeguard as regards hygiene and health, and provide efficient protection against the rigours of the climate and the effects of the war. In no case shall permanent places of internment be situated in unhealthy areas or in districts, the climate of which is injurious to the internees. In all cases where the district, in which a protected person is temporarily interned, is in an unhealthy area or has a climate which is harmful to his health, he shall be removed to a more suitable place of internment as rapidly as circumstances permit.

The premises shall be fully protected from dampness, adequately heated and lighted, in particular between dusk and lights out. The sleeping quarters shall be sufficiently spacious and well ventilated, and the internees shall have suitable bedding and sufficient blankets, account being taken of the climate, and the age, sex, and state of health of the internees.

Internees shall have for their use, day and night, sanitary conveniences which conform to the rules of hygiene, and are constantly maintained in a state of cleanliness. They shall be provided with sufficient water and soap for their daily personal toilet and for washing their personal laundry; installations and facilities necessary for this purpose shall be granted to them. Showers or baths shall also be available. The necessary time shall be set aside for washing and for cleaning.

Whenever it is necessary, as an exceptional and temporary measure, to accommodate women internees who are not members of a family unit in the same place of internment as men, the provision of separate sleeping quarters and sanitary conveniences for the use of such women internees shall be obligatory.

Art. 86. The Detaining Power shall place at the disposal of interned persons, of whatever denomination, premises suitable for the holding of their religious services.

Art. 87. Canteens shall be installed in every place of internment, except where other suitable facilities are available. Their purpose shall be to enable internees to make purchases, at prices not higher than local market prices, of foodstuffs and articles of everyday use, including soap and tobacco, such as would increase their personal well-being and comfort.

Profits made by canteens shall be credited to a welfare fund to be set up for each place of internment, and administered for the benefit of the internees attached to such place of internment. The Internee Committee provided for in Article 102 shall have the right to check the management of the canteen and of the said fund.

When a place of internment is closed down, the balance of the welfare fund shall be transferred to the welfare fund of a place of internment for internees of the same nationality, or, if such a place does not exist, to a central welfare fund which shall be administered for the benefit of all internees remaining in the custody of the Detaining Power. In case of a general release, the said profits shall be kept by the Detaining Power, subject to any agreement to the contrary between the Powers concerned.

Art. 88. In all places of internment exposed to air raids and other hazards of war, shelters adequate in number and structure to ensure the necessary protection shall be installed. In case of alarms, the measures internees shall be free to enter such shelters as quickly as possible, excepting those who remain for the protection of their quarters against the aforesaid hazards. Any protective measures taken in favour of the population shall also apply to them.

All due precautions must be taken in places of internment against the danger of fire.

Chapter III. Food and Clothing

ART. 89. Daily food rations for internees shall be sufficient in quantity, quality and variety to keep internees in a good state of health and prevent the development of nutritional deficiencies. Account shall also be taken of the customary diet of the internees.

Internees shall also be given the means by which they can prepare for themselves any additional food in their possession.

Sufficient drinking water shall be supplied to internees. The use of tobacco shall be permitted.

Internees who work shall receive additional rations in proportion to the kind of labour which they perform.

Expectant and nursing mothers and children under fifteen years of age, shall be given additional food, in proportion to their physiological needs.

ART. 90. When taken into custody, internees shall be given all facilities to provide themselves with the necessary clothing, footwear and change of underwear, and later on, to procure further supplies if required. Should any internees not have sufficient clothing, account being taken of the climate, and be unable to procure any, it shall be provided free of charge to them by the Detaining Power.

The clothing supplied by the Detaining Power to internees and the outward markings placed on their own clothes shall not be ignominious nor expose them to ridicule.

Workers shall receive suitable working outfits, including protective clothing, whenever the nature of their work so requires.

Chapter IV. Hygiene and Medical Attention

ART. 91. Every place of internment shall have an adequate infirmary, under the direction of a qualified doctor, where internees may have the attention they require, as well as an appropriate diet. Isolation wards shall be set aside for cases of contagious or mental diseases.

Maternity cases and internees suffering from serious diseases, or whose condition requires special treatment, a surgical operation or hospital care, must be admitted to any institution where adequate treatment can be given and shall receive care not inferior to that provided for the general population.

Internees shall, for preference, have the attention of medical personnel of their own nationality.

Internees may not be prevented from presenting themselves to the medical authorities for examination. The medical authorities of the Detaining Power shall, upon request, issue to every internee who has undergone treatment an official certificate showing the nature of his illness or injury, and the duration and nature of the treatment given. A duplicate of this certificate shall be forwarded to the Central Agency provided for in Article 140.

Treatment, including the provision of any apparatus necessary for the maintenance of internees in good health, particularly dentures and other artificial appliances and spectacles, shall be free of charge to the internee.

ART. 92. Medical inspections of internees shall be made at least once a month. Their purpose shall be, in particular, to supervise the general state of health, nutrition and cleanliness of internees, and to detect contagious diseases, especially tuberculosis, malaria, and venereal diseases. Such inspections shall include, in particular, the checking of weight of each internee and, at least once a year, radioscopic examination.

Chapter V. Religious, Intellectual and Physical Activities

ART. 93. Internees shall enjoy complete latitude in the exercise of their religious duties, including attendance at the services of their faith, on condition that they comply with the disciplinary routine prescribed by the detaining authorities.

Ministers of religion who are interned shall be allowed to minister freely to the members of their community. For this purpose the Detaining Power shall ensure their equitable allocation amongst the various places of internment in which there are internees speaking the same language and belonging to the same religion. Should such ministers be too few in number, the Detaining Power shall provide them with the necessary facilities, including means of transport, for moving from one place to another, and they shall be authorized to visit any internees who are in hospital. Ministers of religion shall be at liberty to correspond on matters concerning their ministry with the religious authorities in the country of detention and, as far as possible, with the international religious organizations of their faith. Such correspondence shall not be considered as forming a part of the quota mentioned in Article 107. It shall, however, be subject to the provisions of Article 112.

When internees do not have at their disposal the assistance of ministers of their faith, or should these latter be too few in number, the local religious authorities of the same faith may appoint, in agreement with the Detaining Power, a minister of the internees' faith or, if such a course is feasible from a denominational point of view, a minister of similar religion or a qualified layman. The latter shall enjoy the facilities granted to the ministry he has assumed. Persons so appointed shall comply with all regulations laid down by the Detaining Power in the interests of discipline and security.

ART. 94. The Detaining Power shall encourage intellectual, educational and recreational pursuits, sports and games amongst internees, whilst leaving them free to take part in them or not. It shall take all practicable measures to ensure the exercice thereof, in particular by providing suitable premises.

All possible facilities shall be granted to internees to continue their studies or to take up new subjects. The education of children and young people shall be ensured; they shall be allowed to attend schools either within the place of internment or outside.

Internees shall be given opportunities for physical exercise, sports and outdoor games. For this purpose, sufficient open spaces shall be set aside in all places of internment. Special playgrounds shall be reserved for children and young people.

ART. 95. The Detaining Power shall not employ internees as workers, unless they so desire. Employment which, if undertaken under compulsion by a protected person not in internment, would involve a breach of Articles 40 or 51 of the present Convention, and employment on work which is of a degrading or humiliating character are in any case prohibited.

After a working period of six weeks, internees shall be free to give up work at any moment, subject to eight days' notice.

These provisions constitute no obstacle to the right of the Detaining Power to employ interned doctors, dentists and other medical personnel in their professional capacity on behalf of their fellow internees, or to employ internees for administrative and maintenance work in places of internment and to detail such persons for work in the kitchens or for other domestic tasks, or to require such persons to undertake duties connected with the protection of internees against aerial bombardment or other war risks. No internee may, however, be required to perform tasks for which he is, in the opinion of a medical officer, physically unsuited.

The Detaining Power shall take entire responsibility for all working conditions, for medical attention, for the payment of wages, and for ensuring that all employed internees receive compensation for occupational accidents and diseases. The standards prescribed for the said working conditions and for compensation shall be in accordance with the national laws and regulations, and with the existing practice; they shall in no case be inferior to those obtaining for work of the same nature in the same district. Wages for work done shall be determined on an equitable basis by special agreements between the internees, the Detaining Power, and, if the case arises, employers other than the Detaining Power to provide for free maintenance of internees and for the medical attention which their state of health may require. Internees permanently detailed for categories of work mentioned in the third paragraph of this Article, shall be paid fair wages by the Detaining Power. The working conditions and the scale of compensation for occupational accidents and diseases to internees, thusdetailed, shall not be inferior to those applicable to work of the same nature in the same district.

ART. 96. All labour detachments shall remain part of and dependent upon a place of internment. The competent authorities of the Detaining Power and the commandant of a place of internment shall be responsible for the observance in a labour detachment of the provisions of the present Convention. The commandant shall keep an up-to-date list of the labour detachments subordinate to him and shall communicate it to the delegates of the Protecting Power, of the International Committee of the Red Cross and of other humanitarian organizations who may visit the places of internment.

Chapter VI. Personal Property and Financial Resources

ART. 97. Internees shall be permitted to retain articles of personal use. Monies, cheques, bonds, etc., and valuables in their possession may not be taken from them except in accordance with established procedure. Detailed receipts shall be given therefor.

The amounts shall be paid into the account of every internee as provided for in Article 98. Such amounts may not be converted into any other currency unless legislation in force in the territory in which the owner is interned so requires or the internee gives his consent.

Articles which have above all a personal or sentimental value may not be taken away.

A woman internee shall not be searched except by a woman.

On release or repatriation, internees shall be given all articles, monies or other valuables taken from them during internment and shall receive in currency the balance of any credit to their accounts kept in accordance with Article 98, with the exception of any articles or amounts withheld by the Detaining Power by virtue of its legislation in force. If the property of an internee is so withheld, the owner shall receive a detailed receipt.

Family or identity documents in the possession of internees may not be taken away without a receipt being given. At no time shall internees be left without identity documents. If they have none, they shall be issued with special documents drawn up by the detaining authorities, which will serve as their identity papers until the end of their internment.

Internees may keep on their persons a certain amount of money, in cash or in the shape of purchase coupons, to enable them to make purchases.

ART. 98. All internees shall receive regular allowances, sufficient to enable them to purchase goods and articles, such as tobacco, toilet requisites, etc. Such allowances may take the form of credits or purchase coupons.

Furthermore, internees may receive allowances from the Power to which they owe allegiance, the Protecting Powers, the organizations which may assist them, or their families, as well as the income on their property in accordance with the law of the Detaining Power. The amount of allowances granted by the Power to which they owe allegiance shall be the same for each category of internees (infirm, sick, pregnant women, etc.) but may not be allocated by that Power or distributed by the Detaining Power on the basis of discriminations between internees which are prohibited by Article 27 of the present Convention.

The Detaining Power shall open a regular account for every internee, to which shall be credited the allowances named in the present Article, the wages earned and the remittances received, together with such sums taken from him as may be available under the legislation in force in the territory in which he is interned. Internees shall be granted all facilities consistent with the legislation in force in such territory to make remittances to their families and to other dependants. They may draw from their accounts the amounts necessary for their personal expenses, within the limits fixed by the Detaining Power. They shall at all times be afforded reasonable facilities for consulting and obtaining copies of their accounts. A statement of accounts shall be furnished to the Protecting Power, on request, and shall accompany the internee in case of transfer.

Chapter VII. Administration and Discipline

Art. 99. Every place of internment shall be put under the authority of a responsible officer, chosen from the regular military forces or the regular civil administration of the Detaining Power. The officer in charge of the place of internment must have in his possession a copy of the present Convention in the official language, or one of the official languages, of his country and shall be responsible for its application. The staff in control of internees shall be instructed in the provisions of the present Convention and of the administrative measures adopted to ensure its application.

The text of the present Convention and the texts of special agreements concluded under the said Convention shall be posted inside the place of internment, in a language which the internees understand, or shall be in the possession of the Internee Committee.

Regulations, orders, notices and publications of every kind shall be communicated to the internees and posted inside the places of internment, in a language which they understand.

Every order and command addressed to internees individually must, likewise, be given in a language which they understand.

Art. 100. The disciplinary regime in places of internment shall be consistent with humanitarian principles, and shall in no circumstances include regulations imposing on internees any physical exertion dangerous to their health or involving physical or moral victimization. Identification by tattooing or imprinting signs or markings on the body, is prohibited.

In particular, prolonged standing and roll-calls, punishment drill, military drill and manoeuvres, or the reduction of food rations, are prohibited.

Art. 101. Internees shall have the right to present to the authorities in whose power they are, any petition with regard to the conditions of internment to which they are subjected.

They shall also have the right to apply without restriction through the Internee Committee or, if they consider it necessary, direct to the representatives of the Protecting Power, in order to indicate to them any points on which they may have complaints to make with regard to the conditions of internment.

Such petitions and complaints shall be transmitted forthwith and without alteration, and even if the latter are recognized to be unfounded, they may not occasion any punishment.

Periodic reports on the situation in places of internment and as to the needs of the internees may be sent by the Internee Committees to the representatives of the Protecting Powers.

ART. 102. In every place of internment, the internees shall freely elect by secret ballot every six months, the members of a Committee empowered to represent them before the Detaining and the Protecting Powers, the International Committee of the Red Cross and any other organization which may assist them. The members of the Committee shall be eligible for re-election.

Internees so elected shall enter upon their duties after their election has been approved by the detaining authorities. The reasons for any refusals or dismissals shall be communicated to the Protecting Powers concerned.

ART. 103. The Internee Committees shall further the physical, spiritual and intellectual well-being of the internees.

In case the internees decide, in particular, to organize a system of mutual assistance amongst themselves, this organization would be within the competence of the Committees in addition to the special duties entrusted to them under other provisions of the present Convention.

ART. 104. Members of Internee Committees shall not be required to perform any other work, if the accomplishment of their duties is rendered more difficult thereby.

Members of Internee Committees may appoint from amongst the internees such assistants as they may require. All material facilities shall be granted to them, particularly a certain freedom of movement necessary for the accomplishment of their duties (visits to labour detachments, receipt of supplies, etc.).

All facilities shall likewise be accorded to members of Internee Committees for communication by post and telegraph with the detaining authorities, the Protecting Powers, the International Committee of the Red Cross and their delegates, and with the organizations which give assistance to internees. Committee members in labour detachments shall enjoy similar facilities for communication with their Internee Committee in the principal place of internment. Such communications shall not be limited, nor considered as forming a part of the quota mentioned in Article 107.

Members of Internee Committees who are transferred shall be allowed a reasonable time to acquaint their successors with current affairs.

Chaper VIII. Relations with the Exterior

Art. 105. Immediately upon interning protected persons, the Detaining Powers shall inform them, the Power to which they owe allegiance and their Protecting Power of the measures taken for executing the provisions of the present Chapter. The Detaining Powers shall likewise inform the Parties concerned of any subsequent modifications of such measures.

Art. 106. As soon as he is interned, or at the latest not more than one week after his arrival in a place of internment, and likewise in cases of sickness or transfer to another place of internment or to a hospital, every internee shall be enabled to send direct to his family, on the one hand, and to the Central Agency provided for by Article 140, on the other, an internment card similar, if possible, to the model annexed to the present Convention, informing his relatives of his detention, address and state of health. The said cards shall be forwarded as rapidly as possible and may not be delayed in any way.

Art. 107. Internees shall be allowed to send and receive letters and cards. If the Detaining Power deems it necessary to limit the number of letters and cards sent by each internee, the said number shall not be less than two letters and four cards monthly; these shall be drawn up so as to conform as closely as possible to the models annexed to the present Convention. If limitations must be placed on the correspondence addressed to internees, they may be ordered only by the Power to which such internees owe allegiance, possibly at the request of the Detaining Power. Such letters and cards must be conveyed with reasonable despatch; they may not be delayed or retained for disciplinary reasons.

Internees who have been a long time without news, or who find it impossible to receive news from their relatives, or to give them news by the ordinary postal route, as well as those who are at a considerable distance from their homes, shall be allowed to send telegrams, the charges being paid by them in the currency at their disposal. They shall likewise benefit by this provision in cases which are recognized to be urgent.

As a rule, internees' mail shall be written in their own language. The Parties to the conflict may authorize correspondence in other languages.

Art. 108. Internees shall be allowed to receive, by post or by any other means, individual parcels or collective shipments containing in particular foodstuffs, clothing, medical supplies, as well as books and objects of a devotional, educational or recreational character which may meet their needs. Such shipments shall in no way free the Detaining Power from the obligations imposed upon it by virtue of the present Convention.

Should military necessity require the quantity of such shipments to be limited, due notice thereof shall be given to the Protecting Power and to the International Committee of the Red Cross, or to any other organization giving assistance to the internees and responsible for the forwarding of such shipments.

The conditions for the sending of individual parcels and collective shipments shall, if necessary, be the subject of special agreements between the Powers concerned, which may in no case delay the receipt by the internees of relief supplies. Parcels of clothing and foodstuffs may not include books. Medical relief supplies shall, as a rule, be sent in collective parcels.

Art. 109. In the absence of special agreements between Parties to the conflict regarding the conditions for the receipt and distribution of collective relief shipments, the regulations concerning collective relief which are annexed to the present Convention shall be applied.

The special agreements provided for above shall in no case restrict the right of Internee Committees to take possession of collective relief shipments intended for internees, to undertake their distribution and to dispose of them in the interests of the recipients. Nor shall such agreements restrict the right of representatives of the Protecting Powers, the International Committee of the Red Cross, or any other organization giving assistance to internees and responsible for the forwarding of collective shipments, to supervise their distribution to the recipients.

Art. 110. An relief shipments for internees shall be exempt from import, customs and other dues.

All matter sent by mail, including relief parcels sent by parcel post and remittances of money, addressed from other countries to internees or despatched by them through the post office, either direct or through the Information Bureaux provided for in Article 136 and the Central Information Agency provided for in Article 140, shall be exempt from all postal dues both in the countries of origin and destination and in intermediate countries. To this end, in particular, the exemption provided by the Universal Postal Convention of 1947 and by the agreements of the Universal Postal Union in favour of civilians of enemy nationality detained in camps or civilian prisons, shall be extended to the other interned persons protected by the present Convention. The countries not signatory to the above-mentioned agreements shall be bound to grant freedom from charges in the same circumstances.

The cost of transporting relief shipments which are intended for internees and which, by reason of their weight or any other cause, cannot be sent through the post office, shall be borne by the Detaining Power in all the territories under its control. Other Powers which are Parties to the present Convention shall bear the cost of transport in their respective territories.

Costs connected with the transport of such shipments, which are not covered by the above paragraphs, shall be charged to the senders.

The High Contracting Parties shall endeavour to reduce, so far as possible, the charges for telegrams sent by internees, or addressed to them.

ART. 111. Should military operations prevent the Powers concerned from fulfilling their obligation to ensure the conveyance of the mail and relief shipments provided for in Articles 106, 107, 108 and 113, the Protecting Powers concerned, the International Committee of the Red Cross or any other organization duly approved by the Parties to the conflict may undertake the conveyance of such shipments by suitable means (rail, motor vehicles, vessels or aircraft, etc.). For this purpose, the High Contracting Parties shall endeavour to supply them with such transport, and to allow its circulation, especially by granting the necessary safe-conducts.

Such transport may also be used to convey:

- **a.** correspondence, lists and reports exchanged between the Central Information Agency referred to in Article 140 and the National Bureaux referred to in Article 136;
- **b.** correspondence and reports relating to internees which the Protecting Powers, the International Committee of the Red Cross or any other organization assisting the internees exchange either with their own delegates or with the Parties to the conflict.

These provisions in no way detract from the right of any Party to the conflict to arrange other means of transport if it should so prefer, nor preclude the granting of safe-conducts, under mutually agreed conditions, to such means of transport.

The costs occasioned by the use of such means of transport shall be borne, in proportion to the importance of the shipments, by the Parties to the conflict whose nationals are benefited thereby.

Art. 112. The censoring of correspondence addressed to internees or despatched by them shall be done as quickly as possible.

The examination of consignments intended for internees shall not be carried out under conditions that will expose the goods contained in them to deterioration. It shall be done in the presence of the addressee, or of a fellow-internee duly delegated by him. The delivery to internees of individual or collective consignments shall not be delayed under the pretext of difficulties of censorship.

Any prohibition of correspondence ordered by the Parties to the conflict either for military or political reasons, shall be only temporary and its duration shall be as short as possible.

Art. 113. The Detaining Powers shall provide all reasonable execution facilities for the transmission, through the Protecting Power or the Central Agency provided for in Article 140, or as otherwise required, of wills, powers of attorney, letters of authority, or any other documents intended for internees or despatched by them.

In all cases the Detaining Powers shall facilitate the execution and authentication in due legal form of such documents on behalf of internees, in particular by allowing them to consult a lawyer.

Art. 114. The Detaining Power shall afford internees all facilities to enable them to manage their property, provided this is not incompatible with the conditions of internment and the law which is applicable. For this purpose, the said Power may give them permission to leave the place of internment in urgent cases and if circumstances allow.

Art. 115. In all cases where an internee is a party to proceedings in any court, the Detaining Power shall, if he so requests, cause the court to be informed of his detention and shall, within legal limits, ensure that all necessary steps are taken to prevent him from being in any way prejudiced, by reason of his internment, as regards the preparation and conduct of his case or as regards the execution of any judgment of the court.

Art. 116. Every internee shall be allowed to receive visitors, especially near relatives, at regular intervals and as frequently as possible.

As far as is possible, internees shall be permitted to visit their homes in urgent cases, particularly in cases of death or serious illness of relatives.

Chapter IX. Penal and Disciplinary Sanctions

ART. 117. Subject to the provisions of the present Chapter, the laws in force in the territory in which they are detained will continue to apply to internees who commit offences during internment.

If general laws, regulations or orders declare acts committed by internees to be punishable, whereas the same acts are not punishable when committed by persons who are not internees, such acts shall entail disciplinary punishments only.

No internee may be punished more than once for the same act, or on the same count.

ART. 118. The courts or authorities shall in passing sentence take as far as possible into account the fact that the defendant is not a national of the Detaining Power. They shall be free to reduce the penalty prescribed for the offence with which the internee is charged and shall not be obliged, to this end, to apply the minimum sentence prescribed.

Imprisonment in premises without daylight, and, in general, all forms of cruelty without exception are forbidden.

Internees who have served disciplinary or judicial sentences shall not be treated differently from other internees.

The duration of preventive detention undergone by an internee shall be deducted from any disciplinary or judicial penalty involving confinement to which he may be sentenced.

Internee Committees shall be informed of all judicial proceedings instituted against internees whom they represent, and of their result.

ART. 119. The disciplinary punishments applicable to internees shall be the following:

1. a fine which shall not exceed 50 per cent of the wages which the internee would otherwise receive under the provisions of Article 95 during a period of not more than thirty days.
2. discontinuance of privileges granted over and above the treatment provided for by the present Convention
3. fatigue duties, not exceeding two hours daily, in connection with the maintenance of the place of internment.
4. confinement.

In no case shall disciplinary penalties be inhuman, brutal or dangerous for the health of internees. Account shall be taken of the internee's age, sex and state of health.

The duration of any single punishment shall in no case exceed a maximum of thirty consecutive days, even if the internee is answerable for several breaches of discipline when his case is dealt with, whether such breaches are connected or not.

Art. 120. Internees who are recaptured after having escaped or when attempting to escape, shall be liable only to disciplinary punishment in respect of this act, even if it is a repeated offence.

Article 118, paragraph 3, notwithstanding, internees punished as a result of escape or attempt to escape, may be subjected to special surveillance, on condition that such surveillance does not affect the state of their health, that it is exercised in a place of internment and that it does not entail the abolition of any of the safeguards granted by the present Convention.

Internees who aid and abet an escape or attempt to escape, shall be liable on this count to disciplinary punishment only.

Art. 121. Escape, or attempt to escape, even if it is a repeated offence, shall not be deemed an aggravating circumstance in cases where an internee is prosecuted for offences committed during his escape.

The Parties to the conflict shall ensure that the competent authorities exercise leniency in deciding whether punishment inflicted for an offence shall be of a disciplinary or judicial nature, especially in respect of acts committed in connection with an escape, whether successful or not.

Art. 122. Acts which constitute offences against discipline shall be investigated immediately. This rule shall be applied, in particular, in cases of escape or attempt to escape. Recaptured internees shall be handed over to the competent authorities as soon as possible.

In cases of offences against discipline, confinement awaiting trial shall be reduced to an absolute minimum for all internees, and shall not exceed fourteen days. Its duration shall in any case be deducted from any sentence of confinement.

The provisions of Articles 124 and 125 shall apply to internees who are in confinement awaiting trial for offences against discipline.

Art. 123. Without prejudice to the competence of courts and higher authorities, disciplinary punishment may be ordered only by the commandant of the place of internment, or by a responsible officer or official who replaces him, or to whom he has delegated his disciplinary powers.

Before any disciplinary punishment is awarded, the accused internee shall be given precise information regarding the offences of which he is accused, and given an opportunity of explaining his conduct and of defending himself. He shall be permitted, in particular, to call witnesses and to have recourse, if necessary, to the services of a qualified interpreter. The decision shall be announced in the presence of the accused and of a member of the Internee Committee.

The period elapsing between the time of award of a disciplinary punishment and its execution shall not exceed one month.

When an internee is awarded a further disciplinary punishment, a period of at least three days shall elapse between the execution of any two of the punishments, if the duration of one of these is ten days or more.

A record of disciplinary punishments shall be maintained by the commandant of the place of internment and shall be open to inspection by representatives of the Protecting Power.

Art. 124. Internees shall not in any case be transferred to penitentiary establishments (prisons, penitentiaries, convict prisons, etc.) to undergo disciplinary punishment therein.

The premises in which disciplinary punishments are undergone shall conform to sanitary requirements: they shall in particular be provided with adequate bedding. Internees undergoing punishment shall be enabled to keep themselves in a state of cleanliness.

Women internees undergoing disciplinary punishment shall be confined in separate quarters from male internees and shall be under the immediate supervision of women.

Art. 125. Internees awarded disciplinary punishment shall be allowed to exercise and to stay in the open air at least two hours daily.

They shall be allowed, if they so request, to be present at the daily medical inspections. They shall receive the attention which their state of health requires and, if necessary, shall be removed to the infirmary of the place of internment or to a hospital.

They shall have permission to read and write, likewise to send and receive letters. Parcels and remittances of money, however, may be withheld from them until the completion of their punishment; such consignments shall meanwhile be entrusted to the Internee Committee, who will hand over to the infirmary the perishable goods contained in the parcels.

No internee given a disciplinary punishment may be deprived of the benefit of the provisions of Articles 107 and 143 of the present Convention.

ART. 126. The provisions of Articles 71 to 76 inclusive shall apply, by analogy, to proceedings against internees who are in the national territory of the Detaining Power.

Chapter X. Transfers of Internees

ART. 127. The transfer of internees shall always be effected humanely. As a general rule, it shall be carried out by rail or other means of transport, and under conditions at least equal to those obtaining for the forces of the Detaining Power in their changes of station. If, as an exceptional measure, such removals have to be effected on foot, they may not take place unless the internees are in a fit state of health, and may not in any case expose them to excessive fatigue.

The Detaining Power shall supply internees during transfer with drinking water and food sufficient in quantity, quality and variety to maintain them in good health, and also with the necessary clothing, adequate shelter and the necessary medical attention. The Detaining Power shall take all suitable precautions to ensure their safety during transfer, and shall establish before their departure a complete list of all internees transferred.

Sick, wounded or infirm internees and maternity cases shall not be transferred if the journey would be seriously detrimental to them, unless their safety imperatively so demands.

If the combat zone draws close to a place of internment, the internees in the said place shall not be transferred unless their removal can be carried out in adequate conditions of safety, or unless they are exposed to greater risks by remaining on the spot than by being transferred.

When making decisions regarding the transfer of internees, the Detaining Power shall take their interests into account and, in particular, shall not do anything to increase the difficulties of repatriating them or returning them to their own homes.

ART. 128. In the event of transfer, internees shall be officially advised of their departure and of their new postal address. Such notification shall be given in time for them to pack their luggage and inform their next of kin.

They shall be allowed to take with them their personal effects, and the correspondence and parcels which have arrived for them. The weight of such baggage may be limited if the conditions of transfer so require, but in no case to less than twenty-five kilograms per internee.

Mail and parcels addressed to their former place of internment shall be forwarded to them without delay.

The commandant of the place of internment shall take, in agreement with the Internee Committee, any measures needed to ensure the transport of the internees' community property and of the luggage the internees are unable to take with them in consequence of restrictions imposed by virtue of the second paragraph.

Chapter XI. Deaths

ART. 129. The wills of internees shall be received for safe-keeping by the responsible authorities; and if the event of the death of an internee his will shall be transmitted without delay to a person whom he has previously designated.

Deaths of internees shall be certified in every case by a doctor, and a death certificate shall be made out, showing the causes of death and the conditions under which it occurred.

An official record of the death, duly registered, shall be drawn up in accordance with the procedure relating thereto in force in the territory where the place of internment is situated, and a duly certified copy of such record shall be transmitted without delay to the Protecting Power as well as to the Central Agency referred to in Article 140.

ART. 130. The detaining authorities shall ensure that internees who die while interned are honourably buried, if possible according to the rites of the religion to which they belonged and that their graves are respected, properly maintained, and marked in such a way that they can always be recognized.

Deceased internees shall be buried in individual graves unless unavoidable circumstances require the use of collective graves. Bodies may be cremated only for imperative reasons of hygiene, on account of the religion of the deceased or in accordance with his expressed wish to this effect. In case of cremation, the fact shall be stated and the reasons given in the death certificate of the deceased. The ashes shall be retained for safe-keeping by the detaining authorities and shall be transferred as soon as possible to the next of kin on their request.

As soon as circumstances permit, and not later than the close of hostilities, the Detaining Power shall forward lists of graves of deceased internees to the Powers on whom deceased internees depended, through the Information Bureaux provided for in Article 136. Such lists shall include all particulars necessary for the identification of the deceased internees, as well as the exact location of their graves.

Art. 131. Every death or serious injury of an internee, caused or suspected to have been caused by a sentry, another internee or any other person, as well as any death the cause of which is unknown, shall be immediately followed by an official enquiry by the Detaining Power.

A communication on this subject shall be sent immediately to the Protecting Power. The evidence of any witnesses shall be taken, and a report including such evidence shall be prepared and forwarded to the said Protecting Power.

If the enquiry indicates the guilt of one or more persons, the Detaining Power shall take all necessary steps to ensure the prosecution of the person or persons responsible.

Chapter XIII. Release, Repatriation and Accommodation in Neutral Countries

Art. 132. Each interned person shall be released by the Detaining Power as soon as the reasons which necessitated his internment no longer exist.

The Parties to the conflict shall, moreover, endeavour during the course of hostilities, to conclude agreements for the release, the repatriation, the return to places of residence or the accommodation in a neutral country of certain classes of internees, in particular children, pregnant women and mothers with infants and young children, wounded and sick, and internees who have been detained for a long time.

Art. 133. Internment shall cease as soon as possible after the close of hostilities.

Internees in the territory of a Party to the conflict against whom penal proceedings are pending for offences not exclusively subject to disciplinary penalties, may be detained until the close of such proceedings and, if circumstances require, until the completion of the penalty. The same shall apply to internees who have been previously sentenced to a punishment depriving them of liberty.

By agreement between the Detaining Power and the Powers concerned, committees may be set up after the close of hostilities, or of the occupation of territories, to search for dispersed internees.

ART. 134. The High Contracting Parties shall endeavour, upon the close of hostilities or occupation, to ensure the return of all internees to their last place of residence, or to facilitate their repatriation.

ART. 135. The Detaining Power shall bear the expense of returning released internees to the places where they were residing when interned, or, if it took them into custody while they were in transit or on the high seas, the cost of completing their journey or of their return to their point of departure.

Where a Detaining Power refuses permission to reside in its territory to a released internee who previously had his permanent domicile therein, such Detaining Power shall pay the cost of the said internee's repatriation. If, however, the internee elects to return to his country on his own responsibility or in obedience to the Government of the Power to which he owes allegiance, the Detaining Power need not pay the expenses of his journey beyond the point of his departure from its territory. The Detaining Power need not pay the cost of repatriation of an internee who was interned at his own request.

If internees are transferred in accordance with Article 45, the transferring and receiving Powers shall agree on the portion of the above costs to be borne by each.

The foregoing shall not prejudice such special agreements as may be concluded between Parties to the conflict concerning the exchange and repatriation of their nationals in enemy hands.

Section V. Information Bureaux and Central Agency

ART. 136. Upon the outbreak of a conflict and in all cases of occupation, each of the Parties to the conflict shall establish an official Information Bureau responsible for receiving and transmitting information in respect of the protected persons who are in its power.

Each of the Parties to the conflict shall, within the shortest possible period, give its Bureau information of any measure taken by it concerning any protected persons who are kept in custody for more than two weeks, who are subjected to assigned residence or who are interned. It shall, furthermore, require its various departments concerned with such matters to provide the aforesaid Bureau promptly with information concerning all changes pertaining to these protected persons, as, for example, transfers, releases, repatriations, escapes, admittances to hospitals, births and deaths.

Art. 137. Each national Bureau shall immediately forward information concerning protected persons by the most rapid means to the Powers in whose territory they resided, through the intermediary of the Protecting Powers and likewise through the Central Agency provided for in Article 140. The Bureaux shall also reply to all enquiries which may be received regarding protected persons.

Information Bureaux shall transmit information concerning a protected person unless its transmission might be detrimental to the person concerned or to his or her relatives. Even in such a case, the information may not be withheld from the Central Agency which, upon being notified of the circumstances, will take the necessary precautions indicated in Article 140.

All communications in writing made by any Bureau shall be authenticated by a signature or a seal.

Art. 138. The information received by the national Bureau and transmitted by it shall be of such a character as to make it possible to identify the protected person exactly and to advise his next of kin quickly. The information in respect of each person shall include at least his surname, first names, place and date of birth, nationality last residence and distinguishing characteristics, the first name of the father and the maiden name of the mother, the date, place and nature of the action taken with regard to the individual, the address at which correspondence may be sent to him and the name and address of the person to be informed.

Likewise, information regarding the state of health of internees who are seriously ill or seriously wounded shall be supplied regularly and if possible every week.

Art. 139. Each national Information Bureau shall, furthermore, be responsible for collecting all personal valuables left by protected persons mentioned in Article 136, in particular those who have been repatriated or released, or who have escaped or died; it shall forward the said valuables to those concerned, either direct, or, if necessary, through the Central Agency. Such articles shall be sent by the Bureau in sealed packets which shall be accompanied by statements giving clear and full identity particulars of the person to whom the articles belonged, and by a complete list of the contents of the parcel. Detailed records shall be maintained of the receipt and despatch of all such valuables.

ART. 140. A Central Information Agency for protected persons, in particular for internees, shall be created in a neutral country. The International Committee of the Red Cross shall, if it deems necessary, propose to the Powers concerned the organization of such an Agency, which may be the same as that provided for in Article 123 of the Geneva Convention relative to the Treatment of Prisoners of War of 12 August 1949.

The function of the Agency shall be to collect all information of the type set forth in Article 136 which it may obtain through official or private channels and to transmit it as rapidly as possible to the countries of origin or of residence of the persons concerned, except in cases where such transmissions might be detrimental to the persons whom the said information concerns, or to their relatives. It shall receive from the Parties to the conflict all reasonable facilities for effecting such transmissions.

The High Contracting Parties, and in particular those whose nationals benefit by the services of the Central Agency, are requested to give the said Agency the financial aid it may require.

The foregoing provisions shall in no way be interpreted as restricting the humanitarian activities of the International Committee of the Red Cross and of the relief Societies described in Article 142.

ART. 141. The national Information Bureaux and the Central Information Agency shall enjoy free postage for all mail, likewise the exemptions provided for in Article 110, and further, so far as possible, exemption from telegraphic charges or, at least, greatly reduced rates.

PART IV. EXECUTION OF THE CONVENTION

Section I. General Provisions

ART. 142. Subject to the measures which the Detaining Powers may consider essential to ensure their security or to meet any other reasonable need, the representatives of religious organizations, relief societies, or any other organizations assisting the protected persons, shall receive from these Powers, for themselves or their duly accredited agents, all facilities for visiting the protected persons, for distributing relief supplies and material from any source, intended for educational, recreational or religious purposes, or for assisting them in organizing their leisure time within the places of internment. Such societies or organizations may be constituted in the territory of the Detaining Power, or in any other country, or they may have an international character.

The Detaining Power may limit the number of societies and organizations whose delegates are allowed to carry out their activities in its territory and under its supervision, on condition, however, that such limitation shall not hinder the supply of effective and adequate relief to all protected persons.

The special position of the International Committee of the Red Cross in this field shall be recognized and respected at all times.

ART. 143. Representatives or delegates of the Protecting Powers shall have permission to go to all places where protected persons are, particularly to places of internment, detention and work.

They shall have access to all premises occupied by protected persons and shall be able to interview the latter without witnesses, personally or through an interpreter.

Such visits may not be prohibited except for reasons of imperative military necessity, and then only as an exceptional and temporary measure. Their duration and frequency shall not be restricted.

Such representatives and delegates shall have full liberty to select the places they wish to visit. The Detaining or Occupying Power, the Protecting Power and when occasion arises the Power of origin of the persons to be visited, may agree that compatriots of the internees shall be permitted to participate in the visits.

The delegates of the International Committee of the Red Cross shall also enjoy the above prerogatives. The appointment of such delegates shall be submitted to the approval of the Power governing the territories where they will carry out their duties.

ART. 144. The High Contracting Parties undertake, in time of peace as in time of war, to disseminate the text of the present Convention as widely as possible in their respective countries, and, in particular, to include the study thereof in their programmes of military and, if possible, civil instruction, so that the principles thereof may become known to the entire population.

Any civilian, military, police or other authorities, who in time of war assume responsibilities in respect of protected persons, must possess the text of the Convention and be specially instructed as to its provisions.

Art. 145. The High Contracting Parties shall communicate to one another through the Swiss Federal Council and, during hostilities, through the Protecting Powers, the official translations of the present Convention, as well as the laws and regulations which they may adopt to ensure the application thereof.

Art. 146. The High Contracting Parties undertake to enact any legislation necessary to provide effective penal sanctions for persons committing, or ordering to be committed, any of the grave breaches of the present Convention defined in the following Article.

Each High Contracting Party shall be under the obligation to search for persons alleged to have committed, or to have ordered to be committed, such grave breaches, and shall bring such persons, regardless of their nationality, before its own courts. It may also, if it prefers, and in accordance with the provisions of its own legislation, hand such persons over for trial to another High Contracting Party concerned, provided such High Contracting Party has made out a prima facie case.

Each High Contracting Party shall take measures necessary for the suppression of all acts contrary to the provisions of the present Convention other than the grave breaches defined in the following Article.

In all circumstances, the accused persons shall benefit by safeguards of proper trial and defence, which shall not be less favourable than those provided by Article 105 and those following of the Geneva Convention relative to the Treatment of Prisoners of War of 12 August 1949.

Art. 147. Grave breaches to which the preceding Article relates shall be those involving any of the following acts, if committed against persons or

property protected by the present Convention: wilful killing, torture or inhuman treatment, including biological experiments, wilfully causing great suffering or serious injury to body or health, unlawful deportation or transfer or unlawful confinement of a protected person, compelling a protected person to serve in the forces of a hostile Power, or wilfully depriving a protected person of the rights of fair and regular trial prescribed in the present Convention, taking of hostages and extensive destruction and appropriation of property, not justified by military necessity and carried out unlawfully and wantonly.

Art. 148. No High Contracting Party shall be allowed to absolve itself or any other High Contracting Party of any liability incurred by itself or by another High Contracting Party in respect of breaches referred to in the preceding Article.

ART. 149. At the request of a Party to the conflict, an enquiry shall be instituted, in a manner to be decided between the interested Parties, concerning any alleged violation of the Convention.

If agreement has not been reached concerning the procedure for the enquiry, the Parties should agree on the choice of an umpire who will decide upon the procedure to be followed.

Once the violation has been established, the Parties to the conflict shall put an end to it and shall repress it with the least possible delay.

Section II. Final Provisions

ART. 150. The present Convention is established in English and in French. Both texts are equally authentic.

The Swiss Federal Council shall arrange for official translations of the Convention to be made in the Russian and Spanish languages.

ART. 151. The present Convention, which bears the date of this day, is open to signature until 12 February 1950, in the name of the Powers represented at the Conference which opened at Geneva on 21 April 1949.

ART. 152. The present Convention shall be ratified as soon as possible and the ratifications shall be deposited at Berne.

A record shall be drawn up of the deposit of each instrument of ratification and certified copies of this record shall be transmitted by the Swiss Federal Council to all the Powers in whose name the Convention has been signed, or whose accession has been notified.

ART. 153. The present Convention shall come into force six months after not less than two instruments of ratification have been deposited.

Thereafter, it shall come into force for each High Contracting Party six months after the deposit of the instrument of ratification.

ART. 154. In the relations between the Powers who are bound by the Hague Conventions respecting the Laws and Customs of War on Land, whether that of 29 July 1899, or that of 18 October 1907, and who are parties to the present Convention, this last Convention shall be supplementary to Sections II and III of the Regulations annexed to the above-mentioned Conventions of The Hague.

Art. 155. From the date of its coming into force, it shall be open to any Power in whose name the present Convention has not been signed, to accede to this Convention.

Art. 156. Accessions shall be notified in writing to the Swiss Federal Council, and shall take effect six months after the date on which they are received.

The Swiss Federal Council shall communicate the accessions to all the Powers in whose name the Convention has been signed, or whose accession has been notified.

Art. 157. The situations provided for in Articles 2 and 3 shall effective immediate effect to ratifications deposited and accessions notified by the Parties to the conflict before or after the beginning of hostilities or occupation. The Swiss Federal Council shall communicate by the quickest method any ratifications or accessions received from Parties to the conflict.

Art. 158. Each of the High Contracting Parties shall be at liberty to denounce the present Convention.

The denunciation shall be notified in writing to the Swiss Federal Council, which shall transmit it to the Governments of all the High Contracting Parties.

The denunciation shall take effect one year after the notification thereof has been made to the Swiss Federal Council. However, a denunciation of which notification has been made at a time when the denouncing Power is involved in a conflict shall not take effect until peace has been concluded, and until after operations connected with the release, repatriation and re-establishment of the persons protected by the present Convention have been terminated.

The denunciation shall have effect only in respect of the denouncing Power. It shall in no way impair the obligations which the Parties to the conflict shall remain bound to fulfil by virtue of the principles of the law of nations, as they result from the usages established among civilized peoples, from the laws of humanity and the dictates of the public conscience.

Art. 159. The Swiss Federal Council shall register the present Convention with the Secretariat of the United Nations. The Swiss Federal Council shall also inform the Secretariat of the United Nations of all ratifications, accessions and denunciations received by it with respect to the present Convention.

In witness whereof the undersigned, having deposited their respective full powers, have signed the present Convention.

Done at Geneva this twelfth day of August 1949, in the English and French languages. The original shall be deposited in the Archives of the Swiss Confederation. The Swiss Federal Council shall transmit certified copies thereof to each of the signatory and acceding States.

Annex I. Draft Agreement Relating to Hospital and Safety Zones and Localities

ART. 1. Hospital and safety zones shall be strictly reserved for the persons mentioned in Article 23 of the Geneva Convention for the Amelioration of the Condition of the Wounded and Sick in Armed Forces in the Field of 12 August 1949, and in Article 14 of the Geneva Convention relative to the Protection of Civilian Persons in Time of War of 12 August 1949, and for the personnel entrusted with the organization and administration of these zones and localities, and with the care of the persons therein assembled.

Nevertheless, persons whose permanent residence is within such zones shall have the right to stay there.

ART. 2. No persons residing, in whatever capacity, in a hospital and safety zone shall perform any work, either within or without the zone, directly connected with military operations or the production of war material.

ART. 3. The Power establishing a hospital and safety zone shall take all necessary measures to prohibit access to all persons who have no right of residence or entry therein.

ART. 4. Hospital and safety zones shall fulfil the following conditions:

- **a.** they shall comprise only a small part of the territory governed by the Power which has established them
- **b.** they shall be thinly populated in relation to the possibilities of accommodation
- **c.** they shall be far removed and free from all military objectives, or large industrial or administrative establishments
- **d.** they shall not be situated in areas which, according to every probability, may become important for the conduct of the war.

Art. 5. Hospital and safety zones shall be subject to the following obligations:

- **a.** the lines of communication and means of transport which they possess shall not be used for the transport of military personnel or material, even in transit
- **b.** they shall in no case be defended by military means.

Art. 6. Hospital and safety zones shall be marked by means of oblique red bands on a white ground, placed on the buildings and outer precincts.

Zones reserved exclusively for the wounded and sick may be marked by means of the Red Cross (Red Crescent, Red Lion and Sun) emblem on a white ground.

They may be similarly marked at night by means of appropriate illumination.

Art. 7. The Powers shall communicate to all the High Contracting Parties in peacetime or on the outbreak of hostilities, a list of the hospital and safety zones in the territories governed by them. They shall also give notice of any new zones set up during hostilities.

As soon as the adverse party has received the above-mentioned notification, the zone shall be regularly established.

If, however, the adverse party considers that the conditions of the present agreement have not been fulfilled, it may refuse to recognize the zone by giving immediate notice thereof to the Party responsible for the said zone, or may make its recognition of such zone dependent upon the institution of the control provided for in Article 8.

Art. 8. Any Power having recognized one or several hospital and safety zones instituted by the adverse Party shall be entitled to demand control by one or more Special Commissions, for the purpose of ascertaining if the zones fulfil the conditions and obligations stipulated in the present agreement.

For this purpose, members of the Special Commissions shall at all times have free access to the various zones and may even reside there permanently. They shall be given all facilities for their duties of inspection.

Art. 9. Should the Special Commissions note any facts which they consider contrary to the stipulations of the present agreement, they shall at once draw the attention of the Power governing the said zone to these facts, and shall fix a time limit of five days within which the matter should be rectified. They shall duly notify the Power which has recognized the zone.

If, when the time limit has expired, the Power governing the zone has not complied with the warning, the adverse Party may declare that it is no longer bound by the present agreement in respect of the said zone.

Art. 10. Any Power setting up one or more hospital and safety zones, and the adverse Parties to whom their existence has been notified, shall nominate or have nominated by the Protecting Powers or by other neutral Powers, persons eligible to be members of the Special Commissions mentioned in Articles 8 and 9.

Art. 11. In no circumstances may hospital and safety zones be the object of attack. They shall be protected and respected at all times by the Parties to the conflict.

Art. 12. In the case of occupation of a territory, the hospital and safety zones therein shall continue to be respected and utilized as such.

Their purpose may, however, be modified by the Occupying Power, on condition that all measures are taken to ensure the safety of the persons accommodated.

Art. 13. The present agreement shall also apply to localities which the Powers may utilize for the same purposes as hospital and safety zones.

Annex II. Draft Regulations Concerning Collective Relief

Art. 1. The Internee Committees shall be allowed to distribute collective relief shipments for which they are responsible to all internees who are dependent for administration on the said Committee's place of internment, including those internees who are in hospitals, or in prison or other penitentiary establishments.

Art. 2. The distribution of collective relief shipments shall be effected in accordance with the instructions of the donors and with a plan drawn up by the Internee Committees. The issue of medical stores shall, however, be made for preference in agreement with the senior medical officers, and the latter may, in hospitals and infirmaries, waive the said instructions, if the needs of their patients so demand. Within the limits thus defined, the distribution shall always be carried out equitably.

Art. 3. Members of Internee Committees shall be allowed to go to the railway stations or other points of arrival of relief supplies near their places of internment so as to enable them to verify the quantity as well as the quality of the goods received and to make out detailed reports thereon for the donors.

Art. 4. Internee Committees shall be given the facilities necessary for verifying whether the distribution of collective relief in all subdivisions and annexes of their places of internment has been carried out in accordance with their instructions.

Art. 5. Internee Committees shall be allowed to complete, and to cause to be completed by members of the Internee Committees in labour detachments or by the senior medical officers of infirmaries and hospitals, forms or questionnaires intended for the donors, relating to collective relief supplies (distribution, requirements, quantities, etc.). Such forms and questionnaires, duly completed, shall be forwarded to the donors without delay.

Art. 6. In order to secure the regular distribution of collective relief supplies to the internees in their place of internment, and to meet any needs that may arise through the arrival of fresh parties of internees, the Internee Committees shall be allowed to create and maintain sufficient reserve stocks of collective relief. For this purpose, they shall have suitable warehouses at their disposal; each warehouse shall be provided with two locks, the Internee Committee holding the keys of one lock, and the commandant of the place of internment the keys of the other.

Art. 7. The High Contracting Parties, and the Detaining Powers in particular, shall, so far as is in any way possible and subject to the regulations governing the food supply of the population, authorize purchases of goods to be made in their territories for the distribution of collective relief to the internees. They shall likewise facilitate the transfer of funds and other financial measures of a technical or administrative nature taken for the purpose of making such purchases.

Art. 8. The foregoing provisions shall not constitute an obstacle to the right of internees to receive collective relief before their arrival in a place of internment or in the course of their transfer, nor to the possibility of representatives of the Protecting Power, or of the International Committee of the Red Cross or any other humanitarian organization giving assistance to internees and responsible for forwarding such supplies, ensuring the distribution thereof to the recipients by any other means they may deem suitable.

appendix III

CONVENTION AGAINST TORTURE

Convention Against Torture and Other Cruel, Inhuman or Degrading Treatment or Punishment

The States Parties to this Convention,

Considering that, in accordance with the principles proclaimed in the Charter of the United Nations, recognition of the equal and inalienable rights of all members of the human family is the foundation of freedom, justice and peace in the world,

Recognizing that those rights derive from the inherent dignity of the human person,

Considering the obligation of States under the Charter, in particular Article 55, to promote universal respect for, and observance of, human rights and fundamental freedoms,

Having regard to article 5 of the Universal Declaration of Human Rights and article 7 of the International Covenant on Civil and Political Rights, both of which provide that no one may be subjected to torture or to cruel, inhuman or degrading treatment or punishment,

Having regard also to the Declaration on the Protection of All Persons from Being Subjected to Torture and Other Cruel, Inhuman or Degrading Treatment or Punishment, adopted by the General Assembly on 9 December 1975 (resolution 3452 (XXX)),

Desiring to make more effective the struggle against torture and other cruel, inhuman or degrading treatment or punishment throughout the world,

Have agreed as follows:

Part I

Article 1

1. For the purposes of this Convention, torture means any act by which severe pain or suffering, whether physical or mental, is intentionally inflicted on a person for such purposes as obtaining from him or a third person information or a confession, punishing him for an act he or a third person has committed or is suspected of having committed, or intimidating or coercing him or a third person, or for any reason based on discrimination of any kind, when such pain or suffering is inflicted by or at the instigation of or with the consent or acquiescence of a public official or other person acting in an official capacity. It does not include pain or suffering arising only from, inherent in or incidental to lawful sanctions.
2. This article is without prejudice to any international instrument or national legislation which does or may contain provisions of wider application.

Article 2

1. Each State Party shall take effective legislative, administrative, judicial or other measures to prevent acts of torture in any territory under its jurisdiction.
2. No exceptional circumstances whatsoever, whether a state of war or a threat or war, internal political instability or any other public emergency, may be invoked as a justification of torture.
3. An order from a superior officer or a public authority may not be invoked as a justification of torture.

Article 3

1. No State Party shall expel, return ("refouler") or extradite a person to another State where there are substantial grounds for believing that he would be in danger of being subjected to torture.
2. For the purpose of determining whether there are such grounds, the competent authorities shall take into account all relevant considerations including,

where applicable, the existence in the State concerned of a consistent pattern of gross, flagrant or mass violations of human rights.

Article 4

1. Each State Party shall ensure that all acts of torture are offences under its criminal law. The same shall apply to an attempt to commit torture and to an act by any person which constitutes complicity or participation in torture.
2. Each State Party shall make these offences punishable by appropriate penalties which take into account their grave nature.

Article 5

1. Each State Party shall take such measures as may be necessary to establish its jurisdiction over the offences referred to in article 4 in the following cases:
    1. When the offences are committed in any territory under its jurisdiction or on board a ship or aircraft registered in that State;
    2. When the alleged offender is a national of that State;
    3. When the victim was a national of that State if that State considers it appropriate.
2. Each State Party shall likewise take such measures as may be necessary to establish its jurisdiction over such offences in cases where the alleged offender is present in any territory under its jurisdiction and it does not extradite him pursuant to article 8 to any of the States mentioned in Paragraph 1 of this article.
3. This Convention does not exclude any criminal jurisdiction exercised in accordance with internal law.

Article 6

1. Upon being satisfied, after an examination of information available to it, that the circumstances so warrant, any State Party in whose territory a person alleged to have committed any offence referred to in article 4 is present, shall take him into custody or take other legal measures to ensure his presence. The custody and other legal measures shall be as provided in the law of that State but may be continued only for such time as is necessary to enable any criminal or extradition proceedings to be instituted.

2. Such State shall immediately make a preliminary inquiry into the facts.
3. Any person in custody pursuant to paragraph 1 of this article shall be assisted in communicating immediately with the nearest appropriate representative of the State of which he is a national, or, if he is a stateless person, to the representative of the State where he usually resides.
4. When a State, pursuant to this article, has taken a person into custody, it shall immediately notify the States referred to in article 5, paragraph 1, of the fact that such person is in custody and of the circumstances which warrant his detention. The State which makes the preliminary inquiry contemplated in paragraph 2 of this article shall promptly report its findings to the said State and shall indicate whether it intends to exercise jurisdiction.

Article 7

1. The State Party in territory under whose jurisdiction a person alleged to have committed any offence referred to in article 4 is found, shall in the cases contemplated in article 5, if it does not extradite him, submit the case to its competent authorities for the purpose of prosecution.
2. These authorities shall take their decision in the same manner as in the case of any ordinary offence of a serious nature under the law of that State. In the cases referred to in article 5, paragraph 2, the standards of evidence required for prosecution and conviction shall in no way be less stringent than those which apply in the cases referred to in article 5, paragraph 1.
3. Any person regarding whom proceedings are brought in connection with any of the offences referred to in article 4 shall be guaranteed fair treatment at all stages of the proceedings.

Article 8

1. The offences referred to in article 4 shall be deemed to be included as extraditable offences in any extradition treaty existing between States Parties. States Parties undertake to include such offences as extraditable offences in every extradition treaty to be concluded between them.
2. If a State Party which makes extradition conditional on the existence of a treaty receives a request for extradition from another State Party with which it has no extradition treaty, it may consider this Convention as the legal

basis for extradition in respect of such offenses. Extradition shall be subject to the other conditions provided by the law of the requested State.

3. States Parties which do not make extradition conditional on the existence of a treaty shall recognize such offences as extraditable offences between themselves subject to the conditions provided by the law of the requested state.
4. Such offences shall be treated, for the purpose of extradition between States Parties, as if they had been committed not only in the place in which they occurred but also in the territories of the States required to establish their jurisdiction in accordance with article 5, paragraph 1.

Article 9

1. States Parties shall afford one another the greatest measure of assistance in connection with civil proceedings brought in respect of any of the offences referred to in article 4, including the supply of all evidence at their disposal necessary for the proceedings.
2. States Parties shall carry out their obligations under paragraph 1 of this article in conformity with any treaties on mutual judicial assistance that may exist between them.

Article 10

1. Each State Party shall ensure that education and information regarding the prohibition against torture are fully included in the training of law enforcement personnel, civil or military, medical personnel, public officials and other persons who may be involved in the custody, interrogation or treatment of any individual subjected to any form of arrest, detention or imprisonment.
2. Each State Party shall include this prohibition in the rules or instructions issued in regard to the duties and functions of any such persons.

Article 11

Each State Party shall keep under systematic review interrogation rules, instructions, methods and practices as well as arrangements for the custody and treatment of persons subjected to any form of arrest, detention or imprisonment in any territory under its jurisdiction, with a view to preventing any cases of torture.

Article 12

Each State Party shall ensure that its competent authorities proceed to a prompt and impartial investigation, wherever there is reasonable ground to believe that an act of torture has been committee in any territory under its jurisdiction.

Article 13

Each State Party shall ensure that any individual who alleges he has been subjected to torture in any territory under its jurisdiction has the right to complain to and to have his case promptly and impartially examined its competent authorities. Steps shall be taken to ensure that the complainant and witnesses are protected against all ill-treatment or intimidation as a consequence of his complaint or any evidence given.

Article 14

1. Each State Party shall ensure in its legal system that the victim of an act of torture obtains redress and has an enforceable right to fair and adequate compensation including the means for as full rehabilitation as possible. In the event of the death of the victim as a result of an act of torture, his dependents shall be entitled to compensation.
2. Nothing in this article shall affect any right of the victim or other person to compensation which may exist under national law.

Article 15

Each State Party shall ensure that any statement which is established to have been made as a result of torture shall not be invoked as evidence in any proceedings, except against a person accused of torture as evidence that the statement was made.

Article 16

1. Each State Party shall undertake to prevent in any territory under its jurisdiction other acts of cruel, inhuman or degrading treatment or punishment which do not amount to torture as defined in article 1, when such acts are committed by or at the instigation of or with the consent or acquiescence of a public official or other person acting in an official capacity. In

particular, the obligations contained in articles 10, 11, 12 and 13 shall apply with the substitution for references to torture or references to other forms of cruel, inhuman or degrading treatment or punishment.

2. The provisions of this Convention are without prejudice to the provisions of any other international instrument or national law which prohibit cruel, inhuman or degrading treatment or punishment or which relate to extradition or expulsion.

Article 17

1. There shall be established a Committee against Torture (hereinafter referred to as the Committee) which shall carry out the functions hereinafter provided. The Committee shall consist of 10 experts of high moral standing and recognized competence in the field of human rights, who shall serve in their personal capacity. The experts shall be elected by the States Parties, consideration being given to equitable geographical distribution and to the usefulness of the participation of some persons having legal experience.
2. The members of the Committee shall be elected by secret ballot from a list of persons nominated by States Parties. Each State Party may nominate one person from among its own nationals. States Parties shall bear in mind the usefulness of nominating persons who are also members of the Human Rights Committee established under the International Covenant on Civil and Political Rights and are willing to serve on the Committee against Torture.
3. Elections of the members of the Committee shall be held at biennial meetings of States Parties convened by the Secretary-General of the United Nations. At those meetings, for which two thirds of the States Parties shall constitute a quorum, the persons elected to the Committee shall be those who obtain the largest number of votes and an absolute majority of the votes of the representatives of States Parties present and voting.
4. The initial election shall be held no later than six months after the date of the entry into force of this Convention. At least four months before the date of each election, the Secretary-General of the United Nations shall address a letter to the States Parties inviting them to submit their nominations within three months. The Secretary-General shall prepare a list in alphabetical order of all persons thus nominated, indicating the States Parties which have nominated them, and shall submit it to the States Parties.

5. The members of the Committee shall be elected for a term of four years. They shall be eligible for re-election if renominated. However, the term of five of the members elected at the first election shall expire at the end of two years; immediately after the first election the names of these five members shall be chosen by lot by the chairman of the meeting referred to in paragraph 3.
6. If a member of the Committee dies or resigns or for any other cause can no longer perform his Committee duties, the State Party which nominated him shall appoint another expert from among its nationals to serve for the remainder of his term, subject to the approval of the majority of the States Parties. The approval shall be considered given unless half or more of the States Parties respond negatively within six weeks after having been informed by the Secretary-General of the United Nations of the proposed appointment.
7. States Parties shall be responsible for the expenses of the members of the Committee while they are in performance of Committee duties.

Article 18

1. The Committee shall elect its officers for a term of two years. They may be re-elected.
2. The Committee shall establish its own rules of procedure, but these rules shall provide, inter alia, that
    1. Six members shall constitute a quorum;
    2. Decisions of the Committee shall be made by a majority vote of the members present.
3. The Secretary-General of the United Nations shall provide the necessary staff and facilities for the effective performance of the functions of the Committee under this Convention.
4. The Secretary-General of the United Nations shall convene the initial meeting of the Committee. After its initial meeting, the Committee shall meet at such times as shall be provided in its rules of procedure.
5. The State Parties shall be responsible for expenses incurred in connection with the holding of meetings of the States Parties and of the Committee, including reimbursement of the United Nations for any expenses, such as the cost of staff and facilities, incurred by the United Nations pursuant to paragraph 3 above.

Article 19

1. The States Parties shall submit to the Committee, through the Secretary-General of the United Nations, reports on the measures they have taken to give effect to their undertakings under this Convention, within one year after the entry into force of this Convention for the State Party concerned. Thereafter the States Parties shall submit supplementary reports every four years on any new measures taken, and such other reports as the Committee may request.
2. The Secretary-General shall transmit the reports to all States Parties.
3. [Each report shall be considered by the Committee which may make such comments or suggestions on the report as it considers appropriate, and shall forward these to the State Party concerned. That State Party may respond with any observations it chooses to the Committee.
4. The Committee may, at its discretion, decide to include any comments or suggestions made by it in accordance with paragraph 3, together with the observations thereon received from the State Party concerned, in its annual report made in accordance with article 24. If so requested by the State Party concerned, the Committee may also include a copy of the report submitted under paragraph 1.]

Article 20

1. If the Committee receives reliable information which appears to it to contain well-founded indications that torture is being systematically practised in the territory of a State Party, the Committee shall invite that State Party to co-operate in the examination of the information and to this end to submit observations with regard to the information concerned.
2. Taking into account any observations which may have been submitted by the State Party concerned as well as any other relevant information available to it, the Committee may, if it decides that this is warranted, designate one or more of its members to make a confidential inquiry and to report to the Committee urgently.
3. If an inquiry is made in accordance with paragraph 2, the Committee shall seek the co-operation of the State Party concerned. In agreement with that State Party, such an inquiry may include a visit to its territory.
4. After examining the findings of its member or members submitted in accordance with paragraph 2, the Committee shall transmit these findings to

the State Party concerned together with any comments or suggestions which seem appropriate in view of the situation.

5. All the proceedings of the Committee referred to in paragraphs 1 to 4 of this article shall be confidential, and at all stages of the proceedings the co-operation of the State Party shall be sought. After such proceedings have been completed with regard to an inquiry made in accordance with paragraph 2, the Committee may, after consultations with the State Party concerned, decide to include a summary account of the results of the proceedings in its annual report made in accordance with article 24.

Article 21

1. A State Party to this Convention may at any time declare under this article 3 that it recognizes the competence of the Committee to receive and consider communications to the effect that a State Party claims that another State Party is not fulfilling its obligations under this Convention. Such communications may be received and considered according to the procedures laid down in this article only if submitted by a State Party which has made a declaration recognizing in regard to itself the competence of the Committee. No communication shall be dealt with by the Committee under this article if it concerns a State Party which has not made such a declaration. Communications received under this article shall be dealt with in accordance with the following procedure:
    1. If a State Party considers that another State Party is not giving effect to the provisions of this Convention, it may, by written communication, bring the matter to the attention of that State Party. Within three months after the receipt of the communication the receiving State shall afford the State which sent the communication an explanation or any other statement in writing clarifying the matter which should include, to the extent possible and pertinent, references to domestic procedures and remedies taken, pending, or available in the matter.
    2. If the matter is not adjusted to the satisfaction of both States Parties concerned within six months after the receipt by the receiving State of the initial communication, either State shall have the right to refer the matter to the Committee by notice given to the Committee and to the other State.

3. The Committee shall deal with a matter referred to it under this article only after it has ascertained that all domestic remedies have been invoked and exhausted in the matter, in conformity with the generally recognized principles of international law. This shall not be the rule where the application of the remedies is unreasonably prolonged or is unlikely to bring effective relief to the person who is the victim of the violation of this Convention.
4. The Committee shall hold closed meetings when examining communications under this article.
5. Subject to the provisions of subparagraph (c), the Committee shall make available its good offices to the States Parties concerned with a view to a friendly solution of the matter on the basis of respect for the obligations provided for in the present Convention. For this purpose, the Committee may, when appropriate, set up an ad hoc conciliation commission.
6. In any matter referred to it under this article, the Committee may call upon the States Parties concerned, referred to in subparagraph (b), to supply any relevant information.
7. The States Parties concerned, referred to in subparagraph (b), shall have the right to be represented when the matter is being considered by the Committee and to make submissions orally and/or in writing.
8. The Committee shall, within 12 months after the date of receipt of notice under subparagraph (b), submit a report.
    1. If a solution within the terms of subparagraph (e) is reached, the Committee shall confine its report to a brief statement of the facts and of the solution reached.
    2. If a solution within the terms of subparagraph (e) is not reached, the Committee shall confine its report to a brief statement of the facts; the written submissions and record of the oral submissions made by the States Parties concerned shall be attached to the report.

In every matter, the report shall be communicated to the States Parties concerned.

2. The provisions of this article shall come into force when five States Parties to this Convention have made declarations under paragraph 1 of this article. Such declarations shall be deposited by the States Parties with the Secretary-General of the United Nations, who shall transmit copies thereof to the other States Parties. A declaration may be withdrawn at any time by

notification to the Secretary-General. Such a withdrawal shall not prejudice the consideration of any matter which is the subject of a communication already transmitted under this article; no further communication by any State Party shall be received under this article after the notification of withdrawal of the declaration has been received by the Secretary-General, unless the State Party concerned has made a new declaration.

Article 22

1. A State Party to this Convention may at any time declare under this article that it recognizes the competence of the Committee to receive and consider communications from or on behalf of individuals subject to its jurisdiction who claim to be victims of a violation by a State Party of the provisions of the Convention. No communication shall be received by the Committee if it concerns a State Party to the Convention which has not made such a declaration.
2. The Committee shall consider inadmissible any communication under this article which is anonymous, or which it considers to be an abuse of the right of submission of such communications or to be incompatible with the provisions of this Convention.
3. Subject to the provisions of paragraph 2, the Committee shall bring any communication submitted to it under this article to the attention of the State Party to this Convention which has made a declaration under paragraph 1 and is alleged to be violating any provisions of the Convention. Within six months, the receiving State shall submit to the Committee written explanations or statements clarifying the matter and the remedy, if any, that may have been taken by that State.
4. The Committee shall consider communications received under this article in the light of all information made available to it by or on behalf of the individual and by the State Party concerned.
5. The Committee shall not consider any communication from an individual under this article unless it has ascertained that:
    1. The same matter has not been, and is not being examined under another procedure of international investigation or settlement;
    2. The individual has exhausted all available domestic remedies; this shall not be the rule where the application of the remedies is unreasonably prolonged or is unlikely to bring effective relief to the person who is the victim of the violation of this Convention.

6. The Committee shall hold closed meetings when examining communications under this article.
7. The Committee shall forward its views to the State Party concerned and to the individual.
8. The provisions of this article shall come into force when five States Parties to this Convention have made declarations under paragraph 1 of this article. Such declarations shall be deposited by the States Parties with the Secretary-General of the United Nations, who shall transmit parties thereof to the other States Parties. A declaration may be withdrawn at any time by notification to the Secretary-General. Such a withdrawal shall not prejudice the consideration of any matter which is the subject of a communication already transmitted under this article; no further communication by or on behalf of an individual shall be received under this article after the notification of withdrawal of the declaration has been received by the Secretary-General, unless the State Party concerned has made a new declaration.

Article 23

The members of the Committee, and of the ad hoc conciliation commissions which may be appointed under article 21, paragraph 1 (e), shall be entitled to the facilities, privileges and immunities of experts on missions for the United Nations as laid down in the relevant sections of the Convention on the Privileges and Immunities of the United Nations.

Article 24

The Committee shall submit an annual report on its activities under this Convention to the States Parties and to the General Assembly of the United Nations.

PART III

Article 25

1. This Convention is open for signature by all States.
2. This Convention is subject to ratification. Instruments of ratification shall be deposited with the Secretary-General of the United Nations.

Article 26

This Convention is open to accession by all States. Accession shall be effected by the deposit of an instrument of accession with the Secretary-General of the United Nations.

Article 27

1. This Convention shall enter into force on the thirtieth day after the date of the deposit with the Secretary-General of the United Nations of the twentieth instrument of ratification or accession.
2. For each State ratifying this Convention or acceding to it after the deposit of the twentieth instrument of ratification or accession, the Convention shall enter into force on the thirtieth day after the date of the deposit of its own instrument of ratification or accession.

Article 28

1. Each State may, at the time of signature or ratification of this Convention or accession thereto, declare that it does not recognize the competence of the Committee provided for in article 20.

2. Any State Party having made a reservation in accordance with paragraph 1 of this article may, at any time, withdraw this reservation by notification to the Secretary-General of the United Nations.

Article 29

1. Any State Party to this Convention may propose an amendment and file it with the Secretary-General of the United Nations. The Secretary-General shall thereupon communicate the proposed amendment to the States Parties to this Convention with a request that they notify him whether they favour a conference of States Parties for the purpose of considering and voting upon the proposal. In the event that within four months from the date of such communication at least one third of the State Parties favours such a conference, the Secretary-General shall convene the conference under the auspices of the United Nations. Any amendment adopted by a majority of the States Parties present and voting at the conference shall be submitted by the Secretary-General to all the States Parties for acceptance.

2. An amendment adopted in accordance with paragraph 1 shall enter into force when two thirds of the States Parties to this Convention have notified the Secretary-General of the United Nations that they have accepted it in accordance with their respective constitutional processes.
3. When amendments enter into force, they shall be binding on those States Parties which have accepted them, other States Parties still being bound by the provisions of this Convention and any earlier amendments which they have accepted.

Article 30

1. Any dispute between two or more States Parties concerning the interpretation or application of this Convention which cannot be settled through negotiation, shall, at the request of one of them, be submitted to arbitration. If within six months from the date of the request for arbitration the Parties are unable to agree on the organization of the arbitration, any one of those Parties may refer the dispute to the International Court of Justice by request in conformity with the Statute of the Court.
2. Each State may at the time of signature or ratification of this Convention or accession thereto, declare that it does not consider itself bound by the preceding paragraph. The other States Parties shall not be bound by the preceding paragraph with respect to any State Party having made such a reservation.
3. Any State Party having made a reservation in accordance with the preceding paragraph may at any time withdraw this reservation by notification to the Secretary-General of the United Nations.

Article 31

1. A State Party may denounce this Convention by written notification to the Secretary-General of the United Nations. Denunciation becomes effective one year after the date of receipt of the notification by the Secretary-General.
2. Such a denunciation shall not have the effect of releasing the State Party from its obligations under this Convention in regard to any act or omission which occurs prior to the date at which the denunciation becomes effective. Nor shall denunciation prejudice in any way the continued consideration of

any matter which is already under consideration by the Committee prior to the date at which the denunciation becomes effective.

3. Following the date at which the denunciation of a State Party becomes effective, the Committee shall not commence consideration of any new matter regarding that State.

Article 32

The Secretary-General of the United Nations shall inform all members of the United Nations and all States which have signed this Convention or acceded to it, or the following particulars:

1. Signatures, ratifications and accessions under articles 25 and 26;
2. The date of entry into force of this Convention under article 27, and the date of the entry into force of any amendments under article 29;
3. Denunciations under article 31.

Article 33

1. This Convention, of which the Arabic, Chinese, English, French, Russian and Spanish texts are equally authentic, shall be deposited in the archives of the United Nations.
2. The Secretary-General of the United Nations shall transmit certified copies of this Convention to all States.

On February 4, 1985, the Convention was opened for signature at United Nations Headquarters in New York. At that time, representatives of the following countries signed it: Afghanistan, Argentina, Belgium, Bolivia, Costa Rica, Denmark, Dominican Republic, Finland, France, Greece, Iceland, Italy, Netherlands, Norway, Portugal, Senegal, Spain, Sweden, Switzerland and Uruguay. Subsequently, signatures were received from Venezuela on February 15, from Luxembourg and Panama on February 22, from Austria on March 14, and from the United Kingdom on March 15, 1985.

(signatures)

Created on July 16, 1994 / Last edited on January 25, 1997 appendix IV

INTERNATIONAL COVENANT ON CIVIL AND POLITICAL RIGHTS

The States Parties to the present Covenant,

Considering that, in accordance with the principles proclaimed in the Charter of the United Nations, recognition of the inherent dignity and of the equal and inalienable rights of all members of the human family is the foundation of freedom, justice and peace in the world,

Recognizing that these rights derive from the inherent dignity of the human person,

Recognizing that, in accordance with the *Universal Declaration of Human Rights,* the ideal of free human beings enjoying civil and political freedom and freedom from fear and want can only be achieved if conditions are created whereby everyone may enjoy his civil and political rights, as well as his economic, social and cultural rights,

Considering the obligation of States under the Charter of the United Nations to promote universal respect for and observance of, human rights and freedoms,

Realizing that the individual, having duties to other individuals and to the community to which he belongs, is under a responsibility to strive for the promotion and observance of the rights recognized in the present Covenant,

Agree upon the following articles:

PART I

Article 1

1. All peoples have the right of self-determination. By virtue of that right they freely determine their political status and freely pursue their economic, social and cultural development.
2. All peoples may, for their own ends, freely dispose of their natural wealth and resources without prejudice to any obligations arising out of international economic co-operation, based upon the principle of mutual benefit, and international law. In no case may a people be deprived of it its own means of subsistence.
3. The States Parties to the present Covenant, including those having responsibility for the administration of Non-Self-Governing and Trust Territories, shall promote the realization of the right of self-determination, and shall respect that right, in conformity with the provisions of the Charter of the United Nations.

PART II

Article 2

1. Each State Party to the present Covenant undertakes to respect and to ensure to all individuals within its territory and subject to its jurisdiction the rights recognized in the present Covenant, without distinction of any kind, such as race, colour, sex, language, religion, political or other opinion, national or social origin, property, birth or other status.
2. Where not already provided for by existing legislative or other measures, each State Party to the present Covenant undertakes to take the necessary steps, in accordance with its constitutional processes and with the provisions of the present Covenant, to adopt such legislative or other measures as may be necessary to give effect to the rights recognized in the present Covenant.
3. Each State Party to the present Covenant undertakes:
   a. To ensure that any person whose rights or freedoms as herein recognized are violated shall have an effective remedy, notwithstanding that the violation has been committed by persons acting in an official capacity;

b. To ensure that any person claiming such a remedy shall have his right thereto determined by competent judicial, administrative or legislative authorities, or by any other competent authority provided for by the legal system of the State, and to develop the possibilities of judicial remedy;
c. To ensure that the competent authorities shall enforce such remedies when granted.

Article 3

The States Parties to the present Covenant undertake to ensure the equal right of men and women to the enjoyment of all civil and political rights set forth in the present Covenant.

Article 4

1. In time of public emergency which threatens the life of the nation and the existence of which is officially proclaimed, the States Parties to the present Covenant may take measures derogating from their obligations under the present Covenant to the extent strictly required by the exigencies of the situation, provided that such measures are not inconsistent with their other obligations under international law and do not involve discrimination solely on the ground of race, colour, sex, language, religion or social origin.
2. No derogation from articles 6, 7, 8 (paragraphs 1 and 2), 11 ,15, 16 and 18 may be made under this provision.
3. Any State Party to the present Covenant availing itself of the right of derogation shall immediately inform the other States Parties to the present Covenant, through the intermediary of the Secretary-General of the United Nations, of the provisions from which it has derogated and of the reasons by which it was actuated. A further communication shall be made, through the same intermediary, on the date on which it terminates such derogation.

Article 5

1. Nothing in the present Covenant may be interpreted as implying for any State, group or person any right to engage in any activity or perform any act aimed at the destruction of any of the rights and freedoms recognized herein or at their limitation to a greater extent than is provided for in the present Covenant.

2. There shall be no restriction upon or derogation from any of the fundamental human rights recognized or existing in any State Party to the present Covenant pursuant to law, conventions, regulations or custom on the pretext that the present Covenant does not recognize such rights or that it recognizes them to a lesser extent.

PART III

Article 6

1. Every human being has the inherent right to life. This right shall be protected by law. No one shall be arbitrarily deprived of his life.
2. In countries which have not abolished the death penalty, sentence of death may be imposed only for the most serious crimes in accordance with the law in force at the time of the commission of the crime and not contrary to the provisions of the present Covenant and to the Convention on the Prevention and Punishment of the Crime of Genocide. This penalty can only be carried out pursuant to a final judgement rendered by a competent court.
3. When deprivation of life constitutes the crime of genocide, it is understood that nothing in this article shall authorize any State Party to the present Covenant to derogate in any way from any obligation assumed under the provisions of the Convention on the Prevention and Punishment of the Crime of Genocide.
4. Anyone sentenced to death shall have the right to seek pardon or commutation of the sentence. Amnesty, pardon or commutation of the sentence of death may be granted in all cases.
5. Sentence of death shall not be imposed for crimes committed by persons below eighteen years of age and shall not be carried out on pregnant women.
6. Nothing in this article shall be invoked to delay or to prevent the abolition of capital punishment by any State Party to the present Covenant.

Article 7

No one shall be subjected to torture or to cruel, inhuman or degrading treatment or punishment. In particular, no one shall be subjected without his free consent to medical or scientific experimentation.

Article 8

1. No one shall be held in slavery; slavery and the slave-trade in all their forms shall be prohibited.
2. No one shall be held in servitude.
3. **a.** No one shall be required to perform forced or compulsory labour
   b. Paragraph 3 (a) shall not be held to preclude, in countries where imprisonment with hard labour may be imposed as a punishment for a crime, the performance of hard labour in pursuance of a sentence to such punishment by a competent court.
   c. For the purpose of this paragraph the term "forced or compulsory labour" shall not include:
      i. Any work or service, not referred to in sub-paragraph (b), normally required of a person who is under detention in consequence of a lawful order of a court, or of a person during conditional release from such detention;
      ii. Any service of a military character and, in countries where conscientious objection is recognized, any national service required by law of conscientious objectors;
      iii. Any service exacted in cases of emergency or calamity threatening the life or well-being of the community;
      iv. Any work or service which forms part of normal civil obligations.

Article 9

1. Everyone has the right to liberty and security of person. No one shall be subjected to arbitrary arrest or detention. No one shall be deprived of his liberty except on such grounds and in accordance with such procedure as are established by law.
2. Anyone who is arrested shall be informed, at the time of arrest, of the reasons for his arrest and shall be promptly informed of any charges against him.
3. Anyone arrested or detained on a criminal charge shall be brought promptly before a judge or other officer authorized by law to exercise judicial power and shall be entitled to trial within a reasonable time or to release. It shall not be the general rule that persons awaiting trial shall be detained in custody, but release may be subject to guarantees to appear for trial, at any other stage of the judicial proceedings, and, should occasion arise, for execution of the judgement.

4. Anyone who is deprived of his liberty by arrest or detention shall be entitled to take proceedings before a court, in order that that court may decide without delay on the lawfulness of his detention and order his release if the detention is not lawful.
5. Anyone who has been the victim of unlawful arrest or detention shall have an enforceable right to compensation.

Article 10

1. All persons deprived of their liberty shall be treated with humanity and with respect for the inherent dignity of the human person.
2. a. Accused persons shall, save in exceptional circumstances, be segregated from convicted persons and shall be subject to separate treatment appropriate to their status as unconvicted persons;
   b. Accused juvenile persons shall be separated from adults and brought as speedily as possible for adjudication.
3. The penitentiary system shall comprise treatment of prisoners the essential aim of which shall be their reformation and social rehabilitation. Juvenile offenders shall be segregated from adults and be accorded treatment appropriate to their age and legal status.

Article 11

No one shall be imprisoned merely on the ground of inability to fulfil a contractual obligation.

Article 12

1. Everyone lawfully within the territory of a State shall, within that territory, have the right to liberty of movement and freedom to choose his residence.
2. Everyone shall be free to leave any country, including his own.
3. The above-mentioned rights shall not be subject to any restrictions except those which are provided by law, are necessary to protect national security, public order (ordre public), public health or morals or the rights and freedoms of others, and are consistent with the other rights recognized in the present Covenant.
4. No one shall be arbitrarily deprived of the right to enter his own country.

Article 13

An alien lawfully in the territory of a State Party to the present Covenant may be expelled therefrom only in pursuance of a decision reached in accordance with law and shall, except where compelling reasons of national security otherwise require, be allowed to submit the reasons against his expulsion and to have his case reviewed by, and be represented for the purpose before, the competent authority or a person or persons especially designated by the competent authority.

Article 14

1. All persons shall be equal before the courts and tribunals. In the determination of any criminal charge against him, or of his rights and obligations in a suit at law, everyone shall be entitled to a fair and public hearing by a competent, independent and impartial tribunal established by law. The Press and the public may be excluded from all or part of a trial for reasons of morals, public order (ordre public) or national security in a democratic society, or when the interest of the private lives of the parties so requires, or to the extent strictly necessary in the opinion of the court in special circumstances where publicity would prejudice the interests of justice; but any judgement rendered in a criminal case or in a suit at law shall be made public except where the interest of juvenile persons otherwise requires or the proceedings concern matrimonial disputes or the guardianship of children.
2. Everyone charged with a criminal offence shall have the right to be presumed innocent until proved guilty according to law.
3. In the determination of any criminal charge against him, everyone shall be entitled to the following minimum guarantees, in full equality:
   a. To be informed promptly and in detail in a language which he understands of the nature and cause of the charge against him;
   b. To have adequate time and facilities for the preparation of his defence and to communicate with counsel of his own choosing;
   c. To be tried without undue delay;
   d. To be tried in his presence, and to defend himself in person or through legal assistance of his own choosing; to be informed, if he does not have legal assistance, of this right; and to have legal assistance assigned to him, in any case where the interests of justice so require, and without

payment by him in any such case if he does not have sufficient means to pay for it;

e. To examine, or have examined the witnesses against him and to obtain the attendance and examination of witnesses on his behalf under the same conditions as witnesses against him;

f. To have the free assistance of an interpreter if he cannot understand or speak the language used in court;

g. Not to be compelled to testify against himself or to confess guilt.

4. In the case of juvenile persons, the procedure shall be such as will take account of their age and the desirability of promoting their rehabilitation.
5. Everyone convicted of a crime shall have the right to his conviction and sentence being reviewed by a higher tribunal according to law.
6. When a person has by a final decision been convicted of a criminal offence and when subsequently his conviction has been reversed or he has been pardoned on the ground that a new or newly discovered fact shows conclusively that there has been a miscarriage of justice, the person who has suffered punishment as a result of such conviction shall be compensated according to law, unless it is proved that the non-disclosure of the unknown fact in time is wholly or partly attributable to him.
7. No one shall be liable to be tried or punished again for an offence for which he has already been finally convicted or acquitted in accordance with the law and penal procedure of each country.

Article 15

1. No one shall be held guilty of any criminal offence on account of any act or omission which did not constitute a criminal offence, under national or international law, at the time when it was committed. Nor shall a heavier penalty be imposed than the one that was applicable at the time when the criminal offence was committed. If, subsequent to the commission of the offence, provision is made by law for the imposition of a lighter penalty, the offender shall benefit thereby.
2. Nothing in this article shall prejudice the trial and punishment of any person for any act or omission which, at the time when it was committed. was criminal according to the general principles of law recognized by the community of nations.

Article 16

Everyone shall have the right to recognition everywhere as a person before the law.

Article 17

1. No one shall be subjected to arbitrary or unlawful interference with his privacy, family, home or correspondence, nor to unlawful attacks on his honour and reputation.
2. Everyone has the right to the protection of the law against such interference or attacks.

Article 18

1. Everyone shall have the right to freedom of thought, conscience and religion. This right shall include freedom to have or to adopt a religion or belief of his choice, and freedom, either individually or in community with others and in public or private, to manifest his religion or belief in worship, observance, practice and teaching.
2. No one shall be subject to coercion which would impair his freedom to have or to adopt a religion or belief of his choice.
3. Freedom to manifest one's religion or beliefs may be subject only to such limitations as are prescribed by law and are necessary to protect public safety, order, health, or morals or the fundamental rights and freedoms of others.
4. The States Parties to the present Covenant undertake to have respect for the liberty of parents and, when applicable, legal guardians to ensure the religious and moral education of their children in conformity with their own convictions.

Article 19

1. Everyone shall have the right to hold opinions without interference.
2. Everyone shall have the right to freedom of expression; this right shall include freedom to seek, receive and impart information and ideas of all kinds, regardless of frontiers, either orally, in writing or in print, in the form of art, or through any other media of his choice.

3. The exercise of the rights provided for in paragraph 2 of this article carries with it special duties and responsibilities. It may therefore be subject to certain restrictions, but these shall only be such as are provided by law and are necessary:
   a. For respect of the rights or reputations of others;
   b. For the protection of national security or of public order (ordre public), or of public health or morals.

Article 20

1. Any propaganda for war shall be prohibited by law.
2. Any advocacy of national, racial or religious hatred that constitutes incitement to discrimination, hostility or violence shall be prohibited by law.

Article 21

The right of peaceful assembly shall be recognized. No restrictions may be placed on the exercise of this right other than those imposed in conformity with the law and which are necessary in a democratic society in the interests of national security or public safety, public order (ordre public), the protection of public health or morals or the protection of the rights and freedoms of others.

Article 22

1. Everyone shall have the right to freedom of association with others, including the right to form and join trade unions for the protection of his interests.
2. No restrictions may be placed on the exercise of this right other than those which are prescribed by law and which are necessary in a democratic society in the interests of national security or public safety, public order (ordre public), the protection of public health or morals or the protection of the rights and freedoms of others. This article shall not prevent the imposition of lawful restrictions on members of the armed forces and of the police in their exercise of this right.
3. Nothing in this article shall authorize States Parties to the International Labour Organisation Convention of 1948 concerning Freedom of Association and Protection of the Right to Organize to take legislative measures which would prejudice, or to apply the law in such a manner as to prejudice, the guarantees provided for in that Convention.

Article 23

1. The family is the natural and fundamental group unit of society and is entitled to protection by society and the State.
2. The right of men and women of marriageable age to marry and to found a family shall be recognized.
3. No marriage shall be entered into without the free and full consent of the intending spouses.
4. States Parties to the present Covenant shall take appropriate steps to ensure equality of rights and responsibilities of spouses as to marriage, during marriage and at its dissolution. In the case of dissolution, provision shall be made for the necessary protection of any children.

Article 24

1. Every child shall have, without any discrimination as to race, colour sex, language, religion, national or social origin, property or birth, the right to such measures of protection as are required by his status as a minor, on the part of his family, society and the State.
2. Every child shall be registered immediately after birth and shall have a name.
3. Every child has the right to acquire a nationality.

Article 25

Every citizen shall have the right and the opportunity, without any of the distinctions mentioned in article 2 and without unreasonable restrictions:

a. To take part in the conduct of public affairs, directly or through freely chosen representatives;
b. To vote and to be elected at genuine periodic elections which shall be by universal and equal suffrage and shall be held by secret ballot, guaranteeing the free expression of the will of the electors;
c. To have access, on general terms of equality, to public service in his country.

Article 26

All persons are equal before the law and are entitled without any discrimination to the equal protection of the law. In this respect, the law shall prohibit any discrimination and guarantee to all persons equal and effective protection against discrimination on any ground such as race, colour, sex, language, religion, political or other opinion, national or social origin, property, birth or other status.

Article 27

In those States in which ethnic, religious or linguistic minorities exist persons belonging to such minorities shall not be denied the right, in community with the other members of their group, to enjoy their own culture, to profess and practise their own religion, or to use their own language.

PART IV

Article 28

1. There shall be established a Human Rights Committee (hereafter referred to in the present Covenant as the Committee). It shall consist of eighteen members and shall carry out the functions hereinafter provided.
2. The Committee shall be composed of nationals of the States Parties to the present Covenant who shall be persons of high moral character and recognized competence in the field of human rights, consideration being given to the usefulness of the participation of some persons having legal experience.
3. The members of the Committee shall be elected and shall serve in their personal capacity.

Article 29

1. The members of the Committee shall be elected by secret ballot from a list of persons possessing the qualifications prescribed in article 28 and nominated for the purpose by the States Parties to the present Covenant.
2. Each State Party to the present Covenant may nominate not more than two persons. These persons shall be nationals of the nominating State.
3. A person shall be eligible for renomination.

Article 30

1. The initial election shall be held no later than six months after the date of the entry into force of the present Covenant.

2. At least four months before the date of each election to the Committee other than an election to fill a vacancy declared in accordance with article 34, the Secretary-General of the United Nations shall address a written invitation to the States Parties to the present Covenant to submit their nominations for membership of the Committee within three months.
3. The Secretary-General of the United Nations shall prepare a list in alphabetical order of all the persons thus nominated, with an indication of the States Parties which have nominated them, and shall submit it to the States Parties to the present Covenant no later than one month before the date of each election.
4. Elections of the members of the Committee shall be held at a meeting of the States Parties to the present Covenant convened by the Secretary-General of the United Nations at the Headquarters of the United Nations. At that meeting, for which two thirds of the States Parties to the present Covenant shall constitute a quorum, the persons elected to the Committee shall be those nominees who obtain the largest number of votes and an absolute majority of the votes of the representatives of States Parties present and voting.

Article 31

1. The Committee may not include more than one national of the same State.
2. In the election of the Committee, consideration shall be given to equitable geographical distribution of membership and to the representation of the different forms of civilization and of the principal legal systems.

Article 32

1. The members of the Committee shall be elected for a term of four years. They shall be eligible for re-election if renominated. However, the terms of nine of the members elected at the first election shall expire at the end of two years; immediately after the first election, the names of these nine members elected at the first election shall expire at the end of two years; immediately after the first election, the names of these nine members shall be chosen by lot by the Chairman of the meeting referred to in article 30, paragraph 4.
2. Elections at the expiry of office shall be held in accordance with the preceding articles of this part of the present Covenant.

Article 33

1. If, in the unanimous opinion of the other members, a member of the Committee has ceased to carry out his functions for any cause other than absence of a temporary character, the Chairman of the Committee shall notify the Secretary-General of the United Nations, who shall then declare the seat of that member to be vacant.
2. In the event of the death or the resignation of a member of the Committee, the Chairman shall immediately notify the Secretary-General of the United Nations, who shall declare the seat vacant from the date of death or the date on which the resignation takes effect.

Article 34

1. When a vacancy is declared in accordance with article 33 and if the term of office of the member to be replaced does not expire within six months of the declaration of the vacancy, the Secretary-General of the United Nations shall notify each of the States Parties to the present Covenant, which may within two months submit nominations in accordance with article 29 for the purpose of filling the vacancy.
2. The Secretary-General of the United Nations shall prepare a list in alphabetical order of the persons thus nominated and shall submit it to the States Parties to the present Covenant. The election to fill the vacancy shall then take place in accordance with the relevant provisions of this part of the present Covenant.
3. A member of the Committee elected to fill a vacancy declared in accordance with Article 33 shall hold office for the remainder of the term of the member who vacated the seat on the Committee under the provisions of that article.

Article 35

The members of the Committee shall, with the approval of the General Assembly of the United Nations, receive emoluments from United Nations resources on such terms and conditions as the General Assembly may decide, having regard to the importance of the Committee's responsibilities.

Article 36

The Secretary-General of the United Nations shall provide the necessary staff and facilities for the effective performance of the functions of the Committee under the present Covenant.

Article 37

1. The Secretary-General of the United Nations shall convene the initial meeting of the Committee at the Headquarters of the United Nations.
2. After its initial meeting, the Committee shall meet at such times as shall be provided in its rules of procedure.
3. The Committee shall normally meet at the Headquarters of the United Nations or at the United Nations Office at Geneva.

Article 38

Every member of the Committee shall, before taking up his duties, make a solemn declaration in open committee that he will perform his functions impartially and conscientiously.

Article 39

1. The Committee shall elect its officers for a term of two years. They may be re-elected.
2. The Committee shall establish its own rules of procedure, but these rules shall provide, inter alia, that:
   a. Twelve members shall constitute a quorum;
   b. Decisions of the Committee shall be made by a majority vote of the members present.

Article 40

1. The States Parties to the present Covenant undertake to submit reports on the measures they have adopted which give effect to the rights recognized herein and on the progress made in the enjoyment of those rights:
   a. Within one year of the entry into force of the present Covenant for the States Parties concerned;
   b. Thereafter whenever the Committee so requests.

2. All reports shall be submitted to the Secretary-General of the United Nations, who shall transmit them to the Committee for consideration. Reports shall indicate the factors and difficulties, if any, affecting the implementation of the present Covenant.
3. The Secretary-General of the United Nations may, after consultation with the Committee, transmit to the specialized agencies concerned copies of such parts of the reports as may fall within their field of competence.
4. The Committee shall study the reports submitted by the States Parties to the present Covenant. It shall transmit its reports, and such general comments as it may consider appropriate, to the States Parties. The Committee may also transmit to the Economic and Social Council these comments along with the copies of the reports it has received from States Parties to the present Covenant.
5. The States Parties to the present Covenant may submit to the Committee observations on any comments that may be made in accordance with paragraph 4 of this article.

Article 41

1. A State Party to the present Covenant may at any time declare under this article that it recognizes the competence of the Committee to receive and consider communications to the effect that a State Party claims that another State Party is not fulfilling its obligations under the present Covenant. Communications under this article may be received and considered only if submitted by a State Party which has made a declaration recognizing in regard to itself the competence of the Committee. No communication shall be received by the Committee if it concerns a State Party which has not made such a declaration. Communications received under this article shall be dealt with in accordance with the following procedure:
   a. If a State Party to the present Covenant considers that another State Party is not giving effect to the provisions of the present Covenant, it may, by written communication, bring the matter to the attention of that State Party. Within three months after the receipt of the communication, the receiving State shall afford the State which sent the communication an explanation or any other statement in writing clarifying the matter, which should include, to the extent possible and pertinent, reference to domestic procedures and remedies taken, pending, or available in the matter.

- **b.** If the matter is not adjusted to the satisfaction of both States Parties concerned within six months after the receipt by the receiving State of the initial communication, either State shall have the right to refer the matter to the Committee, by notice given to the Committee and to the other State.
- **c.** The Committee shall deal with a matter referred to it only after it has ascertained that all available domestic remedies have been invoked and exhausted in the matter, in conformity with the generally recognized principles of international law. This shall not be the rule where the application of the remedies is unreasonably prolonged.
- **d.** The Committee shall hold closed meetings when examining communications under this article.
- **e.** Subject to the provisions of sub-paragraph (c), the Committee shall make available its good offices to the States Parties concerned with a view to a friendly solution of the matter on the basis of respect for human rights and fundamental freedoms as recognized in the present Covenant.
- **f.** In any matter referred to it, the Committee may call upon the States Parties concerned, referred to in sub-paragraph (b), to supply any relevant information.
- **g.** The States Parties concerned, referred to in sub-paragraph (b), shall have the right to be represented when the matter is being considered in the Committee and to make submissions orally and/or in writing.
- **h.** The Committee shall, within twelve months after the date of receipt of notice under sub-paragraph (b), submit a report:
  - i. If a solution within the terms of sub-paragraph (e) is reached, the Committee shall confine its report to a brief statement of the facts and of the solution reached;
  - ii. If a solution within the terms of sub-paragraph (e) is not reached, the Committee shall confine its report to a brief statement of the facts; the written submissions and record of the oral submissions made by the States Parties concerned shall be attached to the report.

  In every matter, the report shall be communicated to the States Parties concerned.

2. The provisions of this article shall come into force when ten States Parties to the present Covenant have made declarations under paragraph 1 of this article. Such declarations shall be deposited by the States Parties with the Secretary-General of the United Nations, who shall transmit copies thereof to the other States Parties. A declaration may be withdrawn at any time by notification to the Secretary-General. Such a withdrawal shall not prejudice the consideration of any matter which is the subject of a communication already transmitted under this article; no further communication by any State Party shall be received after the notification of withdrawal of the declaration has been received by the Secretary-General, unless the State Party concerned had made a new declaration.

Article 42

1. **a.** If a matter referred to the Committee in accordance with article 41 is not resolved to the satisfaction of the States Parties concerned, the Committee may, with the prior consent of the States Parties concerned, appoint an ad hoc Conciliation Commission (hereinafter referred to as the Commission). The good offices of the Commission shall be made available to the States Parties concerned with a view to an amicable solution of the matter on the basis of respect for the present Covenant;
   b. The Commission shall consist of five persons acceptable to the States Parties concerned. If the States Parties concerned fail to reach agreement within three months on all or part of the composition of the Commission the members of the Commission concerning whom no agreement has been reached shall be elected by secret ballot by a two-thirds majority vote of the Committee from among its members.
2. The members of the Commission shall serve in their personal capacity. They shall not be nationals of the States Parties concerned, or of a State not party to the present Covenant, or of a State Party which has not made a declaration under article 41.
3. The Commission shall elect its own Chairman and adopt its own rules of procedure.
4. The meetings of the Commission shall normally be held at the Headquarters of the United Nations or at the United Nations Office at Geneva. However, they may be held at such other convenient places as the Commission may determine in consultation with the Secretary-General of the United Nations and the States Parties concerned.
5. The secretariat provided in accordance with article 36 shall also service the commissions appointed under this article.
6. The information received and collated by the Committee shall be made available to the Commission and the Commission may call upon the States Parties concerned to supply any other relevant information.

7. When the Commission has fully considered the matter, but in any event not later than twelve months after having been seized of the matter, it shall submit to the Chairman of the Committee a report for communication to the States Parties concerned:
   a. If the Commission is unable to complete its consideration of the matter within twelve months, it shall confine its report to a brief statement of the status of its consideration of the matter;
   b. If an amicable solution to the matter on the basis of respect for human rights as recognized in the present Covenant is reached, the Commission shall confine its report to a brief statement of the facts and of the solution reached;
   c. If a solution within the terms of sub-paragraph (b) is not reached, the Commission's report shall embody its findings on all questions of fact relevant to the issues between the States Parties concerned, and its views on the possibilities of an amicable solution of the matter. This report shall also contain the written submissions and a record of the oral submissions made by the States Parties concerned;
   d. If the Commission's report is submitted under sub-paragraph (c), the States Parties concerned shall, within three months of the receipt of the report, notify the Chairman of the Committee whether or not they accept the contents of the report of the Commission.
8. The provisions of this article are without prejudice to the responsibilities of the Committee under article 41.
9. The States Parties concerned shall share equally all the expenses of the members of the Commission in accordance with estimates to be provided by the Secretary-General of the United Nations .
10. The Secretary-General of the United Nations shall be empowered to pay the expenses of the members of the Commission, if necessary, before reimbursement by the States Parties concerned, in accordance with paragraph 9 of this article.

Article 43

The members of the Committee, and of the ad hoc conciliation commissions which may be appointed under article 42, shall be entitled to the facilities, privileges and immunities of experts on mission for the United Nations as laid down in the relevant sections of the Convention on the Privileges and Immunities of the United Nations.

Article 44

The provisions for the implementation of the present Covenant shall apply without prejudice to the procedures prescribed in the field of human rights by or under the constituent instruments and the conventions of the United Nations and of the specialized agencies and shall not prevent the States Parties to the present Covenant from having recourse to other procedures for settling a dispute in accordance with general or special international agreements in force between them.

Article 45

The Committee shall submit to the General Assembly of the United Nations, through the Economic and Social Council, an annual report on its activities.

PART V

Article 46

Nothing in the present Covenant shall be interpreted as impairing the provisions of the Charter of the United Nations and of the constitutions of the specialized agencies which define the respective responsibilities of the various organs of the United Nations and of the specialized agencies in regard to the matters dealt with in the present Covenant.

Article 47

Nothing in the present Covenant shall be interpreted as impairing the inherent right of all peoples to enjoy and utilize fully and freely their natural wealth and resources.

PART VI

Article 48

1. The present Covenant is open for signature by any State Member of the United Nations or member of any of its specialized agencies, by any State Party to the Statute of the International Court of Justice, and by any other State which has been invited by the General Assembly of the United Nations to become a party to the present Covenant.

2. The present Covenant is subject to ratification. Instruments of ratification shall be deposited with the Secretary-General of the United Nations.
3. The present Covenant shall be open to accession by any State referred to in paragraph 1 of this article.
4. Accession shall be effected by the deposit of an instrument of accession with the Secretary-General of the United Nations.
5. The Secretary-General of the United Nations shall inform all States which have signed this Covenant or acceded to it of the deposit of each instrument of ratification or accession.

Article 49

1. The present Covenant shall enter into force three months after the date of the deposit with the Secretary-General of the United Nations of the thirty-fifth instrument of ratification or instrument of accession.
2. For each State ratifying the present Covenant or acceding to it after the deposit of the thirty-fifth instrument of ratification or instrument of accession, the present Covenant shall enter into force three months after the date of the deposit of its own instrument of ratification or instrument of accession.

Article 50

The provisions of the present Covenant shall extend to all parts of federal States without any limitations or exceptions.

Article 51

1. Any State Party to the present Covenant may propose an amendment and file it with the Secretary-General of the United Nations. The Secretary-General of the United Nations shall thereupon communicate any proposed amendments to the States Parties to the present Covenant with a request that they notify him whether they favour a conference of States Parties for the purpose of considering and voting upon the proposals. In the event that at least one third of the States Parties favours such a conference, the Secretary-General shall convene the conference under the auspices of the United Nations. Any amendment adopted by a majority of the States Parties

present and voting at the conference shall be submitted to the General Assembly of the United Nations for approval.

2. Amendments shall come into force when they have been approved by the General Assembly of the United Nations and accepted by a two-thirds majority of the States Parties to the present Covenant in accordance with their respective constitutional processes.
3. When amendments come into force, they shall be binding on those States Parties which have accepted them, other States Parties still being bound by the provisions of the present Covenant and any earlier amendment which they have accepted.

Article 52

Irrespective of the notifications made under article 48, paragraph 5, the Secretary-General of the United Nations shall inform all States referred to in paragraph 1 of the same article of the following particulars:

a. Signatures, ratifications and accessions under article 48;
b. The date of the entry into force of the present Covenant under article 49 and the date of the entry into force of any amendments under article 51.

Article 53

1. The present Covenant, of which the Chinese, English, French, Russian and Spanish texts are equally authentic, shall be deposited in the archives of the United Nations.
2. The Secretary-General of the United Nations shall transmit certified copies of the present Covenant to all States referred to in article 48.

IN FAITH WHEREOF the undersigned, being duly authorized thereto by their respective Governments, have signed the present Covenant, opened for signature at New York, on the nineteenth day of December, one thousand nine hundred and sixty-six.

International Covenant on Civil and Political Rights

appendix

V ADDITIONAL PROTOCOL I TO THE GENEVA CONVENTIONS OF 1949 (1977)

Protocol Additional to the Geneva Conventions of 12 August 1949, and relating to the Protection of Victims of International Armed Conflicts (Protocol I), 8 June 1977.

PREAMBLE

The High Contracting Parties,

Proclaiming their earnest wish to see peace prevail among peoples,

Recalling that every State has the duty, in conformity with the Charter of the United Nations, to refrain in its international relations from the threat or use of force against the sovereignty, territorial integrity or political independence of any State, or in any other manner inconsistent with the purposes of the United Nations,

Believing it necessary nevertheless to reaffirm and develop the provisions protecting the victims of armed conflicts and to supplement measures intended to reinforce their application,

Expressing their conviction that nothing in this Protocol or in the Geneva Conventions of 12 August 1949 can be construed as legitimizing or authorizing any act of aggression or any other use of force inconsistent with the Charter of the United Nations,

Reaffirming further that the provisions of the Geneva Conventions of 12 August 1949 and of this Protocol must be fully applied in all circumstances to all persons who are protected by those instruments, without any adverse distinction based on the nature or origin of the armed conflict or on the causes espoused by or attributed to the Parties to the conflict,

Have agreed on the following:

Part I. General Provisions

Art. 1. General principles and scope of application

1. The High Contracting Parties undertake to respect and to ensure respect for this Protocol in all circumstances.
2. In cases not covered by this Protocol or by other international agreements, civilians and combatants remain under the protection and authority of the principles of international law derived from established custom, from the principles of humanity and from dictates of public conscience.
3. This Protocol, which supplements the Geneva Conventions of 12 August 1949 for the protection of war victims, shall apply in the situations referred to in Article 2 common to those Conventions.
4. The situations referred to in the preceding paragraph include armed conflicts in which peoples are fighting against colonial domination and alien occupation and against racist regimes in the exercise of their right of self-determination, as enshrined in the Charter of the United Nations and the Declaration on Principles of International Law concerning Friendly Relations and Co-operation among States in accordance with the Charter of the United Nations.

Art. 2. Definitions

For the purposes of this Protocol

a. "First Convention," "Second Convention," "Third Convention" and "Fourth Convention" mean, respectively, the Geneva Convention for the Amelioration of the Condition of the Wounded and Sick in Armed Forces in the Field of 12 August 1949; the Geneva Convention for the Amelioration of the Condition of Wounded, Sick and Ship-wrecked Members of Armed Forces at Sea of 12 August 1949; the Geneva Convention relative to the Treatment of Prisoners of War of 12 August 1949; the Geneva Convention relative to the Protection of Civilian Persons in Time of War of 12 August 1949; "the Conventions" means the four Geneva Conventions of 12 August 1949 for the protection of war victims;

b. "Rules of international law applicable in armed conflict" means the rules applicable in armed conflict set forth in international agreements to which the Parties to the conflict are Parties and the generally recognized principles and rules of international law which are applicable to armed conflict;

c. "Protecting Power" means a neutral or other State not a Party to the conflict which has been designated by a Party to the conflict and accepted by the adverse Party and has agreed to carry out the functions assigned to a Protecting Power under the Conventions and this Protocol;

d. "Substitute" means an organization acting in place of a Protecting Power in accordance with Article 5.

Art. 3. Beginning and end of application

Without prejudice to the provisions which are applicable at all times:

a. the Conventions and this Protocol shall apply from the beginning of any situation referred to in Article 1 of this Protocol.

b. the application of the Conventions and of this Protocol shall cease, in the territory of Parties to the conflict, on the general close of military operations and, in the case of occupied territories, on the termination of the occupation, except, in either circumstance, for those persons whose final release, repatriation or re-establishment takes place thereafter. These persons shall continue to benefit from the relevant provisions of the Conventions and of this Protocol until their final release repatriation or re-establishment.

Art. 4. Legal status of the Parties to the conflict

The application of the Conventions and of this Protocol, as well as the conclusion of the agreements provided for therein, shall not affect the legal status of the Parties to the conflict. Neither the occupation of a territory nor the application of the Conventions and this Protocol shall affect the legal status of the territory in question.

Art. 5. Appointment of Protecting Powers and of their substitute

1. It is the duty of the Parties to a conflict from the beginning of that conflict to secure the supervision and implementation of the Conventions and of this Protocol by the application of the system of Protecting Powers, including inter alia the designation and acceptance of those Powers, in accordance with the following paragraphs. Protecting Powers shall have the duty of safeguarding the interests of the Parties to the conflict.

2. From the beginning of a situation referred to in Article 1, each Party to the conflict shall without delay designate a Protecting Power for the purpose of applying the Conventions and this Protocol and shall, likewise without delay and for the same purpose, permit the activities or a Protecting Power which has been accepted by it as such after designation by the adverse Party.
3. If a Protecting Power has not been designated or accepted from the beginning of a situation referred to in Article 1, the International Committee of the Red Cross, without prejudice to the right of any other impartial humanitarian organization to do likewise, shall offer its good offices to the Parties to the conflict with a view to the designation without delay of a Protecting Power to which the Parties to the conflict consent. For that purpose it may inter alia ask each Party to provide it with a list of at least five States which that Party considers acceptable to act as Protecting Power on its behalf in relation to an adverse Party and ask each adverse Party to provide a list or at least five States which it would accept as the Protecting Power of the first Party; these lists shall be communicated to the Committee within two weeks after the receipt or the request; it shall compare them and seek the agreement of any proposed State named on both lists.
4. If, despite the foregoing, there is no Protecting Power, the Parties to the conflict shall accept without delay an offer which may be made by the International Committee of the Red Cross or by any other organization which offers all guarantees of impartiality and efficacy, after due consultations with the said Parties and taking into account the result of these consultations, to act as a substitute. The functioning of such a substitute is subject to the consent of the Parties to the conflict; every effort shall be made by the Parties to the conflict to facilitate the operations of the substitute in the performance of its tasks under the Conventions and this Protocol.
5. In accordance with Article 4, the designation and acceptance of Protecting Powers for the purpose of applying the Conventions and this Protocol shall not affect the legal status of the Parties to the conflict or of any territory, including occupied territory.
6. The maintenance of diplomatic relations between Parties to the conflict or the entrusting of the protection of a Party's interests and those of its nationals

to a third State in accordance with the rules of international law relating to diplomatic relations is no obstacle to the designation of Protecting Powers for the purpose of applying the Conventions and this Protocol.

7. Any subsequent mention in this Protocol of a Protecting Power includes also a substitute.

ART. 6. Qualified persons

1. The High Contracting Parties shall, also in peacetime, endeavour, with the assistance of the national Red Cross (Red Crescent, Red Lion and Sun) Societies, to train qualified personnel to facilitate the application of the Conventions and of this Protocol, and in particular the activities of the Protecting Powers.
2. The recruitment and training of such personnel are within domestic jurisdiction.
3. The International Committee of the Red Cross shall hold at the disposal of the High Contracting Parties the lists of persons so trained which the High Contracting Parties may have established and may have transmitted to it for that purpose.
4. The conditions governing the employment of such personnel outside the national territory shall, in each case, be the subject of special agreements between the Parties concerned.

ART. 7. Meetings

The depositary of this Protocol shall convene a meeting of the High Contracting Parties, at the request of one or more of the said Parties and upon, the approval of the majority of the said Parties, to consider general problems concerning the application of the Conventions and of the Protocol.

PART II. WOUNDED, SICK AND SHIPWRECKED

Section I. General Protection

ART. 8. Terminology

For the purposes of this Protocol:

a. "Wounded" and "sick" mean persons, whether military or civilian, who, because of trauma, disease or other physical or mental disorder or disability, are in need of medical assistance or care and who refrain from any act of hostility. These terms also cover maternity cases, new-born babies and other persons who may be in need of immediate medical assistance or care, such as the infirm or expectant mothers, and who refrain from any act of hostility;

b. "Shipwrecked" means persons, whether military or civilian, who are in peril at sea or in other waters as a result of misfortune affecting them or the vessel or aircraft carrying them and who refrain from any act of hostility. These persons, provided that they continue to refrain from any act of hostility, shall continue to be considered shipwrecked during their rescue until they acquire another status under the Conventions or this Protocol;

c. "Medical personnel" means those persons assigned, by a Party to the conflict, exclusively to the medical purposes enumerated under e) or to the administration of medical units or to the operation or administration of medical transports. Such assignments may be either permanent or temporary. The term includes:

i. medical personnel of a Party to the conflict, whether military or civilian, including those described in the First and Second Conventions, and those assigned to civil defence organizations;

ii. medical personnel of national Red Cross (Red Crescent, Red Lion and Sun) Societies and other national voluntary aid societies duly recognized and authorized by a Party to the conflict;

iii. medical personnel or medical units or medical transports described in Article 9, paragraph 2.

d. "Religious personnel" means military or civilian persons, such as chaplains, who are exclusively engaged in the work of their ministry and attached:

i. to the armed forces of a Party to the conflict;

ii. to medical units or medical transports of a Party to the conflict;

iii. to medical units or medical transports described in Article 9, Paragraph 2; or

iv. to civil defence organizations of a Party to the conflict.

The attachment of religious personnel may be either permanent or temporary, and the relevant provisions mentioned under k) apply to them;

e. "Medical units" means establishments and other units, whether military or civilian, organized for medical purposes, namely the search for, collection, transportation, diagnosis or treatment—including first-aid treatment—of the wounded, sick and shipwrecked, or for the prevention of disease.

The term includes for example, hospitals and other similar units, blood transfusion centres, preventive medicine centres and institutes, medical depots and the medical and pharmaceutical stores of such units. Medical units may be fixed or mobile, permanent or temporary;

f. "Medical transportation" means the conveyance by land, water or air of the wounded, sick, shipwrecked, medical personnel, religious personnel, medical equipment or medical supplies protected by the Conventions and by this Protocol;

g. "Medical transports" means any means of transportation, whether military or civilian, permanent or temporary, assigned exclusively to medical transportation and under the control of a competent authority of a Party to the conflict;

h. "Medical vehicles" means any medical transports by land;

i. "Medical ships and craft" means any medical transports by water;

j. "Medical aircraft" means any medical transports by air;

k. "Permanent medical personnel," "permanent medical units" and "permanent medical transports" mean those assigned exclusively to medical purposes for an indeterminate period. "Temporary medical personnel," "temporary medical-units" and "temporary medical transports" mean those devoted exclusively to medical purposes for limited periods during the whole of such periods. Unless otherwise specified, the terms "medical personnel," "medical units" and "medical transports" cover both permanent and temporary categories;

l. "Distinctive emblem" means the distinctive emblem of the red cross, red crescent or red lion and sun on a white ground when used for the protection of medical units and transports, or medical and religious personnel, equipment or supplies;

m. "Distinctive signal" means any signal or message specified for the identification exclusively of medical units or transports in Chapter III of Annex I to this Protocol.

Art. 9. Field of application

1. This Part, the provisions of which are intended to ameliorate the condition of the wounded, sick and shipwrecked, shall apply to all those affected by a situation referred to in Article 1, without any adverse distinction founded on race, colour, sex, language, religion or belief political or other opinion, national or social origin, wealth, birth or other status, or on any other similar criteria.

2. The relevant provisions of Articles 27 and 32 of the First Convention shall apply to permanent medical units and transports (other than hospital ships, to which Article 25 of the Second Convention applies) and their personnel made available to a Party to the conflict for humanitarian purposes:
   a. by a neutral or other State which is not a Party to that conflict;
   b. by a recognized and authorized aid society of such a State;
   c. by an impartial international humanitarian organization.

Art. 10. Protection and care

1. All the wounded, sick and shipwrecked, to whichever Party they belong, shall be respected and protected.
2. In all circumstances they shall be treated humanely and shall receive, to the fullest extent practicable and with the least possible delay, the medical care and attention required by their condition. There shall be no distinction among them founded on any grounds other than medical ones.

Art. 11. Protection of persons

1. The physical or mental health and integrity of persons who are in the power of the adverse Party or who are interned, detained or otherwise deprived of liberty as a result of a situation referred to in Article 1 shall not be endangered by any unjustified act or omission. Accordingly, it is prohibited to subject the persons described in this Article to any medical procedure which is not indicated by the state of health of the person concerned and which is not consistent with generally accepted medical standards which would be applied under similar medical circumstances to persons who are nationals of the Party conducting the procedure and who are in no way deprived of liberty.
2. It is, in particular, prohibited to carry out on such persons, even with their consent:
   a. physical mutilations;
   b. medical or scientific experiments;
   c. removal of tissue or organs for transplantation, except where these acts are justified in conformity with the conditions provided for in paragraph 1.
3. Exceptions to the prohibition in paragraph 2 (c) may be made only in the case of donations of blood for transfusion or of skin for grafting, provided that they are given voluntarily and without any coercion or inducement,

and then only for therapeutic purposes, under conditions consistent with generally accepted medical standards and controls designed for the benefit of both the donor and the recipient.

4. Any wilful act or omission which seriously endangers the physical or mental health or integrity of any person who is in the power of a Party other than the one on which he depends and which either violates any of the prohibitions in paragraphs 1 and 2 or fails to comply with the requirements of paragraph 3 shall be a grave breach of this Protocol.
5. The persons described in paragraph 1 have the right to refuse any surgical operation. In case of refusal, medical personnel shall endeavour to obtain a written statement to that effect, signed or acknowledged by the patient.
6. Each Party to the conflict shall keep a medical record for every donation of blood for transfusion or skin for grafting by persons referred to in paragraph 1, if that donation is made under the responsibility of that Party. In addition, each Party to the conflict shall endeavour to keep a record of all medical procedures undertaken with respect to any person who is interned, detained or otherwise deprived of liberty as a result of a situation referred to in Article 1. These records shall be available at all times for inspection by the Protecting Power.

ART. 12. Protection of medical units

1. Medical units shall be respected and protected at all times and shall not be the object of attack.
2. Paragraph 1 shall apply to civilian medical units, provided that they:
   a. belong to one of the Parties to the conflict;
   b. are recognized and authorized by the competent authority of one of the Parties to the conflict; or
   c. are authorized in conformity with Article 9, paragraph 2, of this Protocol or Article 27 of the First Convention.
3. The Parties to the conflict are invited to notify each other of the location of their fixed medical units. The absence of such notification shall not exempt any of the Parties from the obligation to comply with the provisions of paragraph 1.
4. Under no circumstances shall medical units be used in an attempt to shield military objectives from attack. Whenever possible, the Parties to the conflict shall ensure that medical units are so sited that attacks against military objectives do not imperil their safety.

Art. 13. Discontinuance of protection of civilian medical units

1. The protection to which civilian medical units are entitled shall not cease unless they are used to commit, outside their humanitarian function, acts harmful to the enemy. Protection may, however, cease only after a warning has been given setting, whenever appropriate, a reasonable time-limit, and after such warning has remained unheeded.
2. The following shall not be considered as acts harmful to the enemy:
    - **a.** that the personnel of the unit are equipped with light individual weapons for their own defence or for that of the wounded and sick in their charge;
    - **b.** that the unit is guarded by a picket or by sentries or by an escort;
    - **c.** that small arms and ammunition taken from the wounded and sick, and not yet handed to the proper service, are found in the units;
    - **d.** that members of the armed forces or other combatants are in the unit for medical reasons.

Art. 14. Limitations on requisition of civilian medical units

1. The Occupying Power has the duty to ensure that the medical needs of the civilian population in occupied territory continue to be satisfied.
2. The Occupying Power shall not, therefore, requisition civilian medical units, their equipment, their materiel or the services of their personnel, so long as these resources are necessary for the provision of adequate medical services for the civilian population and for the continuing medical care of any wounded and sick already under treatment.
3. Provided that the general rule in paragraph 2 continues to be observed, the Occupying Power may requisition the said resources, subject to the following particular conditions:
    - **a.** that the resources are necessary for the adequate and immediate medical treatment of the wounded and sick members of the armed forces of the Occupying Power or of prisoners of war;
    - **b.** that the requisition continues only while such necessity exists; and
    - **c.** that immediate arrangements are made to ensure that the medical needs of the civilian population, as well as those of any wounded and sick under treatment who are affected by the requisition, continue to be satisfied.

Art. 15. Protection of civilian medical and religious personnel

1. Civilian medical personnel shall be respected and protected.
2. If needed, all available help shall be afforded to civilian medical personnel in an area where civilian medical services are disrupted by reason of combat activity.
3. The Occupying Power shall afford civilian medical personnel in occupied territories every assistance to enable them to perform, to the best of their ability, their humanitarian functions. The Occupying Power may not require that, in the performance of those functions, such personnel shall give priority to the treatment of any person except on medical grounds. They shall not be compelled to carry out tasks which are not compatible with their humanitarian mission.
4. Civilian medical personnel shall have access to any place where their services are essential, subject to such supervisory and safety measures as the relevant Party to the conflict may deem necessary.
5. Civilian religious personnel shall be respected and protected. The provisions of the Conventions and of this Protocol concerning the protection and identification of medical personnel shall apply equally to such persons.

Art. 16. General protection of medical duties

1. Under no circumstances shall any person be punished for carrying out medical activities compatible with medical ethics, regardless of the person benefiting therefrom.
2. Persons engaged in medical activities shall not be compelled to perform acts or to carry out work contrary to the rules of medical ethics or to other medical rules designed for the benefit of the wounded and sick or to the provisions of the Conventions or of this Protocol, or to refrain from performing acts or from carrying out work required by those rules and provisions.
3. No person engaged in medical activities shall be compelled to give to anyone belonging either to an adverse Party, or to his own Party except as required by the law of the latter Party, any information concerning the wounded and sick who are, or who have been, under his care, if such information would, in his opinion, prove harmful to the patients concerned or to their families. Regulations for the compulsory notification of communicable diseases shall, however, be respected.

ART. 17. Role of the civilian population and of aid societies

1. The civilian population shall respect the wounded, sick and shipwrecked, even if they belong to the adverse Party, and shall commit no act of violence against them. The civilian population and aid societies, such as national Red Cross (Red Crescent, Red Lion and Sun) Societies, shall be permitted, even on their own initiative, to collect and care for the wounded, sick and shipwrecked, even in invaded or occupied areas. No one shall be harmed, prosecuted, convicted or punished for such humanitarian acts.
2. The Parties to the conflict may appeal to the civilian population and the aid societies referred to in paragraph 1 to collect and care for the wounded, sick and shipwrecked, and to search for the dead and report their location; they shall grant both protection and the necessary facilities to those who respond to this appeal. If the adverse Party gains or regains control of the area, that Party also shall afford the same protection and facilities for as long as they are needed.

ART. 18. Identification

1. Each Party to the conflict shall endeavour to ensure that medical and religious personnel and medical units and transports are identifiable.
2. Each Party to the conflict shall also endeavour to adopt and to implement methods and procedures which will make it possible to recognize medical units and transports which use the distinctive emblem and distinctive signals.
3. In occupied territory and in areas where fighting is taking place or is likely to take place, civilian medical personnel and civilian religious personnel should be recognizable by the distinctive emblem and an identity card certifying their status.
4. With the consent of the competent authority, medical units and transports shall be marked by the distinctive emblem. The ships and craft referred to in Article 22 of this Protocol shall be marked in accordance with the provisions of the Second Convention.
5. In addition to the distinctive emblem, a Party to the conflict may, as provided in Chapter III of Annex I to this Protocol, authorize the use of distinctive signals to identify medical units and transports. Exceptionally, in the special cases covered in that Chapter, medical transports may use distinctive signals without displaying the distinctive emblem.

6. The application of the provisions of paragraphs 1 to 5 of this article is governed by Chapters I to III of Annex I to this Protocol. Signals designated in Chapter III of the Annex for the exclusive use of medical units and transports shall not, except as provided therein, be used for any purpose other than to identify the medical units and transports specified in that Chapter.
7. This article does not authorize any wider use of the distinctive emblem in peacetime than is prescribed in Article 44 of the First Convention.
8. The provisions of the Conventions and of this Protocol relating to supervision of the use of the distinctive emblem and to the prevention and repression of any misuse thereof shall be applicable to distinctive signals.

Art. 19. Neutral and other States not Parties to the conflict

Neutral and other States not Parties to the conflict shall apply the relevant provisions of this Protocol to persons protected by this Part who may be received or interned within their territory, and to any dead of the Parties to that conflict whom they may find.

Art. 20. Prohibition of reprisals

Reprisals against the persons and objects protected by this Part are prohibited.

Section II. Medical Transportation

Art. 21. Medical vehicles

Medical vehicles shall be respected and protected in the same way as mobile medical units under the Conventions and this Protocol.

Art. 22. Hospital ships and coastal rescue craft

1. The provisions of the Conventions relating to:
    - **a.** vessels described in Articles 22, 24, 25 and 27 of the Second Convention,
    - **b.** their lifeboats and small craft,
    - **c.** their personnel and crews, and
    - **d.** the wounded; sick and shipwrecked on board.

    shall also apply where these vessels carry civilian wounded, sick and shipwrecked who do not belong to any of the categories mentioned in Article 13 of the Second Convention. Such civilians shall not, however, be subject to surrender to any Party which is not their own, or to capture at sea. If they find themselves in the power of a Party to the conflict other than their own they shall be covered by the Fourth Convention and by this Protocol.

2. The protection provided by the Conventions to vessels described in Article 25 of the Second Convention shall extend to hospital ships made available for humanitarian purposes to a Party to the conflict:

   a. by a neutral or other State which is not a Party to that conflict; or
   b. by an impartial international humanitarian organization,

   provided that, in either case, the requirements set out in that Article are complied with.

3. Small craft described in Article 27 of the Second Convention shall be protected, even if the notification envisaged by that Article has not been made. The Parties to the conflict are, nevertheless, invited to inform each other of any details of such craft which will facilitate their identification and recognition.

Art. 23. Other medical ships and craft

1. Medical ships and craft other than those referred to in Article 22 of this Protocol and Article 38 of the Second Convention shall, whether at sea or in other waters, be respected and protected in the same way as mobile medical units under the Conventions and this Protocol. Since this protection can only be effective if they can be identified and recognized as medical ships or craft, such vessels should be marked with the distinctive emblem and as far as possible comply with the second paragraph of Article 43 of the Second Convention.
2. The ships and craft referred to in paragraph 1 shall remain subject to the laws of war. Any warship on the surface able immediately to enforce its command may order them to stop, order them off, or make them take a certain course, and they shall obey every such command. Such ships and craft may not in any other way be diverted from their medical mission so long as they are needed for the wounded, sick and shipwrecked on board.
3. The protection provided in paragraph 1 shall cease only under the conditions set out in Articles 34 and 35 of the Second Convention. A clear refusal to obey a command given in accordance with paragraph 2 shall be an act harmful to the enemy under Article 34 of the Second Convention.
4. A Party to the conflict may notify any adverse Party as far in advance of sailing as possible of the name, description, expected time of sailing, course

and estimated speed of the medical ship or craft, particularly in the case of ships of over 2,000 gross tons, and may provide any other information which would facilitate identification and recognition. The adverse Party shall acknowledge receipt of such information.

5. The provisions of Article 37 of the Second Convention shall apply to medical and religious personnel in such ships and craft.
6. The provisions of the Second Convention shall apply to the wounded, sick and shipwrecked belonging to the categories referred to in Article 13 of the Second Convention and in Article 44 of this Protocol who may be on board such medical ships and craft. Wounded, sick and shipwrecked civilians who do not belong to any or the categories mentioned in Article 13 of the Second Convention shall not be subject, at sea, either to surrender to any Party which is not their own, or to removal from such ships or craft; if they find themselves in the power of a Party to the conflict other than their own, they shall be covered by the Fourth Convention and by this Protocol.

ART. 24. Protection of medical Aircraft

Medical aircraft shall be respected and protected, subject to the provisions of this Part.

ART. 25. Medical aircraft in areas not controlled by an adverse Party

In and over land areas physically controlled by friendly forces, or in and over sea areas not physically controlled by an adverse Party, the respect and protection of medical aircraft of a Party to the conflict is not dependent on any agreement with an adverse Party. For greater safety, however, a Party to the conflict operating its medical aircraft in these areas may notify the adverse Party, as provided in Article 29, in particular when such aircraft are making flights bringing them within range of surface-to-air weapons systems of the adverse Party.

ART. 26. Medical aircraft in contact or similar zones

1. In and over those parts of the contact zone which are physically controlled by friendly forces and in and over those areas the physical control of which is not clearly established, protection for medical aircraft can be fully effective only by prior agreement between the competent military authorities of the Parties to the conflict, as provided for in Article 29. Although, in the absence of such an agreement, medical aircraft operate at their own risk, they shall nevertheless be respected after they have been recognized as such.

2. "Contact zone" means any area on land where the forward elements of opposing forces are in contact with each other, especially where they are exposed to direct fire from the ground.

Art. 27. Medical aircraft in areas controlled by an adverse Party

1. The medical aircraft of a Party to the conflict shall continue to be protected while flying over land or sea areas physically controlled by an adverse Party, provided that prior agreement to such flights has been obtained from the competent authority of that adverse Party.
2. A medical aircraft which flies over an area physically controlled by an adverse Party without, or in deviation from the terms of, an agreement provided for in paragraph 1, either through navigational error or because of an emergency affecting the safety of the flight, shall make every effort to identify itself and to inform the adverse Party of the circumstances. As soon as such medical aircraft has been recognized by the adverse Party, that Party shall make all reasonable efforts to give the order to land or to alight on water, referred to in Article 30, paragraph 1, or to take other measures to safeguard its own interests, and, in either case, to allow the aircraft time for compliance, before resorting to an attack against the aircraft.

Art. 28. Restrictions on operations of medical aircraft

1. The Parties to the conflict are prohibited from using their medical aircraft to attempt to acquire any military advantage over an adverse Party. The presence of medical aircraft shall not be used in an attempt to render military objectives immune from attack.
2. Medical aircraft shall not be used to collect or transmit intelligence data and shall not carry any equipment intended for such purposes. They are prohibited from carrying any persons or cargo not included within the definition in Article 8 (6). The carrying on board of the personal effects of the occupants or of equipment intended solely to facilitate navigation, communication or identification shall not be considered as prohibited,
3. Medical aircraft shall not carry any armament except small arms and ammunition taken from the wounded, sick and shipwrecked on board and not yet handed to the proper service, and such light individual weapons as may be necessary to enable the medical personnel on board to defend themselves and the wounded, sick and shipwrecked in their charge.

4. While carrying out the flights referred to in Articles 26 and 27, medical aircraft shall not, except by prior agreement with the adverse Party, be used to search for the wounded, sick and shipwrecked.

Art. 29. Notifications and agreements concerning medical aircraft

1. Notifications under Article 25, or requests for prior agreement under Articles 26, 27, 28, paragraph 4, or 31 shall state the proposed number of medical aircraft, their flight plans and means of identification, and shall be understood to mean that every flight will be carried out in compliance with Article 28.
2. A Party which receives a notification given under Article 25 shall at once acknowledge receipt of such notification. 3. A Party which receives a request for prior agreement under Articles 25, 27, 28, paragraph 4, or 31 shall, as rapidly as possible, notify the requesting Party:
   a. that the request is agreed to;
   b. that the request is denied; or
   c. of reasonable alternative proposals to the request. It may also propose prohibition or restriction of other flights in the area during the time involved. If the Party which submitted the request accepts the alternative proposals, it shall notify the other Party of such acceptance.
4. The Parties shall take the necessary measures to ensure that notifications and agreements can be made rapidly.
5. The Parties shall also take the necessary measures to disseminate rapidly the substance of any such notifications and agreements to the military units concerned and shall instruct those units regarding the means of identification that will be used by the medical aircraft in question.

Art. 30. Landing and inspection of medical aircraft

1. Medical aircraft flying over areas which are physically controlled by an adverse Party, or over areas the physical control of which is not clearly established, may be ordered to land or to alight on water, as appropriate, to permit inspection in accordance with the following paragraphs. Medical aircraft shall obey any such order.
2. If such an aircraft lands or alights on water, whether ordered to do so or for other reasons, it may be subjected to inspection solely to determine the matters referred to in paragraphs 3 and 4. Any such inspection shall be commenced without delay and shall be conducted expeditiously. The

inspecting Party shall not require the wounded and sick to be removed from the aircraft unless their removal is essential for the inspection. That Party shall in any event ensure that the condition of the wounded and sick is not adversely affected by the inspection or by the removal.

3. If the inspection discloses that the aircraft:
   - **a.** is a medical aircraft within the meaning of Article 8, sub-paragraph j),
   - **b.** is not in violation of the conditions prescribed in Article 28, and
   - **c.** has not flown without or in breach of a prior agreement where such agreement is required,

   the aircraft and those of its occupants who belong to the adverse Party or to a neutral or other State not a Party to the conflict shall be authorized to continue the flight without delay.
4. If the inspection discloses that the aircraft:
   - **a.** is not a medical aircraft within the meaning of Article 8, sub-paragraph j),
   - **b.** is in violation or the conditions prescribed in Article 28, or
   - **c.** has flown without or in breach of a prior agreement where such agreement is required,

   the aircraft may be seized. Its occupants shall be treated in conformity with the relevant provisions of the Conventions and of this Protocol. Any aircraft seized which had been assigned as a permanent medical aircraft may be used thereafter only as a medical aircraft.

ART. 31. Neutral or other States not Parties to the conflict

1. Except by prior agreement, medical aircraft shall not fly over or land in the territory of a neutral or other State not a Party to the conflict. However, with such an agreement, they shall be respected throughout their flight and also for the duration of any calls in the territory. Nevertheless they shall obey any summons to land or to alight on water, as appropriate.
2. Should a medical aircraft, in the absence of an agreement or in deviation from the terms of an agreement, fly over the territory of a neutral or other State not a Party to the conflict, either through navigational error or because of an emergency affecting the safety of the flight, it shall make every effort to give notice of the flight and to identify itself. As soon as such medical aircraft is recognized, that State shall make all reasonable efforts to give the order to land or to alight on water referred to in Article 30, paragraph 1, or to take other measures to safeguard its own interests, and, in either

case, to allow the aircraft time for compliance, before resorting to an attack against the aircraft.

3. If a medical aircraft, either by agreement or in the circumstances mentioned in paragraph 2, lands or alights on water in the territory of a neutral or other State not Party to the conflict, whether ordered to do so or for other reasons, the aircraft shall be subject to inspection for the purposes of determining whether it is in fact a medical aircraft. The inspection shall be commenced without delay and shall be conducted expeditiously. The inspecting Party shall not require the wounded and sick of the Party operating the aircraft to be removed from it unless their removal is essential for the inspection. The inspecting Party shall in any event ensure that the condition of the wounded and sick is not adversely affected by the inspection or the removal. If the inspection discloses that the aircraft is in fact a medical aircraft, the aircraft with its occupants, other than those who must be detained in accordance with the rules of international law applicable in armed conflict, shall be allowed to resume its flight, and reasonable facilities shall be given for the continuation of the flight. If the inspection discloses that the aircraft is not a medical aircraft, it shall be seized and the occupants treated in accordance with paragraph 4.
4. The wounded, sick and shipwrecked disembarked, otherwise than temporarily, from a medical aircraft with the consent of the local authorities in the territory of a neutral or other State not a Party to the conflict shall, unless agreed otherwise between that State and the Parties to the conflict, be detained by that State where so required by the rules of international law applicable in armed conflict, in such a manner that they cannot again take part in the hostilities. The cost of hospital treatment and internment shall be borne by the State to which those persons belong.
5. Neutral or other States not Parties to the conflict shall apply any conditions and restrictions on the passage of medical aircraft over, or on the landing of medical aircraft in, their territory equally to all Parties to the conflict.

Section III. Missing and Dead Persons

ART. 32. General principle

In the implementation of this Section, the activities of the High Contracting Parties, of the Parties to the conflict and of the international humanitarian organizations mentioned in the Conventions and in this Protocol shall be prompted mainly by the right of families to know the fate of their relatives.

ART. 33. Missing persons

1. As soon as circumstances permit, and at the latest from the end of active hostilities, each Party to the conflict shall search for the persons who have been reported missing by an adverse Party. Such adverse Party shall transmit all relevant information concerning such persons in order to facilitate such searches.
2. In order to facilitate the gathering of information pursuant to the preceding paragraph, each Party to the conflict shall, with respect to persons who would not receive more favourable consideration under the Conventions and this Protocol:
   a. record the information specified in Article 138 of the Fourth Convention in respect of such persons who have been detained, imprisoned or otherwise held in captivity for more than two weeks as a result of hostilities or occupation, or who have died during any period of detention;
   b. to the fullest extent possible, facilitate and, if need be, carry out the search for and the recording of information concerning such persons if they have died in other circumstances as a result of hostilities or occupation.
3. Information concerning persons reported missing pursuant to paragraph 1 and requests for such information shall be transmitted either directly or through the Protecting Power or the Central Tracing Agency of the International Committee of the Red Cross or national Red Cross (Red Crescent, Red Lion and Sun) Societies. Where the information is not transmitted through the International Committee of the Red Cross and its Central Tracing Agency, each Party to the conflict shall ensure that such information is also supplied to the Central Tracing Agency.
4. The Parties to the conflict shall endeavour to agree on arrangements for teams to search for, identify and recover the dead from battlefield areas, including arrangements, if appropriate, for such teams to be accompanied by personnel of the adverse Party while carrying out these missions in areas controlled by the adverse Party. Personnel of such teams shall be respected and protected while exclusively carrying out these duties.

ART. 34. Remains of deceased

1. The remains of persons who have died for reasons related to occupation or in detention resulting from occupation or hostilities and those or persons not nationals of the country in which they have died as a result of hostilities shall be respected, and the gravesites of all such persons shall be respected, maintained and marked as provided for in Article 130 of the Fourth Convention, where their remains or gravesites would not receive more favourable consideration under the Conventions and this Protocol.
2. As soon as circumstances and the relations between the adverse Parties permit, the High Contracting Parties in whose territories graves and, as the case may be, other locations of the remains of persons who have died as a result of hostilities or during occupation or in detention are situated, shall conclude agreements in order:
   - **a.** to facilitate access to the gravesites by relatives of the deceased and by representatives of official graves registration services and to regulate the practical arrangements for such access;
   - **b.** to protect and maintain such gravesites permanently;
   - **c.** to facilitate the return of the remains of the deceased and of personal effects to the home country upon its request or, unless that country objects, upon the request of the next of kin.
3. In the absence of the agreements provided for in paragraph 2 (b) or (c) and if the home country or such deceased is not willing to arrange at its expense for the maintenance of such gravesites, the High Contracting Party in whose territory the gravesites are situated may offer to facilitate the return of the remains of the deceased to the home country. Where such an offer has not been accepted the High Contracting Party may, after the expiry of five years from the date of the offer and upon due notice to the home country, adopt the arrangements laid down in its own laws relating to cemeteries and graves.
4. A High Contracting Party in whose territory the grave sites referred to in this Article are situated shall be permitted to exhume the remains only:
   - **a.** in accordance with paragraphs 2 (c) and 3, or
   - **b.** where exhumation is a matter or overriding public necessity, including cases of medical and investigative necessity, in which case the High Contracting Party shall at all times respect the remains, and shall give notice to the home country or its intention to exhume the remains together with details of the intended place of reinterment.

PART III. METHODS AND MEANS OF WARFARE COMBATANT AND PRISONERS-OF-WAR

Section I. Methods and Means of Warfare

ART. 35. Basic rules

1. In any armed conflict, the right of the Parties to the conflict to choose methods or means of warfare is not unlimited.
2. It is prohibited to employ weapons, projectiles and material and methods of warfare of a nature to cause superfluous injury or unnecessary suffering.
3. It is prohibited to employ methods or means of warfare which are intended, or may be expected, to cause widespread, long-term and severe damage to the natural environment.

ART. 36. New weapons

In the study, development, acquisition or adoption of a new weapon, means or method of warfare, a High Contracting Party is under an obligation to determine whether its employment would, in some or all circumstances, be prohibited by this Protocol or by any other rule of international law applicable to the High Contracting Party.

ART. 37. Prohibition of Perfidy

1. It is prohibited to kill, injure or capture an adversary by resort to perfidy. Acts inviting the confidence of an adversary to lead him to believe that he is entitled to, or is obliged to accord, protection under the rules of international law applicable in armed conflict, with intent to betray that confidence, shall constitute perfidy. The following acts are examples of perfidy:
   a. the feigning of an intent to negotiate under a flag of truce or of a surrender;
   b. the feigning of an incapacitation by wounds or sickness;
   c. the feigning of civilian, non-combatant status; and
   d. the feigning of protected status by the use of signs, emblems or uniforms of the United Nations or of neutral or other States not Parties to the conflict.
2. Ruses of war are not prohibited. Such ruses are acts which are intended to mislead an adversary or to induce him to act recklessly but which infringe no rule of international law applicable in armed conflict and which are not perfidious because they do not invite the confidence of an adversary with

respect to protection under that law. The following are examples of such ruses: the use of camouflage, decoys, mock operations and misinformation.

Art. 38. Recognized emblems

1. It is prohibited to make improper use of the distinctive emblem of the red cross, red crescent or red lion and sun or of other emblems, signs or signals provided for by the Conventions or by this Protocol. It is also prohibited to misuse deliberately in an armed conflict other internationally recognized protective emblems, signs or signals, including the flag of truce, and the protective emblem of cultural property.
2. It is prohibited to make use of the distinctive emblem of the United Nations, except as authorized by that Organization.

Art. 39. Emblems of nationality

1. It is prohibited to make use in an armed conflict of the flags or military emblems, insignia or uniforms of neutral or other States not Parties to the conflict.
2. It is prohibited to make use of the flags or military emblems, insignia or uniforms of adverse Parties while engaging in attacks or in order to shield, favour, protect or impede military operations.
3. Nothing in this Article or in Article 37, paragraph 1 (d), shall affect the existing generally recognized rules of international law applicable to espionage or to the use of flags in the conduct of armed conflict at sea.

Art. 40. Quarter

It is prohibited to order that there shall be no survivors, to threaten an adversary therewith or to conduct hostilities on this basis.

Art. 41. Safeguard of an enemy hors de combat

1. A person who is recognized or who, in the circumstances, should be recognized to be hors de combat shall not be made the object of attack.
2. A person is hors de combat if:
   - **a.** he is in the power of an adverse Party;
   - **b.** he clearly expresses an intention to surrender; or
   - **c.** he has been rendered unconscious or is otherwise incapacitated by wounds or sickness, and therefore is incapable of defending himself;

provided that in any of these cases he abstains from any hostile act and does not attempt to escape.

3. When persons entitled to protection as prisoners of war have fallen into the power of an adverse Party under unusual conditions of combat which prevent their evacuation as provided for in Part III, Section I, of the Third Convention, they shall be released and all feasible precautions shall be taken to ensure their safety.

ART. 42. Occupants of aircraft

1. No person parachuting from an aircraft in distress shall be made the object of attack during his descent.
2. Upon reaching the ground in territory controlled by an adverse Party, a person who has parachuted from an aircraft in distress shall be given an opportunity to surrender before being made the object of attack, unless it is apparent that he is engaging in a hostile act.
3. Airborne troops are not protected by this Article.

Section II. Combatants and Prisoners of War

ART. 43. Armed forces

1. The armed forces of a Party to a conflict consist of all organized armed forces, groups and units which are under a command responsible to that Party for the conduct or its subordinates, even if that Party is represented by a government or an authority not recognized by an adverse Party. Such armed forces shall be subject to an internal disciplinary system which, inter alia, shall enforce compliance with the rules of international law applicable in armed conflict.
2. Members of the armed forces of a Party to a conflict (other than medical personnel and chaplains covered by Article 33 of the Third Convention) are combatants, that is to say, they have the right to participate directly in hostilities.
3. Whenever a Party to a conflict incorporates a paramilitary or armed law enforcement agency into its armed forces it shall so notify the other Parties to the conflict.

ART. 44. Combatants and prisoners of war

1. Any combatant, as defined in Article 43, who falls into the power of an adverse Party shall be a prisoner of war.

2. While all combatants are obliged to comply with the rules of international law applicable in armed conflict, violations of these rules shall not deprive a combatant of his right to be a combatant or, if he falls into the power of an adverse Party, of his right to be a prisoner of war, except as provided in paragraphs 3 and 4.
3. In order to promote the protection of the civilian population from the effects of hostilities, combatants are obliged to distinguish themselves from the civilian population while they are engaged in an attack or in a military operation preparatory to an attack. Recognizing, however, that there are situations in armed conflicts where, owing to the nature of the hostilities an armed combatant cannot so distinguish himself, he shall retain his status as a combatant, provided that, in such situations, he carries his arms openly:
   a. during each military engagement, and
   b. during such time as he is visible to the adversary while he is engaged in a military deployment preceding the launching of an attack in which he is to participate.

   Acts which comply with the requirements of this paragraph shall not be considered as perfidious within the meaning of Article 37, paragraph 1 (c).
4. A combatant who falls into the power of an adverse Party while failing to meet the requirements set forth in the second sentence of paragraph 3 shall forfeit his right to be a prisoner of war, but he shall, nevertheless, be given protections equivalent in all respects to those accorded to prisoners of war by the Third Convention and by this Protocol. This protection includes protections equivalent to those accorded to prisoners of war by the Third Convention in the case where such a person is tried and punished for any offences he has committed.
5. Any combatant who falls into the power of an adverse Party while not engaged in an attack or in a military operation preparatory to an attack shall not forfeit his rights to be a combatant and a prisoner of war by virtue of his prior activities .
6. This Article is without prejudice to the right of any person to be a prisoner of war pursuant to Article 4 of the Third Convention.
7. This Article is not intended to change the generally accepted practice of States with respect to the wearing of the uniform by combatants assigned to the regular, uniformed armed units of a Party to the conflict.
8. In addition to the categories of persons mentioned in Article 13 of the First and Second Conventions, all members of the armed forces of a Party to the

conflict, as defined in Article 43 of this Protocol, shall be entitled to protection under those Conventions if they are wounded or sick or, in the case of the Second Convention, shipwrecked at sea or in other waters.

Art. 45. Protection of persons who have taken part in hostilities

1. A person who takes part in hostilities and falls into the power of an adverse Party shall be presumed to be a prisoner of war, and therefore shall be protected by the Third Convention, if he claims the status of prisoner of war, or if he appears to be entitled to such status, or if the Party on which he depends claims such status on his behalf by notification to the detaining Power or to the Protecting Power. Should any doubt arise as to whether any such person is entitled to the status of prisoner of war, he shall continue to have such status and, therefore, to be protected by the Third Convention and this Protocol until such time as his status has been determined by a competent tribunal.
2. If a person who has fallen into the power of an adverse Party is not held as a prisoner of war and is to be tried by that Party for an offence arising out of the hostilities, he shall have the right to assert his entitlement to prisoner-of-war status before a judicial tribunal and to have that question adjudicated. Whenever possible under the applicable procedure, this adjudication shall occur before the trial for the offence. The representatives of the Protecting Power shall be entitled to attend the proceedings in which that question is adjudicated, unless, exceptionally, the proceedings are held in camera in the interest of State security. In such a case the detaining Power shall advise the Protecting Power accordingly.
3. Any person who has taken part in hostilities, who is not entitled to prisoner-of-war status and who does not benefit from more favourable treatment in accordance with the Fourth Convention shall have the right at all times to the protection of Article 75 of this Protocol. In occupied territory, any such person, unless he is held as a spy, shall also be entitled, notwithstanding Article 5 of the Fourth Convention, to his rights of communication under that Convention.

Art. 46. Spies

1. Notwithstanding any other provision of the Conventions or of this Protocol, any member of the armed forces of a Party to the conflict who falls into the

power of an adverse Party while engaging in espionage shall not have the right to the status of prisoner of war and may be treated as a spy.

2. A member of the armed forces of a Party to the conflict who, on behalf of that Party and in territory controlled by an adverse Party, gathers or attempts to gather information shall not be considered as engaging in espionage if, while so acting, he is in the uniform of his armed forces.
3. A member of the armed forces of a Party to the conflict who is a resident of territory occupied by an adverse Party and who, on behalf of the Party on which he depends, gathers or attempts to gather information of military value within that territory shall not be considered as engaging in espionage unless he does so through an act of false pretences or deliberately in a clandestine manner. Moreover, such a resident shall not lose his right to the status of prisoner of war and may not be treated as a spy unless he is captured while engaging in espionage.
4. A member of the armed forces of a Party to the conflict who is not a resident of territory occupied by an adverse Party and who has engaged in espionage in that territory shall not lose his right to the status of prisoner of war and may not be treated as a spy unless he is captured before he has rejoined the armed forces to which he belongs.

ART. 47. Mercenaries

1. A mercenary shall not have the right to be a combatant or a prisoner of war.
2. A mercenary is any person who:
   - **a.** is specially recruited locally or abroad in order to fight in an armed conflict;
   - **b.** does, in fact, take a direct part in the hostilities;
   - **c.** is motivated to take part in the hostilities essentially by the desire for private gain and, in fact, is promised, by or on behalf of a Party to the conflict, material compensation substantially in excess of that promised or paid to combatants of similar ranks and functions in the armed forces of that Party;
   - **d.** is neither a national of a Party to the conflict nor a resident of territory controlled by a Party to the conflict;
   - **e.** is not a member of the armed forces of a Party to the conflict; and
   - **f.** has not been sent by a State which is not a Party to the conflict on official duty as a member of its armed forces.

PART IV. CIVILIAN POPULATION

Section I. General Protection Against Effects of Hostilities

Chapter I. Basic Rule and Field of Application

ART. 48. Basic rule

In order to ensure respect for and protection of the civilian population and civilian objects, the Parties to the conflict shall at all times distinguish between the civilian population and combatants and between civilian objects and military objectives and accordingly shall direct their operations only against military objectives.

ART. 49. Definition of attacks and scope of application

1. "Attacks" means acts of violence against the adversary, whether in offence or in defence.
2. The provisions of this Protocol with respect to attacks apply to all attacks in whatever territory conducted, including the national territory belonging to a Party to the conflict but under the control of an adverse Party.
3. The provisions of this section apply to any land, air or sea warfare which may affect the civilian population, individual civilians or civilian objects on land. They further apply to all attacks from the sea or from the air against objectives on land but do not otherwise affect the rules of international law applicable in armed conflict at sea or in the air.
4. The provisions of this section are additional to the rules concerning humanitarian protection contained in the Fourth Convention, particularly in part II thereof, and in other international agreements binding upon the High Contracting Parties, as well as to other rules of international law relating to the protection of civilians and civilian objects on land, at sea or in the air against the effects of hostilities.

Chapter II. Civilians and Civilian Population

ART. 50. Definition of civilians and civilian population

1. A civilian is any person who does not belong to one of the categories of persons referred to in Article 4 (A) (1), (2), (3) and (6) of the Third Convention and in Article 43 of this Protocol. In case of doubt whether a person is a civilian, that person shall be considered to be a civilian.

2. The civilian population comprises all persons who are civilians.
3. The presence within the civilian population of individuals who do not come within the definition of civilians does not deprive the population of its civilian character.

ART. 51. Protection of the civilian population

1. The civilian population and individual civilians shall enjoy general protection against dangers arising from military operations. To give effect to this protection, the following rules, which are additional to other applicable rules of international law, shall be observed in all circumstances.
2. The civilian population as such, as well as individual civilians, shall not be the object of attack. Acts or threats of violence the primary purpose of which is to spread terror among the civilian population are prohibited.
3. Civilians shall enjoy the protection afforded by this section, unless and for such time as they take a direct part in hostilities.
4. Indiscriminate attacks are prohibited. Indiscriminate attacks are:
   - **a.** those which are not directed at a specific military objective;
   - **b.** those which employ a method or means of combat which cannot be directed at a specific military objective; or
   - **c.** those which employ a method or means of combat the effects of which cannot be limited as required by this Protocol;

   and consequently, in each such case, are of a nature to strike military objectives and civilians or civilian objects without distinction.
5. Among others, the following types of attacks are to be considered as indiscriminate:
   - **a.** an attack by bombardment by any methods or means which treats as a single military objective a number of clearly separated and distinct military objectives located in a city, town, village or other area containing a similar concentration of civilians or civilian objects; and
   - **b.** an attack which may be expected to cause incidental loss of civilian life, injury to civilians, damage to civilian objects, or a combination thereof, which would be excessive in relation to the concrete and direct military advantage anticipated.
6. Attacks against the civilian population or civilians by way of reprisals are prohibited.

7. The presence or movements of the civilian population or individual civilians shall not be used to render certain points or areas immune from military operations, in particular in attempts to shield military objectives from attacks or to shield, favour or impede military operations. The Parties to the conflict shall not direct the movement of the civilian population or individual civilians in order to attempt to shield military objectives from attacks or to shield military operations.
8. Any violation of these prohibitions shall not release the Parties to the conflict from their legal obligations with respect to the civilian population and civilians, including the obligation to take the precautionary measures provided for in Article 57.

Chapter III. Civilian Objects

Art. 52. General Protection of civilian objects

1. Civilian objects shall not be the object of attack or of reprisals. Civilian objects are all objects which are not military objectives as defined in paragraph 2.
2. Attacks shall be limited strictly to military objectives. In so far as objects are concerned, military objectives are limited to those objects which by their nature, location, purpose or use make an effective contribution to military action and whose total or partial destruction, capture or neutralization, in the circumstances ruling at the time, offers a definite military advantage.
3. In case of doubt whether an object which is normally dedicated to civilian purposes, such as a place of worship, a house or other dwelling or a school, is being used to make an effective contribution to military action, it shall be presumed not to be so used.

Art. 53. Protection of cultural objects and of places of worship

Without prejudice to the provisions of the Hague Convention for the Protection of Cultural Property in the Event of Armed Conflict of 14 May 1954, and of other relevant international instruments, it is prohibited:

a. to commit any acts of hostility directed against the historic monuments, works of art or places of worship which constitute the cultural or spiritual heritage of peoples;
b. to use such objects in support of the military effort;
c. to make such objects the object of reprisals.

Art. 54. Protection of objects indispensable to the survival of the civilian population

1. Starvation of civilians as a method of warfare is prohibited.
2. It is prohibited to attack, destroy, remove or render useless objects indispensable to the survival of the civilian population, such as food-stuffs, agricultural areas for the production of food-stuffs, crops, livestock, drinking water installations and supplies and irrigation works, for the specific purpose of denying them for their sustenance value to the civilian population or to the adverse Party, whatever the motive, whether in order to starve out civilians, to cause them to move away, or for any other motive.
3. The prohibitions in paragraph 2 shall not apply to such of the objects covered by it as are used by an adverse Party:
   a. as sustenance solely for the members of its armed forces; or
   b. if not as sustenance, then in direct support of military action, provided, however, that in no event shall actions against these objects be taken which may be expected to leave the civilian population with such inadequate food or water as to cause its starvation or force its movement.
4. These objects shall not be made the object of reprisals.
5. In recognition of the vital requirements of any Party to the conflict in the defence of its national territory against invasion, derogation from the prohibitions contained in paragraph 2 may be made by a Party to the conflict within such territory under its own control where required by imperative military necessity.

Art. 55. Protection of the natural environment

1. Care shall be taken in warfare to protect the natural environment against widespread, long-term and severe damage. This protection includes a prohibition of the use of methods or means of warfare which are intended or may be expected to cause such damage to the natural environment and thereby to prejudice the health or survival of the population.
2. Attacks against the natural environment by way of reprisals are prohibited.

Art. 56. Protection of works and installations containing dangerous forces

1. Works or installations containing dangerous forces, namely dams, dykes and nuclear electrical generating stations, shall not be made the object of attack, even where these objects are military objectives, if such attack may

cause the release of dangerous forces and consequent severe losses among the civilian population. Other military objectives located at or in the vicinity of these works or installations shall not be made the object of attack if such attack may cause the release of dangerous forces from the works or installations and consequent severe losses among the civilian population.

2. The special protection against attack provided by paragraph 1 shall cease:
   a. for a dam or a dyke only if it is used for other than its normal function and in regular, significant and direct support of military operations and if such attack is the only feasible way to terminate such support;
   b. for a nuclear electrical generating station only if it provides electric power in regular, significant and direct support of military operations and if such attack is the only feasible way to terminate such support;
   c. for other military objectives located at or in the vicinity of these works or installations only if they are used in regular, significant and direct support of military operations and if such attack is the only feasible way to terminate such support.
3. In all cases, the civilian population and individual civilians shall remain entitled to all the protection accorded them by international law, including the protection of the precautionary measures provided for in Article 57. If the protection Ceases and any of the works, installations or military objectives mentioned in paragraph 1 is attacked, all practical precautions shall be taken to avoid the release of the dangerous forces.
4. It is prohibited to make any of the works, installations or military objectives mentioned in paragraph 1 the object of reprisals.
5. The Parties to the conflict shall endeavour to avoid locating any military objectives in the vicinity of the works or installations mentioned in paragraph 1. Nevertheless, installations erected for the sole purpose of defending the protected works or installations from attack are permissible and shall not themselves be made the object of attack, provided that they are not used in hostilities except for defensive actions necessary to respond to attacks against the protected works or installations and that their armament is limited to weapons capable only of repelling hostile action against the protected works or installations.
6. The High Contracting Parties and the Parties to the conflict are urged to conclude further agreements among themselves to provide additional protection for objects containing dangerous forces.

7. In order to facilitate the identification of the objects protected by this article, the Parties to the conflict may mark them with a special sign consisting of a group of three bright orange circles placed on the same axis, as specified in Article 16 of Annex I to this Protocol [Article 17 of Amended Annex]. The absence of such marking in no way relieves any Party to the conflict of its obligations under this Article.

Chapter IV. Precautionary Measures

Art. 57. Precautions in attack

1. In the conduct of military operations, constant care shall be taken to spare the civilian population, civilians and civilian objects.
2. With respect to attacks, the following precautions shall be taken:
   a. those who plan or decide upon an attack shall:
      i. do everything feasible to verify that the objectives to be attacked are neither civilians nor civilian objects and are not subject to special protection but are military objectives within the meaning of paragraph 2 of Article 52 and that it is not prohibited by the provisions of this Protocol to attack them;
      ii. take all feasible precautions in the choice of means and methods of attack with a view to avoiding, and in any event to minimizing, incidental loss or civilian life, injury to civilians and damage to civilian objects;
      iii. refrain from deciding to launch any attack which may be expected to cause incidental loss of civilian life, injury to civilians, damage to civilian objects, or a combination thereof, which would be excessive in relation to the concrete and direct military advantage anticipated;
   b. an attack shall be cancelled or suspended if it becomes apparent that the objective is not a military one or is subject to special protection or that the attack may be expected to cause incidental loss of civilian life, injury to civilians, damage to civilian objects, or a combination thereof, which would be excessive in relation to the concrete and direct military advantage anticipated;
   c. effective advance warning shall be given of attacks which may affect the civilian population, unless circumstances do not permit.

3. When a choice is possible between several military objectives for obtaining a similar military advantage, the objective to be selected shall be that the attack on which may be expected to cause the least danger to civilian lives and to civilian objects.
4. In the conduct of military operations at sea or in the air, each Party to the conflict shall, in conformity with its rights and duties under the rules of international law applicable in armed conflict, take all reasonable precautions to avoid losses of civilian lives and damage to civilian objects.
5. No provision of this article may be construed as authorizing any attacks against the civilian population, civilians or civilian objects.

ART. 58. Precautions against the effects of attacks

The Parties to the conflict shall, to the maximum extent feasible:

a. without prejudice to Article 49 of the Fourth Convention, endeavour to remove the civilian population, individual civilians and civilian objects under their control from the vicinity of military objectives;
b. avoid locating military objectives within or near densely populated areas;
c. take the other necessary precautions to protect the civilian population, individual civilians and civilian objects under their control against the dangers resulting from military operations.

Chapter V. Localities and Zones Under Special Protection

ART. 59. Non-defended localities

1. It is prohibited for the Parties to the conflict to attack, by any means whatsoever, non-defended localities.
2. The appropriate authorities of a Party to the conflict may declare as a non-defended locality any inhabited place near or in a zone where armed forces are in contact which is open for occupation by an adverse Party.

   Such a locality shall fulfil the following conditions:

   a. all combatants, as well as mobile weapons and mobile military equipment must have been evacuated;
   b. no hostile use shall be made of fixed military installations or establishments;
   c. no acts of hostility shall be committed by the authorities or by the population; and
   d. no activities in support of military operations shall be undertaken.

3. The presence, in this locality, of persons specially protected under the Conventions and this Protocol, and of police forces retained for the sole purpose of maintaining law and order, is not contrary to the conditions laid down in paragraph 2.
4. The declaration made under paragraph 2 shall be addressed to the adverse Party and shall define and describe, as precisely as possible, the limits of the non-defended locality. The Party to the conflict to which the declaration is addressed shall acknowledge its receipt and shall treat the locality as a non-defended locality unless the conditions laid down in paragraph 2 are not in fact fulfilled, in which event it shall immediately so inform the Party making the declaration. Even if the conditions laid down in paragraph 2 are not fulfilled, the locality shall continue to enjoy the protection provided by the other provisions of this Protocol and the other rules of international law applicable in armed conflict.
5. The Parties to the conflict may agree on the establishment of non-defended localities even if such localities do not fulfil the conditions laid down in paragraph 2. The agreement should define and describe, as precisely as possible, the limits of the non-defended locality; if necessary, it may lay down the methods of supervision.
6. The Party which is in control of a locality governed by such an agreement shall mark it, so far as possible, by such signs as may be agreed upon with the other Party, which shall be displayed where they are clearly visible, especially on its perimeter and limits and on highways.
7. A locality loses its status as a non-defended locality when its ceases to fulfil the conditions laid down in paragraph 2 or in the agreement referred to in paragraph 5. In such an eventuality, the locality shall continue to enjoy the protection provided by the other provisions of this Protocol and the other rules of international law applicable in armed conflict.

Art. 60. Demilitarized zones

1. It is prohibited for the Parties to the conflict to extend their military operations to zones on which they have conferred by agreement the status of demilitarized zone, if such extension is contrary to the terms of this agreement.
2. The agreement shall be an express agreement, may be concluded verbally or in writing, either directly or through a Protecting Power or any impartial humanitarian organization, and may consist of reciprocal and concordant

declarations. The agreement may be concluded in peacetime, as well as after the outbreak of hostilities, and should define and describe, as precisely as possible, the limits of the demilitarized zone and, if necessary, lay down the methods of supervision.

3. The subject of such an agreement shall normally be any zone which fulfils the following conditions:
   a. all combatants, as well as mobile weapons and mobile military equipment, must have been evacuated;
   b. no hostile use shall be made of fixed military installations or establishments;
   c. no acts of hostility shall be committed by the authorities or by the population; and
   d. any activity linked to the military effort must have ceased.

   The Parties to the conflict shall agree upon the interpretation to be given to the condition laid down in subparagraph (d) and upon persons to be admitted to the demilitarized zone other than those mentioned in paragraph 4.
4. The presence, in this zone, of persons specially protected under the Conventions and this Protocol, and of police forces retained for the sole purpose of maintaining law and order, is not contrary to the conditions laid down in paragraph 3.
5. The Party which is in control of such a zone shall mark it, so far as possible, by such signs as may be agreed upon with the other Party, which shall be displayed where they are clearly visible, especially on its perimeter and limits and on highways.
6. If the fighting draws near to a demilitarized zone, and if the Parties to the conflict have so agreed, none of them may use the zone for purposes related to the conduct of military operations or unilaterally revoke its status.
7. If one of the Parties to the conflict commits a material breach of the provisions of paragraphs 3 or 6, the other Party shall be released from its obligations under the agreement conferring upon the zone the status of demilitarized zone. In such an eventuality, the zone loses its status but shall continue to enjoy the protection provided by the other provisions of this Protocol and the other rules of international law applicable in armed conflict.

Chapter VI. Civil Defence

Art. 61. Definitions and scope

For the purpose of this Protocol:

1. "Civil defence" means the performance of some or all of the undermentioned humanitarian tasks intended to protect the civilian population against the dangers, and to help it to recover from the immediate effects, of hostilities or disasters and also to provide the conditions necessary for its survival. These tasks are:
   - **a.** warning;
   - **b.** evacuation;
   - **c.** management of shelters;
   - **d.** management of blackout measures;
   - **e.** rescue;
   - **f.** medical services, including first aid, and religious assistance;
   - **g.** fire-fighting;
   - **h.** detection and marking of danger areas;
   - **i.** decontamination and similar protective measures;
   - **j.** provision of emergency accommodation and supplies;
   - **k.** emergency assistance in the restoration and maintenance of order in distressed areas;
   - **l.** emergency repair of indispensable public utilities;
   - **m.** emergency disposal of the dead;
   - **n.** assistance in the preservation of objects essential for survival;
   - **o.** complementary activities necessary to carry out any of the tasks mentioned above, including, but not limited to, planning and organization;
2. "Civil defence organizations" means those establishments and other units which are organized or authorized by the competent authorities of a Party to the conflict to perform any of the tasks mentioned under (1), and which are assigned and devoted exclusively to such tasks; (3) "Personnel" of civil defence organizations means those persons assigned by a Party to the conflict exclusively to the performance of the tasks mentioned under (1), including personnel assigned by the competent authority of that Party exclusively to the administration of these organizations;
4. "Matériel" of civil defence organizations means equipment, supplies and transports used by these organizations for the performance of the tasks mentioned under (1).

Art. 62. General protection

1. Civilian civil defence organizations and their personnel shall be respected and protected, subject to the provisions of this Protocol, particularly the provisions of this section. They shall be entitled to perform their civil defence tasks except in case of imperative military necessity.
2. The provisions of paragraph 1 shall also apply to civilians who, although not members of civilian civil defence organizations, respond to an appeal from the competent authorities and perform civil defence tasks under their control.
3. Buildings and matériel used for civil defence purposes and shelters provided for the civilian population are covered by Article 52. Objects used for civil defence purposes may not be destroyed or diverted from their proper use except by the Party to which they belong.

Art. 63. Civil defence in occupied territories

1. In occupied territories, civilian civil defence organizations shall receive from the authorities the facilities necessary for the performance of their tasks. In no Circumstances shall their personnel be compelled to perform activities which would interfere with the proper performance of these tasks. The Occupying Power shall not change the structure or personnel of such organizations in any way which might jeopardize the efficient performance of their mission. These organizations shall not be required to give priority to the nationals or interests of that Power.
2. The Occupying Power shall not compel, coerce or induce civilian civil defence organizations to perform their tasks in any manner prejudicial to the interests of the civilian population.
3. The Occupying Power may disarm civil defence personnel for reasons of security.
4. The Occupying Power shall neither divert from their proper use nor requisition buildings or matériel belonging to or used by civil defence organizations if such diversion or requisition would be harmful to the civilian population.
5. Provided that the general rule in paragraph 4 continues to be observed, the Occupying Power may requisition or divert these resources, subject to the following particular conditions:
    a. that the buildings or matériel are necessary for other needs of the civilian population; and

b. that the requisition or diversion continues only while such necessity exists.

6. The Occupying Power shall neither divert nor requisition shelters provided for the use of the civilian population or needed by such population.

ART. 64. Civilian civil defence organizations of neutral or other States not Parties to the conflict and international co-ordinating organizations

1. Articles 62, 63, 65 and 66 shall also apply to the personnel and matériel of civilian civil defence organizations of neutral or other States not Parties to the conflict which perform civil defence tasks mentioned in Article 61 in the territory of a Party to the conflict, with the consent and under the control of that Party. Notification of such assistance shall be given as soon as possible to any adverse Party concerned. In no circumstances shall this activity be deemed to be an interference in the conflict. This activity should, however, be performed with due regard to the security interests of the Parties to the conflict concerned.

2. The Parties to the conflict receiving the assistance referred to in paragraph 1 and the High Contracting Parties granting it should facilitate international co-ordination of such civil defence actions when appropriate. In such cases the relevant international organizations are covered by the provisions of this Chapter.

3. In occupied territories, the Occupying Power may only exclude or restrict the activities of civilian civil defence organizations of neutral or other States not Parties to the conflict and of international co-ordinating organizations if it can ensure the adequate performance of civil defence tasks from its own resources or those of the occupied territory.

ART. 65. Cessation of protection

1. The protection to which civilian civil defence organizations, their personnel, buildings, shelters and matériel are entitled shall not cease unless they commit or are used to commit, outside their proper tasks, acts harmful to the enemy. Protection may, however, cease only after a warning has been given setting, whenever appropriate, a reasonable time-limit, and after such warning has remained unheeded.

2. The following shall not be considered as acts harmful to the enemy:

a. that civil defence tasks are carried out under the direction or control of military authorities;

b. that civilian civil defence personnel co-operate with military personnel in the performance of civil defence tasks, or that some military personnel are attached to civilian civil defence organizations;
c. that the performance of civil defence tasks may incidentally benefit military victims, particularly those who are hors de combat.

3. It shall also not be considered as an act harmful to the enemy that civilian civil defence personnel bear light individual weapons for the purpose of maintaining order or for self-defence. However, in areas where land fighting is taking place or is likely to take place, the Parties to the conflict shall undertake the appropriate measures to limit these weapons to handguns, such as pistols or revolvers, in order to assist in distinguishing between civil defence personnel and combatants. Although civil defence personnel bear other light individual weapons in such areas, they shall nevertheless be respected and protected as soon as they have been recognized as such.
4. The formation of civilian civil defence organizations along military lines, and compulsory service in them, shall also not deprive them of the protection conferred by this Chapter.

ART. 66. Identification

1. Each Party to the conflict shall endeavour to ensure that its civil defence organizations, their personnel, buildings and matériel are identifiable while they are exclusively devoted to the performance of civil defence tasks. Shelters provided for the civilian population should be similarly identifiable.
2. Each Party to the conflict shall also endeavour to adopt and implement methods and procedures which will make it possible to recognize civilian shelters as well as civil defence personnel, buildings and matériel on which the international distinctive sign of civil defence is displayed.
3. In occupied territories and in areas where fighting is taking place or is likely to take place, civilian civil defence personnel should be recognizable by the international distinctive sign of civil defence and by an identity card certifying their status.
4. The international distinctive sign of civil defence is an equilateral blue triangle on an orange ground when used for the protection of civil defence organizations, their personnel, buildings and matériel and for civilian shelters.
5. In addition to the distinctive sign, Parties to the conflict may agree upon the use of distinctive signals for civil defence identification purposes.

6. The application of the provisions of paragraphs 1 to 4 is governed by Chapter V of Annex I to this Protocol.

7. In time of peace, the sign described in paragraph 4 may, with the consent of the competent national authorities, be used for civil defence identification purposes.

8. The High Contracting Parties and the Parties to the conflict shall take the measures necessary to supervise the display of the international distinctive sign of civil defence and to prevent and repress any misuse thereof.

9. The identification of civil defence medical and religious personnel, medical units and medical transports is also governed by Article 18.

ART. 67. Members of the armed forces and military units assigned to civil defence organizations

1. Members of the armed forces and military units assigned to civil defence organizations shall be respected and protected, provided that:

- **a.** such personnel and such units are permanently assigned and exclusively devoted to the performance of any of the tasks mentioned in Article 61;
- **b.** if so assigned, such personnel do not perform any other military duties during the conflict;
- **c.** such personnel are clearly distinguishable from the other members of the armed forces by prominently displaying the international distinctive sign of civil defence, which shall be as large as appropriate, and such personnel are provided with the identity card referred to in Chapter V of Annex I to this Protocol certifying their status;
- **d.** such personnel and such units are equipped only with light individual weapons for the purpose of maintaining order or for self-defence. The provisions of Article 65, paragraph 3 shall also apply in this case;
- **e.** such personnel do not participate directly in hostilities, and do not commit, or are not used to commit, outside their civil defence tasks, acts harmful to the adverse Party
- **f.** such personnel and such units perform their civil defence tasks only within the national territory of their Party.

The non-observance of the conditions stated in (e) above by any member of the armed forces who is bound by the conditions prescribed in (a) and (b) above is prohibited.

2. Military personnel serving within civil defence organizations shall, if they fall into the power of an adverse Party, be prisoners of war. In occupied territory they may, but only in the interest of the civilian population of that territory, be employed on civil defence tasks in so far as the need arises, provided however that, if such work is dangerous, they volunteer for such tasks.
3. The buildings and major items of equipment and transports of military units assigned to civil defence organizations shall be clearly marked with the international distinctive sign of civil defence. This distinctive sign shall be as large as appropriate.
4. The matériel and buildings of military units permanently assigned to civil defence organizations and exclusively devoted to the performance of civil defence tasks shall, if they fall into the hands of an adverse Party, remain subject to the laws of war. They may not be diverted from their civil defence purpose so long as they are required for the performance of civil defence tasks, except in case of imperative military necessity, unless previous arrangements have been made for adequate provision for the needs of the civilian population.

Section II. Relief in Favour of the Civilian Population

ART. 68. Field of application

The provisions of this Section apply to the civilian population as defined in this Protocol and are supplementary to Articles 23, 55, 59, 60, 61 and 62 and other relevant provisions of the Fourth Convention.

ART. 69. Basic needs in occupied territories

1. In addition to the duties specified in Article 55 of the Fourth Convention concerning food and medical supplies, the Occupying Power shall, to the fullest extent of the means available to it and without any adverse distinction, also ensure the provision of clothing, bedding, means of shelter, other supplies essential to the survival of the civilian population of the occupied territory and objects necessary for religious worship.
2. Relief actions for the benefit of the civilian population of occupied territories are governed by Articles 59, 60, 61, 62, 108, 109, 110 and 111 of the Fourth Convention, and by Article 71 of this Protocol, and shall be implemented without delay.

Art. 70. Relief actions

1. If the civilian population of any territory under the control of a Party to the conflict, other than occupied territory, is not adequately provided with the supplies mentioned in Article 69, relief actions which are humanitarian and impartial in character and conducted without any adverse distinction shall be undertaken, subject to the agreement of the Parties concerned in such relief actions. Offers of such relief shall not be regarded as interference in the armed conflict or as unfriendly acts. In the distribution of relief consignments, priority shall be given to those persons, such as children, expectant mothers, maternity cases and nursing mothers, who, under the Fourth Convention or under this Protocol, are to be accorded privileged treatment or special protection.
2. The Parties to the conflict and each High Contracting Party shall allow and facilitate rapid and unimpeded passage of all relief consignments, equipment and personnel provided in accordance with this Section, even if such assistance is destined for the civilian population of the adverse Party.
3. The Parties to the conflict and each High Contracting Party which allow the passage of relief consignments, equipment and personnel in accordance with paragraph 2:
    a. shall have the right to prescribe the technical arrangements, including search, under which such passage is permitted;
    b. may make such permission conditional on the distribution of this assistance being made under the local supervision of a Protecting Power;
    c. shall, in no way whatsoever, divert relief consignments from the purpose for which they are intended nor delay their forwarding, except in cases of urgent necessity in the interest of the civilian population concerned.
4. The Parties to the conflict shall protect relief consignments and facilitate their rapid distribution.
5. The Parties to the conflict and each High Contracting Party concerned shall encourage and facilitate effective international co-ordination of the relief actions referred to in paragraph 1.

Art. 71. Personnel participating in relief actions

1. Where necessary, relief personnel may form part of the assistance provided in any relief action, in particular for the transportation and distribution of relief consignments; the participation of such personnel shall be subject to the approval of the Party in whose territory they will carry out their duties.

2. Such personnel shall be respected and protected.
3. Each Party in receipt of relief consignments shall, to the fullest extent practicable, assist the relief personnel referred to in paragraph 1 in carrying out their relief mission. Only in case of imperative military necessity may the activities of the relief personnel be limited or their movements temporarily restricted.
4. Under no circumstances may relief personnel exceed the terms of their mission under this Protocol. In particular they shall take account of the security requirements of the Party in whose territory they are carrying out their duties. The mission of any of the personnel who do not respect these conditions may be terminated.

Section III. Treatment of Persons in the Power of a Party to the Conflict

Chapter I. Field of Application and Protection of Persons and Objects

ART. 72. Field of application

The provisions of this Section are additional to the rules concerning humanitarian protection of civilians and civilian objects in the power of a Party to the conflict contained in the Fourth Convention, particularly Parts I and III thereof, as well as to other applicable rules of international law relating to the protection of fundamental human rights during international armed conflict.

ART. 73. Refugees and stateless persons

Persons who, before the beginning of hostilities, were considered as stateless persons or refugees under the relevant international instruments accepted by the Parties concerned or under the national legislation of the State of refuge or State of residence shall be protected persons within the meaning of Parts I and III of the Fourth Convention, in all circumstances and without any adverse distinction.

ART. 74. Reunion of dispersed families

The High Contracting Parties and the Parties to the conflict shall facilitate in every possible way the reunion of families dispersed as a result of armed conflicts and shall encourage in particular the work of the humanitarian organizations engaged in this task in accordance with the provisions of the Conventions and of this Protocol and in conformity with their respective security regulations.

Art. 75. Fundamental guarantees

1. In so far as they are affected by a situation referred to in Article 1 of this Protocol, persons who are in the power of a Party to the conflict and who do not benefit from more favourable treatment under the Conventions or under this Protocol shall be treated humanely in all circumstances and shall enjoy, as a minimum, the protection provided by this Article without any adverse distinction based upon race, colour, sex, language, religion or belief, political or other opinion, national or social origin, wealth, birth or other status, or on any other similar criteria. Each Party shall respect the person, honour, convictions and religious practices of all such persons.
2. The following acts are and shall remain prohibited at any time and in any place whatsoever, whether committed by civilian or by military agents:
   a. violence to the life, health, or physical or mental well-being of persons, in particular:
      i. murder;
      ii. torture of all kinds, whether physical or mental;
      iii. corporal punishment; and
      iv. mutilation;
   b. outrages upon personal dignity, in particular humiliating and degrading treatment, enforced prostitution and any form of indecent assault;
   c. the taking of hostages;
   d. collective punishments; and
   e. threats to commit any of the foregoing acts.
3. Any person arrested, detained or interned for actions related to the armed conflict shall be informed promptly, in a language he understands, of the reasons why these measures have been taken. Except in cases of arrest or detention for penal offences, such persons shall be released with the minimum delay possible and in any event as soon as the circumstances justifying the arrest, detention or internment have ceased to exist.
4. No sentence may be passed and no penalty may be executed on a person found guilty of a penal offence related to the armed conflict except pursuant to a conviction pronounced by an impartial and regularly constituted court respecting the generally recognized principles of regular judicial procedure, which include the following:
   a. the procedure shall provide for an accused to be informed without delay of the particulars of the offence alleged against him and shall

afford the accused before and during his trial all necessary rights and means of defence;

b. no one shall be convicted of an offence except on the basis of individual penal responsibility;

c. no one shall be accused or convicted of a criminal offence on account or any act or omission which did not constitute a criminal offence under the national or international law to which he was subject at the time when it was committed; nor shall a heavier penalty be imposed than that which was applicable at the time when the criminal offence was committed; if, after the commission of the offence, provision is made by law for the imposition of a lighter penalty, the offender shall benefit thereby;

d. anyone charged with an offence is presumed innocent until proved guilty according to law;

e. anyone charged with an offence shall have the right to be tried in his presence;

f. no one shall be compelled to testify against himself or to confess guilt;

g. anyone charged with an offence shall have the right to examine, or have examined, the witnesses against him and to obtain the attendance and examination of witnesses on his behalf under the same conditions as witnesses against him;

h. no one shall be prosecuted or punished by the same Party for an offence in respect of which a final judgement acquitting or convicting that person has been previously pronounced under the same law and judicial procedure;

i. anyone prosecuted for an offence shall have the right to have the judgement pronounced publicly; and

j. a convicted person shall be advised on conviction or his judicial and other remedies and of the time-limits within which they may be exercised.

5. Women whose liberty has been restricted for reasons related to the armed conflict shall be held in quarters separated from men's quarters. They shall be under the immediate supervision of women. Nevertheless, in cases where families are detained or interned, they shall, whenever possible, be held in the same place and accommodated as family units.

6. Persons who are arrested, detained or interned for reasons related to the armed conflict shall enjoy the protection provided by this Article until their final release, repatriation or re-establishment, even after the end of the armed conflict.

7. In order to avoid any doubt concerning the prosecution and trial of persons accused of war crimes or crimes against humanity, the following principles shall apply:
   a. persons who are accused or such crimes should be submitted for the purpose of prosecution and trial in accordance with the applicable rules of international law; and
   b. any such persons who do not benefit from more favourable treatment under the Conventions or this Protocol shall be accorded the treatment provided by this Article, whether or not the crimes of which they are accused constitute grave breaches of the Conventions or of this Protocol.
8. No provision of this Article may be construed as limiting or infringing any other more favourable provision granting greater protection, under any applicable rules of international law, to persons covered by paragraph 1

Chapter II. Measures in Favour of Women and Children

ART. 76. Protection of women

1. Women shall be the object of special respect and shall be protected in particular against rape, forced prostitution and any other form of indecent assault.
2. Pregnant women and mothers having dependent infants who are arrested, detained or interned for reasons related to the armed conflict, shall have their cases considered with the utmost priority.
3. To the maximum extent feasible, the Parties to the conflict shall endeavour to avoid the pronouncement of the death penalty on pregnant women or mothers having dependent infants, for an offence related to the armed conflict. The death penalty for such offences shall not be executed on such women.

ART. 77. Protection of children

1. Children shall be the object of special respect and shall be protected against any form of indecent assault. The Parties to the conflict shall provide them with the care and aid they require, whether because of their age or for any other reason.

2. The Parties to the conflict shall take all feasible measures in order that children who have not attained the age of fifteen years do not take a direct part in hostilities and, in particular, they shall refrain from recruiting them into their armed forces. In recruiting among those persons who have attained the age of fifteen years but who have not attained the age of eighteen years the Parties to the conflict shall endeavour to give priority to those who are oldest.
3. If, in exceptional cases, despite the provisions of paragraph 2, children who have not attained the age of fifteen years take a direct part in hostilities and fall into the power of an adverse Party, they shall continue to benefit from the special protection accorded by this Article, whether or not they are prisoners of war.
4. If arrested, detained or interned for reasons related to the armed conflict, children shall be held in quarters separate from the quarters of adults, except where families are accommodated as family units as provided in Article 75, paragraph 5.
5. The death penalty for an offence related to the armed conflict shall not be executed on persons who had not attained the age of eighteen years at the time the offence was committed.

Art. 78. Evacuation of children

1. No Party to the conflict shall arrange for the evacuation of children, other than its own nationals, to a foreign country except for a temporary evacuation where compelling reasons of the health or medical treatment of the children or, except in occupied territory, their safety, so require. Where the parents or legal guardians can be found, their written consent to such evacuation is required. If these persons cannot be found, the written consent to such evacuation of the persons who by law or custom are primarily responsible for the care of the children is required. Any such evacuation shall be supervised by the Protecting Power in agreement with the Parties concerned, namely, the Party arranging for the evacuation, the Party receiving the children and any Parties whose nationals are being evacuated. In each case, all Parties to the conflict shall take all feasible precautions to avoid endangering the evacuation.
2. Whenever an evacuation occurs pursuant to paragraph 1, each child's education, including his religious and moral education as his parents desire, shall be provided while he is away with the greatest possible continuity.

3. With a view to facilitating the return to their families and country of children evacuated pursuant to this Article, the authorities of the Party arranging for the evacuation and, as appropriate, the authorities of the receiving country shall establish for each child a card with photographs, which they shall send to the Central Tracing Agency of the International Committee of the Red Cross. Each card shall bear, whenever possible, and whenever it involves no risk of harm to the child, the following information:
   a. surname(s) of the child;
   b. the child's first name(s);
   c. the child's sex;
   d. the place and date of birth (or, if that date is not known, the approximate age);
   e. the father's full name;
   f. the mother's full name and her maiden name;
   g. the child's next-of-kin;
   h. the child's nationality;
   i. the child's native language, and any other languages he speaks;
   j. the address of the child's family;
   k. any identification number for the child;
   l. the child's state of health;
   m. the child's blood group;
   n. any distinguishing features;
   o. the date on which and the place where the child was found;
   p. the date on which and the place from which the child left the country;
   q. the child's religion, if any;
   r. the child's present address in the receiving country;
   s. should the child die before his return, the date, place and circumstances of death and place of interment.

Chapter III. Journalists

ART. 79. Measures or protection for journalists

1. Journalists engaged in dangerous professional missions in areas of armed conflict shall be considered as civilians within the meaning of Article 50, paragraph 1.
2. They shall be protected as such under the Conventions and this Protocol, provided that they take no action adversely affecting their status as civilians, and without prejudice to the right of war correspondents accredited

to the armed forces to the status provided for in Article 4 (A) (4) of the Third Convention.

3. They may obtain an identity card similar to the model in Annex II of this Protocol. This card, which shall be issued by the government of the State of which the Journalist is a national or in whose territory he resides or in which the news medium employing him is located, shall attest to his status as a journalist.

PART V. EXECUTION OF THE CONVENTIONS AND OF ITS PROTOCOLS

Section I. General Provisions

ART. 80. Measures for execution

1. The High Contracting Parties and the Parties to the conflict shall without delay take all necessary measures for the execution of their obligations under the Conventions and this Protocol.
2. The High Contracting Parties and the Parties to the conflict shall give orders and instructions to ensure observance of the Conventions and this Protocol, and shall supervise their execution.

ART. 81. Activities of the Red Cross and other humanitarian organizations

1. The Parties to the conflict shall grant to the International Committee of the Red Cross all facilities, within their power so as to enable it to carry out the humanitarian functions assigned to it by the Conventions and this Protocol in order to ensure protection and assistance to the victims of conflicts; the International Committee of the Red Cross may also carry out any other humanitarian activities in favour of these victims, subject to the consent of the Parties to the conflict concerned.
2. The Parties to the conflict shall grant to their respective Red Cross (Red Crescent, Red Lion and Sun) organizations the facilities necessary for carrying out their humanitarian activities in favour of the victims of the conflict, in accordance with the provisions of the Conventions and this Protocol and the fundamental principles of the Red Cross as formulated by the International Conferences of the Red Cross.
3. The High Contracting Parties and the Parties to the conflict shall facilitate in every possible way the assistance which Red Cross (Red Crescent, Red

Lion and Sun) organizations and the League of Red Cross Societies extend to the victims of conflicts in accordance with the provisions of the Conventions and this Protocol and with the fundamental principles of the red Cross as formulated by the International Conferences of the Red Cross.

4. The High Contracting Parties and the Parties to the conflict shall, as far as possible, make facilities similar to those mentioned in paragraphs 2 and 3 available to the other humanitarian organizations referred to in the Conventions and this Protocol which are duly authorized by the respective Parties to the conflict and which perform their humanitarian activities in accordance with the provisions of the Conventions and this Protocol.

ART. 82. Legal advisers in armed forces

The High Contracting Parties at all times, and the Parties to the conflict in time of armed conflict, shall ensure that legal advisers are available, when necessary, to advise military commanders at the appropriate level on the application of the Conventions and this Protocol and on the appropriate instruction to be given to the armed forces on this subject.

ART. 83. Dissemination

1. The High Contracting Parties undertake, in time of peace as in time of armed conflict, to disseminate the Conventions and this Protocol as widely as possible in their respective countries and, in particular, to include the study thereof in their programmes of military instruction and to encourage the study thereof by the civilian population, so that those instruments may become known to the armed forces and to the civilian population.
2. Any military or civilian authorities who, in time of armed conflict, assume responsibilities in respect of the application of the Conventions and this Protocol shall be fully acquainted with the text thereof.

ART. 84. Rules of application

The High Contracting Parties shall communicate to one another, as soon as possible, through the depositary and, as appropriate, through the Protecting Powers, their official translations of this Protocol, as well as the laws and regulations which they may adopt to ensure its application.

Section II. Repression of Breaches of the Conventions and of this Protocol

ART. 85. Repression of breaches of this Protocol

1. The provisions of the Conventions relating to the repression of breaches and grave breaches, supplemented by this Section, shall apply to the repression of breaches and grave breaches of this Protocol.
2. Acts described as grave breaches in the Conventions are grave breaches of this Protocol if committed against persons in the power of an adverse Party protected by Articles 44, 45 and 73 of this Protocol, or against the wounded, sick and shipwrecked of the adverse Party who are protected by this Protocol, or against those medical or religious personnel, medical units or medical transports which are under the control of the adverse Party and are protected by this Protocol.
3. In addition to the grave breaches defined in Article 11, the following acts shall be regarded as grave breaches of this Protocol, when committed wilfully, in violation of the relevant provisions of this Protocol, and causing death or serious injury to body or health:
   a. making the civilian population or individual civilians the object of attack;
   b. launching an indiscriminate attack affecting the civilian population or civilian objects in the knowledge that such attack will cause excessive loss of life, injury to civilians or damage to civilian objects, as defined in Article 57, paragraph 2 (a)(iii);
   c. launching an attack against works or installations containing dangerous forces in the knowledge that such attack will cause excessive loss of life, injury to civilians or damage to civilian objects, as defined in Article 57, paragraph 2 (a)(iii);
   d. making non-defended localities and demilitarized zones the object of attack;
   e. making a person the object of attack in the knowledge that he is hors de combat;
   f. the perfidious use, in violation of Article 37, of the distinctive emblem of the red cross, red crescent or red lion and sun or of other protective signs recognized by the Conventions or this Protocol.
4. In addition to the grave breaches defined in the preceding paragraphs and in the Conventions, the following shall be regarded as grave breaches of this Protocol, when committed wilfully and in violation of the Conventions or the Protocol:

- **a.** the transfer by the occupying Power of parts of its own civilian population into the territory it occupies, or the deportation or transfer of all or parts of the population of the occupied territory within or outside this territory, in violation of Article 49 of the Fourth Convention;
- **b.** unjustifiable delay in the repatriation of prisoners of war or civilians;
- **c.** practices of apartheid and other inhuman and degrading practices involving outrages upon personal dignity, based on racial discrimination;
- **d.** making the clearly-recognized historic monuments, works of art or places of worship which constitute the cultural or spiritual heritage of peoples and to which special protection has been given by special arrangement, for example, within the framework of a competent international organization, the object of attack, causing as a result extensive destruction thereof, where there is no evidence of the violation by the adverse Party of Article 53, subparagraph (b), and when such historic monuments, works of art and places of worship are not located in the immediate proximity of military objectives;
- **e.** depriving a person protected by the Conventions or referred to in paragraph 2 of this Article of the rights of fair and regular trial.

5. Without prejudice to the application of the Conventions and of this Protocol, grave breaches of these instruments shall be regarded as war crimes.

ART. 86. Failure to act

1. The High Contracting Parties and the Parties to the conflict shall repress grave breaches, and take measures necessary to suppress all other breaches, of the Conventions or of this Protocol which result from a failure to act when under a duty to do so.
2. The fact that a breach of the Conventions or of this Protocol was committed by a subordinate does not absolve his superiors from penal or disciplinary responsibility, as the case may be, if they knew, or had information which should have enabled them to conclude in the circumstances at the time, that he was committing or was going to commit such a breach and if they did not take all feasible measures within their power to prevent or repress the breach.

ART. 87. Duty of commanders

1. The High Contracting Parties and the Parties to the conflict shall require military commanders, with respect to members of the armed forces under their command and other persons under their control, to prevent and, where necessary, to suppress and to report to competent authorities breaches of the Conventions and of this Protocol.
2. In order to prevent and suppress breaches, High Contracting Parties and Parties to the conflict shall require that, commensurate with their level of responsibility, commanders ensure that members of the armed forces under their command are aware of their obligations under the Conventions and this Protocol.
3. The High Contracting Parties and Parties to the conflict shall require any commander who is aware that subordinates or other persons under his control are going to commit or have committed a breach of the Conventions or of this Protocol, to initiate such steps as are necessary to prevent such violations of the Conventions or this Protocol, and, where appropriate, to initiate disciplinary or penal action against violators thereof.

ART. 88. Mutual assistance in criminal matters

1. The High Contracting Parties shall afford one another the greatest measure of assistance in connexion with criminal proceedings brought in respect of grave breaches of the Conventions or of this Protocol.
2. Subject to the rights and obligations established in the Conventions and in Article 85, paragraph 1 of this Protocol, and when circumstances permit, the High Contracting Parties shall co-operate in the matter of extradition. They shall give due consideration to the request of the State in whose territory the alleged offence has occurred.
3. The law of the High Contracting Party requested shall apply in all cases. The provisions of the preceding paragraphs shall not, however, affect the obligations arising from the provisions of any other treaty of a bilateral or multilateral nature which governs or will govern the whole or part of the subject of mutual assistance in criminal matters.

ART. 89. Co-operation

In situations of serious violations of the Conventions or of this Protocol, the High Contracting Parties undertake to act jointly or individually, in co-operation with the United Nations and in conformity with the United Nations Charter.

ART. 90. International Fact-Finding Commission

1. **a.** An International Fact-Finding Commission (hereinafter referred to as "the Commission") consisting of 15 members of high moral standing and acknowledged impartiality shall be established;
   b. When not less than 20 High Contracting Parties have agreed to accept the competence of the Commission pursuant to paragraph 2, the depositary shall then, and at intervals of five years thereafter, convene a meeting of representatives of those High Contracting Parties for the purpose of electing the members of the Commission. At the meeting, the representatives shall elect the members of the Commission by secret ballot from a list of persons to which each of those High Contracting Parties may nominate one person;
   b. The members of the Commission shall serve in their personal capacity and shall hold office until the election of new members at the ensuing meeting;
   c. At the election, the High Contracting Parties shall ensure that the persons to be elected to the Commission individually possess the qualifications required and that, in the Commission as a whole, equitable geographical representation is assured;
   d. In the case of a casual vacancy, the Commission itself shall fill the vacancy, having due regard to the provisions of the preceding subparagraphs;
   f. The depositary shall make available to the Commission the necessary administrative facilities for the performance of its functions.
2. **a.** The High Contracting Parties may at the time of signing, ratifying or acceding to the Protocol, or at any other subsequent time, declare that they recognize ipso facto and without special agreement, in relation to any other High Contracting Party accepting the same obligation, the competence of the Commission to inquire into allegations by such other Party, as authorized by this Article;
   b. The declarations referred to above shall be deposited with the depositary, which shall transmit copies thereof to the High Contracting Parties;
   c. The Commission shall be competent to:
      i. inquire into any facts alleged to be a grave breach as defined in the Conventions and this Protocol or other serious violation of the Conventions or of this Protocol;

ii. facilitate, through its good offices, the restoration of an attitude of respect for the Conventions and this Protocol;

d. In other situations, the Commission shall institute an inquiry at the request of a Party to the conflict only with the consent of the other Party or Parties concerned;

e. Subject to the foregoing provisions or this paragraph, the provisions of Article 52 of the First Convention, Article 53 of the Second Convention, Article 132 or the Third Convention and Article 149 of the Fourth Convention shall continue to apply to any alleged violation of the Conventions and shall extend to any alleged violation of this Protocol.

3. a. Unless otherwise agreed by the Parties concerned, all inquiries shall be undertaken by a Chamber consisting of seven members appointed as follows:

i. five members of the Commission, not nationals of any Party to the conflict, appointed by the President of the Commission on the basis of equitable representation of the geographical areas, after consultation with the Parties to the conflict;

ii. two ad hoc members, not nationals of any Party to the conflict, one to be appointed by each side;

b. Upon receipt of the request for an inquiry, the President of the Commission shall specify an appropriate time-limit for setting up a Chamber. If any ad hoc member has not been appointed within the time-limit, the President shall immediately appoint such additional member or members of the Commission as may be necessary to complete the membership of the Chamber.

4. a. The Chamber set up under paragraph 3 to undertake an inquiry shall invite the Parties to the conflict to assist it and to present evidence. The Chamber may also seek such other evidence as it deems appropriate and may carry out an investigation of the situation in loco;

b. All evidence shall be fully disclosed to the Parties, which shall have the right to comment on it to the Commission;

c. Each Party shall have the right to challenge such evidence.

5. a. The Commission shall submit to the Parties a report on the findings of fact of the Chamber, with such recommendations as it may deem appropriate;

b. If the Chamber is unable to secure sufficient evidence for factual and impartial findings, the Commission shall state the reasons for that inability;

c. The Commission shall not report its findings publicly, unless all the Parties to the conflict have requested the Commission to do so.

6. The Commission shall establish its own rules, including rules for the presidency or the Commission and the presidency of the Chamber. Those rules shall ensure that the functions of the President of the Commission are exercised at all times and that, in the case of an inquiry, they are exercised by a person who is not a national of a Party to the conflict.
7. The administrative expenses of the Commission shall be met by contributions from the High Contracting Parties which made declarations under paragraph 2, and by voluntary contributions. The Party or Parties to the conflict requesting an inquiry shall advance the necessary funds for expenses incurred by a Chamber and shall be reimbursed by the Party or Parties against which the allegations are made to the extent of 50 per cent of the costs of the Chamber. Where there are counter-allegations before the Chamber each side shall advance 50 per cent of the necessary funds.

ART. 91. Responsibility

A Party to the conflict which violates the provisions of the Conventions or of this Protocol shall, if the case demands, be liable to pay compensation. It shall be responsible for all acts committed by persons forming part of its armed forces.

PART IV. FINAL RESOLUTIONS

ART. 92. Signature

This Protocol shall be open for signature by the Parties to the Conventions six months after the signing of the Final Act and will remain open for a period or twelve months.

ART. 93. Ratification

This Protocol shall be ratified as soon as possible. The instruments of ratification shall be deposited with the Swiss Federal Council, depositary of the Conventions.

ART. 94. Accession

This Protocol shall be open for accession by any Party to the Conventions which has not signed it. The instruments of accession shall be deposited with the depositary.

Art. 95. Entry into force

1. This Protocol shall enter into force six months after two instruments of ratification or accession have been deposited.
2. For each Party to the Conventions thereafter ratifying or acceding to this Protocol, it shall enter into force six months after the deposit by such Party of its instrument of ratification or accession.

Art. 96. Treaty relations upon entry into force or this Protocol

1. When the Parties to the Conventions are also Parties to this Protocol, the Conventions shall apply as supplemented by this Protocol.
2. When one of the Parties to the conflict is not bound by this Protocol, the Parties to the Protocol shall remain bound by it in their mutual relations. They shall furthermore be bound by this Protocol in relation to each of the Parties which are not bound by it, if the latter accepts and applies the provisions thereof.
3. The authority representing a people engaged against a High Contracting Party in an armed conflict of the type referred to in Article 1, paragraph 4, may undertake to apply the Conventions and this Protocol in relation to that conflict by means of a unilateral declaration addressed to the depositary. Such declaration shall, upon its receipt by the depositary, have in relation to that conflict the following effects:
   a. the Conventions and this Protocol are brought into force for the said authority as a Party to the conflict with immediate effect;
   b. the said authority assumes the same rights and obligations as those which have been assumed by a High Contracting Party to the Conventions and this Protocol; and
   c. the Conventions and this Protocol are equally binding upon all Parties to the conflict.

Art. 97. Amendment

1. Any High Contracting Party may propose amendments to this Protocol. The text of any proposed amendment shall be communicated to the depositary, which shall decide, after consultation with all the High Contracting Parties and the International Committee of the Red Cross, whether a conference should be convened to consider the proposed amendment.

2. The depositary shall invite to that conference all the High Contracting Parties as well as the Parties to the Conventions, whether or not they are signatories or this Protocol.

Art. 98. Revision of Annex I

1. Not later than four years after the entry into force of this Protocol and thereafter at intervals of not less than four years, the International Committee of the Red Cross shall consult the High Contracting Parties concerning Annex I to this Protocol and, if it considers it necessary, may propose a meeting of technical experts to review Annex I and to propose such amendments to it as may appear to be desirable. Unless, within six months of the communication of a proposal for such a meeting to the High Contracting Parties, one third of them object, the International Committee of the Red Cross shall convene the meeting, inviting also observers of appropriate international organizations. Such a meeting shall also be convened by the International Committee of the Red Cross at any time at the request of one third of the High Contracting Parties.
2. The depositary shall convene a conference of the High Contracting Parties and the Parties to the Conventions to consider amendments proposed by the meeting of technical experts if, after that meeting, the International Committee of the Red Cross or one third of the High Contracting Parties so request.
3. Amendments to Annex I may be adopted at such a conference by a two-thirds majority of the High Contracting Parties present and voting.
4. The depositary shall communicate any amendment so adopted to the High Contracting Parties and to the Parties to the Conventions. The amendment shall be considered to have been accepted at the end of a period of one year after it has been so communicated, unless within that period a declaration of non-acceptance of the amendment has been communicated to the depositary by not less than one third of the High Contracting Parties.
5. An amendment considered to have been accepted in accordance with paragraph 4 shall enter into force three months after its acceptance for all High Contracting Parties other than those which have made a declaration of non-acceptance in accordance with that paragraph. Any Party making such a declaration may at any time withdraw it and the amendment shall then enter into force for that Party three months thereafter.

6. The depositary shall notify the High Contracting Parties and the Parties to the Conventions of the entry into force of any amendment, of the Parties bound thereby, of the date of its entry into force in relation to each Party, of declarations of non-acceptance made in accordance with paragraph 4, and of withdrawals of such declarations.

Art. 99. Denunciation

1. In case a High Contracting Party should denounce this Protocol, the denunciation shall only take effect one year after receipt of the instrument of denunciation. If, however, on the expiry of that year the denouncing Party is engaged in one of the situations referred to in Article I, the denunciation shall not take effect before the end of the armed conflict or occupation and not, in any case, before operations connected with the final release, repatriation or re-establishment of the persons protected by the Convention or this Protocol have been terminated.
2. The denunciation shall be notified in writing to the depositary, which shall transmit it to all the High Contracting Parties.
3. The denunciation shall have effect only in respect of the denouncing Party.
4. Any denunciation under paragraph 1 shall not affect the obligations already incurred, by reason of the armed conflict, under this Protocol by such denouncing Party in respect of any act committed before this denunciation becomes effective.

Art. 100. Notifications

The depositary shall inform the High Contracting Parties as well as the Parties to the Conventions, whether or not they are signatories of this Protocol, of:

- **a.** signatures affixed to this Protocol and the deposit of instruments of ratification and accession under Articles 93 and 94;
- **b.** the date of entry into force of this Protocol under Article 95;
- **c.** communications and declarations received under Articles 84, 90 and 97;
- **d.** declarations received under Article 96, paragraph 3, which shall be communicated by the quickest methods; and
- **e.** denunciations under Article 99.

ART. 101. Registration

1. After its entry into force, this Protocol shall be transmitted by the depositary to the Secretariat of the United Nations for registration and publication, in accordance with Article 102 of the Charter of the United Nations.
2. The depositary shall also inform the Secretariat of the United Nations of all ratifications, accessions and denunciations received by it with respect to this Protocol.

ART. 102. Authentic texts

The original of this Protocol, of which the Arabic, Chinese, English, French, Russian and Spanish texts are equally authentic, shall be deposited with the depositary, which shall transmit certified true copies thereof to all the Parties to the Conventions.

appendix VI

ADDITIONAL PROTOCOL II TO THE GENEVA CONVENTIONS OF 1949 (1977)

Protocol Additional to the Geneva Conventions of 12 August 1949, and relating to the Protection of Victims of Non-International Armed Conflicts (Protocol II), 8 June 1977.

PREAMBLE

The High Contracting Parties, Recalling that the humanitarian principles enshrined in Article 3 common to the Geneva Conventions of 12 August 1949, constitute the foundation of respect for the human person in cases of armed conflict not of an international character,

Recalling furthermore that international instruments relating to human rights offer a basic protection to the human person,

Emphasizing the need to ensure a better protection for the victims of those armed conflicts,

Recalling that, in cases not covered by the law in force, the human person remains under the protection of the principles of humanity and the dictates of the public conscience,

Have agreed on the following:

PART I. SCOPE OF THIS PROTOCOL

ART. 1. Material field of application

1. This Protocol, which develops and supplements Article 3 common to the Geneva Conventions of 12 August 1949 without modifying its existing conditions or application, shall apply to all armed conflicts which are not covered by Article 1 of the Protocol Additional to the Geneva Conventions of 12 August 1949, and relating to the Protection of Victims of International Armed Conflicts (Protocol I) and which take place in the territory of a High Contracting Party between its armed forces and dissident armed forces or other organized armed groups which, under responsible command, exercise such control over a part of its territory as to enable them to carry out sustained and concerted military operations and to implement this Protocol.
2. This Protocol shall not apply to situations of internal disturbances and tensions, such as riots, isolated and sporadic acts of violence and other acts of a similar nature, as not being armed conflicts.

ART. 2. Personal field of application

1. This Protocol shall be applied without any adverse distinction founded on race, colour, sex, language, religion or belief, political or other opinion, national or social origin, wealth, birth or other status, or on any other similar criteria (hereinafter referred to as "adverse distinction") to all persons affected by an armed conflict as defined in Article 1.
2. At the end of the armed conflict, all the persons who have been deprived of their liberty or whose liberty has been restricted for reasons related to such conflict, as well as those deprived of their liberty or whose liberty is restricted after the conflict for the same reasons, shall enjoy the protection of Articles 5 and 6 until the end of such deprivation or restriction of liberty.

ART. 3. Non-intervention

1. Nothing in this Protocol shall be invoked for the purpose of affecting the sovereignty of a State or the responsibility of the government, by all legitimate means, to maintain or re-establish law and order in the State or to defend the national unity and territorial integrity of the State.

2. Nothing in this Protocol shall be invoked as a justification for intervening, directly or indirectly, for any reason whatever, in the armed conflict or in the internal or external affairs of the High Contracting Party in the territory of which that conflict occurs.

PART II. HUMANE TREATMENT

ART. 4. Fundamental guarantees

1. All persons who do not take a direct part or who have ceased to take part in hostilities, whether or not their liberty has been restricted, are entitled to respect for their person, honour and convictions and religious practices. They shall in all circumstances be treated humanely, without any adverse distinction. It is prohibited to order that there shall be no survivors.
2. Without prejudice to the generality of the foregoing, the following acts against the persons referred to in paragraph I are and shall remain prohibited at any time and in any place whatsoever:
   a. violence to the life, health and physical or mental well-being of persons, in particular murder as well as cruel treatment such as torture, mutilation or any form of corporal punishment;
   b. collective punishments;
   c. taking of hostages;
   d. acts of terrorism;
   e. outrages upon personal dignity, in particular humiliating and degrading treatment, rape, enforced prostitution and any form or indecent assault;
   f. slavery and the slave trade in all their forms;
   g. pillage;
   h. threats to commit any or the foregoing acts.
3. Children shall be provided with the care and aid they require, and in particular:
   a. they shall receive an education, including religious and moral education, in keeping with the wishes of their parents, or in the absence of parents, of those responsible for their care;
   b. all appropriate steps shall be taken to facilitate the reunion of families temporarily separated;

- **c.** children who have not attained the age of fifteen years shall neither be recruited in the armed forces or groups nor allowed to take part in hostilities;
- **d.** the special protection provided by this Article to children who have not attained the age of fifteen years shall remain applicable to them if they take a direct part in hostilities despite the provisions of subparagraph (c) and are captured;
- **e.** measures shall be taken, if necessary, and whenever possible with the consent of their parents or persons who by law or custom are primarily responsible for their care, to remove children temporarily from the area in which hostilities are taking place to a safer area within the country and ensure that they are accompanied by persons responsible for their safety and well-being.

ART. 5. Persons whose liberty has been restricted

1. In addition to the provisions of Article 4 the following provisions shall be respected as a minimum with regard to persons deprived of their liberty for reasons related to the armed conflict, whether they are interned or detained;
   - **a.** the wounded and the sick shall be treated in accordance with Article 7;
   - **b.** the persons referred to in this paragraph shall, to the same extent as the local civilian population, be provided with food and drinking water and be afforded safeguards as regards health and hygiene and protection against the rigours of the climate and the dangers of the armed conflict;
   - **c.** they shall be allowed to receive individual or collective relief;
   - **d.** they shall be allowed to practise their religion and, if requested and appropriate, to receive spiritual assistance from persons, such as chaplains, performing religious functions;
   - **e.** they shall, if made to work, have the benefit of working conditions and safeguards similar to those enjoyed by the local civilian population.
2. Those who are responsible for the internment or detention of the persons referred to in paragraph 1 shall also, within the limits of their capabilities, respect the following provisions relating to such persons:
   - **a.** except when men and women of a family are accommodated together, women shall be held in quarters separated from those of men and shall be under the immediate supervision of women;
   - **b.** they shall be allowed to send and receive letters and cards, the number of which may be limited by competent authority if it deems necessary;

- **c.** places of internment and detention shall not be located close to the combat zone. The persons referred to in paragraph 1 shall be evacuated when the places where they are interned or detained become particularly exposed to danger arising out of the armed conflict, if their evacuation can be carried out under adequate conditions of safety;
- **d.** they shall have the benefit of medical examinations;
- **e.** their physical or mental health and integrity shall not be endangered by any unjustified act or omission. Accordingly, it is prohibited to subject the persons described in this Article to any medical procedure which is not indicated by the state of health of the person concerned, and which is not consistent with the generally accepted medical standards applied to free persons under similar medical circumstances.

3. Persons who are not covered by paragraph 1 but whose liberty has been restricted in any way whatsoever for reasons related to the armed conflict shall be treated humanely in accordance with Article 4 and with paragraphs 1 (a), (c) and (d), and 2 (b) of this Article.

4. If it is decided to release persons deprived of their liberty, necessary measures to ensure their safety shall be taken by those so deciding.

ART. 6. Penal prosecutions

1. This Article applies to the prosecution and punishment of criminal offences related to the armed conflict.

2. No sentence shall be passed and no penalty shall be executed on a person found guilty of an offence except pursuant to a conviction pronounced by a court offering the essential guarantees of independence and impartiality.
In particular:

- **a.** the procedure shall provide for an accused to be informed without delay of the particulars of the offence alleged against him and shall afford the accused before and during his trial all necessary rights and means of defence;
- **b.** no one shall be convicted of an offence except on the basis of individual penal responsibility;
- **c.** no one shall be held guilty of any criminal offence on account of any act or omission which did not constitute a criminal offence, under the law, at the time when it was committed; nor shall a heavier penalty be imposed than that which was applicable at the time when the criminal

offence was committed; if, after the commission of the offence, provision is made by law for the imposition of a lighter penalty, the offender shall benefit thereby;

d. anyone charged with an offence is presumed innocent until proved guilty according to law;

e. anyone charged with an offence shall have the right to be tried in his presence;

f. no one shall be compelled to testify against himself or to confess guilt.

3. A convicted person shall be advised on conviction of his judicial and other remedies and of the time-limits within which they may be exercised.

4. The death penalty shall not be pronounced on persons who were under the age of eighteen years at the time of the offence and shall not be carried out on pregnant women or mothers of young children.

5. At the end of hostilities, the authorities in power shall endeavour to grant the broadest possible amnesty to persons who have participated in the armed conflict, or those deprived of their liberty for reasons related to the armed conflict, whether they are interned or detained.

PART III. WOUNDED, SICK AND SHIPWRECKED

ART. 7. Protection and care

1. All the wounded, sick and shipwrecked, whether or not they have taken part in the armed conflict, shall be respected and protected.

2. In all circumstances they shall be treated humanely and shall receive to the fullest extent practicable and with the least possible delay, the medical care and attention required by their condition. There shall be no distinction among them founded on any grounds other than medical ones.

ART. 8. Search

Whenever circumstances permit and particularly after an engagement, all possible measures shall be taken, without delay, to search for and collect the wounded, sick and shipwrecked, to protect them against pillage and ill-treatment, to ensure their adequate care, and to search for the dead, prevent their being despoiled, and decently dispose of them.

Art. 9. Protection of medical and religious personnel

1. Medical and religious personnel shall be respected and protected and shall be granted all available help for the performance of their duties. They shall not be compelled to carry out tasks which are not compatible with their humanitarian mission.
2. In the performance of their duties medical personnel may not be required to give priority to any person except on medical grounds.

Art. 10. General protection of medical duties

1. Under no circumstances shall any person be punished for having carried out medical activities compatible with medical ethics, regardless of the person benefiting therefrom.
2. Persons engaged in medical activities shall neither be compelled to perform acts or to carry out work contrary to, nor be compelled to refrain from acts required by, the rules of medical ethics or other rules designed for the benefit of the wounded and sick, or this Protocol.
3. The professional obligations of persons engaged in medical activities regarding information which they may acquire concerning the wounded and sick under their care shall, subject to national law, be respected.
4. Subject to national law, no person engaged in medical activities may be penalized in any way for refusing or failing to give information concerning the wounded and sick who are, or who have been, under his care.

Art. 11. Protection of medical units and transports

1. Medical units and transports shall be respected and protected at all times and shall not be the object of attack.
2. The protection to which medical units and transports are entitled shall not cease unless they are used to commit hostile acts, outside their humanitarian function. Protection may, however, cease only after a warning has been given, setting, whenever appropriate, a reasonable time-limit, and after such warning has remained unheeded.

Art. 12. The distinctive emblem

Under the direction of the competent authority concerned, the distinctive emblem of the red cross, red crescent or red lion and sun on a white ground shall be displayed by medical and religious personnel and medical units, and on medical transports. It shall be respected in all circumstances. It shall not be used improperly.

PART IV. CIVILIAN POPULATION

ART. 13. Protection of the civilian population

1. The civilian population and individual civilians shall enjoy general protection against the dangers arising from military operations. To give effect to this protection, the following rules shall be observed in all circumstances.
2. The civilian population as such, as well as individual civilians, shall not be the object of attack. Acts or threats of violence the primary purpose of which is to spread terror among the civilian population are prohibited.
3. Civilians shall enjoy the protection afforded by this part, unless and for such time as they take a direct part in hostilities.

ART. 14. Protection of objects indispensable to the survival of the civilian population

Starvation of civilians as a method of combat is prohibited. It is therefore prohibited to attack, destroy, remove or render useless for that purpose, objects indispensable to the survival of the civilian population such as food-stuffs, agricultural areas for the production of food-stuffs, crops, livestock, drinking water installations and supplies and irrigation works.

ART. 15. Protection of works and installations containing dangerous forces

Works or installations containing dangerous forces, namely dams, dykes and nuclear electrical generating stations, shall not be made the object of attack, even where these objects are military objectives, if such attack may cause the release of dangerous forces and consequent severe losses among the civilian population.

ART. 16. Protection of cultural objects and of places of worship

Without prejudice to the provisions of the Hague Convention for the Protection of Cultural Property in the Event of Armed Conflict of 14 May 1954, it is prohibited to commit any acts of hostility directed against historic monuments, works of art or places of worship which constitute the cultural or spiritual heritage of peoples, and to use them in support of the military effort.

Art. 17. Prohibition of forced movement of civilians

1. The displacement of the civilian population shall not be ordered for reasons related to the conflict unless the security of the civilians involved or imperative military reasons so demand. Should such displacements have to be carried out, all possible measures shall be taken in order that the civilian population may be received under satisfactory conditions of shelter, hygiene, health, safety and nutrition.
2. Civilians shall not be compelled to leave their own territory for reasons connected with the conflict.

Art. 18. Relief societies and relief actions

1. Relief societies located in the territory of the High Contracting Party, such as Red Cross (Red Crescent, Red Lion and Sun) organizations may offer their services for the performance of their traditional functions in relation to the victims of the armed conflict. The civilian population may, even on its own initiative, offer to collect and care for the wounded, sick and shipwrecked.
2. If the civilian population is suffering undue hardship owing to a lack of the supplies essential for its survival, such as food-stuffs and medical supplies, relief actions for the civilian population which are of an exclusively humanitarian and impartial nature and which are conducted without any adverse distinction shall be undertaken subject to the consent of the High Contracting Party concerned.

Part V. Final Provisions

Art. 19. Dissemination

This Protocol shall be disseminated as widely as possible.

Art. 20. Signature

This Protocol shall be open for signature by the Parties to the Conventions six months after the signing of the Final Act and will remain open for a period of twelve months.

Art. 21. Ratification

This Protocol shall be ratified as soon as possible. The instruments of ratification shall be deposited with the Swiss Federal Council, depositary of the Conventions.

Art. 22. Accession

This Protocol shall be open for accession by any Party to the Conventions which has not signed it. The instruments of accession shall be deposited with the depositary.

Art. 23. Entry into force

1. This Protocol shall enter into force six months after two instruments of ratification or accession have been deposited.
2. For each Party to the Conventions thereafter ratifying or acceding to this Protocol, it shall enter into force six months after the deposit by such Party of its instrument of ratification or accession.

Art. 24. Amendment

1. Any High Contracting Party may propose amendments to this Protocol. The text of any proposed amendment shall be communicated to the depositary which shall decide, after consultation with all the High Contracting Parties and the International Committee of the Red Cross, whether a conference should be convened to consider the proposed amendment.
2. The depositary shall invite to that conference all the High Contracting Parties as well as the Parties to the Conventions, whether or not they are signatories of this Protocol.

Art. 25. Denunciation

1. In case a High Contracting Party should denounce this Protocol, the denunciation shall only take effect six months after receipt of the instrument of denunciation. If, however, on the expiry of six months, the denouncing Party is engaged in the situation referred to in Article 1, the denunciation shall not take effect before the end of the armed conflict. Persons who have been deprived of liberty, or whose liberty has been restricted, for reasons related to the conflict shall nevertheless continue to benefit from the provisions of this Protocol until their final release.
2. The denunciation shall be notified in writing to the depositary, which shall transmit it to all the High Contracting Parties.

Art. 26. Notifications

The depositary shall inform the High Contracting Parties as well as the Parties to the Conventions, whether or not they are signatories of this Protocol, of:

- **a.** signatures affixed to this Protocol and the deposit of instruments of ratification and accession under Articles 21 and 22;
- **b.** the date of entry into force of this Protocol under Article 23; and
- **c.** communications and declarations received under Article 24.

Art. 27. Registration

1. After its entry into force, this Protocol shall be transmitted by the depositary to the Secretariat of the United Nations for registration and publication, in accordance with Article 102 of the Charter of the United Nations.
2. The depositary shall also inform the Secretariat of the United Nations of all ratifications, accessions and denunciations received by it with respect to this Protocol.

Art. 28. Authentic texts

The original of this Protocol, of which the Arabic, Chinese, English, French, Russian and Spanish texts are equally authentic, shall be deposited with the depositary, which shall transmit certified true copies thereof to all the Parties to the Conventions.

appendix VII

TORTURE VICTIM PROTECTION ACT

Torture Victim Protection Act of 1991

(Enrolled as Agreed to or Passed by Both House and Senate)

H.R.2092

One Hundred Second Congress of the United States of America
AT THE SECOND SESSION

Begun and held at the City of Washington on Friday, the third day of January, one thousand nine hundred and ninety-two

AN ACT

To carry out obligations of the United States under the United Nations Charter and other international agreements pertaining to the protection of human rights by establishing a civil action for recovery of damages from an individual who engages in torture or extrajudicial killing.

Be it enacted by the Senate and House of Representatives of the United States of America in Congress assembled,

SECTION 1. SHORT TITLE

This Act may be cited as the 'Torture Victim Protection Act of 1991'.

SECTION 2. ESTABLISHMENT OF CIVIL ACTION

a. Liability—An individual who, under actual or apparent authority, or color of law, of any foreign nation—

  1. subjects an individual to torture shall, in a civil action, be liable for damages to that individual; or

  2. subjects an individual to extrajudicial killing shall, in a civil action, be liable for damages to the individual's legal representative, or to any person who may be a claimant in an action for wrongful death.

b. Exhaustion of Remedies—A court shall decline to hear a claim under this section if the claimant has not exhausted adequate and available remedies in the place in which the conduct giving rise to the claim occurred.

c. Statute of Limitations—No action shall be maintained under this section unless it is commenced within 10 years after the cause of action arose.

SECTION 3. DEFINITIONS

a. Extrajudicial Killing—For the purposes of this Act, the term `extrajudicial killing' means a deliberated killing not authorized by a previous judgment pronounced by a regularly constituted court affording all the judicial guarantees which are recognized as indispensable by civilized peoples. Such term, however, does not include any such killing that, under international law, is lawfully carried out under the authority of a foreign nation.

b. Torture—For the purposes of this Act—

  1. the term 'torture' means any act, directed against an individual in the offender's custody or physical control, by which severe pain or suffering (other than pain or suffering arising only from or inherent in, or incidental to, lawful sanctions), whether physical or mental, is intentionally inflicted on that individual for such purposes as obtaining from that individual or a third person information or a confession, punishing that individual for an act that individual or a third person has committed or is suspected of having committed, intimidating or coercing that individual or a third person, or for any reason based on discrimination of any kind; and

2. mental pain or suffering refers to prolonged mental harm caused by or resulting from—
   A. the intentional infliction or threatened infliction of severe physical pain or suffering;
   B. the administration or application, or threatened administration or application, of mind altering substances or other procedures calculated to disrupt profoundly the senses or the personality;
   C. the threat of imminent death; or
   D. the threat that another individual will imminently be subjected to death, severe physical pain or suffering, or the administration or application of mind altering substances or other procedures calculated to disrupt profoundly the senses or personality.

Speaker of the House of Representatives.
Vice President of the United States and
President of the Senate.

appendix VIII

WAR CRIMES ACT OF 1996 (AS AMENDED)

18 U.S.C. § 2441. War Crimes

a. Offense.—Whoever, whether inside or outside the United States, commits a war crime, in any of the circumstances described in subsection (b), shall be fined under this title or imprisoned for life or any term of years, or both, and if death results to the victim, shall also be subject to the penalty of death.
b. Circumstances.—The circumstances referred to in subsection (a) are that the person committing such breach or the victim of such war crime is a member of the Armed Forces of the United States or a national of the United State (as defined in section 101 of the Immigration and Nationality Act).
c. Definition.—As used in this section the term 'war crime' means any conduct—
    1. defined as a grave breach in any of the international conventions signed at Geneva 12 August 1949, or any protocol to such convention to which the United States is a party;
    2. prohibited by Article 23, 25, 27, or 28 of the Annex to the Hague Convention IV, Respecting the Laws and Customs of War on Land, signed 18 October 1907;
    3. which constitutes a violation of common Article 3 of the international conventions signed at Geneva, 12 August 1949, or any protocol to such

convention to which the United States is a party and which deals with non-international armed conflict; or

4. of a person who, in relation to an armed conflict and contrary to the provisions of the Protocol on Prohibitions or Restrictions on the Use of Mines, Booby-Traps and Other Devices as amended at Geneva on 3 May 1996 (Protocol II as amended on 3 May 1996), when the United States is a party to such Protocol, willfully kills or causes serious injury to civilians.

appendix IX

UNITED STATES NATIONAL SECURITY STRATEGY, 2002

INTRODUCTION

The great struggles of the twentieth century between liberty and totalitarianism ended with a decisive victory for the forces of freedom—and a single sustainable model for national success: freedom, democracy, and free enterprise. In the twenty-first century, only nations that share a commitment to protecting basic human rights and guaranteeing political and economic freedom will be able to unleash the potential of their people and assure their future prosperity. People everywhere want to say what they think; choose who will govern them; worship as they please; educate their children—male and female; own property; and enjoy the benefits of their labor. These values of freedom are right and true for every person, in every society—and the duty of protecting these values against their enemies is the common calling of freedom-loving people across the globe and across the ages.

Today, the United States enjoys a position of unparalleled military strength and great economic and political influence. In keeping with our heritage and principles, we do not use our strength to press for unilateral advantage. We seek instead to create a balance of power that favors human freedom: conditions in which all nations and all societies can choose for themselves the rewards and challenges of political and economic liberty. By making the world safer, we allow the people of the world to make their own lives better. We will defend this just peace against threats from terrorists and tyrants. We will preserve the peace by building good relations among the great powers. We will extend the peace by encouraging free and open societies on every continent.

Defending our Nation against its enemies is the first and fundamental commitment of the Federal Government. Today, that task has changed dramatically. Enemies in the past needed great armies and great industrial capabilities to endanger America. Now, shadowy networks of individuals can bring great chaos and suffering to our shores for less than it costs to purchase a single tank. Terrorists are organized to penetrate open societies and to turn the power of modern technologies against us.

To defeat this threat we must make use of every tool in our arsenal—from better homeland defenses and law enforcement to intelligence and cutting off terrorist financing. The war against terrorists of global reach is a global enterprise of uncertain duration. America will help nations that need our assistance in combating terror. And America will hold to account nations that are compromised by terror—because the allies of terror are the enemies of civilization. The United States and countries cooperating with us must not allow the terrorists to develop new home bases. Together, we will seek to deny them sanctuary at every turn.

The gravest danger our Nation faces lies at the crossroads of radicalism and technology. Our enemies have openly declared that they are seeking weapons of mass destruction, and evidence indicates that they are doing so with determination. The United States will not allow these efforts to succeed. We will build defenses against ballistic missiles and other means of delivery. We will cooperate with other nations to deny, contain, and curtail our enemies' efforts to acquire dangerous technologies. And, as a matter of common sense and self-defense, America will act against such emerging threats before they are fully formed. We cannot defend America and our friends by hoping for the best. So we must be prepared to defeat our enemies' plans, using the best intelligence and proceeding with deliberation. History will judge harshly those who saw this coming danger but failed to act. In the new world we have entered, the only path to safety is the path of action.

As we defend the peace, we will also take advantage of an historic opportunity to preserve the peace. Today, the international community has the best chance since the rise of the nation-state in the seventeenth century to build a world where great powers compete in peace instead of continually prepare for war. Today, the world's great powers find ourselves on the same side—united by common dangers of terrorist violence and chaos. The United States will build on these common interests to promote global security. We are also increasingly united by common values. Russia is in the midst of a hopeful transition, reaching for its democratic future and a partner in the war on terror. Chinese leaders are discovering that economic freedom is the only source of national wealth. In time, they will find that social and political freedom is the only source of national greatness. America will encourage the advancement of democracy and economic openness in both nations, because these are the best foundations for domestic stability and international order. We will strongly resist aggression from other great powers—even as we welcome their peaceful pursuit of prosperity, trade, and cultural advancement.

Finally, the United States will use this moment of opportunity to extend the benefits of freedom across the globe. We will actively work to bring the hope of democracy, development, free markets, and free trade to every corner of the world. The events of September 11, 2001, taught us that weak states, like Afghanistan, can pose as great a danger to our national interests as strong states. Poverty does not make poor people into terrorists and murderers. Yet poverty, weak institutions, and corruption can make weak states vulnerable to terrorist networks and drug cartels within their borders.

The United States will stand beside any nation determined to build a better future by seeking the rewards of liberty for its people. Free trade and free markets have proven their ability to lift whole societies out of poverty—so the United States will work with individual nations, entire regions, and the entire global trading community to build a world that trades in freedom and therefore grows in prosperity. The United States will deliver greater development assistance through the New Millennium Challenge Account to nations that govern justly, invest in their people, and encourage economic freedom. We will also continue to lead the world in efforts to reduce the terrible toll of AIDS and other infectious diseases.

In building a balance of power that favors freedom, the United States is guided by the conviction that all nations have important responsibilities. Nations that enjoy freedom must actively fight terror. Nations that depend on international stability must help prevent the spread of weapons of mass destruction. Nations that seek international aid must govern themselves wisely, so that aid is well spent. For freedom to thrive, accountability must be expected and required.

We are also guided by the conviction that no nation can build a safer, better world alone. Alliances and multilateral institutions can multiply the strength of freedom-loving nations. The United States is committed to lasting institutions like the United Nations, the World Trade Organization, the Organization of American States, and NATO as well as other long-standing alliances. Coalitions of the willing can augment these permanent institutions. In all cases, international obligations are to be taken seriously. They are not to be undertaken symbolically to rally support for an ideal without furthering its attainment.

Freedom is the non-negotiable demand of human dignity; the birthright of every person—in every civilization. Throughout history, freedom has been threatened by war and terror; it has been challenged by the clashing wills of powerful states and the evil designs of tyrants; and it has been tested by widespread poverty and disease. Today, humanity holds in its hands the opportunity to further freedom's triumph over all these foes. The United States welcomes our responsibility to lead in this great mission.

I. Overview of America's International Strategy

> "Our Nation's cause has always been larger than our Nation's defense. We fight, as we always fight, for a just peace—a peace that favors liberty. We will defend the peace against the threats from terrorists and tyrants. We will preserve the peace by building good relations among the great powers. And we will extend the peace by encouraging free and open societies on every continent."
>
> President Bush
> West Point, New York
> June 1, 2002

The United States possesses unprecedented—and unequaled—strength and influence in the world. Sustained by faith in the principles of liberty, and the value of a free society, this position comes with unparalleled responsibilities, obligations, and opportunity. The great strength of this nation must be used to promote a balance of power that favors freedom.

For most of the twentieth century, the world was divided by a great struggle over ideas: destructive totalitarian visions versus freedom and equality.

That great struggle is over. The militant visions of class, nation, and race which promised utopia and delivered misery have been defeated and discredited. America is now threatened less by conquering states than we are by failing ones. We are menaced less by fleets and armies than by catastrophic technologies in the hands of the embittered few. We must defeat these threats to our Nation, allies, and friends.

This is also a time of opportunity for America. We will work to translate this moment of influence into decades of peace, prosperity, and liberty. The U.S. national security strategy will be based on a distinctly American internationalism that reflects the union of our values and our national interests. The aim of this strategy is to help make the world not just safer but better. Our goals on the path to progress are clear: political and economic freedom, peaceful relations with other states, and respect for human dignity.

And this path is not America's alone. It is open to all.

To achieve these goals, the United States will:

- ✦ champion aspirations for human dignity;
- ✦ strengthen alliances to defeat global terrorism and work to prevent attacks against us and our friends;
- ✦ work with others to defuse regional conflicts;
- ✦ prevent our enemies from threatening us, our allies, and our friends, with weapons of mass destruction;
- ✦ ignite a new era of global economic growth through free markets and free trade;
- ✦ expand the circle of development by opening societies and building the infrastructure of democracy;
- ✦ develop agendas for cooperative action with other main centers of global power; and
- ✦ transform America's national security institutions to meet the challenges and opportunities of the twenty-first century.

II. Champion Aspirations for Human Dignity

> "Some worry that it is somehow undiplomatic or impolite to speak the language of right and wrong. I disagree. Different circumstances require different methods, but not different moralities."
>
> President Bush
> West Point, New York
> June 1, 2002

In pursuit of our goals, our first imperative is to clarify what we stand for: the United States must defend liberty and justice because these principles are right and true for all people everywhere. No nation owns these aspirations, and no nation is exempt from them. Fathers and mothers in all societies want their children to be educated and to live free from poverty and violence. No people on earth yearn to be oppressed, aspire to servitude, or eagerly await the midnight knock of the secret police.

America must stand firmly for the nonnegotiable demands of human dignity: the rule of law; limits on the absolute power of the state; free speech; freedom of worship; equal justice; respect for women; religious and ethnic tolerance; and respect for private property.

These demands can be met in many ways. America's constitution has served us well. Many other nations, with different histories and cultures, facing different circumstances, have successfully incorporated these core principles into their own systems of governance. History has not been kind to those nations which ignored or flouted the rights and aspirations of their people.

Our own history is a long struggle to live up to our ideals. But even in our worst moments, the principles enshrined in the Declaration of Independence were there to guide us. As a result, America is not just a stronger, but is a freer and more just society.

Today, these ideals are a lifeline to lonely defenders of liberty. And when openings arrive, we can encourage change—as we did in central and eastern Europe between 1989 and 1991, or in Belgrade in 2000. When we see democratic processes take hold among our friends in Taiwan or in the Republic of Korea, and see elected leaders replace generals in Latin America and Africa, we see examples of how authoritarian systems can evolve, marrying local history and traditions with the principles we all cherish.

Embodying lessons from our past and using the opportunity we have today, the national security strategy of the United States must start from these core beliefs and look outward for possibilities to expand liberty.

Our principles will guide our government's decisions about international cooperation, the character of our foreign assistance, and the allocation of resources. They will guide our actions and our words in international bodies.

We will:

- speak out honestly about violations of the nonnegotiable demands of human dignity using our voice and vote in international institutions to advance freedom;

- use our foreign aid to promote freedom and support those who struggle non-violently for it, ensuring that nations moving toward democracy are rewarded for the steps they take;

- make freedom and the development of democratic institutions key themes in our bilateral relations, seeking solidarity and cooperation from other democracies while we press governments that deny human rights to move toward a better future; and
- take special efforts to promote freedom of religion and conscience and defend it from encroachment by repressive governments.

We will champion the cause of human dignity and oppose those who resist it.

III. Strengthen Alliances to Defeat Global Terrorism and Work to Prevent Attacks Against Us and Our Friends

> "Just three days removed from these events, Americans do not yet have the distance of history. But our responsibility to history is already clear: to answer these attacks and rid the world of evil. War has been waged against us by stealth and deceit and murder. This nation is peaceful, but fierce when stirred to anger. The conflict was begun on the timing and terms of others. It will end in a way, and at an hour, of our choosing."
>
> President Bush
> Washington, D.C. (The National Cathedral)
> September 14, 2001

The United States of America is fighting a war against terrorists of global reach. The enemy is not a single political regime or person or religion or ideology. The enemy is terrorism—premeditated, politically motivated violence perpetrated against innocents.

In many regions, legitimate grievances prevent the emergence of a lasting peace. Such grievances deserve to be, and must be, addressed within a political process. But no cause justifies terror. The United States will make no concessions to terrorist demands and strike no deals with them. We make no distinction between terrorists and those who knowingly harbor or provide aid to them.

The struggle against global terrorism is different from any other war in our history. It will be fought on many fronts against a particularly elusive enemy over an extended period of time. Progress will come through the persistent accumulation of successes—some seen, some unseen.

Today our enemies have seen the results of what civilized nations can, and will, do against regimes that harbor, support, and use terrorism to achieve their political goals. Afghanistan has been liberated; coalition forces continue to hunt down the Taliban and al-Qaida. But it is not only this battlefield on which we will engage terrorists. Thousands of trained terrorists remain at large with cells in North America, South America, Europe, Africa, the Middle East, and across Asia.

Our priority will be first to disrupt and destroy terrorist organizations of global reach and attack their leadership; command, control, and communications; material support; and finances. This will have a disabling effect upon the terrorists' ability to plan and operate.

We will continue to encourage our regional partners to take up a coordinated effort that isolates the terrorists. Once the regional campaign localizes the threat to a particular state, we will help ensure the state has the military, law enforcement, political, and financial tools necessary to finish the task.

The United States will continue to work with our allies to disrupt the financing of terrorism. We will identify and block the sources of funding for terrorism, freeze the assets of terrorists and those who support them, deny terrorists access to the international financial system, protect legitimate charities from being abused by terrorists, and prevent the movement of terrorists' assets through alternative financial networks.

However, this campaign need not be sequential to be effective, the cumulative effect across all regions will help achieve the results we seek.

We will disrupt and destroy terrorist organizations by:

- direct and continuous action using all the elements of national and international power. Our immediate focus will be those terrorist organizations of global reach and any terrorist or state sponsor of terrorism which attempts to gain or use weapons of mass destruction (WMD) or their precursors;
- defending the United States, the American people, and our interests at home and abroad by identifying and destroying the threat before it reaches our borders. While the United States will constantly strive to enlist the support of the international community, we will not hesitate to act alone, if necessary, to exercise our right of self-defense by acting preemptively against such terrorists, to prevent them from doing harm against our people and our country; and
- denying further sponsorship, support, and sanctuary to terrorists by convincing or compelling states to accept their sovereign responsibilities.

We will also wage a war of ideas to win the battle against international terrorism. This includes:

- using the full influence of the United States, and working closely with allies and friends, to make clear that all acts of terrorism are illegitimate so that terrorism will be viewed in the same light as slavery, piracy, or genocide: behavior that no respectable government can condone or support and all must oppose;
- supporting moderate and modern government, especially in the Muslim world, to ensure that the conditions and ideologies that promote terrorism do not find fertile ground in any nation;
- diminishing the underlying conditions that spawn terrorism by enlisting the international community to focus its efforts and resources on areas most at risk; and
- using effective public diplomacy to promote the free flow of information and ideas to kindle the hopes and aspirations of freedom of those in societies ruled by the sponsors of global terrorism.

While we recognize that our best defense is a good offense we are also strengthening America's homeland security to protect against and deter attack.

This Administration has proposed the largest government reorganization since the Truman Administration created the National Security Council and the Department of Defense. Centered on a new Department of Homeland Security and including a new unified military command and a fundamental reordering of the FBI, our comprehensive plan to secure the homeland encompasses every level of government and the cooperation of the public and the private sector.

This strategy will turn adversity into opportunity. For example, emergency management systems will be better able to cope not just with terrorism but with all hazards. Our medical system will be strengthened to manage not just bioterror, but all infectious diseases and mass-casualty dangers. Our border controls will not just stop terrorists, but improve the efficient movement of legitimate traffic.

While our focus is protecting America, we know that to defeat terrorism in today's globalized world we need support from our allies and friends. Wherever possible, the United States will rely on regional organizations and state powers to meet their obligations to fight terrorism. Where governments find the fight against terrorism beyond their capacities, we will match their willpower and their resources with whatever help we and our allies can provide.

As we pursue the terrorists in Afghanistan, we will continue to work with international organizations such as the United Nations, as well as non-governmental organizations, and other countries to provide the humanitarian, political, economic, and security assistance necessary to rebuild Afghanistan so that it will never again abuse its people, threaten its neighbors, and provide a haven for terrorists

In the war against global terrorism, we will never forget that we are ultimately fighting for our democratic values and way of life. Freedom and fear are at war, and there will be no quick or easy end to this conflict. In leading the campaign against terrorism, we are forging new, productive international relationships and redefining existing ones in ways that meet the challenges of the twenty-first century.

IV. Work with Others to Defuse Regional Conflicts

> "We build a world of justice, or we will live in a world of coercion. The magnitude of our shared responsibilities makes our disagreements look so small."
>
> President Bush
> Berlin, Germany
> May 23, 2002

Concerned nations must remain actively engaged in critical regional disputes to avoid explosive escalation and minimize human suffering. In an increasingly interconnected world, regional crisis can strain our alliances, rekindle rivalries among the major powers, and create horrifying affronts to human dignity. When violence erupts and states falter, the United States will work with friends and partners to alleviate suffering and restore stability.

No doctrine can anticipate every circumstance in which U.S. action—direct or indirect—is warranted. We have finite political, economic, and military resources to meet our global priorities. The United States will approach each case with these strategic principles in mind:

- ✦ The United States should invest time and resources into building international relationships and institutions that can help manage local crises when they emerge.

- ✦ The United States should be realistic about its ability to help those who are unwilling or unready to help themselves. Where and when people are ready to do their part, we will be willing to move decisively.

Policies in several key regions offer some illustrations of how we will apply these principles:

The Israeli-Palestinian conflict is critical because of the toll of human suffering, because of America's close relationship with the state of Israel and key Arab states, and because of that region's importance to other global priorities of the United States. There can be no peace for either side without freedom for both sides. America stands committed to an independent and democratic Palestine, living beside Israel in peace and security. Like all other people, Palestinians deserve a government that serves their interests, and listens to their voices, and counts their votes. The United States will continue to encourage all parties to step up to their responsibilities as we seek a just and comprehensive settlement to the conflict.

The United States, the international donor community, and the World Bank stand ready to work with a reformed Palestinian government on economic development, increased humanitarian assistance and a program to establish, finance, and monitor a truly independent judiciary. If Palestinians embrace democracy, and the rule of law, confront corruption, and firmly reject terror, they can count on American support for the creation of a Palestinian state.

Israel also has a large stake in the success of a democratic Palestine. Permanent occupation threatens Israel's identity and democracy. So the United States continues to challenge Israeli leaders to take concrete steps to support the emergence of a viable, credible Palestinian state. As there is progress towards security, Israel forces need to withdraw fully to positions they held prior to September 28, 2000. And consistent with the recommendations of the Mitchell Committee, Israeli settlement activity in the occupied territories must stop. As violence subsides, freedom of movement should be restored, permitting innocent Palestinians to resume work and normal life. The United States can play a crucial role but, ultimately, lasting peace can only come when Israelis and Palestinians resolve the issues and end the conflict between them.

In South Asia, the United States has also emphasized the need for India and Pakistan to resolve their disputes. This administration invested time and resources building strong bilateral relations with India and Pakistan. These strong relations then gave us leverage to play a constructive role when tensions in the region became acute. With Pakistan, our bilateral relations have been bolstered by Pakistan's choice to join the war against terror and move toward building a more open and tolerant society. The Administration sees India's potential to become one of the great democratic powers of the twenty-first century and has worked hard to transform our relationship accordingly. Our involvement in this regional dispute, building on earlier investments in bilateral relations, looks first to concrete steps by India and Pakistan that can help defuse military confrontation.

Indonesia took courageous steps to create a working democracy and respect for the rule of law. By tolerating ethnic minorities, respecting the rule of law, and accepting open markets, Indonesia may be able to employ the engine of opportunity that has helped lift some of its neighbors out of poverty and desperation. It is the initiative by Indonesia that allows U.S. assistance to make a difference.

In the Western Hemisphere we have formed flexible coalitions with countries that share our priorities, particularly Mexico, Brazil, Canada, Chile, and Colombia. Together we will promote a truly democratic hemisphere where our integration advances security, prosperity, opportunity, and hope. We will work with regional institutions, such as the Summit of the Americas process, the Organization of American States (OAS), and the Defense Ministerial of the Americas for the benefit of the entire hemisphere.

Parts of Latin America confront regional conflict, especially arising from the violence of drug cartels and their accomplices. This conflict and unrestrained narcotics trafficking could imperil the health and security of the United States. Therefore we have developed an active strategy to help the Andean nations adjust their economies, enforce their laws, defeat terrorist organizations, and cut off the supply of drugs, while—as important—we work to reduce the demand for drugs in our own country.

In Colombia, we recognize the link between terrorist and extremist groups that challenge the security of the state and drug trafficking activities that help finance the operations of such groups. We are working to help Colombia defend its democratic institutions and defeat illegal armed groups of both the left and right by extending effective sovereignty over the entire national territory and provide basic security to the Colombian people.

In Africa, promise and opportunity sit side by side with disease, war, and desperate poverty. This threatens both a core value of the United States—preserving human dignity—and our strategic priority—combating global terror. American interests and American principles, therefore, lead in the same direction: we will work with others for an African continent that lives in liberty, peace, and growing prosperity. Together with our European allies, we must help strengthen Africa's fragile states, help build indigenous capability to secure porous borders, and help build up the law enforcement and intelligence infrastructure to deny havens for terrorists.

An ever more lethal environment exists in Africa as local civil wars spread beyond borders to create regional war zones. Forming coalitions of the willing and cooperative security arrangements are key to confronting these emerging transnational threats.

Africa's great size and diversity requires a security strategy that focuses bilateral engagement, and builds coalitions of the willing. This administration will focus on three interlocking strategies for the region:

- ✦ countries with major impact on their neighborhood such as South Africa, Nigeria, Kenya, and Ethiopia are anchors for regional engagement and require focused attention;
- ✦ coordination with European allies and international institutions is essential for constructive conflict mediation and successful peace operations; and
- ✦ Africa's capable reforming states and sub-regional organizations must be strengthened as the primary means to address transnational threats on a sustained basis.

Ultimately the path of political and economic freedom presents the surest route to progress in sub-Saharan Africa, where most wars are conflicts over material resources and political access often tragically waged on the basis of ethnic and religious difference. The transition to the African Union with its stated commitment to good governance and a common responsibility for democratic political systems offers opportunities to strengthen democracy on the continent.

V. Prevent Our Enemies from Threatening Us, Our Allies, and Our Friends with Weapons of Mass Destruction

> "The gravest danger to freedom lies at the crossroads of radicalism and technology. When the spread of chemical and biological and nuclear weapons, along with ballistic missile technology—when that occurs, even weak states and small groups could attain a catastrophic power to strike great nations. Our enemies have declared this very intention, and have been caught seeking these terrible weapons. They want the capability to blackmail us, or to harm us, or to harm our friends—and we will oppose them with all our power."
>
> President Bush
West Point, New York
June 1, 2002

The nature of the Cold War threat required the United States—with our allies and friends—to emphasize deterrence of the enemy's use of force, producing a grim strategy of mutual assured destruction. With the collapse of the Soviet

Union and the end of the Cold War, our security environment has undergone profound transformation.

Having moved from confrontation to cooperation as the hallmark of our relationship with Russia, the dividends are evident: an end to the balance of terror that divided us; an historic reduction in the nuclear arsenals on both sides; and cooperation in areas such as counterterrorism and missile defense that until recently were inconceivable.

But new deadly challenges have emerged from rogue states and terrorists. None of these contemporary threats rival the sheer destructive power that was arrayed against us by the Soviet Union. However, the nature and motivations of these new adversaries, their determination to obtain destructive powers hitherto available only to the world's strongest states, and the greater likelihood that they will use weapons of mass destruction against us, make today's security environment more complex and dangerous.

In the 1990s we witnessed the emergence of a small number of rogue states that, while different in important ways, share a number of attributes. These states:

- brutalize their own people and squander their national resources for the personal gain of the rulers;
- display no regard for international law, threaten their neighbors, and callously violate international treaties to which they are party;
- are determined to acquire weapons of mass destruction, along with other advanced military technology, to be used as threats or offensively to achieve the aggressive designs of these regimes;
- sponsor terrorism around the globe; and
- reject basic human values and hate the United States and everything for which it stands.

At the time of the Gulf War, we acquired irrefutable proof that Iraq's designs were not limited to the chemical weapons it had used against Iran and its own people, but also extended to the acquisition of nuclear weapons and biological agents. In the past decade North Korea has become the world's principal purveyor of ballistic missiles, and has tested increasingly capable missiles while developing its own WMD arsenal. Other rogue regimes seek nuclear, biological, and chemical weapons as well. These states' pursuit of, and global trade in, such weapons has become a looming threat to all nations.

We must be prepared to stop rogue states and their terrorist clients before they are able to threaten or use weapons of mass destruction against the United States and our allies and friends. Our response must take full advantage of strengthened alliances, the establishment of new partnerships with former adversaries, innovation in the use of military forces, modern technologies, including the development of an effective missile defense system, and increased emphasis on intelligence collection and analysis.

Our comprehensive strategy to combat WMD includes:

- ✦ Proactive counterproliferation efforts. We must deter and defend against the threat before it is unleashed. We must ensure that key capabilities—detection, active and passive defenses, and counterforce capabilities—are integrated into our defense transformation and our homeland security systems. Counterproliferation must also be integrated into the doctrine, training, and equipping of our forces and those of our allies to ensure that we can prevail in any conflict with WMD-armed adversaries.

- ✦ Strengthened nonproliferation efforts to prevent rogue states and terrorists from acquiring the materials, technologies and expertise necessary for weapons of mass destruction. We will enhance diplomacy, arms control, multilateral export controls, and threat reduction assistance that impede states and terrorists seeking WMD, and when necessary, interdict enabling technologies and materials. We will continue to build coalitions to support these efforts, encouraging their increased political and financial support for nonproliferation and threat reduction programs. The recent G-8 agreement to commit up to $20 billion to a global partnership against proliferation marks a major step forward.

- ✦ Effective consequence management to respond to the effects of WMD use, whether by terrorists or hostile states. Minimizing the effects of WMD use against our people will help deter those who possess such weapons and dissuade those who seek to acquire them by persuading enemies that they cannot attain their desired ends. The United States must also be prepared to respond to the effects of WMD use against our forces abroad, and to help friends and allies if they are attacked.

It has taken almost a decade for us to comprehend the true nature of this new threat. Given the goals of rogue states and terrorists, the United States can no longer solely rely on a reactive posture as we have in the past. The inability to deter a potential attacker, the immediacy of today's threats, and the magnitude of potential harm that could be caused by our adversaries' choice of weapons, do not permit that option. We cannot let our enemies strike first.

- In the Cold War, especially following the Cuban missile crisis, we faced a generally status quo, risk-averse adversary. Deterrence was an effective defense. But deterrence based only upon the threat of retaliation is far less likely to work against leaders of rogue states more willing to take risks, gambling with the lives of their people, and the wealth of their nations.
- In the Cold War, weapons of mass destruction were considered weapons of last resort whose use risked the destruction of those who used them. Today, our enemies see weapons of mass destruction as weapons of choice. For rogue states these weapons are tools of intimidation and military aggression against their neighbors. These weapons may also allow these states to attempt to blackmail the United States and our allies to prevent us from deterring or repelling the aggressive behavior of rogue states. Such states also see these weapons as their best means of overcoming the conventional superiority of the United States.
- Traditional concepts of deterrence will not work against a terrorist enemy whose avowed tactics are wanton destruction and the targeting of innocents; whose so-called soldiers seek martyrdom in death and whose most potent protection is statelessness. The overlap between states that sponsor terror and those that pursue WMD compels us to action.

For centuries, international law recognized that nations need not suffer an attack before they can lawfully take action to defend themselves against forces that present an imminent danger of attack. Legal scholars and international jurists often conditioned the legitimacy of preemption on the existence of an imminent threat—most often a visible mobilization of armies, navies, and air forces preparing to attack.

We must adapt the concept of imminent threat to the capabilities and objectives of today's adversaries. Rogue states and terrorists do not seek to attack us using conventional means. They know such attacks would fail. Instead, they rely on acts of terrorism and, potentially, the use of weapons of mass destruction—weapons that can be easily concealed and delivered covertly and without warning.

The targets of these attacks are our military forces and our civilian population, in direct violation of one of the principal norms of the law of warfare. As was demonstrated by the losses on September 11, 2001, mass civilian casualties is the specific objective of terrorists and these losses would be exponentially more severe if terrorists acquired and used weapons of mass destruction.

The United States has long maintained the option of preemptive actions to counter a sufficient threat to our national security. The greater the threat, the greater is the risk of inaction—and the more compelling the case for taking anticipatory action to defend ourselves, even if uncertainty remains as to the time and place of the enemy's attack. To forestall or prevent such hostile acts by our adversaries, the United States will, if necessary, act preemptively.

The United States will not use force in all cases to preempt emerging threats, nor should nations use preemption as a pretext for aggression. Yet in an age where the enemies of civilization openly and actively seek the world's most destructive technologies, the United States cannot remain idle while dangers gather.

We will always proceed deliberately, weighing the consequences of our actions. To support preemptive options, we will:

- build better, more integrated intelligence capabilities to provide timely, accurate information on threats, wherever they may emerge;
- coordinate closely with allies to form a common assessment of the most dangerous threats; and
- continue to transform our military forces to ensure our ability to conduct rapid and precise operations to achieve decisive results.

The purpose of our actions will always be to eliminate a specific threat to the United States or our allies and friends. The reasons for our actions will be clear, the force measured, and the cause just.

VI. Ignite a New Era of Global Economic Growth through Free Markets and Free Trade

> "When nations close their markets and opportunity is hoarded by a privileged few, no amount—no amount—of development aid is ever enough. When nations respect their people, open markets, invest in better health and education, every dollar of aid, every dollar of trade revenue and domestic capital is used more effectively."
>
> President Bush
> Monterrey, Mexico
> March 22, 2002

A strong world economy enhances our national security by advancing prosperity and freedom in the rest of the world. Economic growth supported by free trade and free markets creates new jobs and higher incomes. It allows people to lift their lives out of poverty, spurs economic and legal reform, and the fight against corruption, and it reinforces the habits of liberty.

We will promote economic growth and economic freedom beyond America's shores. All governments are responsible for creating their own economic policies and responding to their own economic challenge. We will use our economic engagement with other countries to underscore the benefits of policies that generate higher productivity and sustained economic growth, including:

- pro-growth legal and regulatory policies to encourage business investment, innovation, and entrepreneurial activity;
- tax policies—particularly lower marginal tax rates—that improve incentives for work and investment;
- rule of law and intolerance of corruption so that people are confident that they will be able to enjoy the fruits of their economic endeavors;
- strong financial systems that allow capital to be put to its most efficient use;
- sound fiscal policies to support business activity;
- investments in health and education that improve the well-being and skills of the labor force and population as a whole; and
- free trade that provides new avenues for growth and fosters the diffusion of technologies and ideas that increase productivity and opportunity.

The lessons of history are clear: market economies, not command-and-control economies with the heavy hand of government, are the best way to promote prosperity and reduce poverty. Policies that further strengthen market incentives and market institutions are relevant for all economies—industrialized countries, emerging markets, and the developing world.

A return to strong economic growth in Europe and Japan is vital to U.S. national security interests. We want our allies to have strong economies for their own sake, for the sake of the global economy, and for the sake of global security. European efforts to remove structural barriers in their economies are particularly important in this regard, as are Japan's efforts to end deflation and address the problems of non-performing loans in the Japanese banking system. We will continue to use our regular consultations with Japan and our European partners—including through the Group of Seven (G-7)—to discuss policies they are adopting to promote growth in their economies and support higher global economic growth.

Improving stability in emerging markets is also key to global economic growth. International flows of investment capital are needed to expand the productive potential of these economies. These flows allow emerging markets and developing countries to make the investments that raise living standards and reduce poverty. Our long-term objective should be a world in which all countries have investment-grade credit ratings that allow them access to international capital markets and to invest in their future.

We are committed to policies that will help emerging markets achieve access to larger capital flows at lower cost. To this end, we will continue to pursue reforms aimed at reducing uncertainty in financial markets. We will work actively with other countries, the International Monetary Fund (IMF), and the private sector to implement the G-7 Action Plan negotiated earlier this year for preventing financial crises and more effectively resolving them when they occur.

The best way to deal with financial crises is to prevent them from occurring, and we have encouraged the IMF to improve its efforts doing so. We will continue to work with the IMF to streamline the policy conditions for its lending and to focus its lending strategy on achieving economic growth through sound fiscal and monetary policy, exchange rate policy, and financial sector policy.

The concept of "free trade" arose as a moral principle even before it became a pillar of economics. If you can make something that others value, you should be able to sell it to them. If others make something that you value, you should be able to buy it. This is real freedom, the freedom for a person—or a nation—to make a living. To promote free trade, the Unites States has developed a comprehensive strategy:

- Seize the global initiative. The new global trade negotiations we helped launch at Doha in November 2001 will have an ambitious agenda, especially in agriculture, manufacturing, and services, targeted for completion in 2005. The United States has led the way in completing the accession of China and a democratic Taiwan to the World Trade Organization. We will assist Russia's preparations to join the WTO.
- Press regional initiatives. The United States and other democracies in the Western Hemisphere have agreed to create the Free Trade Area of the Americas, targeted for completion in 2005. This year the United States will advocate market-access negotiations with its partners, targeted on agriculture, industrial

goods, services, investment, and government procurement. We will also offer more opportunity to the poorest continent, Africa, starting with full use of the preferences allowed in the African Growth and Opportunity Act, and leading to free trade.

- Move ahead with bilateral free trade agreements. Building on the free trade agreement with Jordan enacted in 2001, the Administration will work this year to complete free trade agreements with Chile and Singapore. Our aim is to achieve free trade agreements with a mix of developed and developing countries in all regions of the world. Initially, Central America, Southern Africa, Morocco, and Australia will be our principal focal points.
- Renew the executive-congressional partnership. Every administration's trade strategy depends on a productive partnership with Congress. After a gap of 8 years, the Administration reestablished majority support in the Congress for trade liberalization by passing Trade Promotion Authority and the other market opening measures for developing countries in the Trade Act of 2002. This Administration will work with Congress to enact new bilateral, regional, and global trade agreements that will be concluded under the recently passed Trade Promotion Authority.
- Promote the connection between trade and development. Trade policies can help developing countries strengthen property rights, competition, the rule of law, investment, the spread of knowledge, open societies, the efficient allocation of resources, and regional integration—all leading to growth, opportunity, and confidence in developing countries. The United States is implementing The Africa Growth and Opportunity Act to provide market-access for nearly all goods produced in the 35 countries of sub-Saharan Africa. We will make more use of this act and its equivalent for the Caribbean Basin and continue to work with multilateral and regional institutions to help poorer countries take advantage of these opportunities. Beyond market access, the most important area where trade intersects with poverty is in public health. We will ensure that the WTO intellectual property rules are flexible enough to allow developing nations to gain access to critical medicines for extraordinary dangers like HIV/AIDS, tuberculosis, and malaria.
- Enforce trade agreements and laws against unfair practices. Commerce depends on the rule of law; international trade depends on enforceable agreements. Our top priorities are to resolve ongoing disputes with the European Union, Canada, and Mexico and to make a global effort to address

new technology, science, and health regulations that needlessly impede farm exports and improved agriculture. Laws against unfair trade practices are often abused, but the international community must be able to address genuine concerns about government subsidies and dumping. International industrial espionage which undermines fair competition must be detected and deterred.

- Help domestic industries and workers adjust. There is a sound statutory framework for these transitional safeguards which we have used in the agricultural sector and which we are using this year to help the American steel industry. The benefits of free trade depend upon the enforcement of fair trading practices. These safeguards help ensure that the benefits of free trade do not come at the expense of American workers. Trade adjustment assistance will help workers adapt to the change and dynamism of open markets.
- Protect the environment and workers. The United States must foster economic growth in ways that will provide a better life along with widening prosperity. We will incorporate labor and environmental concerns into U.S. trade negotiations, creating a healthy "network" between multilateral environmental agreements with the WTO, and use the International Labor Organization, trade preference programs, and trade talks to improve working conditions in conjunction with freer trade.
- Enhance energy security. We will strengthen our own energy security and the shared prosperity of the global economy by working with our allies, trading partners, and energy producers to expand the sources and types of global energy supplied, especially in the Western Hemisphere, Africa, Central Asia, and the Caspian region. We will also continue to work with our partners to develop cleaner and more energy efficient technologies.

Economic growth should be accompanied by global efforts to stabilize greenhouse gas concentrations associated with this growth, containing them at a level that prevents dangerous human interference with the global climate. Our overall objective is to reduce America's greenhouse gas emissions relative to the size of our economy, cutting such emissions per unit of economic activity by 18 percent over the next 10 years, by the year 2012. Our strategies for attaining this goal will be to:

- remain committed to the basic U.N. Framework Convention for international cooperation;

- obtain agreements with key industries to cut emissions of some of the most potent greenhouse gases and give transferable credits to companies that can show real cuts;
- develop improved standards for measuring and registering emission reductions;
- promote renewable energy production and clean coal technology, as well as nuclear power—which produces no greenhouse gas emissions, while also improving fuel economy for U.S. cars and trucks;
- increase spending on research and new conservation technologies, to a total of $4.5 billion—the largest sum being spent on climate change by any country in the world and a $700 million increase over last year's budget; and
- assist developing countries, especially the major greenhouse gas emitters such as China and India, so that they will have the tools and resources to join this effort and be able to grow along a cleaner and better path.

VII. Expand the Circle of Development by Opening Societies and Building the Infrastructure of Democracy

> "In World War II we fought to make the world safer, then worked to rebuild it. As we wage war today to keep the world safe from terror, we must also work to make the world a better place for all its citizens."
>
> President Bush
> Washington, D.C.
> (Inter-American Development Bank)
> March 14, 2002

A world where some live in comfort and plenty, while half of the human race lives on less than $2 a day, is neither just nor stable. Including all of the world's poor in an expanding circle of development—and opportunity—is a moral imperative and one of the top priorities of U.S. international policy.

Decades of massive development assistance have failed to spur economic growth in the poorest countries. Worse, development aid has often served to prop up failed policies, relieving the pressure for reform and perpetuating misery. Results of aid are typically measured in dollars spent by donors, not in the rates of growth and poverty reduction achieved by recipients. These are the indicators of a failed strategy.

Working with other nations, the United States is confronting this failure. We forged a new consensus at the U.N. Conference on Financing for Development in Monterrey that the objectives of assistance—and the strategies to achieve those objectives—must change.

This Administration's goal is to help unleash the productive potential of individuals in all nations. Sustained growth and poverty reduction is impossible without the right national policies. Where governments have implemented real policy changes we will provide significant new levels of assistance. The United States and other developed countries should set an ambitious and specific target: to double the size of the world's poorest economies within a decade.

The United States Government will pursue these major strategies to achieve this goal:

- ✦ Provide resources to aid countries that have met the challenge of national reform. We propose a 50 percent increase in the core development assistance given by the United States. While continuing our present programs, including humanitarian assistance based on need alone, these billions of new dollars will form a new Millennium Challenge Account for projects in countries whose governments rule justly, invest in their people, and encourage economic freedom. Governments must fight corruption, respect basic human rights, embrace the rule of law, invest in health care and education, follow responsible economic policies, and enable entrepreneurship. The Millennium Challenge Account will reward countries that have demonstrated real policy change and challenge those that have not to implement reforms.
- ✦ Improve the effectiveness of the World Bank and other development banks in raising living standards. The United States is committed to a comprehensive reform agenda for making the World Bank and the other multilateral development banks more effective in improving the lives of the world's poor. We have reversed the downward trend in U.S. contributions and proposed an 18 percent increase in the U.S. contributions to the International Development Association (IDA)—the World Bank's fund for the poorest countries—and the African Development Fund. The key to raising living standards and reducing poverty around the world is increasing productivity growth, especially in the poorest countries. We will continue to press the

multilateral development banks to focus on activities that increase economic productivity, such as improvements in education, health, rule of law, and private sector development. Every project, every loan, every grant must be judged by how much it will increase productivity growth in developing countries.

✦ Insist upon measurable results to ensure that development assistance is actually making a difference in the lives of the world's poor. When it comes to economic development, what really matters is that more children are getting a better education, more people have access to health care and clean water, or more workers can find jobs to make a better future for their families. We have a moral obligation to measure the success of our development assistance by whether it is delivering results. For this reason, we will continue to demand that our own development assistance as well as assistance from the multilateral development banks has measurable goals and concrete benchmarks for achieving those goals. Thanks to U.S. leadership, the recent IDA replenishment agreement will establish a monitoring and evaluation system that measures recipient countries' progress. For the first time, donors can link a portion of their contributions to IDA to the achievement of actual development results, and part of the U.S. contribution is linked in this way. We will strive to make sure that the World Bank and other multilateral development banks build on this progress so that a focus on results is an integral part of everything that these institutions do.

✦ Increase the amount of development assistance that is provided in the form of grants instead of loans. Greater use of results-based grants is the best way to help poor countries make productive investments, particularly in the social sectors, without saddling them with ever-larger debt burdens. As a result of U.S. leadership, the recent IDA agreement provided for significant increases in grant funding for the poorest countries for education, HIV/AIDS, health, nutrition, water, sanitation, and other human needs. Our goal is to build on that progress by increasing the use of grants at the other multilateral development banks. We will also challenge universities, nonprofits, and the private sector to match government efforts by using grants to support development projects that show results.

✦ Open societies to commerce and investment. Trade and investment are the real engines of economic growth. Even if government aid increases, most money for development must come from trade, domestic capital, and foreign investment. An effective strategy must try to expand these flows as well. Free markets and free trade are key priorities of our national security strategy.

✦ Secure public health. The scale of the public health crisis in poor countries is enormous. In countries afflicted by epidemics and pandemics like HIV/AIDS, malaria, and tuberculosis, growth and development will be threatened until these scourges can be contained. Resources from the developed world are necessary but will be effective only with honest governance, which supports prevention programs and provides effective local infrastructure. The United States has strongly backed the new global fund for HIV/AIDS organized by U.N. Secretary General Kofi Annan and its focus on combining prevention with a broad strategy for treatment and care. The United States already contributes more than twice as much money to such efforts as the next largest donor. If the global fund demonstrates its promise, we will be ready to give even more.

✦ Emphasize education. Literacy and learning are the foundation of democracy and development. Only about 7 percent of World Bank resources are devoted to education. This proportion should grow. The United States will increase its own funding for education assistance by at least 20 percent with an emphasis on improving basic education and teacher training in Africa. The United States can also bring information technology to these societies, many of whose education systems have been devastated by AIDS.

✦ Continue to aid agricultural development. New technologies, including biotechnology, have enormous potential to improve crop yields in developing countries while using fewer pesticides and less water. Using sound science, the United States should help bring these benefits to the 800 million people, including 300 million children, who still suffer from hunger and malnutrition.

VIII. Develop Agendas for Cooperative Action with the Other Main Centers of Global Power

"We have our best chance since the rise of the nation-state in the 17th century to build a world where the great powers compete in peace instead of prepare for war."

President Bush
West Point, New York
June 1, 2002

America will implement its strategies by organizing coalitions—as broad as practicable—of states able and willing to promote a balance of power that favors freedom. Effective coalition leadership requires clear priorities, an appreciation of others' interests, and consistent consultations among partners with a spirit of humility.

There is little of lasting consequence that the United States can accomplish in the world without the sustained cooperation of its allies and friends in Canada and Europe. Europe is also the seat of two of the strongest and most able international institutions in the world: the North Atlantic Treaty Organization (NATO), which has, since its inception, been the fulcrum of transatlantic and inter-European security, and the European Union (EU), our partner in opening world trade.

The attacks of September 11 were also an attack on NATO, as NATO itself recognized when it invoked its Article V self-defense clause for the first time. NATO's core mission—collective defense of the transatlantic alliance of democracies—remains, but NATO must develop new structures and capabilities to carry out that mission under new circumstances. NATO must build a capability to field, at short notice, highly mobile, specially trained forces whenever they are needed to respond to a threat against any member of the alliance.

The alliance must be able to act wherever our interests are threatened, creating coalitions under NATO's own mandate, as well as contributing to mission-based coalitions. To achieve this, we must:

- ✦ expand NATO's membership to those democratic nations willing and able to share the burden of defending and advancing our common interests;
- ✦ ensure that the military forces of NATO nations have appropriate combat contributions to make in coalition warfare;
- ✦ develop planning processes to enable those contributions to become effective multinational fighting forces;
- ✦ take advantage of the technological opportunities and economies of scale in our defense spending to transform NATO military forces so that they dominate potential aggressors and diminish our vulnerabilities;
- ✦ streamline and increase the flexibility of command structures to meet new operational demands and the associated requirements of training, integrating, and experimenting with new force configurations; and
- ✦ maintain the ability to work and fight together as allies even as we take the necessary steps to transform and modernize our forces.

If NATO succeeds in enacting these changes, the rewards will be a partnership as central to the security and interests of its member states as was the case during the Cold War. We will sustain a common perspective on the threats to our societies and improve our ability to take common action in defense of our nations and their interests. At the same time, we welcome our European allies' efforts to forge a greater foreign policy and defense identity with the EU, and commit ourselves to close consultations to ensure that these developments work with NATO. We cannot afford to lose this opportunity to better prepare the family of transatlantic democracies for the challenges to come.

The attacks of September 11 energized America's Asian alliances. Australia invoked the ANZUS Treaty to declare the September 11 was an attack on Australia itself, following that historic decision with the dispatch of some of the world's finest combat forces for Operation Enduring Freedom. Japan and the Republic of Korea provided unprecedented levels of military logistical support within weeks of the terrorist attack. We have deepened cooperation on counter-terrorism with our alliance partners in Thailand and the Philippines and received invaluable assistance from close friends like Singapore and New Zealand.

The war against terrorism has proven that America's alliances in Asia not only underpin regional peace and stability, but are flexible and ready to deal with new challenges. To enhance our Asian alliances and friendships, we will:

- look to Japan to continue forging a leading role in regional and global affairs based on our common interests, our common values, and our close defense and diplomatic cooperation;
- work with South Korea to maintain vigilance towards the North while preparing our alliance to make contributions to the broader stability of the region over the longer-term;
- build on 50 years of U.S.-Australian alliance cooperation as we continue working together to resolve regional and global problems—as we have so many times from the Battle of Leyte Gulf to Tora Bora;
- maintain forces in the region that reflect our commitments to our allies, our requirements, our technological advances, and the strategic environment; and
- build on stability provided by these alliances, as well as with institutions such as ASEAN and the Asia-Pacific Economic Cooperation forum, to develop a mix of regional and bilateral strategies to manage change in this dynamic region.

We are attentive to the possible renewal of old patterns of great power competition. Several potential great powers are now in the midst of internal transition—most importantly Russia, India, and China. In all three cases, recent developments have encouraged our hope that a truly global consensus about basic principles is slowly taking shape.

With Russia, we are already building a new strategic relationship based on a central reality of the twenty-first century: the United States and Russia are no longer strategic adversaries. The Moscow Treaty on Strategic Reductions is emblematic of this new reality and reflects a critical change in Russian thinking that promises to lead to productive, long-term relations with the Euro-Atlantic community and the United States. Russia's top leaders have a realistic assessment of their country's current weakness and the policies—internal and external—needed to reverse those weaknesses. They understand, increasingly, that Cold War approaches do not serve their national interests and that Russian and American strategic interests overlap in many areas.

United States policy seeks to use this turn in Russian thinking to refocus our relationship on emerging and potential common interests and challenges. We are broadening our already extensive cooperation in the global war on terrorism. We are facilitating Russia's entry into the World Trade Organization, without lowering standards for accession, to promote beneficial bilateral trade and investment relations. We have created the NATO-Russia Council with the goal of deepening security cooperation among Russia, our European allies, and ourselves. We will continue to bolster the independence and stability of the states of the former Soviet Union in the belief that a prosperous and stable neighborhood will reinforce Russia's growing commitment to integration into the Euro-Atlantic community.

At the same time, we are realistic about the differences that still divide us from Russia and about the time and effort it will take to build an enduring strategic partnership. Lingering distrust of our motives and policies by key Russian elites slows improvement in our relations. Russia's uneven commitment to the basic values of free-market democracy and dubious record in combating the proliferation of weapons of mass destruction remain matters of great concern. Russia's very weakness limits the opportunities for cooperation. Nevertheless, those opportunities are vastly greater now than in recent years—or even decades.

The United States has undertaken a transformation in its bilateral relationship with India based on a conviction that U.S. interests require a strong relationship with India. We are the two largest democracies, committed to political freedom protected by representative government. India is moving toward greater economic freedom as well. We have a common interest in the free flow of commerce, including through the vital sea lanes of the Indian Ocean. Finally, we share an interest in fighting terrorism and in creating a strategically stable Asia.

Differences remain, including over the development of India's nuclear and missile programs, and the pace of India's economic reforms. But while in the past these concerns may have dominated our thinking about India, today we start with a view of India as a growing world power with which we have common strategic interests. Through a strong partnership with India, we can best address any differences and shape a dynamic future.

The United States relationship with China is an important part of our strategy to promote a stable, peaceful, and prosperous Asia-Pacific region. We welcome the emergence of a strong, peaceful, and prosperous China. The democratic development of China is crucial to that future. Yet, a quarter century after beginning the process of shedding the worst features of the Communist legacy, China's leaders have not yet made the next series of fundamental choices about the character of their state. In pursuing advanced military capabilities that can threaten its neighbors in the Asia-Pacific region, China is following an outdated path that, in the end, will hamper its own pursuit of national greatness. In time, China will find that social and political freedom is the only source of that greatness.

The United States seeks a constructive relationship with a changing China. We already cooperate well where our interests overlap, including the current war on terrorism and in promoting stability on the Korean peninsula. Likewise, we have coordinated on the future of Afghanistan and have initiated a comprehensive dialogue on counter-terrorism and similar transitional concerns. Shared health and environmental threats, such as the spread of HIV/AIDS, challenge us to promote jointly the welfare of our citizens.

Addressing these transnational threats will challenge China to become more open with information, promote the development of civil society, and enhance individual human rights. China has begun to take the road to political openness, permitting many personal freedoms and conducting village-level elections, yet remains strongly committed to national one-party rule by the Communist Party. To make that nation truly accountable to its citizen's needs and aspirations, however, much work remains to be done. Only by allowing the Chinese people to think, assemble, and worship freely can China reach its full potential.

Our important trade relationship will benefit from China's entry into the World Trade Organization, which will create more export opportunities and ultimately more jobs for American farmers, workers, and companies. China is our fourth largest trading partner, with over $100 billion in annual two-way trade. The power of market principles and the WTO's requirements for transparency and accountability will advance openness and the rule of law in China to help establish basic protections for commerce and for citizens. There are, however, other areas in which we have profound disagreements. Our commitment to the self-defense of Taiwan under the Taiwan Relations Act is one. Human rights is another. We expect China to adhere to its nonproliferation commitments. We will work to narrow differences where they exist, but not allow them to preclude cooperation where we agree.

The events of September 11, 2001, fundamentally changed the context for relations between the United States and other main centers of global power, and opened vast, new opportunities. With our long-standing allies in Europe and Asia, and with leaders in Russia, India, and China, we must develop active agendas of cooperation lest these relationships become routine and unproductive.

Every agency of the United States Government shares the challenge. We can build fruitful habits of consultation, quiet argument, sober analysis, and common action. In the long-term, these are the practices that will sustain the supremacy of our common principles and keep open the path of progress.

IX. Transform America's National Security Institutions to Meet the Challenges and Opportunities of the Twenty-First Century

> "Terrorists attacked a symbol of American prosperity. They did not touch its source. America is successful because of the hard work, creativity, and enterprise of our people."
>
> President Bush
> Washington, D.C. (Joint Session of Congress)
> September 20, 2001

The major institutions of American national security were designed in a different era to meet different requirements. All of them must be transformed.

It is time to reaffirm the essential role of American military strength. We must build and maintain our defenses beyond challenge. Our military's highest priority is to defend the United States. To do so effectively, our military must:

- assure our allies and friends;
- dissuade future military competition;

- deter threats against U.S. interests, allies, and friends; and
- decisively defeat any adversary if deterrence fails.

The unparalleled strength of the United States armed forces, and their forward presence, have maintained the peace in some of the world's most strategically vital regions. However, the threats and enemies we must confront have changed, and so must our forces. A military structured to deter massive Cold War-era armies must be transformed to focus more on how an adversary might fight rather than where and when a war might occur. We will channel our energies to overcome a host of operational challenges.

The presence of American forces overseas is one of the most profound symbols of the U.S. commitments to allies and friends. Through our willingness to use force in our own defense and in defense of others, the United States demonstrates its resolve to maintain a balance of power that favors freedom. To contend with uncertainty and to meet the many security challenges we face, the United States will require bases and stations within and beyond Western Europe and Northeast Asia, as well as temporary access arrangements for the long-distance deployment of U.S. forces.

Before the war in Afghanistan, that area was low on the list of major planning contingencies. Yet, in a very short time, we had to operate across the length and breadth of that remote nation, using every branch of the armed forces. We must prepare for more such deployments by developing assets such as advanced remote sensing, long-range precision strike capabilities, and transformed maneuver and expeditionary forces. This broad portfolio of military capabilities must also include the ability to defend the homeland, conduct information operations, ensure U.S. access to distant theaters, and protect critical U.S. infrastructure and assets in outer space.

Innovation within the armed forces will rest on experimentation with new approaches to warfare, strengthening joint operations, exploiting U.S. intelligence advantages, and taking full advantage of science and technology. We must also transform the way the Department of Defense is run, especially in financial management and recruitment and retention. Finally, while maintaining near-term readiness and the ability to fight the war on terrorism, the goal must be to provide the President with a wider range of military options to discourage aggression or any form of coercion against the United States, our allies, and our friends.

We know from history that deterrence can fail; and we know from experience that some enemies cannot be deterred. The United States must and will maintain the capability to defeat any attempt by an enemy—whether a state or non-state actor—to impose its will on the United States, our allies, or our friends. We will maintain the forces sufficient to support our obligations, and to defend freedom. Our forces will be strong enough to dissuade potential adversaries from pursuing a military build-up in hopes of surpassing, or equaling, the power of the United States.

Intelligence—and how we use it—is our first line of defense against terrorists and the threat posed by hostile states. Designed around the priority of gathering enormous information about a massive, fixed object—the Soviet bloc—the intelligence community is coping with the challenge of following a far more complex and elusive set of targets.

We must transform our intelligence capabilities and build new ones to keep pace with the nature of these threats. Intelligence must be appropriately integrated with our defense and law enforcement systems and coordinated with our allies and friends. We need to protect the capabilities we have so that we do not arm our enemies with the knowledge of how best to surprise us. Those who would harm us also seek the benefit of surprise to limit our prevention and response options and to maximize injury.

We must strengthen intelligence warning and analysis to provide integrated threat assessments for national and homeland security. Since the threats inspired by foreign governments and groups may be conducted inside the United States, we must also ensure the proper fusion of information between intelligence and law enforcement.

Initiatives in this area will include:

- strengthening the authority of the Director of Central Intelligence to lead the development and actions of the Nation's foreign intelligence capabilities;
- establishing a new framework for intelligence warning that provides seamless and integrated warning across the spectrum of threats facing the nation and our allies;
- continuing to develop new methods of collecting information to sustain our intelligence advantage;
- investing in future capabilities while working to protect them through a more vigorous effort to prevent the compromise of intelligence capabilities; and
- collecting intelligence against the terrorist danger across the government with all-source analysis.

As the United States Government relies on the armed forces to defend America's interests, it must rely on diplomacy to interact with other nations. We will ensure that the Department of State receives funding sufficient to ensure the success of American diplomacy. The State Department takes the lead in managing our bilateral relationships with other governments. And in this new era, its people and institutions must be able to interact equally adroitly with non-governmental organizations and international institutions. Officials trained mainly in international politics must also extend their reach to understand complex issues of domestic governance around the world, including public health, education, law enforcement, the judiciary, and public diplomacy.

Our diplomats serve at the front line of complex negotiations, civil wars, and other humanitarian catastrophes. As humanitarian relief requirements are better understood, we must also be able to help build police forces, court systems, and legal codes, local and provincial government institutions, and electoral systems. Effective international cooperation is needed to accomplish these goals, backed by American readiness to play our part.

Just as our diplomatic institutions must adapt so that we can reach out to others, we also need a different and more comprehensive approach to public information efforts that can help people around the world learn about and understand America. The war on terrorism is not a clash of civilizations. It does, however, reveal the clash inside a civilization, a battle for the future of the Muslim world. This is a struggle of ideas and this is an area where America must excel.

We will take the actions necessary to ensure that our efforts to meet our global security commitments and protect Americans are not impaired by the potential for investigations, inquiry, or prosecution by the International Criminal Court (ICC), whose jurisdiction does not extend to Americans and which we do not accept. We will work together with other nations to avoid complications in our military operations and cooperation, through such mechanisms as multilateral and bilateral agreements that will protect U.S. nationals from the ICC. We will implement fully the American Servicemembers Protection Act, whose provisions are intended to ensure and enhance the protection of U.S. personnel and officials.

We will make hard choices in the coming year and beyond to ensure the right level and allocation of government spending on national security. The United States Government must strengthen its defenses to win this war. At home, our most important priority is to protect the homeland for the American people.

Today, the distinction between domestic and foreign affairs is diminishing. In a globalized world, events beyond America's borders have a greater impact inside them. Our society must be open to people, ideas, and goods from across the globe. The characteristics we most cherish—our freedom, our cities, our systems of movement, and modern life—are vulnerable to terrorism. This vulnerability will persist long after we bring to justice those responsible for the September eleventh attacks. As time passes, individuals may gain access to means of destruction that until now could be wielded only by armies, fleets, and squadrons. This is a new condition of life. We will adjust to it and thrive—in spite of it.

In exercising our leadership, we will respect the values, judgment, and interests of our friends and partners. Still, we will be prepared to act apart when our interests and unique responsibilities require. When we disagree on particulars, we will explain forthrightly the grounds for our concerns and strive to forge viable alternatives. We will not allow such disagreements to obscure our determination to secure together, with our allies and our friends, our shared fundamental interests and values.

Ultimately, the foundation of American strength is at home. It is in the skills of our people, the dynamism of our economy, and the resilience of our institutions. A diverse, modern society has inherent, ambitious, entrepreneurial energy. Our strength comes from what we do with that energy. That is where our national security begins.

appendix X

BOUMEDIENE et al. v. BUSH

SUPREME COURT OF THE UNITED STATES

BOUMEDIENE et al. v. BUSH, PRESIDENT OF THE UNITED STATES, et al.

CERTIORARI TO THE UNITED STATES COURT OF APPEALS FOR THE DISTRICT OF COLUMBIA CIRCUIT

Argued December 5, 2007—Decided June 12, No. 06–1195. 2008**

In the Authorization for Use of Military Force (AUMF), Congress empowered the President "to use all necessary and appropriate force against those . . . he determines planned, authorized, committed, or aided the terrorist attacks . . . on September 11, 2001." In *Hamdi* v. *Rumsfeld*, 542 U.S. 507, five Justices recognized that detaining individuals captured while fighting against the United States in Afghanistan for the duration of that conflict was a fundamental and accepted incident to war. Thereafter, the Defense Department established Combatant Status Review Tribunals (CSRTs) to determine whether individuals detained at the U. S. Naval Station at Guantanamo Bay, Cuba, were "enemy combatants."

Petitioners are aliens detained at Guantanamo after being captured in Afghanistan or elsewhere abroad and designated enemy combatants by CSRTs. Denying membership in the al Qaeda terrorist network that carried out the September 11 attacks and the Taliban regime that supported al Qaeda, each petitioner sought a writ of habeas corpus in the District Court, which ordered the cases dismissed for lack of jurisdiction because Guantanamo is outside sovereign U.S. territory. The D.C. Circuit affirmed, but this Court reversed, holding that 28 U.S. C. §2241 extended statutory habeas jurisdiction to Guantanamo. See *Rasul* v. *Bush,* 542 U.S. 466. Petitioners' cases were then consolidated into two proceedings. In the first, the district judge granted the Government's motion to dismiss, holding that the detainees had no rights that could be vindicated in a habeas action. In the second, the judge held that the detainees had due process rights.

While appeals were pending, Congress passed the Detainee Treatment Act of 2005 (DTA), §1005(e) of which amended 28 U.S.C. §2241 to provide that "no court, justice, or judge shall have jurisdiction to . . . consider . . . an application for . . . habeas corpus filed by or on behalf of an alien detained . . . at Guantanamo," and gave the D.C. Court of Appeals "exclusive" jurisdiction to review CSRT decisions. In *Hamdan* v. *Rumsfeld,* 548 U.S. 557, the Court held this provision inapplicable to cases (like petitioners') pending when the DTA was enacted. Congress responded with the Military Commissions Act of 2006 (MCA), §7(a) of which amended §2241(e)(1) to deny jurisdiction with respect to habeas actions by detained aliens determined to be enemy combatants, while §2241(e)(2) denies jurisdiction as to "any other action against the United States . . . relating to any aspect of the detention, transfer, treatment, trial, or conditions of confinement" of a detained alien determined to be an enemy combatant. MCA §7(b) provides that the 2241(e) amendments "shall take effect on the date of the enactment of this Act, and shall apply to all cases, without exception, pending on or after [that] date . . . which relate to any aspect of the detention, transfer, treatment, trial, or conditions of detention of an alien detained . . . since September 11, 2001."

The D.C. Court of Appeals concluded that MCA §7 must be read to strip from it, and all federal courts, jurisdiction to consider petitioners' habeas applications; that petitioners are not entitled to habeas or the protections of the Suspension Clause, U.S. Const., Art. I, §9, cl. 2, which provides that "[t]he Privilege of the Writ of Habeas Corpus shall not be suspended, unless when in Cases of Rebellion or Invasion the public Safety may require it"; and that it was therefore unnecessary to consider whether the DTA provided an adequate and effective substitute for habeas.

Held:

1. MCA §7 denies the federal courts jurisdiction to hear habeas actions, like the instant cases, that were pending at the time of its enactment. Section §7(b)'s effective date provision undoubtedly applies to habeas actions, which, by definition, "relate to . . . detention" within that section's meaning.

Petitioners argue to no avail that §7(b) does not apply to a §2241(e)(1) habeas action, but only to "any other action" under §2241(e)(2), because it largely repeats that section's language. The phrase "other action" in §2241(e)(2) cannot be understood without referring back to §2241(e)(1), which explicitly mentions the "writ of habeas corpus." Because the two paragraphs' structure implies that habeas is a type of action "relating to any aspect of . . . detention," etc., pending habeas actions are in the category of cases subject to the statute's jurisdictional bar. This is confirmed by the MCA's legislative history. Thus, if MCA §7 is valid, petitioners' cases must be dismissed. Pp. 5–8.

2. Petitioners have the constitutional privilege of habeas corpus. They are not barred from seeking the writ or invoking the Suspension Clause's protections because they have been designated as enemy combatants or because of their presence at Guantanamo. Pp. 8–41.

   a. A brief account of the writ's history and origins shows that protection for the habeas privilege was one of the few safeguards of liberty specified in a Constitution that, at the outset, had no Bill of Rights; in the system the Framers conceived, the writ has a centrality that must inform proper interpretation of the Suspension Clause. That the Framers considered the writ a vital instrument for the protection of individual liberty is evident from the care taken in the Suspension Clause to specify the limited grounds for its suspension: The writ may be suspended only when public safety requires it in times of rebellion or invasion. The Clause is designed to protect against cyclical abuses of the writ by the Executive and Legislative Branches. It protects detainee rights by a means consistent with the Constitution's essential design, ensuring that, except during periods of formal suspension, the Judiciary will have a time-tested device, the writ, to maintain the "delicate balance of governance." *Hamdi, supra,* at 536. Separation-of-powers principles, and the history that influenced their design, inform the Clause's reach and purpose. Pp. 8–15.

   b. A diligent search of founding-era precedents and legal commentaries reveals no certain conclusions. None of the cases the parties cite reveal whether a common-law court would have granted, or refused to hear for lack of jurisdiction, a habeas petition by a prisoner deemed an enemy combatant, under a standard like the Defense Department's in these cases, and when held in a territory, like Guantanamo, over which the Government has total military and civil control. The evidence as to the writ's geographic scope at common law is informative, but, again, not dispositive. Petitioners argue that the site of their detention is analogous to two territories outside England to which the common-law writ ran, the exempt jurisdictions and India, but critical differences between these places and Guantanamo render these claims unpersuasive. The Government argues that Guantanamo is more closely analogous to Scotland and Hanover, where the writ did not run, but it is unclear whether the common-law courts lacked the power to issue the writ there, or whether they refrained from doing so for prudential reasons. The parties' arguments that the very lack of a precedent on point supports their respective positions are premised upon the doubtful assumptions that the historical record is complete and that the common law, if properly understood, yields a definite answer to the questions before the Court. Pp. 15–22.

c. The Suspension Clause has full effect at Guantanamo. The Government's argument that the Clause affords petitioners no rights because the United States does not claim sovereignty over the naval station is rejected. Pp. 22–42.
    i. The Court does not question the Government's position that Cuba maintains sovereignty, in the legal and technical sense, over Guantanamo, but it does not accept the Government's premise that *de jure* sovereignty is the touchstone of habeas jurisdiction. Common-law habeas' history provides scant support for this proposition, and it is inconsistent with the Court's precedents and contrary to fundamental separation-of-powers principles. Pp. 22–25.
    ii. Discussions of the Constitution's extraterritorial application in cases involving provisions other than the Suspension Clause undermine the Government's argument. Fundamental questions regarding the Constitution's geographic scope first arose when the Nation acquired Hawaii and the noncontiguous Territories ceded by Spain after the Spanish-American War, and Congress discontinued its prior practice of extending constitutional rights to territories by statute. In the so-called Insular Cases, the Court held that the Constitution had independent force in the territories that was not contingent upon acts of legislative grace. See, *e.g.*, *Dorr* v. *United States*, 195 U.S. 138. Yet because of the difficulties and disruption

inherent in transforming the former Spanish colonies' civil-law system into an Anglo-American system, the Court adopted the doctrine of territorial incorporation, under which the Constitution applies in full in incorporated Territories surely destined for statehood but only in part in unincorporated Territories. See, *e.g.*, *id.*, at 143. Practical considerations likewise influenced the Court's analysis in *Reid* v. *Covert*, 354 U.S. 1, where, in applying the jury provisions of the Fifth and Sixth Amendments to American civilians being tried by the U.S. military abroad, both the plurality and the concurrences noted the relevance of practical considerations, related not to the petitioners' citizenship, but to the place of their confinement and trial. Finally, in holding that habeas jurisdiction did not extend to enemy aliens, convicted of violating the laws of war, who were detained in a German prison during the Allied Powers' post-World War II occupation, the Court, in *Johnson* v. *Eisentrager*, 339 U.S. 763, stressed the practical difficulties of ordering the production of the prisoners, *id.*, at 779. The Government's reading of *Eisentrager* as adopting a formalistic test for determining the Suspension Clause's reach is rejected because: (1) the discussion of practical considerations in that case was integral to a part of the Court's opinion that came before it announced its holding, see *id.*, at 781; (2) it mentioned the concept of territorial sovereignty only twice in its opinion, in contrast to its significant discussion of practical barriers to the running of the writ; and (3) if the Government's reading were correct, the opinion would have marked not only a change in, but a complete repudiation of, the Insular Cases' (and later *Reid*'s) functional approach. A constricted reading of *Eisentrager* overlooks what the Court sees as a common thread uniting all these cases: The idea that extraterritoriality questions turn on objective factors and practical concerns, not formalism. Pp. 25–34.

iii. The Government's sovereignty-based test raises troubling separation-of-powers concerns, which are illustrated by Guantanamo's political history. Although the United States has maintained complete and uninterrupted control of Guantanamo for over 100 years, the Government's view is that the Constitution has no effect there, at least as to noncitizens, because the United States disclaimed formal sovereignty in its 1903 lease with Cuba. The Nation's basic charter cannot be contracted away like this. The Constitution grants Congress and the President the power to acquire, dispose of, and govern territory, not the power to decide when and where its terms apply. To hold that the political branches may switch the Constitution on or off at will would lead to a regime in which they, not this Court, say "what the law is." *Marbury* v. *Madison,* 1 Cranch 137, 177. These concerns have particular bearing upon the Suspension Clause question here, for the habeas writ is itself an indispensable mechanism for monitoring the separation of powers. Pp. 34–36.

iv. Based on *Eisentrager, supra,* at 777, and the Court's reasoning in its other extraterritoriality opinions, at least three factors are relevant in determining the Suspension Clause's reach: (1) the detainees' citizenship and status and the adequacy of the process through which that status was determined; (2) the nature of the sites where apprehension and then detention took place; and (3) the practical obstacles inherent in resolving the prisoner's entitlement to the writ. Application of this framework reveals, first, that petitioners' status is in dispute: They are not American citizens, but deny they are enemy combatants; and although they have been afforded some process in CSRT proceedings, there has been no *Eisentrager*–style trial by military commission for violations of the laws of war. Second, while the sites of petitioners' apprehension and detention weigh against finding they have Suspension Clause rights, there are critical differences between *Eisentrager*'s German prison, circa 1950, and the Guantanamo Naval Station in 2008, given the Government's absolute and indefinite control over the naval station. Third, although the Court is sensitive to the financial and administrative costs of holding the Suspension Clause applicable in a case of military detention abroad, these factors are not dispositive because the Government presents no credible arguments that the military mission at Guantanamo would be compromised if habeas courts had jurisdiction. The situation in *Eisentrager* was far different, given the historical context and nature of the military's mission in post-War Germany. Pp. 36–41.

d. Petitioners are therefore entitled to the habeas privilege, and if that privilege is to be denied them, Congress must act in accordance with the Suspension Clause's requirements. Cf. Rasul, 542 U.S., at 564. Pp. 41–42.

3. Because the DTA's procedures for reviewing detainees' status are not an adequate and effective substitute for the habeas writ, MCA §7 operates as an unconstitutional suspension of the writ. Pp. 42–64.

a. Given its holding that the writ does not run to petitioners, the D. C. Circuit found it unnecessary to consider whether there was an adequate substitute for habeas. This Court usually remands for consideration of questions not decided below, but departure from this rule is appropriate in "exceptional" circumstances, see, *e.g., Cooper Industries, Inc.* v. *Aviall Services, Inc.,* 543 U.S. 157, here, the grave separation-of-powers issues raised by these cases and the fact that petitioners have been denied meaningful access to a judicial forum for years. Pp. 42–44.

b. Historically, Congress has taken care to avoid suspensions of the writ. For example, the statutes at issue in the Court's two leading cases addressing habeas substitutes, *Swain* v. *Pressley,* 430 U.S. 372, and *United States* v. *Hayman,* 342 U.S. 205, were attempts to streamline habeas relief, not to cut it back. Those cases provide little guidance here because, *inter alia,* the statutes in question gave the courts broad remedial powers to secure the historic office of the writ, and included saving clauses to preserve habeas review as an avenue of last resort. In contrast, Congress intended the DTA and the MCA to circumscribe habeas review, as is evident from the unequivocal nature of MCA §7's jurisdiction-stripping language, from the DTA's text limiting the Court of Appeals' jurisdiction to assessing whether the CSRT complied with the "standards and procedures specified by the Secretary of Defense," DTA §1005(e)(2)(C), and from the absence of a saving clause in either Act. That Congress intended to create a more limited procedure is also confirmed by the legislative history and by a comparison of the DTA and the habeas statute that would govern in MCA §7's absence, 28 U.S.C. §2241. In §2241, Congress authorized "any justice" or "circuit judge" to issue the writ, thereby accommodating the necessity for factfinding that will arise in some cases by allowing the appellate judge or Justice to transfer the case to a district court. See §2241(b). However, by granting the D.C. Circuit "exclusive" jurisdiction over petitioners' cases, see

DTA §1005(e)(2)(A), Congress has foreclosed that option in these cases. Pp. 44–49.

c. This Court does not endeavor to offer a comprehensive summary of the requisites for an adequate habeas substitute. It is uncontroversial, however, that the habeas privilege entitles the prisoner to a meaningful opportunity to demonstrate that he is being held pursuant to "the erroneous application or interpretation" of relevant law, *INS* v. *St. Cyr,* 533 U.S. 289, and the habeas court must have the power to order the conditional release of an individual unlawfully detained. But more may be required depending on the circumstances. Petitioners identify what they see as myriad deficiencies in the CSRTs, the most relevant being the constraints upon the detainee's ability to rebut the factual basis for the Government's assertion that he is an enemy combatant. At the CSRT stage the detainee has limited means to find or present evidence to challenge the Government's case, does not have the assistance of counsel, and may not be aware of the most critical allegations that the Government relied upon to order his detention. His opportunity to confront witnesses is likely to be more theoretical than real, given that there are no limits on the admission of hearsay. The Court therefore agrees with petitioners that there is considerable risk of error in the tribunal's findings of fact. And given that the consequence of error may be detention for the duration of hostilities that may last a generation or more, the risk is too significant to ignore. Accordingly, for the habeas writ, or its substitute, to function as an effective and meaningful remedy in this context, the court conducting the collateral proceeding must have some ability to correct any errors, to assess the sufficiency of the Government's evidence, and to admit and consider relevant exculpatory evidence that was not introduced during the earlier proceeding. *In re Yamashita,* 327 U.S. 1, and *Ex parte Quirin,* 317 U.S. 1, distinguished. Pp. 49–57.

d. Petitioners have met their burden of establishing that the DTA review process is, on its face, an inadequate substitute for habeas. Among the constitutional infirmities from which the DTA potentially suffers are the absence of provisions allowing petitioners to challenge the President's authority under the AUMF to detain them indefinitely, to contest the CSRT's findings of fact, to supplement the record on review with exculpatory evidence discovered after the CSRT proceedings, and to request release. The statute cannot be read to contain each of these constitutionally required procedures. MCA §7 thus effects an unconstitutional suspension of the writ. There is no jurisdictional bar to the District Court's entertaining petitioners' claims. Pp. 57–64.

4. Nor are there prudential barriers to habeas review. Pp. 64–70.

   a. Petitioners need not seek review of their CSRT determinations in the D.C. Circuit before proceeding with their habeas actions in the District Court. If these cases involved detainees held for only a short time while awaiting their CSRT determinations, or were it probable that the Court of Appeals could complete a prompt review of their applications, the case for requiring temporary abstention or exhaustion of alternative remedies would be much stronger. But these qualifications no longer pertain here. In some instances six years have elapsed without the judicial oversight that habeas corpus or an adequate substitute demands. To require these detainees to pursue the limited structure of DTA review before proceeding with habeas actions would be to require additional months, if not years, of delay. This holding should not be read to imply that a habeas court should intervene the moment an enemy combatant steps foot in a territory where the writ runs. Except in cases of undue delay, such as the present, federal courts should refrain from entertaining an enemy combatant's habeas petition at least until after the CSRT has had a chance to review his status. Pp. 64–67.

   b. In effectuating today's holding, certain accommodations—including channeling future cases to a single district court and requiring that court to use its discretion to accommodate to the greatest extent possible the Government's legitimate interest in protecting sources and intelligence gathering methods—should be made to reduce the burden habeas proceedings will place on the military, without impermissibly diluting the writ's protections. Pp. 67–68.

5. In considering both the procedural and substantive standards used to impose detention to prevent acts of terrorism, the courts must accord proper deference to the political branches. However, security subsists, too, in fidelity to freedom's first principles, chief among them being freedom from arbitrary and unlawful restraint and the personal liberty that is secured by adherence to the separation of powers. Pp. 68–70.

476 F. 3d 981, reversed and remanded.

Kennedy, J., delivered the opinion of the Court, in which Stevens, Souter, Ginsburg, and Breyer, JJ., joined. Souter, J., filed a concurring opinion, in which Ginsburg and Breyer, JJ., joined. Roberts, C. J., filed a dissenting opinion, in which Scalia, Thomas, and Alito, JJ., joined. Scalia, J., filed a dissenting opinion, in which Roberts, C. J., and Thomas and Alito, JJ., joined.

Notes

**Together with No. 06–1196, Al Odah, Next Friend of Al Odah, et al. v. United States et al., also on certiorari to the same court.

appendix XI

HAMDAN v. RUMSFELD

SUPREME COURT OF THE UNITED STATES

HAMDAN v. RUMSFELD, SECRETARY OF DEFENSE, et al.

CERTIORARI TO THE UNITED STATES COURT OF APPEALS FOR THE DISTRICT OF COLUMBIA CIRCUIT

Argued March 28, 2006—Decided June 29, No. 05–184. 2006

Pursuant to Congress' Joint Resolution authorizing the President to "use all necessary and appropriate force against those nations, organizations, or persons he determines planned, authorized, committed or aided" the September 11, 2001, al Qaeda terrorist attacks (AUMF), U.S. Armed Forces invaded Afghanistan. During the hostilities, in 2001, militia forces captured petitioner Hamdan, a Yemeni national, and turned him over to the U.S. military, which, in 2002, transported him to prison in Guantanamo Bay, Cuba. Over a year later, the President deemed Hamdan eligible for trial by military commission for then-unspecified crimes. After another year, he was charged with conspiracy "to commit . . . offenses triable by military commission." In habeas and mandamus petitions, Hamdan asserted that the military commission lacks authority to try him because (1) neither congressional Act nor the common law of war supports trial by this commission for conspiracy, an offense that, Hamdan says, is not a violation of the law of war; and (2) the procedures adopted to try him violate basic tenets of military and international law, including the principle that a defendant must be permitted to see and hear the evidence against him.

The District Court granted habeas relief and stayed the commission's proceedings, concluding that the President's authority to establish military commissions extends only to offenders or offenses triable by such a commission under the law of war; that such law includes the Third Geneva Convention; that Hamdan is entitled to that Convention's full protections until adjudged, under it, not to be a prisoner of war; and that, whether or not Hamdan is properly classified a prisoner of war, the commission convened to try him was established in violation of both the Uniform Code of Military Justice (UCMJ), 10 U.S.C. §801 *et seq*., and Common Article 3 of the Third Geneva Convention because it had the power to convict based on evidence the accused would never see or hear. The D.C. Circuit reversed. Although it declined the Government's invitation to abstain from considering Hamdan's challenge, cf. *Schlesinger* v. *Councilman*, 420 U.S. 738, the appeals court ruled, on the merits, that Hamdan was not entitled to relief because the Geneva Conventions are not judicially enforceable. The court also concluded that *Ex parte Quirin*, 317 U.S. 1, foreclosed any separation-of-powers objection to the military commission's jurisdiction, and that Hamdan's trial before the commission would violate neither the UCMJ nor Armed Forces regulations implementing the Geneva Conventions.

Held: The judgment is reversed, and the case is remanded.

415 F. 3d 33, reversed and remanded.

Justice Stevens delivered the opinion of the Court, except as to Parts V and VI–D–iv, concluding:

1. The Government's motion to dismiss, based on the Detainee Treatment Act of 2005 (DTA), is denied. DTA §1005(e)(1) provides that "no court . . . shall have jurisdiction to hear or consider . . . an application for . . . habeas corpus filed by . . . an alien detained . . . at Guantanamo Bay." Section 1005(h)(2) provides that §§1005(e)(2) and (3)—which give the D.C. Circuit "exclusive" jurisdiction to review the final decisions of, respectively, combatant status review tribunals and military commissions—"shall apply with respect to any claim whose review is . . . pending on" the DTA's effective date, as was Hamdan's case. The Government's argument that §§1005(e)(1) and (h) repeal this Court's jurisdiction to review the decision below is rebutted by ordinary principles of statutory construction. A negative inference may be drawn from Congress' failure to include

§1005(e)(1) within the scope of §1005(h)(2). Cf., *e.g., Lindh* v. *Murphy,* 521 U.S. 320. "If . . . Congress was reasonably concerned to ensure that [§§1005(e)(2) and (3)] be applied to pending cases, it should have been just as concerned about [§1005(e)(1)], unless it had the different intent that the latter [section] not be applied to the general run of pending cases." *Id.*, at 329. If anything, the evidence of deliberate omission is stronger here than it was in *Lindh.* The legislative history shows that Congress not only considered the respective temporal reaches of §§1005(e)(1), (2), and (3) together at every stage, but omitted paragraph (1) from its directive only after having *rejected* earlier proposed versions of the statute that would have included what is now paragraph (1) within that directive's scope. Congress' rejection of the very language that would have achieved the result the Government urges weighs heavily against the Government's interpretation. See *Doe* v. *Chao,* 540 U.S. 614. Pp. 7–20.

2. The Government argues unpersuasively that abstention is appropriate under *Councilman,* which concluded that, as a matter of comity, federal courts should normally abstain from intervening in pending courts-martial against service members, see 420 U.S., at 740. Neither of the comity considerations *Councilman* identified weighs in favor of abstention here. First, the assertion that military discipline and, therefore, the Armed Forces' efficient operation, are best served if the military justice system acts without regular interference from civilian courts, see *id.,* at 752, is inapt because Hamdan is not a service member. Second, the view that federal courts should respect the balance Congress struck when it created "an integrated system of military courts and review procedures" is inapposite, since the tribunal convened to try Hamdan is not part of that integrated system. Rather than *Councilman,* the most relevant precedent is *Ex parte Quirin,* where the Court, far from abstaining pending the conclusion of ongoing military proceedings, expedited its review because of (1) the public importance of the questions raised, (2) the Court's duty, in both peace and war, to preserve the constitutional safeguards of civil liberty, and (3) the public interest in a decision on those questions without delay, 317 U.S, at 19. The Government has identified no countervailing interest that would permit federal courts to depart from their general duty to exercise the jurisdiction Congress has conferred on them. Pp. 20–25.
3. The military commission at issue is not expressly authorized by any congressional Act. *Quirin* held that Congress had, through Article of War 15,

sanctioned the use of military commissions to try offenders or offenses against the law of war. 317 U.S., at 28. UCMJ Art. 21, which is substantially identical to the old Art. 15, reads: "The jurisdiction [of] courts-martial shall not be construed as depriving military commissions . . . of concurrent jurisdiction in respect of offenders or offenses that by statute or by the law of war may be tried by such . . . commissions." 10 U.S.C. §821. Contrary to the Government's assertion, even *Quirin* did not view that authorization as a sweeping mandate for the President to invoke military commissions whenever he deems them necessary. Rather, *Quirin* recognized that Congress had simply preserved what power, under the Constitution and the common law of war, the President already had to convene military commissions—with the express condition that he and those under his command comply with the law of war. See 317 U.S., at 28–29. Neither the AUMF nor the DTA can be read to provide specific, overriding authorization for the commission convened to try Hamdan. Assuming the AUMF activated the President's war powers, see *Hamdi* v. *Rumsfeld,* 542 U.S. 507, and that those powers include authority to convene military commissions in appropriate circumstances, see, e.g., *id.,* at 518, there is nothing in the AUMF's text or legislative history even hinting that Congress intended to expand or alter the authorization set forth in UCMJ Art. 21. Cf. *Ex parte Yerger,* 8 Wall. 85, 105. Likewise, the DTA cannot be read to authorize this commission. Although the DTA, unlike either Art. 21 or the AUMF, was enacted after the President convened Hamdan's commission, it contains no language authorizing that tribunal or any other at Guantanamo Bay. Together, the UCMJ, the AUMF, and the DTA at most acknowledge a general Presidential authority to convene military commissions in circumstances where justified under the Constitution and laws, including the law of war. Absent a more specific congressional authorization, this Court's task is, as it was in *Quirin,* to decide whether Hamdan's military commission is so justified. Pp. 25–30.

4. The military commission at issue lacks the power to proceed because its structure and procedures violate both the UCMJ and the four Geneva Conventions signed in 1949. Pp. 49–72.
   a. The commission's procedures, set forth in Commission Order No. 1, provide, among other things, that an accused and his civilian counsel may be excluded from, and precluded from ever learning what evidence was presented during, any part of the proceeding the official

who appointed the commission or the presiding officer decides to "close." Grounds for closure include the protection of classified information, the physical safety of participants and witnesses, the protection of intelligence and law enforcement sources, methods, or activities, and "other national security interests." Appointed military defense counsel must be privy to these closed sessions, but may, at the presiding officer's discretion, be forbidden to reveal to the client what took place therein. Another striking feature is that the rules governing Hamdan's commission permit the admission of any evidence that, in the presiding officer's opinion, would have probative value to a reasonable person. Moreover, the accused and his civilian counsel may be denied access to classified and other "protected information," so long as the presiding officer concludes that the evidence is "probative" and that its admission without the accused's knowledge would not result in the denial of a full and fair trial. Pp. 49–52.

b. The Government objects to this Court's consideration of a procedural challenge at this stage on the grounds, *inter alia,* that Hamdan will be able to raise such a challenge following a final decision under the DTA, and that there is no basis to presume, before the trial has even commenced, that it will not be conducted in good faith and according to law. These contentions are unsound. First, because Hamdan apparently is not subject to the death penalty (at least as matters now stand) and may receive a prison sentence shorter than 10 years, he has no automatic right to federal-court review of the commission's "final decision" under DTA §1005(e)(3). Second, there *is* a basis to presume that the procedures employed during Hamdan's trial will violate the law: He will be, and *indeed already has been,* excluded from his own trial. Thus, review of the procedures in advance of a "final decision" is appropriate. Pp. 52–53.

c. Because UCMJ Article 36 has not been complied with here, the rules specified for Hamdan's commission trial are illegal. The procedures governing such trials historically have been the same as those governing courts-martial. Although this uniformity principle is not inflexible and does not preclude all departures from courts-martial procedures, any such departure must be tailored to the exigency that necessitates it. That understanding is reflected in Art. 36(b), which provides that the procedural rules the President promulgates for courts-martial and military commissions alike must be "uniform insofar as practicable," 10 U.S.C. §836(b). The "practicability" determination the President has made is insufficient to justify variances from the procedures governing courts-martial. The President here has determined, pursuant to the requirement of *Art. 36(a)*, that it is impracticable to apply the rules and principles of law that govern "the trial of criminal cases in the United States district courts" to Hamdan's commission. The President has not, however, made a similar official determination that it is impracticable to apply the rules for courts-martial. And even if subsection (b)'s requirements could be satisfied without an official practicability determination, that subsection's requirements are not satisfied here. Nothing in the record demonstrates that it would be impracticable to apply court-martial rules here. There is no suggestion, *e.g.*, of any logistical difficulty in securing properly sworn and authenticated evidence or in applying the usual principles of relevance and admissibility. It is not evident why the danger posed by international terrorism, considerable though it is, should require, in the case of Hamdan's trial, any variance from the courts-martial rules. The absence of any showing of impracticability is particularly disturbing when considered in light of the clear and admitted failure to apply one of the most fundamental protections afforded not just by the Manual for Courts-Martial but also by the UCMJ itself: The right to be present. See 10 U.S.C.A. §839(c). Because the jettisoning of so basic a right cannot lightly be excused as "practicable," the courts-martial rules must apply. Since it is undisputed that Commission Order No. 1 deviates in many significant respects from those rules, it necessarily violates Art. 36(b). Pp. 53–62.

d. The procedures adopted to try Hamdan also violate the Geneva Conventions. The D.C. Circuit dismissed Hamdan's challenge in this regard on the grounds, *inter alia,* that the Conventions are not judicially enforceable and that, in any event, Hamdan is not entitled to their protections. Neither of these grounds is persuasive. Pp. 62–68.

   i. The appeals court relied on a statement in *Johnson* v. *Eisentrager,* 339 U.S. 763, n. 14, suggesting that this Court lacked power even to consider the merits of a Convention argument because the political and military authorities had sole responsibility for observing and enforcing prisoners' rights under the Convention. However, *Eisentrager* does not control here because, regardless of the nature of the rights conferred on Hamdan, cf. *United States* v. *Rauscher,* 119 U.S. 407, they are indisputably part of the law of war, see *Hamdi,* 542 U.S., at 520–521, compliance with which is the condition upon which UCMJ Art. 21 authority is granted. Pp. 63–65.

ii. Alternatively, the appeals court agreed with the Government that the Conventions do not apply because Hamdan was captured during the war with al Qaeda, which is not a Convention signatory, and that conflict is distinct from the war with signatory Afghanistan. The Court need not decide the merits of this argument because there is at least one provision of the Geneva Conventions that applies here even if the relevant conflict is not between signatories. Common Article 3, which appears in all four Conventions, provides that, in a "conflict not of an international character occurring in the territory of one of the High Contracting Parties [*i.e.*, signatories], each Party to the conflict shall be bound to apply, as a minimum," certain provisions protecting "[p]ersons . . . placed *hors de combat* by . . . detention," including a prohibition on "the passing of sentences . . . without previous judgment . . . by a regularly constituted court affording all the judicial guarantees . . . recognized as indispensable by civilized peoples." The D.C. Circuit ruled Common Article 3 inapplicable to Hamdan because the conflict with al Qaeda is international in scope and thus not a "conflict not of an international character. " That reasoning is erroneous. That the quoted phrase bears its literal meaning and is used here in contradistinction to a conflict between nations is demonstrated by Common Article 2, which limits its own application to any armed conflict between signatories and provides that signatories must abide by all terms of the Conventions even if another party to the conflict is a nonsignatory, so long as the nonsignatory "accepts and applies" those terms. Common Article 3, by contrast, affords some minimal protection, falling short of full protection under the Conventions, to individuals associated with neither a signatory nor even a nonsignatory who are involved in a conflict "in the territory of" a signatory. The latter kind of conflict does not involve a clash between nations (whether signatories or not). Pp. 65–68.

iii. While Common Article 3 does not define its "regularly constituted court" phrase, other sources define the words to mean an "ordinary military cour[t]" that is "established and organized in accordance with the laws and procedures already in force in a country." The regular military courts in our system are the courts-martial established by congressional statute. At a minimum, a military commission can be "regularly constituted" only if some practical need explains deviations from court-martial practice. No such need has been demonstrated here. Pp. 69–70.

iv. Common Article 3's requirements are general, crafted to accommodate a wide variety of legal systems, but they are *requirements* nonetheless. The commission convened to try Hamdan does not meet those requirements. P. 72.

d. Even assuming that Hamden is a dangerous individual who would cause great harm or death to innocent civilians given the opportunity, the Executive nevertheless must comply with the prevailing rule of law in undertaking to try him and subject him to criminal punishment. P. 72.

Justice Stevens, joined by Justice Souter, Justice Ginsburg, and Justice Breyer, concluded in Parts V and VI–D–iv:

1. The Government has not charged Hamdan with an "offense . . . that by the law of war may be tried by military commission," 10 U.S.C. §821. Of the three sorts of military commissions used historically, the law-of-war type used in *Quirin* and other cases is the only model available to try Hamdan. Among the preconditions, incorporated in Article of War 15 and, later, UCMJ Art. 21, for such a tribunal's exercise of jurisdiction are, *inter alia*, that it must be limited to trying offenses committed within the convening commander's field of command, *i.e.*, within the theater of war, and that the offense charged must have been committed during, not before or after, the war. Here, Hamdan is not alleged to have committed any overt act in a theater of war or on any specified date after September 11, 2001. More importantly, the offense alleged is not triable by law-of-war military commission. Although the common law of war may render triable by military commission certain offenses not defined by statute, *Quirin*, 317 U.S., at 30, the precedent for doing so with respect to a particular offense must be plain and unambiguous, cf., *e.g.*, *Loving* v. *United States*, 517 U.S. 748. That burden is far from satisfied here. The crime of "conspiracy" has rarely if ever been tried as such in this country by any law-of-war military commission not exercising some other form of jurisdiction, and does not appear in either the Geneva Conventions or the Hague Conventions—the major treaties on the law of war. Moreover, that conspiracy is not a recognized violation of the law of war is confirmed by other international sources, including, *e.g.*, the International Military Tribunal at Nuremberg, which pointedly refused to recognize conspiracy to commit war crimes as such a violation. Because the conspiracy charge does not support the commission's jurisdiction, the commission lacks authority to try Hamdan. Pp. 30–49.

2. The phrase "all the guarantees . . . recognized as indispensable by civilized peoples" in Common Article 3 of the Geneva Conventions is not defined, but it must be understood to incorporate at least the barest of the trial protections recognized by customary international law. The procedures adopted to try Hamdan deviate from those governing courts-martial in ways not justified by practical need, and thus fail to afford the requisite guarantees. Moreover, various provisions of Commission Order No. 1 dispense with the principles, which are indisputably part of customary international law, that an accused must, absent disruptive conduct or consent, be present for his trial and must be privy to the evidence against him. Pp. 70–72.

Justice Kennedy, agreeing that Hamdan's military commission is unauthorized under the Uniform Code of Military Justice, 10 U.S.C. §§836 and 821, and the Geneva Conventions, concluded that there is therefore no need to decide whether Common Article 3 of the Conventions requires that the accused have the right to be present at all stages of a criminal trial or to address the validity of the conspiracy charge against Hamdan. Pp. 17–19.

Stevens, J., announced the judgment of the Court and delivered the opinion of the Court with respect to Parts I through IV, VI through VI–D–iii, VI–D–v, and VII, in which Kennedy, Souter, Ginsburg, and Breyer, JJ., joined, and an opinion with respect to Parts V and VI–D–iv, in which Souter, Ginsburg, and Breyer, JJ., joined. Breyer, J., filed a concurring opinion, in which Kennedy, Souter, and Ginsburg, JJ., joined. Kennedy, J., filed an opinion concurring in part, in which Souter, Ginsburg, and Breyer, JJ., joined as to Parts I and II. Scalia, J., filed a dissenting opinion, in which Thomas and Alito, JJ., joined. Thomas, J., filed a dissenting opinion, in which Scalia, J., joined, and in which Alito, J., joined as to all but Parts I, II–C–1, and III–B–2. Alito, J., filed a dissenting opinion, in which Scalia and Thomas, JJ., joined as to Parts I through III. Roberts, C. J., took no part in the consideration or decision of the case.

appendix XII

RASUL et al. v. BUSH

SUPREME COURT OF THE UNITED STATES

RASUL et al. v. BUSH, PRESIDENT OF THE UNITED STATES, et al.

CERTIORARI TO THE UNITED STATES COURT OF APPEALS FOR THE DISTRICT OF COLUMIBA CIRCUIT

No. 03–334. Argued April 20, 2004—Decided June 28, 2004

Pursuant to Congress' joint resolution authorizing the use of necessary and appropriate force against nations, organizations, or persons that planned, authorized, committed, or aided in the September 11, 2001, al Qaeda terrorist attacks, the President sent Armed Forces into Afghanistan to wage a military campaign against al Qaeda and the Taliban regime that had supported it. Petitioners, 2 Australians and 12 Kuwaitis captured abroad during the hostilities, are being held in military custody at the Guantanamo Bay, Cuba, Naval Base, which the United States occupies under a lease and treaty recognizing Cuba's ultimate sovereignty, but giving this country complete jurisdiction and control for so long as it does not abandon the leased areas. Petitioners filed suits under federal law challenging the legality of their detention, alleging that they had never been combatants against the United States or engaged in terrorist acts, and that they have never been charged with wrongdoing, permitted to consult counsel, or provided access to courts or other tribunals. The District Court construed the suits as habeas petitions and dismissed them for want of jurisdiction, holding that, under *Johnson* v. *Eisentrager,* 339 U.S. 763, aliens detained outside United States sovereign territory may not invoke habeas relief. The Court of Appeals affirmed.

Held: United States courts have jurisdiction to consider challenges to the legality of the detention of foreign nationals captured abroad in connection with hostilities and incarcerated at Guantanamo Bay. Pp. 4—17.

a. The District Court has jurisdiction to hear petitioners' habeas challenges under 28 U.S.C. §2241, which authorizes district courts, "within their respective jurisdictions," to entertain habeas applications by persons claiming to be held "in custody in violation of the . . . laws . . . of the United States," §§2241(a), (c)(3). Such jurisdiction extends to aliens held in a territory over which the United States exercises plenary and exclusive jurisdiction, but not "ultimate sovereignty." Pp. 4–16.

1. The Court rejects respondents' primary submission that these cases are controlled by *Eisentrager*'s holding that a District Court lacked authority to grant habeas relief to German citizens captured by U.S. forces in China, tried and convicted of war crimes by an American military commission headquartered in Nanking, and incarcerated in occupied Germany. Reversing a Court of Appeals judgment finding jurisdiction, the *Eisentrager* Court found six critical facts: The German prisoners were (a) enemy aliens who (b) had never been or resided in the United States, (c) were captured outside U.S. territory and there held in military custody, (d) were there tried and convicted by the military (e) for offenses committed there, and (f) were imprisoned there at all times. 339 U.S., at 777. Petitioners here differ from the *Eisentrager* detainees in important respects: They are not nationals of countries at war with the United States, and they deny that they have engaged in or plotted acts of aggression against this country; they have never been afforded access to any tribunal, much less charged with and convicted of wrongdoing; and for more than two years they have been imprisoned in territory over which the United States exercises exclusive jurisdiction and control. The *Eisentrager* Court also made clear that all six of the noted critical facts were relevant only to the question of the prisoners' *constitutional* entitlement to habeas review. *Ibid.* The Court's only statement on their statutory entitlement was a passing reference to its absence.

Id., at 768. This cursory treatment is explained by the Court's then-recent decision in *Ahrens* v. *Clark*, 335 U.S. 188, in which it held that the District Court for the District of Columbia lacked jurisdiction to entertain the habeas claims of aliens detained at Ellis Island because the habeas statute's phrase "within their respective jurisdictions" required the petitioners' presence within the court's territorial jurisdiction, *id.*, at 192. However, the Court later held, in *Braden* v. *30th Judicial Circuit Court of Ky.*, 410 U.S. 484, 494–495, that such presence is not "an invariable prerequisite" to the exercise of §2241 jurisdiction because habeas acts upon the person holding the prisoner, not the prisoner himself, so that the court acts "within [its] respective jurisdiction" if the custodian can be reached by service of process. Because *Braden* overruled the statutory predicate to *Eisentrager*'s holding, *Eisentrager* does not preclude the exercise of §2241 jurisdiction over petitioners' claims. Pp. 6–11.

2. Also rejected is respondents' contention that §2241 is limited by the principle that legislation is presumed not to have extraterritorial application unless Congress clearly manifests such an intent, *EEOC* v. *Arabian American Oil Co.*, 499 U.S. 244, 248. That presumption has no application to the operation of the habeas statute with respect to persons detained within "the [United States'] territorial jurisdiction." *Foley Bros., Inc.* v. *Filardo*, 336 U.S. 281, 285. By the express terms of its agreements with Cuba, the United States exercises complete jurisdiction and control over the Guantanamo Base, and may continue to do so permanently if it chooses. Respondents concede that the habeas statute would create federal-court jurisdiction over the claims of an American citizen held at the base. Considering that §2241 draws no distinction between Americans and aliens held in federal custody, there is little reason to think that Congress intended the statute's geographical coverage to vary depending on the detainee's citizenship. Aliens held at the base, like American citizens, are entitled to invoke the federal courts' §2241 authority. Pp. 12–15.
3. Petiti oners contend that they are being held in federal custody in violation of United States laws, and the District Court's jurisdiction over petitioners' custodians is unquestioned, cf. *Braden*, 410 U.S., at 495. Section 2241 requires nothing more and therefore confers jurisdiction on the District Court. Pp. 15–16.

b. The District Court also has jurisdiction to hear the *Al Odah* petitioners' complaint invoking 28 U.S.C. §1331, the federal question statute, and §1350, the Alien Tort Statute. The Court of Appeals, again relying on *Eisentrager,* held that the District Court correctly dismissed these claims for want of jurisdiction because the petitioners lacked the privilege of litigation in U.S. courts. Nothing in *Eisentrager* or any other of the Court's cases categorically excludes aliens detained in military custody outside the United States from that privilege. United States courts have traditionally been open to nonresident aliens. Cf. *Disconto Gesellschaft* v. *Umbreit,* 208 U.S. 570, 578. And indeed, §1350 explicitly confers the privilege of suing for an actionable "tort . . . committed in violation of the law of nations or a treaty of the United States" on aliens alone. The fact that petitioners are being held in military custody is immaterial. Pp. 16–17.

c. Whether and what further proceedings may become necessary after respondents respond to the merits of petitioners' claims are not here addressed. P. 17.

321 F.3d 1134, reversed and remanded.

Stevens, J., delivered the opinion of the Court, in which O'Connor, Souter, Ginsburg, and Breyer, JJ., joined. Kennedy, J., filed an opinion concurring in the judgment. Scalia, J., dissenting opinion, in which Rehnquist, C. J., and Thomas, J., joined.

appendix XIII

SUMMARY OF THE INTERNATIONAL COURT OF JUSTICE

Decision in Avena and Other Mexican Nationals; Mexico v. United States of America

AVENA AND OTHER MEXICAN NATIONALS (MEXICO v. UNITED STATES OF AMERICA)

THE COURT FINDS THAT THE UNITED STATES OF AMERICA HAS BREACHED ITS OBLIGATIONS TO MR. AVENA AND 50 OTHER MEXICAN NATIONALS AND TO MEXICO UNDER THE VIENNA CONVENTION ON CONSULAR RELATIONS

THE HAGUE, 31 March 2004. Today the International Court of Justice, the principal judicial organ of the United Nations, delivered its Judgment in the case concerning Avena and Other Mexican Nationals (Mexico v. United States of America).

In its Judgment, which is final, without appeal and binding on the Parties, the Court, with regard to the merits of the dispute,

- "*finds* by fourteen votes to one that, by not informing, without delay upon their detention, the 51 Mexican nationals referred to in paragraph 106 (1) above of their rights under Article 36, paragraph 1 (*b*), of the Vienna Convention on Consular Relations of 24 April 1963, the United States of America breached the obligations incumbent upon it under that subparagraph;
- *finds* by fourteen votes to one that, by not notifying the appropriate Mexican consular post without delay of the detention of the 49 Mexican nationals

referred to in paragraph 106 (2) above and thereby depriving the United Mexican States of the right, in a timely fashion, to render the assistance provided for by the Vienna Convention to the individuals concerned, the United States of America breached the obligations incumbent upon it under Article 36, paragraph 1 (*b*);

✦ *finds* by fourteen votes to one that, in relation to the 49 Mexican nationals referred to in paragraph 106 (3) above, the United States of America deprived the United Mexican States of the right, in a timely fashion, to communicate with and have access to those nationals and to visit them in detention, and thereby breached the obligations incumbent upon it under Article 36, paragraph 1 (*a*) and (*c*), of the Convention;

✦ *finds* by fourteen votes to one that, in relation to the 34 Mexican nationals referred to in paragraph 106 (4) above, the United States of America deprived the United Mexican States of the right, in a timely fashion, to arrange for legal representation of those nationals, and thereby breached the obligations incumbent upon it under Article 36, paragraph 1 (*c*), of the Convention;

✦ *finds* by fourteen votes to one that, by not permitting the review and reconsideration, in the light of the rights set forth in the Convention, of the conviction and sentences of Mr. César Roberto Fierro Reyna, Mr. Roberto Moreno Ramos and Mr. Osvaldo Torres Aguilera, after the violations referred to in subparagraph (4) above had been established in respect of those individuals, the United States of America breached the obligations incumbent upon it under Article 36, paragraph 2, of the Convention;

✦ *finds* by fourteen votes to one that the appropriate reparation in this case consists in the obligation of the United States of America to provide, by means of its own choosing, review and reconsideration of the convictions and sentences of the Mexican nationals referred to in subparagraphs (4), (5), (6) and (7) above, by taking account both of the violation of the rights set forth in Article 36 of the Convention and of paragraphs 138 to 141 of this Judgment;

✦ unanimously *takes note* of the commitment undertaken by the United States of America to ensure implementation of the specific measures adopted in performance of its obligations under Article 36, paragraph 1 (*b*), of the Vienna Convention; and finds that this commitment must be regarded as meeting the request by the United Mexican States for guarantees and assurances of non-repetition;

✦ unanimously *finds* that, should Mexican nationals nonetheless be sentenced to severe penalties, without their rights under Article 36, paragraph 1 (*b*), of the Convention having been respected, the United States of America shall provide, by means of its own choosing, review and reconsideration of the conviction and sentence, so as to allow full weight to be given to the violation of the rights set forth in the Convention, taking account of paragraphs 138 to 141 of this Judgment."

REASONING OF THE COURT

In its Judgment the Court begins by outlining the history of the case. It recalls that on 9 January 2003 Mexico instituted proceedings against the United States of America in a dispute concerning alleged breaches of Articles 5 and 36 of the Vienna Convention on Consular Relations of 24 April 1963 in relation to the treatment of a number of Mexican nationals who had been tried, convicted and sentenced to death in criminal proceedings in the United States. The original claim related to 54 such persons, but as a result of subsequent adjustments by Mexico, only 52 individual cases are involved. On 9 January 2003 Mexico also asked the Court to indicate provisional measures, and in particular to order the United States to take all measures necessary to ensure that no Mexican national was executed pending a final decision of the Court. On 5 February 2003 the Court unanimously adopted an Order indicating such measures, stating *inter alia* that the "United States of America shall take all measures necessary to ensure that Mr. César Roberto Fierro Reyna, Mr. Roberto Moreno Ramos and Mr. Osvaldo Torres Aguilera . . . are not executed pending final judgment in these proceedings."

The Court then examines four objections of the United States to the Court's jurisdiction and five to the admissibility of the claims of Mexico. It rejects those objections after first having rejected the objection of Mexico to the admissibility of the United States objections.

Ruling on the merits of the case, the Court first addresses the question of whether the 52 individuals concerned had Mexican nationality only, or whether some of them were also United States nationals, as claimed by that State. Concluding that the United States has not proved that claim, the Court finds that the United States did have obligations (to provide consular information) under

Article 36, paragraph 1 (*b*), of the Vienna Convention towards the 52 Mexican nationals.

The Court then examines the meaning of the expression "without delay" used in paragraph 1 (*b*) of Article 36. It finds that the duty to provide consular information exists once it is realized that the person is a foreign national, or once there are grounds to think so, but considers that, in the light *inter alia* of the Convention's *travaux préparatoires* the term "without delay" is not necessarily to be interpreted as meaning "immediately upon arrest." The Court then concludes that, on the basis of this interpretation, the United States has nonetheless violated its obligation to provide consular notification in all of the cases save one.

The Court then takes note of the interrelated nature of the three subparagraphs (*a*), (*b*) and (*c*) of paragraph 1 of Article 36 of the Vienna Convention and finds, in 49 of the cases, that the United States has also violated its obligation under subparagraph (*a*) to enable Mexican consular officers to communicate with, have access to and visit their nationals; while, in 34 cases, it finds that the United States has also, in addition, violated its obligation under subparagraph (*c*) to enable Mexican consular officers to arrange for legal representation of their nationals.

The Court then turns to Mexico's submission in relation to paragraph 2 of Article 36, whereby it claims that the United States violated its obligations under that paragraph by failing to provide "meaningful and effective review and reconsideration of convictions and sentences impaired by a violation of Article 36 (1)," *inter alia* as a result of the operation of the "procedural default" rule. The Court begins by observing that the procedural default rule has not been revised since it drew attention in its Judgment in the *LaGrand* case to the problems which its application could cause for defendants who sought to rely on violations of the Vienna Convention in appeal proceedings. The Court finds that in three cases paragraph 2 of Article 36 has been violated by the United States, but that the possibility of judicial re-examination is still open in 49 of the cases.

Turning to the legal consequences of the above-found breaches and to what legal remedies should be considered, the Court notes that Mexico seeks reparation in the form of "*restitutio in integrum,*" that is to say partial or total annulment of conviction and sentence, as the "necessary and sole remedy." The Court, citing the decision of its predecessor, the Permanent Court of International Justice, in the *Chorzów Factory* case, points out that what is required to make good the breach of an obligation under international law is "reparation in an adequate form." Following its Judgment in the *LaGrand* case the Court finds that in the present case adequate reparation for violations of Article 36 should be provided by review and reconsideration of the convictions and sentences of the Mexican nationals by United States courts.

The Court considers that the choice of means for review and reconsideration should be left to the United States, but that it is to be carried out by taking account of the violation of rights under the Vienna Convention.

The Court then addresses the function of executive clemency. Having found that it is the judicial process that is suited for the task of review and reconsideration, the Court finds that the clemency process, as currently practised within the United States criminal justice system, is not sufficient in itself to serve that purpose, although appropriate clemency procedures can supplement judicial review and reconsideration.

Finally, with regard to Mexico's request for the cessation of wrongful acts by the United States, the Court finds no evidence of a "regular and continuing" pattern of breaches by the United States of Article 36 of the Vienna Convention. And as to its request for guarantees and assurances of non-repetition the Court recognizes the United States efforts to encourage implementation of its obligations under the Vienna Convention and considers that that commitment by the United States meets Mexico's request.

At the end of its reasoning, the Court emphasizes that, in the present case, it has been addressing issues of principle from the viewpoint of the general application of the Vienna Convention. It observes that, while the present case concerns only Mexicans, its Judgment cannot be taken to imply that the Court's conclusions do not apply to other foreign nationals finding themselves in similar situations in the United States.

The Court finally points out that its Order of 5 February 2003 indicating provisional measures mentioned above, according to its terms and to Article 41 of the Statute, was effective pending final judgment, and that the obligations of the United States in that respect are, with effect from the date of the Judgment, replaced by those declared in this Judgment. The Court observes that it has found in relation to the three persons concerned in the Order (among others), that the United States has committed breaches of its obligations under Article 36, paragraph 1, of the Vienna Convention; and that moreover, in respect of those three persons alone, the United States has also committed breaches of Article 36, paragraph 2. The review and reconsideration of conviction and sentence required by Article 36, paragraph 2, which is the appropriate remedy for breaches of Article 36, paragraph 1, has not been carried out. The Court considers that in these three cases it is for the United States to find an appropriate remedy having the nature of review and reconsideration according to the criteria indicated in the Judgment.

Composition of the Court

The Court was composed as follows: President Shi; Vice-President Ranjeva; Judges Guillaume, Koroma, Vereshchetin, Higgins, Parra-Aranguren, Kooijmans, Rezek, Al-Khasawneh, Buergenthal, Elaraby, Owada, Tomka; Judge *ad hoc* Sepúlveda; Registrar Couvreur.

President Shi and Vice-President Ranjeva append declarations to the Judgment of the Court; Judges Vereshchetin, Parra-Aranguren and Tomka and Judge *ad hoc* Sepúlveda append separate opinions to the Judgment of the Court.

appendix

XIV MEDELLIN v. TEXAS

SUPREME COURT OF THE UNITED STATES

MEDELLIN v. TEXAS

CERTIORARI TO THE COURT OF CRIMINAL APPEALS OF TEXAS

Argued October 10, 2007—Decided March 25, No. 06–984. 2008

In the *Case Concerning Avena and Other Mexican Nationals* (*Mex.* v. *U.S.*), 2004 I.C.J. 12 (*Avena*), the International Court of Justice (ICJ) held that the United States had violated Article 36(1)(b) of the Vienna Convention on Consular Relations (Vienna Convention or Convention) by failing to inform 51 named Mexican nationals, including petitioner Medelln, of their Vienna Convention rights. The ICJ found that those named individuals were entitled to review and reconsideration of their U.S. state-court convictions and sentences regardless of their failure to comply with generally applicable state rules governing challenges to criminal convictions. In *Sanchez-Llamas* v. *Oregon*, 548 U.S. 331—issued after *Avena* but involving individuals who were not named in the Avena judgment—this Court held, contrary to the ICJ's determination, that the Convention did not preclude the application of state default rules. The President then issued a memorandum (President's Memorandum or Memorandum) stating that the United States would "discharge its international obligations" under *Avena* "by having State courts give effect to the decision."

Relying on *Avena* andthe President's Memorandum, Medellin filed a second Texas state-court habeas application challenging his state capital murder conviction and death sentence on the ground that he had not been informed of his Vienna Convention rights. The Texas Court of Criminal Appeals dismissed Medelln's application as an abuse of the writ, concluding that neither *Avena* nor the President's Memorandum was binding federal law that could displace the State's limitations on filing successive habeas applications.

Held: Neither *Avena* nor the President's Memorandum constitutes directly enforceable federal law that pre-empts state limitations on the filing of successive habeas petitions. Pp. 8–37.

1. The *Avena* judgment is not directly enforceable as domestic law in state court. Pp. 8–27.
   a. While a treaty may constitute an international commitment, it is not binding domestic law unless Congress has enacted statutes implementing it or the treaty itself conveys an intention that it be "self-executing" and is ratified on that basis. See, *e.g., Foster* v. *Neilson,* 2 Pet. 253, 314. The *Avena* judgment creates an international law obligation on the part of the United States, but it is not automatically binding domestic law because none of the relevant treaty sources—the Optional Protocol, the U.N. Charter, or the ICJ Statute—creates binding federal law in the absence of implementing legislation, and no such legislation has been enacted.

   The most natural reading of the Optional Protocol is that it is a bare grant of jurisdiction. The Protocol says nothing about the effect of an ICJ decision, does not commit signatories to comply therewith, and is silent as to any enforcement mechanism. The obligation to comply with ICJ judgments is derived from Article 94 of the U.N. Charter, which provides that "[e]ach . . . Member . . . undertakes to comply with the [ICJ's] decision . . . in any case to which it is a party." The phrase "undertakes to comply" is simply a commitment by member states to take future action through their political branches. That language does not indicate that the Senate, in ratifying the Optional Protocol, intended to vest ICJ decisions with immediate legal effect in domestic courts.

This reading is confirmed by Article 94(2)—the enforcement provision—which provides the sole remedy for noncompliance: referral to the U.N. Security Council by an aggrieved state. The provision of an express diplomatic rather than judicial remedy is itself evidence that ICJ judgments were not meant to be enforceable in domestic courts. See *Sanchez-Llamas*, 548 U. S., at 347. Even this "quintessentially *international* remed[y]," *id.*, at 355, is not absolute. It requires a Security Council resolution, and the President and Senate were undoubtedly aware that the United States retained the unqualified right to exercise its veto of any such resolution. Medelln's construction would eliminate the option of noncompliance contemplated by Article 94(2), undermining the ability of the political branches to determine whether and how to comply with an ICJ judgment.

The ICJ Statute, by limiting disputes to those involving nations, not individuals, and by specifying that ICJ decisions have no binding force except between those nations, provides further evidence that the *Avena* judgment does not automatically constitute federal law enforceable in U.S. courts. Medellin, an individual, cannot be considered a party to the *Avena* decision. Finally, the United States' interpretation of a treaty "is entitled to great weight," *Sumitomo Shoji America, Inc.* v. *Avagliano*, 457 U.S., at 184–185, and the Executive Branch has unfailingly adhered to its view that the relevant treaties do not create domestically enforceable federal law. Pp. 8–17.

b. The foregoing interpretive approach—parsing a treaty's text to determine if it is self-executing—is hardly novel. This Court has long looked to the language of a treaty to determine whether the President who negotiated it and the Senate that ratified it intended for the treaty to automatically create domestically enforceable federal law. See, *e.g.*, *Foster, supra.* Pp. 18–20.

c. The Court's conclusion that *Avena* does not by itself constitute binding federal law is confirmed by the "postratification understanding" of signatory countries. See *Zicherman* v. *Korean Air Lines Co.*, 516 U.S. 217. There are currently 47 nations that are parties to the Optional Protocol and 171 nations that are parties to the Vienna Convention. Yet neither Medellin nor his *amici* have identified a single nation that treats ICJ judgments as binding in domestic courts. The lack of any basis for supposing that any other country would treat ICJ judgments as directly enforceable as a matter of their domestic law strongly suggests that the treaty should not be so viewed in our courts. See *Sanchez-Llamas,* 548 U.S., at 343–344, and n. 3.

The Court's conclusion is further supported by general principles of interpretation. Given that the forum state's procedural rules govern a treaty's implementation absent a clear and express statement to the contrary, see *e.g., id.,* at 351, one would expect the ratifying parties to the relevant treaties to have clearly stated any intent to give ICJ judgments such effect. There is no statement in the Optional Protocol, the U.N. Charter, or the ICJ Statute that supports this notion. Moreover, the consequences of Medellin's argument give pause: neither Texas nor this Court may look behind an ICJ decision and quarrel with its reasoning or result, despite this Court's holding in *Sanchez-Llamas* that"[n]othing in the [ICJ's] structure or purpose . . . suggests that its interpretations were intended to be conclusive on our courts." *id.,* at 354. Pp. 20–24.

d. The Court's holding does not call into question the ordinary enforcement of foreign judgments. An agreement to abide by the result of an international adjudication can be a treaty obligation like any other, so long as the agreement is consistent with the Constitution. In addition, Congress is up to the task of implementing non-self-executing treaties, even those involving complex commercial disputes. Medelln contends that domestic courts generally give effect to foreign judgments, but the judgment Medelln asks us to enforce is hardly typical: It would enjoin the operation of state law and force the State to take action to "review and reconside[r]" his case. Foreign judgments awarding injunctive relief against private parties, let alone sovereign States, "are not generally entitled to enforcement." Restatement (Third) of Foreign Relations Law of the United States §481, Comment *b,* p. 595 (1986). Pp. 24–27.

2. The President's Memorandum does not independently require the States to provide review and reconsideration of the claims of the 51 Mexican nationals named in *Avena* without regard to state procedural default rules. Pp. 27–37.

a. The President seeks to vindicate plainly compelling interests in ensuring the reciprocal observance of the Vienna Convention, protecting relations with foreign governments, and demonstrating commitment to the role of international law. But those interests do not allow the

Court to set aside first principles. The President's authority to act, as with the exercise of any governmental power, "must stem either from an act of Congress or from the Constitution itself." *Youngstown Sheet & Tube Co.* v. *Sawyer,* 343 U.S. 579.

Justice Jackson's familiar tripartite scheme provides the accepted framework for evaluating executive action in this area. First, "[w]hen the President acts pursuant to an express or implied authorization of Congress, his authority is at its maximum, for it includes all that he possesses in his own right plus all that Congress can delegate." *Youngstown,* 343 U.S., at 635 (Jackson, J., concurring). Second, "[w]hen the President acts in absence of either a congressional grant or denial of authority, he can only rely upon his own independent powers, but there is a zone of twilight in which he and Congress may have concurrent authority, or in which its distribution is uncertain." *Id.,* at 637. In such a circumstance, Presidential authority can derive support from "congressional inertia, indifference or quiescence." *Ibid.* Finally, "[w]hen the President takes measures incompatible with the expressed or implied will of Congress, his power is at its lowest ebb," and the Court can sustain his actions "only by disabling the Congress from acting upon the subject." *Id.,* at 637–638. Pp. 28–29.

b. The United States marshals two principal arguments in favor of the President's authority to establish binding rules of decision that preempt contrary state law. The United States argues that the relevant treaties give the President the authority to implement the *Avena* judgment and that Congress has acquiesced in the exercise of such authority. The United States also relies upon an "independent" international dispute-resolution power. We find these arguments, as well as Medelln's additional argument that the President's Memorandum is a valid exercise of his "Take Care" power, unpersuasive. Pp. 29–37.

i. The United States maintains that the President's Memorandum is implicitly authorized by the Optional Protocol and the U.N. Charter. But the responsibility for transforming an international obligation arising from a non-self-executing treaty into domestic law falls to Congress, not the Executive. *Foster,* 2 Pet., at 315. It is a fundamental constitutional principle that " '[t]he power to make the necessary laws is in Congress; the power to execute in the President.' " *Hamdan* v. *Rumsfeld,* 548 U.S. 557. A non-self-executing treaty, by definition, is one that was ratified with the understanding that it is not to have domestic effect of its own force. That understanding precludes the assertion that Congress has implicitly authorized the President—acting on his own—to achieve precisely the same result. Accordingly, the President's Memorandum does not fall within the first category of the *Youngstown* framework. Indeed, because the non-self-executing character of the relevant treaties not only refutes the notion that the ratifying parties vested the President with the authority to unilaterally make treaty obligations binding on domestic courts, but also implicitly prohibits him from doing so, the President's assertion of authority is within *Youngstown*'s third category, not the first or even the second.

The United States maintains that congressional acquiescence requires that the President's Memorandum be given effect as domestic law. But such acquiescence is pertinent when the President's action falls within the second *Youngstown* category, not the third. In any event, congressional acquiescence does not exist here. Congress' failure to act following the President's resolution of prior ICJ controversies does not demonstrate acquiescence because in none of those prior controversies did the President assert the authority to transform an international obligation into domestic law and thereby displace state law. The United States' reliance on the President's "related" statutory responsibilities and on his "established role" in litigating foreign policy concerns is also misplaced. The President's statutory authorization to represent the United States before the U. N., the ICJ, and the U. N. Security Council speaks to his *international* responsibilities, not to any unilateral authority to create domestic law.

The combination of a non-self-executing treaty and the lack of implementing legislation does not preclude the President from acting to comply with an international treaty obligation by other means, so long as those means are consistent with the Constitution. But the President may not rely upon a non-self-executing treaty to establish binding rules of decision that pre-empt contrary state law. Pp. 30–35.

ii. The United States also claims that—independent of the United States' treaty obligations—the Memorandum is a valid exercise of the President's foreign affairs authority to resolve claims disputes. See, *e.g., American Ins. Assn.* v. *Garamendi,* 539 U.S. 396. This Court's claims-settlement cases involve a narrow set of circumstances: the making of executive agreements to settle civil claims between American citizens and foreign governments or foreign nationals. They are based on the view that "a systematic, unbroken, executive practice, long pursued to the knowledge of the Congress and never before questioned," can "raise a presumption that the [action] had been [taken] in pursuance of its consent." *Dames & Moore* v. *Regan,* 453 U.S. 654. But "[p]ast practice does not, by itself, create power." *Ibid.* The President's Memorandum—a directive issued to state courts that would compel those courts to reopen final criminal judgments and set aside neutrally applicable state laws—is not supported by a "particularly longstanding practice." The Executive's limited authority to settle international claims disputes pursuant to an executive agreement cannot stretch so far. Pp. 35–37.

iii. Medelln's argument that the President's Memorandum is a valid exercise of his power to "Take Care" that the laws be faithfully executed, U.S. Const., Art. II, §3, fails because the ICJ's decision in *Avena* is not domestic law. P. 37.

223 S. W. 3d 315, affirmed.

Roberts, C. J., delivered the opinion of the Court, in which Scalia, Kennedy, Thomas, and Alito, JJ., joined. Stevens, J., filed an opinion concurring in the judgment. Breyer, J., filed a dissenting opinion, in which Souter and Ginsburg, JJ., joined.

appendix XV

SANCHEZ-LLAMAS v. OREGON

SUPREME COURT OF THE UNITED STATES

SANCHEZ-LLAMAS v. OREGON

CERTIORARI TO THE SUPREME COURT OF OREGON

Argued March 29, 2006—Decided June 28, No. 04–10566. 2006*

Article 36(1)(b) of the Vienna Convention on Consular Relations provides that if a person detained by a foreign country "so requests, the competent authorities of the receiving State shall, without delay, inform the consular post of the sending State" of such detention, and "inform the [detainee] of his rights under this sub-paragraph." Article 36(2) specifies: "The rights referred to in paragraph 1 . . . shall be exercised in conformity with the laws and regulations of the receiving State, subject to the proviso . . . that the said laws . . . must enable full effect to be given to the purposes for which the rights accorded under this Article are intended." Along with the Convention, the United States ratified the Optional Protocol Concerning the Compulsory Settlement of Disputes, which provides: "Disputes arising out of the . . . Convention shall lie within the compulsory jurisdiction of the International Court of Justice [(ICJ)]." The United States withdrew from the Protocol on March 7, 2005.

Petitioner in No. 04–10566, Moises Sanchez-Llamas, is a Mexican national. When he was arrested after an exchange of gunfire with police, officers did not inform him that he could ask to have the Mexican Consulate notified of his detention. During interrogation, he made incriminating statements regarding the shootout. Before his trial for attempted murder and other offenses, Sanchez-Llamas moved to suppress those statements on the ground, *inter alia,* that the authorities had failed to comply with Article 36. The state court denied that motion and Sanchez-Llamas was convicted and sentenced to prison, and the Oregon Court of Appeals affirmed. The State Supreme Court also affirmed, concluding that Article 36 does not create rights to consular access or notification that a detained individual can enforce in a judicial proceeding.

Petitioner in No. 05–51, Mario Bustillo, a Honduran national, was arrested and charged with murder, but police never informed him that he could request that the Honduran Consulate be notified of his detention. He was convicted and sentenced to prison, and his conviction and sentence were affirmed on appeal. He then filed a habeas petition in state court arguing, for the first time, that authorities had violated his right to consular notification under Article 36. The court dismissed that claim as procedurally barred because he had failed to raise it at trial or on appeal. The Virginia Supreme Court found no reversible error.

Held: Even assuming without deciding that the Convention creates judicially enforceable rights, suppression is not an appropriate remedy for a violation, and a State may apply its regular procedural default rules to Convention claims. Pp. 7–25.

a. Because petitioners are not in any event entitled to relief, the Court need not resolve whether the Convention grants individuals enforceable rights, but assumes, without deciding, that Article 36 does so. Pp. 7–8.

b. Neither the Convention itself nor this Court's precedents applying the exclusionary rule support suppression of a defendant's statements to police as a remedy for an Article 36 violation.

The Convention does not mandate suppression or any other specific remedy, but expressly leaves Article 36's implementation to domestic law: Article 36 rights must "be exercised in conformity with the laws . . . of the receiving State." Art. 36(2). Sanchez-Llamas' argument that suppression is appropriate under United States law and should be required under the Court's authority to develop remedies for the enforcement of federal law in state-court criminal proceedings is rejected. "It is beyond dispute that [this Court does] not hold a supervisory power over the [state] courts." *Dickerson* v. *United States,* 530 U.S. 428. The exclusionary rule cases on which Sanchez-Llamas principally relies are inapplicable because they rest on the Court's supervisory authority over federal courts.

The Court's authority to create a judicial remedy applicable in state court must therefore lie, if anywhere, in the treaty itself. Where a treaty provides for a particular judicial remedy, courts must apply it as a requirement of federal law. Cf., *e.g., United States v. Giordano,* 416 U.S. 505. But where a treaty does not provide a particular remedy, either expressly or implicitly, it is not for the federal courts to impose one on the States through lawmaking of their own. Even if the "full effect" language of Article 36(2) implicitly requires a judicial remedy, as Sanchez-Llamas claims, that Article equally requires that Article 36(1) rights be exercised in conformity with domestic law. Under domestic law, the exclusionary rule is not a remedy this Court applies lightly. It has been used primarily to deter certain Fourth and *Fifth Amendment* violations, including, *e.g.*, unconstitutional searches and seizures, *Mapp v. Ohio,* 367 U.S. 643, and confessions exacted in violation of the right against compelled self-incrimination or due process, *Dickerson, supra,* at 435. In contrast, Article 36 has nothing to do with searches or interrogations and, indeed, does not guarantee defendants any assistance at all. It secures for foreign nationals only the right to have their consulate *informed* of their arrest or detention—not to have their consulate intervene, or to have police cease their investigation pending any such notice or intervention. Moreover, the failure to inform a defendant of his Article 36 rights is unlikely, with any frequency, to produce unreliable confessions, see *Watkins* v. *Sowders,* 449 U.S. 341, or to give the police any practical advantage in obtaining incriminating evidence, see *Elkins* v. *United States,* 364 U.S. 206. Suppression would also be a vastly disproportionate remedy for an Article 36 violation. The interests Sanchez-Llamas claims Article 36 advances are effectively protected by other constitutional and statutory requirements, including the right to an attorney and to protection against compelled self-incrimination. Finally, suppression is not the only means of vindicating Article 36 rights. For example, diplomatic avenues—the primary means of enforcing the Vienna Convention—remain open. Pp. 8–15.

c. States may subject Article 36 claims to the same procedural default rules that apply generally to other federal-law claims.

This question is controlled by the Court's holding in *Breard* v. *Greene,* 523 U.S. 371, that the petitioner's failure to raise an Article 36 claim in state court prevented him from having the claim heard in a subsequent federal habeas proceeding. Bustillo's two reasons why *Breard* does not control are rejected.

First, he argues that *Breard*'s procedural default holding was unnecessary to the result because the petitioner there could not demonstrate prejudice from the default and because, in any event, the later enacted Antiterrorism and Effective Death Penalty Act of 1996 superseded any right the petitioner had under the Vienna Convention to have his claim heard on collateral review. Resolution of the procedural default question, however, was the principal reason for denying the *Breard* petitioner's claim, and the discussion of the issue occupied the bulk of the Court's reasoning. See 523 U.S., at 375–377. It is no answer to argue that the procedural default holding was unnecessary simply because the petitioner had several other ways to lose.

Second, Bustillo asserts that since *Breard*, the ICJ's *LaGrand* and *Avena* decisions have interpreted the Convention to preclude the application of procedural default rules to Article 36 claims. Although the ICJ's interpretation deserves "respectful consideration," *Breard, supra*, at 375, it does not compel the Court to reconsider *Breard*'s understanding of the Convention. "The judicial Power of the United States" is "vested in one supreme Court . . . and . . . inferior courts." U.S. Const., Art. III, §1. That "power . . . extend[s] to . . . treaties," Art. III, §2, and includes the duty "to say what the law is," *Marbury* v. *Madison*, 1 Cranch 137, 177. If treaties are to be given effect as federal law, determining their meaning as a matter of federal law "is emphatically the province and duty of the judicial department," headed by the "one supreme Court." *Ibid.* Nothing in the ICJ's structure or purpose suggests that its interpretations were intended to be binding on U.S. courts. Even according "respectful consideration," the ICJ's interpretation cannot overcome the plain import of Article 36(2), which states that the rights it implements "shall be exercised in conformity with the laws . . . of the receiving State." In the United States, this means that the rule of procedural default—which applies even to claimed violations of our own Constitution, see *Engle* v. *Isaac*, 456 U.S. 107—applies also to Vienna Convention claims. Bustillo points to nothing in the drafting history of Article 36 or in the contemporary practice of other Convention signatories that undermines this conclusion. *LaGrand*'s conclusion that applying the procedural default rule denies "full effect" to the purposes of Article 36, by preventing courts from attaching legal significance to an Article 36 violation, is inconsistent with the basic framework of an adversary system. Such a system relies chiefly on the *parties* to raise significant issues and present them to the courts in the appropriate manner at the appropriate time for adjudication. See *Castro* v. *United States,* 540 U.S. 375. Procedural default rules generally take on greater importance in an adversary system than in the sort of magistrate-directed, inquisitorial legal system characteristic of many of the other Convention signatories. Under the ICJ's reading of "full effect," Article 36 claims could trump not only procedural default rules, but any number of other rules requiring parties to present their legal claims at the appropriate time for adjudication, such as statutes of limitations and prohibitions against filing successive habeas petitions. This sweeps too broadly, for it reads the "full effect" proviso in a way that leaves little room for the clear instruction in Article 36(2) that Article 36 rights "be exercised in conformity with the laws . . . of the receiving State." A comparison with a suspect's rights under *Miranda* v. *Arizona,* 384 U.S. 436, disposes of Bustillo's "full effect" claim. Although the failure to inform defendants of their right to consular notification may prevent them from becoming aware of their Article 36 rights and asserting them at trial, precisely the same thing is true of *Miranda* rights. Nevertheless, if a defendant fails to raise his *Miranda* claim at trial, procedural default rules may bar him from raising the claim in a subsequent postconviction proceeding. *Wainwright* v. *Sykes,* 433 U.S. 72. Bustillo's attempt to analogize an Article 36 claim to a claim under *Brady* v. *Maryland,* 373 U.S. 83, that the prosecution failed to disclose exculpatory evidence is inapt. Finally, his argument that Article 36 claims are most appropriately raised post-trial or on collateral review under *Massaro* v. *United States,* 538 U.S. 500, is rejected. See *Dickerson, supra,* at 438. Pp. 15–25.

d. The Court's holding in no way disparages the Convention's importance. It is no slight to the Convention to deny petitioners' claims under the same principles this Court would apply to claims under an Act of Congress or the Constitution itself. P. 25.

No. 04–10566, 338 Ore. 267, 108 P. 3d 573, and No. 05–51, affirmed.

Roberts, C. J., delivered the opinion of the Court, in which Scalia, Kennedy, Thomas, and Alito, JJ., joined. Ginsburg, J., filed an opinion concurring in the judgment. Breyer, J., filed a dissenting opinion, in which Stevens and Souter, JJ., joined, and in which Ginsburg, J., joined as to Part II.

Notes

* Together with No. 05–51, Bustillo v. Johnson, Director, Virginia Department of Corrections, on certiorari to the Supreme Court of Virginia.

INDEX

S

T

U

V

W

Y

Z

www.ingramcontent.com/pod-product-compliance
Lightning Source LLC
LaVergne TN
LVHW080117011026
849160LV00013B/1124
* 9 7 8 0 7 5 7 5 6 0 6 9 9 *